THE LETTERS OF
SAMUEL PEPYS

THE LETTERS OF
SAMUEL PEPYS
1656–1703

Selected and edited by

Guy de la Bédoyère

THE BOYDELL PRESS

First published 2006
The Boydell Press, Woodbridge

ISSN 1 84383 197 X

The Boydell Press is an imprint of Boydell & Brewer Ltd
PO Box 9, Woodbridge, Suffolk IP12 3DF, UK
and of Boydell & Brewer Inc.
668 Mt. Hope Avenue, Rochester, NY 14620, USA
website: www.boydellandbrewer.com

A CIP catalogue record of this publication is available
from the British Library

This publication is printed on acid-free paper

Printed in Great Britain by
Cromwell Press, Trowbridge, Wiltshire

CONTENTS

Introduction

SAMUEL PEPYS is of course best known from his Diary, which covers his life from the beginning of 1660 until the last day of May in 1669. There is no doubt that this extraordinary work is one of the most important documents in the English language. Not only is it an exceptional record of an exceptional period in England's history, but it is also a work of literature in its own right. The full publication of the Diary by Robert Latham and William Matthews has justifiably had plaudits heaped upon it and it is unlikely ever to be superseded.

There have been many books written about Samuel Pepys but in order to cover his whole life biographers have had to look more deeply into the vast numbers of manuscripts produced, or received, by Pepys. A relentless archivist, Pepys almost invented the modern concept of administration, reflected as much in his personal papers as those that he presided over as Clerk of the Acts and later as Secretary of the Admiralty. These records formed the bedrock of his naval reforms, but they also include older documents of great historical value to any understanding of the evolution of English naval power. Amongst these one of the most important is the Anthony Roll, which illustrates fifty-eight ships of Henry VIII's Navy in 1546. Pepys was given two of the three rolls by Charles II and had them bound for his library, where they survive today. John Evelyn also gave Pepys an important collection of state and other documents of the sixteenth and early seventeenth centuries, acquired by him from his father-in-law, Sir Richard Browne. These too were bound and placed in Pepys's library.

It was this interest in recording and archiving that makes Pepys such an important figure to us, and not just because of the professional role that he played in his own time. His carefully preserved books and papers form a unique resource for the period. These archives also included Pepys's extensive correspondence. The extant letters date from the 1650s to Pepys's death in 1703. In the seventeenth century letters had more significance than they do now. They were the normal medium not only for the exchange of private and public news between friends and family members, but also the manner in which much military, political and state business was conducted. Pepys's letters involve all these aspects of his busy and complicated life, ranging from the management of the Earl of Sandwich's household and his own personal affairs to naval matters and his darkest hours while imprisoned during the hysteria of the Popish Plot. Although the physical transmission of letters was generally far slower than today, it often comes as a surprise to see that Pepys and his correspondents sometimes exchanged letters at a high rate, occasionally even within the same day.

THE DISPERSAL OF THE CORRESPONDENCE

Initially, all the papers that Pepys left passed to his nephew and heir, John Jackson. Although the terms of Pepys's will that the library, including the Diary, be bequeathed to Magdalene College at Cambridge on Jackson's death in 1723 were fulfilled, there was no such requirement that the letters follow the same path. Some in fact did go to Cambridge where they still are, while the Pepys-Cockerell papers remained with Jackson's descendants. The latter were sold in 1931. Today most of the Pepys-Cockerell papers remain in private hands though the copybook containing letters from 1662–79 was acquired by the National Maritime Museum in Greenwich.

In 1700 Pepys moved to Clapham from York Buildings, his home for many years. It seems likely that he left some of his papers behind, including many letters, from where they probably came into the possession of an antiquarian and collector called Thomas Rawlinson (1681–1725). After Thomas Rawlinson's death in 1725 Richard Rawlinson (1690–1755) catalogued his brother's papers and added many to his own collection of manuscripts. It is unlikely that Richard was the first owner since he was only thirteen at the time of Pepys's death, but the possibility remains that the manuscripts belonged to someone else other than his brother Thomas before he obtained them.

On Richard Rawlinson's death, these papers passed to the Bodleian Library in Oxford, where they remain. The Bodleian also holds manuscripts owned by Thomas Carte (1686–1754), who had acquired them from the archives of the earls of Sandwich. Other archives at the Bodleian, such as those of Thomas Tanner, include some of the Pepys correspondence.

More letters found their way into the hands of an autograph collector called William Upcott (1779–1845). He had discovered them amongst the John Evelyn manuscripts at Wotton House in Surrey, the seat of the Evelyn family. Many of these letters are now in the British Library though the circuitous routes by which some of them reached this safe haven are now untraceable. A number of Pepys's letters to Evelyn in Upcott's collection were loaned to John Smith, who published them in his 1841 edition of the correspondence. Smith also published letters to and from Pepys for which he did not specify a source and the whereabouts of which are now unknown. Until 1996 these included the two letters from John Jackson to Evelyn about Pepys's death. These have resurfaced and are now in the British Library while others remain lost. Braybrooke also appears to have removed some of the letters he used, since a few he published are no longer in the Pepys-Cockerell collection and have found their way to various different homes around the world.

To add to the confusion, in 1889 an autograph collector and dealer called Samuel J. Davey (1863–90) issued a catalogue of Pepys's letters and other manuscripts for sale. Mostly corresponding to gaps in the Pepys-Cockerell collection and the Rawlinson manuscripts for the 1670s and 1680s, they must have been extracted from one or the other before 1825 since neither Braybrooke nor Smith apparently knew about any of them. The letters offered for sale also included a few from the early 1660s, a period poorly represented in the other extant archives of Pepys's correspondence. How Davey obtained the collection remains a mystery. Many of the letters offered for sale were by John Evelyn to Pepys. Fortunately, most of these have now been traced and published. William John Evelyn MP (1822–1908), a collateral descendant of Evelyn's, bought some and they remain in the Evelyn archive now at the British Library. Others have found their way to institutional homes, but several remain lost. Davey almost certainly held on to some letters himself, which were not featured in the 1889 catalogue, and which were dispersed after his death in 1890. This would explain a small number of other letters from Evelyn to Pepys appearing on the market many years later.[1]

---

[1] The letter of 1 Jan 1700 (PF E1), for example, did not surface until a sale in 1979.

PUBLISHING THE LETTERS

The significance of the content of some of the letters, and the identity of some of Pepys's correspondents, meant that the letters attracted attention at the same time as the Diary. Braybrooke included letters in his 1825 edition of the Diary and in 1841 John Smith, the first transcriber of the Diary, published a selection of letters along with the Second (Tangier) Diary. Braybrooke's edition appeared in numerous reprints throughout the nineteenth century, while Smith's appeared only once. Unfortunately, neither Smith nor Braybrooke had much interest in generating authoritative texts and adjusted them as they saw fit.

It was not until 1926 that J. R. Tanner produced a selection of Pepys's correspondence from 1679–1703. It was followed in 1929 by his selection from the 1662–79 copybook. Tanner's selections were taken exclusively from the Pepys-Cockerell manuscripts, which were then still in the hands of descendants of Pepys's nephew John Jackson. Until the present edition, the only collection of Pepys's letters drawn from all available sources, and covering all aspects of his life, was by R. G. Howarth, published in 1932 in a book scarcely known today. The following year Edwin Chappell's edition of shorthand letters from the 1662–79 copybook appeared. Bryant's biographical trilogy includes a number of letters published either in full or in the form of substantial quotations. Thereafter, the only subsequent collections issued were Helen Truesdell Heath's 1955 edition of Pepys's family letters, and the present editor's edition of the Pepys-Evelyn correspondence (1997 and 2005).

Letters to and from Pepys exist today in institutions all round the world, while new ones continue to materialize in sales. Amongst these are, for example, a copybook containing correspondence between Pepys and John Matthews, a cousin, who took care of the education of his nephews. This is now at Harvard. Some letters listed in those sale catalogues have unfortunately disappeared completely.

THE LETTERS

Pepys was a prolific correspondent. His brief Second Diary, compiled on the 1683 expedition to Tangier, includes such references as '[October] 5. Friday – Morning. Busy at the office. Afternoon. Writing letters to go by post to Cadiz: to Mr Houblon a very grave letter ...' Such entries are familiar to any reader of the more famous Diary of the 1660s, for example, 'To the office to finish my letters, and then home to bed' (10 June 1665). Incoming letters were endorsed, replied to, sometimes copied, and stored appropriately. Draft replies were sometimes made on the sheets of the incoming letter. In the earlier part of his life Pepys wrote these drafts himself. Later on, concerned for his eyesight, he relied more on assistants, but not exclusively. Pepys also compiled copies or drafts of letters in books, or in other collections such as his Navy White Book.

Pepys sometimes used shorthand for letter drafts and copies, which of course was what he used for the Diary. Transcribing Pepys's shorthand has presented scholars with a formidable challenge since the early 1800s. The preparatory work for this selection of letters involved learning the shorthand. Thomas Shelton's *Tachygraphy* is cumbersome and prone to ambiguity, especially with some longer words. This encourages the use of simpler and more easily remembered signs, resulting in repetitious turns of phrase and the recurrence of the same or similar words rather than a more varied vocabulary. This is apparent throughout the Diary, and is of course partly attributable to the manner in which diaries are characteristically punctuated by key phrases and references to familiar daily events, such as 'so home to supper and to bed'. These help to break up the text into easily recognizable consecutive chronological blocks.

However, the limitations of Shelton's shorthand system probably did contribute rather more to the literary style of Pepys's Diary than Latham and Matthews really acknowledge. For example, they discuss his compression of 'so long as' to 'so' or 'faintheartedness' to 'faintness' as if these reflect his personal idiosyncratic use of the English language, without acknowledging that when composing in shorthand these are attractive and more convenient alternatives to fuller expression. 'Faintness' can be represented by three simple signs, whereas 'faintheartedness' requires five. 'So' requires one, rather than the three of 'so long as'. Some of the more peculiar or archaic spellings in the Diary are also easily explained by the ingenuity required to spell out more modern words or specific sounds. The archaic 'ketched', for example, is far easier to write unambiguously in shorthand than 'caught', because 'augh' is not easily represented and obliges the writer to record the word as 'cot'.[2]

Echoes of Pepys's spoken voice in the Diary come about because speech tends towards simpler, more familiar, terms that are easier to record in his shorthand than carefully written longhand text. Indeed, it almost seems with some passages that Pepys composed the Diary so that he could maximize his use of simpler signs, only resorting to longhand for names or words which would have been too complicated to set out in shorthand. The shorthand can also be written fast enough to reflect all the unrefined infelicities of normal speech such as his characteristic phrasal inversions, and erratic tensing. All these aspects of Pepys's Diary style are inevitably less evident in the letters for which Pepys seems to have preferred longhand when drafting or copying. It was less essential that the contents of letters be kept secret, though in fact the Diary was easily decipherable by anyone familiar with Shelton's system. Moreover, copies or drafts of official letters at least presumably needed to be kept in a form that could be read by more people than just those versed in the shorthand. The letters therefore tend to be written in a less impulsive and more disciplined fashion, though this of course also reflects their very different nature. Of the 940 letters preserved in the 1662–79 copybook now at Greenwich, just 56 are either wholly or partly in shorthand.

The letters Pepys sent occasionally survive in his correspondents' or official archives. However, many of Pepys's letters exist now only in the form of his retained copies, some of which were made in books, and some on loose sheets filed with the incoming correspondence to which they related. He occasionally recorded the practice, 'I ... wrote a letter to send to Mr Coventry with a piece of plate along with it – which I do preserve among my other letters' (Diary 6 June 1661).

As it happens neither this letter nor whole copybook for the period have survived. Moreover, Pepys did not copy all his letters – this much is plain from extant letters-sent not represented in the copybooks – and he also weeded out his archive. On 9 December 1666 he spent a whole afternoon and night 'looking over and tearing and burning all the unnecessary letters which I have had upon my File for four or five years backward – which I entend to do quite through all my papers, that I may have nothing by me but what is worth keeping, and fit to be seen should I miscarry'. By 'miscarry' Pepys means if he were come to fail in his work or somehow come to professional grief. In this he was unwittingly prophetic, or perhaps given his astute

2 Vol. X, 221ff.

perceptiveness of human nature he was very aware that the higher he climbed, the more enemies he would amass. His skills at compiling evidence to support his activities would stand him in good stead later on, but it also means we will perhaps now never know what he chose to weed from his archives.

It is less clear what Pepys's policy was with private letters. On 4 May 1660 he received a letter from his wife telling him she had been unwell, and replied to her. It can hardly have been the only letter he received from her, but not a single piece of writing by Elizabeth Pepys, or a letter to her from her husband, survives. Indeed, on 9 January 1663 Pepys records destroying a bundle of papers during a quarrel that included letters they had exchanged. Virtually no letters to or from his later female acquaintances, such as Mrs Steward and her sister Elizabeth, Lady Mordaunt, and Julia Shelcross, survive either yet it is plain from the one surviving letter (his retained copy) to Mrs Steward of 20 September 1695 that she had frequently written to him. On 11 December 1666 Pepys recorded his intention to write to Lady Mordaunt 'every month'. If he did, no letter has survived. Incoming letters from such sources have also not survived either because Pepys discarded them, or because any archive he kept of them happens not to have been preserved. He seems generally not to have bothered with making drafts or copies of his replies to them.[3] Either way it is hard to explain the preservation of other letters that are no more trivial or less important unless Pepys was simply more haphazard in his storage of this kind of correspondence. In other instances he was more careful. Letters from his nephew John Jackson for example, while on his Grand Tour, were carefully archived.

The survival of the physical letters that Pepys sent depends largely on whether the recipient and his (or her) descendants preserved their correspondence. Both Lady Mordaunt and her sister, for example, were widows and childless. John Evelyn on the other hand was an obsessive archivist, with a loyal grandson to take care of his estate. His extant papers preserved a number of Pepys's letters, including a copy of one he had forwarded and which would now otherwise be lost.[4] More often it is Pepys's own retained copies, however dispersed, that we have to rely on.

Copying letters was common sense, and was what we would now call backing-up data. Indeed, since copying involved creating 'hard copy' it was a relatively reliable process though also laborious, which explains why Pepys did not copy everything. During the work on the Pepys-Evelyn correspondence, it was possible to compare some of Pepys's copies with the letters he had physically sent. In every case the texts were virtually identical. This means that it is possible for us to rely on retained copies of letters-sent, even where those are the only versions that have survived. Drafts are probably less reliable, though even then Pepys usually marked intended deletions or other alterations. Conversely, in John Evelyn's case his drafts and letters-sent often differ in significant detail. Pepys was a very different personality; his instincts as an administrator and record-keeper would have discouraged him from being able to do this himself, even if he had felt so inclined.

As a letter writer himself Pepys is usually fairly businesslike. Few of his letters are protracted though he had difficulty ending sentences. In this respect the letters often differ from the uninhibited revelations and observations distributed throughout

---

[3] Letters nos. 230 and 234 are the only known exceptions.
[4] P's letter to Evelyn of 7 November 1694 (PF D25) survives only as a copy made by E, who had forwarded the original to Sidney, Lord Godolphin. No draft or copy by P exists. The complex history of the Evelyn archive is discussed in *Particular Friends*, pp. 15-24.

the Diary. Nevertheless, the letters also include many references that complement the personality so vividly displayed in the Diary. His letters to Edward Mountagu in the 1650s for example are filled with his excited observations on the high drama being played out in London during the last days of the Protectorate.

Like most letter-writers of the day, Pepys and his correspondents followed an accepted protocol that reflected relative rank. The texts are almost invariably civil to the point of obsequiousness, regardless of the subject matter under discussion. The writer usually allocates a section of the letter to deprecate his or her own abilities or status and to emphasize total dependence on the goodwill, generosity and talents of the addressee. This was simply a question of good manners, but nevertheless the words used functioned as well-established code that indicated the relative order of social precedence and the degree of familiarity in the personal relationship. Thus Will Hewer, despite his accumulating wealth, is 'Mr Hewer' or 'Sir', but he almost invariably addresses Pepys as 'Honoured Sir'. Likewise, the Earl of Sandwich addresses him as 'Mr Pepys'. Amongst equals 'Sir' is the normal form, though 'My Worthy Friend' and 'Dearest Sir' also appear. However, almost all the letters, regardless of to whom they were addressed, end with a declaration that the writer is the addressee's humble servant, with variations of 'faithful', 'obedient' and 'affectionate' (or their omission), depending on the exact personal relationship. The copy-letters and drafts are inevitably less fulsome in this respect, with the pay-offs frequently being abbreviated. J. R. Tanner's transcriptions usually omit these passages, since they normally add nothing to the substantive content of the letter.

THE LETTER TEXTS
In order to compile this selection of Pepys's letters, the texts have been drawn from a variety of sources including all the previous printed editions, and the original manuscripts. Everything that could be done practicably to verify the contents and details has been undertaken. Most of the letters included in this selection are the fullest text possible apart from the omission in some cases of the social niceties and other cuts made by J. R. Tanner. During the work for the Pepys-Evelyn correspondence it became clear that there was no good reason generally to doubt the transcriptions made by Tanner, Howarth, Bryant and Heath, where they had been able to consult original manuscripts though both Howarth and Bryant occasionally misread words or dates.

This is an observation, not a criticism. Transcribing manuscripts of this era is often extremely difficult for a variety of reasons, and even the most meticulous work contains imperfections. Any editor correcting a predecessor's errors does so in the full knowledge that his or her own work will contain mistakes. Unfortunately this is not something that can be easily passed to a second pair of eyes for checking. However, John Smith was inclined to modify the texts by rearranging the structure of sentences and omitting words or even whole phrases. It is not clear whether this was simply the result of carelessness or deliberate 'improvement'. Braybrooke's treatment was equally unsatisfactory, veering between accurate readings and comprehensive bowdlerization to the point of fraud. Smith's transcriptions of Pepys's shorthand depended on his own technique of decipherment, since he did not know the Pepysian Library contained a copy of Thomas Shelton's *Tachygraphy*. Wherever Smith could not understand a shorthand sign he omitted it or made something up. Even so, thanks to the shortcomings of Shelton's system no transcription is entirely reliable. Wherever possible transcriptions by Smith and

Braybrooke have been avoided but in some instances there is no choice. Some of the original manuscripts were consulted and thirty of the letters included here are published here for the first time from these sources.

As has already been explained, much (but by no means all) of Pepys's outgoing correspondence is known only from drafts or copies made by him or one of his clerks. Conversely, most incoming correspondence is the letter-sent.[5] For example, the letters exchanged by Samuel Newton and Pepys on 8 August 1695 include Newton's original, and a copy or draft of Pepys's reply written on the same sheet.[6] The actual letter sent by Pepys has not survived.

The criteria for selection have varied according to the contents, the date and the broader historical context. Letters have been chosen so that almost every part of Pepys's adult life is represented: his various professional and private interests, his relationships with his business and private equals, his superiors and his inferiors, and petitioners, especially the relentless calls made on his patronage by his brother-in-law Balthazar St Michel and the Skinner family. However, there are key periods that deserve more detailed attention. The Diary period is the most obvious but others include his time before the Brooke House Committee in 1670, the allegations made about him during the Popish Plot of 1679 and then the end of his career in early 1689. Wherever possible short sequences in correspondence have been included. Several letters referred to and quoted from by Pepys's biographers, such as the one to John Tyrrell, and that from Samuel Newton, have been transcribed in full here from the original manuscripts for the first time.[7]

Pepys's years of retirement have for the most part dominated previously published collections. More than half of the letters published by Tanner in 1926 belong to 1700–3 alone. Although intrinsically interesting in their own right, including a significant proportion of them here would have been at the expense of periods when Pepys was in the forefront of historical events. Moreover, the publication of his correspondence with John Evelyn in *Particular Friends*, which provides the full text of 132 letters, includes 50 from the period of Pepys's retirement. Therefore only a representative sample from those latter years has been included here.

Whatever the criteria, inevitably many letters of equal merit have had to be omitted. Pepys's surviving correspondence is vast and even today previously unknown individual letters or documents continue to turn up. Nevertheless, it is worth stressing that some of Pepys's correspondence is routine and, while of interest to specialists in naval history particularly, it has been relatively easy to justify passing most of these by for the present selection.

The editorial treatment of any seventeenth-century texts is a controversial subject in its own right. In *Particular Friends* all the original spelling was retained but abbreviations were expanded. This worked, despite Evelyn's idiosyncratic and erratic spelling, because only two letter-writers were involved. In this selection many more individuals are represented, resulting in an array of different spellings and grammar (or lack of). In deference to a modern audience and in order to cope with the various different forms of names of persons and places in the original texts, and the different policies adopted by previous editors, the spelling has been

---

[5] See p. 275.
[6] Nos. 227-8.
[7] Nos. 165, and 227, quoted from by Bryant iii, 101, and Tomalin, 364, respectively.

modernized throughout except where words have no equivalent today. Although desirable for purely scholarly purposes, original spellings render some letters almost incomprehensible to the modern reader.

It is important to present the texts so that their meaning and content are as readily accessible to a modern reader as they would have been to the original author, regardless of the latter's shortcomings. Where necessary (and where there was no doubt) the proper names of places or persons have been modified to reflect modern usage, and to make them consistent, thereby doing away with a proliferation of confusing phonetic variants.[8] For example, 'Woolwich' has replaced the 'Wollage' or 'Woolage' of the originals, and Cadiz rather than 'Cales'. George Mackenzie, Lord Tarbat, is now just 'Tarbat' rather than variously 'Tarbat' or 'Tarbutt'.

Readers of Pepys's Diary have been accustomed to largely modern English spellings because the text has had to be transcribed from the shorthand original. Other publications, for example Pepys's *Navy White Book* published in 1995 and Knighton's 2004 edition of *Pepys's Later Diaries*, feature modernized texts. In his 1935 edition of Pepys's *Tangier Papers*, Edwin Chappell discussed the issues involved and pointed out that 'no useful purpose' is served by the 'fetish of literal accuracy'. In this he was primarily concerned with the expansion of shorthand texts, but the point is no less relevant when dealing with letters written in a haphazard and inconsistent fashion. The fact is that variant spellings may in a few cases have some contemporary implications for pronunciation, but in general have no relevance to the substantive meaning of a word. More often the added 'e' at the end of words was used to a variable degree by most writers, but has no significance for the meaning.

Modernizing the letters has had a variable impact on the texts. Some originals are long lost and the only texts available are the modernized versions published by Smith or Braybrooke. The treatment of other texts by more recent editors concerned to retain the flavour of the original spellings also varies from no intervention at all to differing levels of expanded abbreviations and other clarifications. Of course, modernizing can distance the reader from the period and the writer's level of education but on balance this seems a small price to pay for coherence, especially as the letter-writers could hardly have intended to be incoherent and – had they had the opportunity – would scarcely have countenanced the publication of their letters at the time in an uncorrected form. Pepys's father and brother-in-law, and James Houblon, for example, wrote letters that were replete with phonetic spellings and haphazard or non-existent punctuation.[9]

Such letters are really now difficult to read without numerous annotations unless the reader is an expert in seventeenth-century English. Apart from modernizing the spelling, punctuation and paragraphing have been introduced where absolutely essential to make the sense clearer but no intervention has been made to modify the readings apart from these changes. The order of words is unaltered as are various other inconsistencies in style, such as signing off, which vary from letter to letter, and between letters-sent, drafts, and copies. However, it should be added that some words that seem familiar have changed their meaning across the centuries. Readers should beware of this. A brief glossary covers some of the more archaic terms, but

---

[8] The general model for names of persons has been the form given in the DNB and also Latham and Matthews, vol. X 'Companion'. These are not always in agreement though: DNB gives Montagu, L & M Mountagu. Since P uses the latter, that has been preferred.

[9] For example Letters nos. 20 and 111 (compare with Heath, no. 7 and Howarth, no. 57).

the best source of reference is the glossary of terms included in every volume of the Latham and Matthews' edition of the Diary.

Dates have been converted to a common format of day, month and year. English 'Old-style' dates based on the Julian calendar where New Year's Day came on 25 March have been converted as well. Thus a date such as 11 March 1655 would be by our reckoning 11 March 1656, and is given as such here. Some letters written from the Continent were dated ten days later according to the Gregorian calendar, but often carried the English date as well. To avoid confusion, since this is a strictly chronological selection, the English date has been given in these instances as well. Where the difference in dates is relevant to the content, this has been noted.

The letters are set out in chronological order with a very few exceptions depending on the date of receipt by Pepys or the order in which he recorded them. They are accompanied by a running commentary in order to place each letter firmly in the context of Samuel Pepys's remarkable life, and the history of the period. A list of personalities provides brief biographical detail about Pepys's correspondents and most of the other individuals mentioned. But with so much outstanding reference material available for Pepys, the reader is strongly advised to take advantage of the Companion volume to the Latham and Matthews' edition of the Diary, and some of the excellent biographies of Pepys produced over the years. Amongst these, Arthur Bryant's trilogy, and those by Richard Ollard and Claire Tomalin are specially recommended. The publication of Pepys's *White Book* and the *Brooke House Papers* in an edition edited by Robert Latham provides a valuable insight into the management of the Second Dutch War. C. S. Knighton's recent *Pepys and the Navy* and *Pepys's Later Diaries*, the latter a collection of Pepys's later diary notes concerned with specific events, are also extremely useful additions to the available material.[10] However, the research for this book uncovered new information about the origins of Mary Skinner's family, and also the probable identities of Mrs Bagwell and Mrs Steward. These are noted in some detail in the section about personalities, and also where relevant in the main text.

I would like to thank Richard Barber, Caroline Palmer, Anna Morton, and Pru Harrison at Boydell, Adrian Carey, the Pepysian Library at Magdalene College, Cambridge, for allowing access to Pepys's letterbooks, the Navy Records Society, the National Maritime Museum in Greenwich, the Institute of Historical Research in London, the Bodleian Library, the British Library, Princeton University Library, and the book-dealers Krown and Spellman of Culver City, California, who kindly made available the unpublished letter of Pepys to Edward Southwell then in their stock.

Thanks are also due to Claire Tomalin for her assistance with some enquiries concerning Pepys's relatives and friends. Finally, full acknowledgement of the efforts of previous editors like J. R. Tanner, R. G. Howarth, and Helen Truesdell Heath should be made.

The book text was designed, laid out, and set in Microsoft Word to camera-ready copy by me. The transcription of the shorthand letter of 27 June 1660 is also by me. Therefore, any mistakes that remain are entirely my responsibility.

Guy de la Bédoyère
Welby, Lincolnshire 2005

[10] All these books are listed in the Bibliography on pp. 283-4.

Abbreviations and references

* – not previously published

BHP – Brooke House Papers in Latham 1995

BL AM – British Library Additional Manuscripts

Bryant i, ii and iii. See Bryant 1933, 1935 and 1938 respectively in the Bibliography

Diary – Samuel Pepys's Diary (see Latham and Matthew). Evelyn's and Hooke's diaries are referred to as 'diary' (lower case)

DNB – *Dictionary of National Biography*

HMC – Historical Manuscripts Commission. Report on the Pepys Manuscripts preserved at Magdalene College, Cambridge, London 1911

MS Rawl – Rawlinson Manuscripts at the Bodleian Library

NWB – Pepys's *Navy White Book*, Latham 1995

OBSessP – Old Bailey Session Papers

PC – the Pepys-Cockerell papers, part published by Tanner (1926 and 1929). Note that those from 1662–April 1679 are at the National Maritime Museum, Greenwich, and the later papers are in private ownership.

PC Sale – Sotheby's 1 April 1931, *Catalogue of the well-known collection of relics of Samuel Pepys, the property of the late John Pepys Cockerell*

Pepysiana – Wheatley 1918

PF – *Particular Friends*, de la Bédoyère 1997 and 2005

Pforz – Carl H. Pforzheimer Collection, Harry Ransom Humanities Research Center, University of Texas at Austin.

PL – Pepysian Library, Cambridge

T1926 – Tanner 1926

T1929 – Tanner 1929

1 Pepys's Early Life and Career: 1633–60

ALTHOUGH PEPYS was born in London and spent almost his entire life there, like so many Londoners of the time and since his immediate family's remoter origins were rural. He had many relatives in Cambridgeshire and Huntingdonshire. His father, John Pepys, was born on 14 January 1601 at Eaton in Cambridgeshire and christened that day at Impington. John Pepys became a tailor's apprentice in London by 1615 and on 15 October 1626 he married Margaret Kite (or Kight), sister of a butcher, at Newington in Middlesex. They produced eleven children, only four of whom reached adulthood, a completely normal experience for the period. John Pepys continued to work as a tailor from the family home in Salisbury Court next to St Bride's churchyard until he inherited a house in Brampton near Huntingdon from his brother Robert in 1661. He moved there with Margaret that year and after her death in 1667 he moved in with his daughter Paulina, by then Mrs John Jackson. He died in 1680.

These comparatively modest origins belied the small window of opportunity that awaited Samuel. His half-great-aunt Paulina by his great-grandfather's second marriage had married Sir Sidney Mountagu in 1618. Their son Edward Mountagu (1625–72) rose to prominence in the Parliamentary forces in the Civil War, later distinguishing himself in the Navy under the Commonwealth, and then made Earl of Sandwich after the Restoration. His patronage played a crucial role in Pepys's career and was probably the most decisive factor in the diarist's early life.

Samuel Pepys was born on 23 February 1633. His immediate family might have been modest but in a time of enormous social upheaval it was not particularly unusual that his extended family included the Mountagu connection, and also lawyers and even a doctor. One of these men, Pepys's cousin Sir Richard Pepys (1588–1659), even rose to become Lord Chief Justice of Ireland in 1654.

By the mid-1640s Samuel had been sent to Huntingdon Grammar School, most likely lodging with his uncle Robert Pepys. By 1646 he had been brought back to London to attend St Paul's School. During this time he witnessed the execution of Charles I and later was embarrassed to be reminded by a former schoolfellow called Christmas that he was known as a 'great roundhead' at that time (Diary 1 Nov 1660). The young Pepys had boasted how he would preach on the King with the subject 'the memory of the wicked shall rot'. Given his later loyalty to Charles II and James II, it was not a time he subsequently remembered with pride.

In 1650 Pepys went to university at Magdalene College, Cambridge, being elected to a scholarship in April 1651. The original plan had been to go to Trinity Hall, and Samuel's name had been entered there the previous June. But life turns on chance events and in this case it was almost certainly connected with the new master of Magdalene, John Sadler, Town Clerk of London. Sadler happened to live at Salisbury Court. This is too much of a coincidence to have had nothing to do with the change of college. But even if it was merely a coincidence, and not a demonstration of neighbourly patronage, Samuel's tutor Samuel Morland knew

Mountagu so well that in 1659 he even wrote a report on his potential to act as a supporter for the restoration of the monarchy.

In spite of the important step this marked in Pepys's life, we know almost nothing about his time at Cambridge. But in about 1653 he took a walk while there, and drank a large quantity of water. To this he attributed the arrival of a kidney stone in his bladder, flushed there by the copious quantities of water that he had consumed. It resulted in so much pain that eventually in 1658 he felt he had no choice but to risk a potentially lethal operation.

Pepys came down from Cambridge in 1654. By now his short life had already transcended some of the most momentous events in English history since the Battle of Hastings. Charles I was dead and the Commonwealth of England was now in power with royal blood on its hands. In December 1653 the MPs resigned their powers to Cromwell and the Protectorate was established. By early 1655 Cromwell had overseen the division of England into eleven military districts, each ruled by a major-general. Throughout this time the new order was already fighting its first international war, using the Navy as its principal instrument. The transformation of the Navy into a serious force began under the Commonwealth and its admiral Robert Blake. Blake had already successfully pursued the Royalists under Prince Rupert into the Mediterranean and led the defeat of the Dutch in the Downs off Kent in May 1652 before the First Dutch War was officially declared in July. A year later the Navy under George Monck had defeated the Dutch at the Battle of the Texel and killed their admiral, van Trump. Blake continued to promote English maritime interests in the West Indies before dying from fever in 1657.

It was by the mid-1650s that Edward Mountagu started to play his decisive part in Samuel's future. He had served in the Parliamentary army during the Civil War. By 1654 he was on Cromwell's fifteen-strong Council of State, and by 1656 was joint general-at-sea with Blake and five others, commanding the Navy in the Downs the following year. During this time he seems to have offered Samuel a position, or at any rate granted a request to offer him one. By the end of 1655 Pepys was managing Mountagu's household as a sort of all-purpose runner who dealt with minor administrative, staff and financial matters on his master's behalf. It is in this capacity that Samuel Pepys first appears in the extant correspondence. Mountagu's own career defined Samuel's and from the very beginning he had been propelled not only into naval affairs, but also to the forefront of the great political and military events of the day.

Pepys's household had a limited staff – just two maids, a boy called Tom and an old messenger called East. On 1 December 1655 he had married Elizabeth Marchant de St Michel at St Margaret's church at Westminster. The location was appropriate. In 1642 Edward Mountagu had married Jemimah Crew in the same place. Mrs Elizabeth Pepys was fifteen, the daughter of a Huguenot immigrant, and brought Pepys nothing but herself. We might very well have expected the young, ambitious, Pepys to choose a wife who brought money and position. Since in every respect the marriage would have been regarded a reckless indulgence by his peers, and Elizabeth and her own family a costly addition to his existing family liabilities, the only reason he can have married her is because he was infatuated with the young woman. Nevertheless, perhaps in deference to her youth, they did not live together until 10 October 1656. Significantly, Pepys seems to have gone to great lengths to avoid any contact with her family at this time.

Meanwhile, the correspondence opens in the early spring of 1656, a little over a year after the establishment of the major-generals and the failed Royalist insurrection known as Penruddock's Uprising, when Pepys received a letter from his master. It is an instruction to change Spanish money into English money at a fixed rate of exchange, based on the bullion values of gold and silver.

The letter was sent from onboard the *Naseby*, pride of the Protectorate fleet and built in 1655, then moored in St Helen's (in the original spelled 'Ellen's') Road in the Solent off the north-east coast of the Isle of Wight. Pepys received it at his master's London suite in Whitehall Palace. Mountagu depended on his servants to manage his affairs while he was at sea, but it soon became plain that Pepys could provide more than just day-to-day administration.

1. EDWARD MOUNTAGU TO SAMUEL PEPYS

For my Servant Samuel
Pepys at my Lodgings in Whitehall

11 March 1656

SAM PEPYS
You are upon sight hereof to pay unto Captain Hare or his assignees the sum of one hundred and fourscore pounds lawful money of England for so much received of him h[ereby?] in pieces of eight and doubloons at 4s 6d the piece of eight. Hereof you are not to fail.

Dated March 11th 1655 on board the *Naseby* frigate in St Helen's Road.

E. MOUNTAGU

The next letter vividly reveals the young administrator cutting his teeth in managing his master's personal and public affairs. Pepys refers to other correspondence sent two days before and continues to deal with a variety of domestic issues including Mountagu's children's clothing, and the issue of the young Marquis de Bades, captured just a few weeks before off Cadiz and now under Mountagu's care.

Pepys goes on to act as a conduit for the latest news. At the time the most potent issue was whether or not Cromwell ('His Highness') would accept the crown and establish a new dynasty of monarchs. He did not, but he increasingly posed in the guise of a king. In 1656 some preparatory work was made to produce a new milled coinage, with Cromwell portrayed in the style of a Roman emperor but described as Protector in a Latin legend. This was an astonishing repudiation of the anti-popish stance of the English Revolution. The new coins started to seep into circulation in 1658 but were stalled when Cromwell died in September that year.

2. SAMUEL PEPYS TO EDWARD MOUNTAGU

27 November 1656

SIR
By Tuesday post I acquainted your Honour with Mr Meadows' answers to both the questions, as likewise particularly to what your last letter commanded me. Yesterday my Lady Pickering came hither to pack up the small glasses, which I hope will all

come whole to your hands. Speaking to her Ladyship further concerning the bed, she took occasion to talk to me concerning the Marquis' expenses, which I was the day before with Sir Gilbert about, and upon some discourse desired me to show her the bill before I made my address to the committee: her intention is to see it made more for your Honour's advantage than she fears you would willingly make it, viz. to set down a suite of hangings, and not reckon a particular servant for the Marquis but put it into the future accompt of his table. I desire to know your further commands concerning this. I have sent swords and belts black and modish, with two caps for your Honour and two for Mistress Jemimah, two pair of spurs for yourself and two for the Gentlemen[1] with two riding coats for them, as handsome as the Monsieur can make, and I hope they will please. A pair of slippers too for one of the Gentlemen: for all things else, I have writ particularly to Mr Barnwell, I hope and have endeavoured everything to your Honour's liking. Here is nothing publicly past worth your hearing, only this morning his Highness went to the Parliament, and in the Painted Chamber signed eleven bills (five public, six private). The common vogue is the old story of the Protector's kingship, which is now said to be merely opposed by the Major-General[2] and soldiers in the House.

> My Lord, your honour's faithful servant
> SAMUEL PEPYS

In the next letter Pepys once more commences by detailing the various domestic issues he was charged with. However, he progresses to a more detailed update on political affairs, particularly the great issue of the day: whether or not the Protectorate was about to become a hereditary office or an elective one. He closes with a subject probably more dear to his heart than any other – music.

3. SAMUEL PEPYS TO EDWARD MOUNTAGU

For the Right Honourable General Mountagu
At Hinchingbrooke Near Huntingdon

Whitehall
11 December 1656

MY LORD

Your Honour's enclosed to Mr Wheeler I have delivered, and sent the dozen stools, and half-dozen cushions. My Lady Pickering was herself here and see the books and silver bedstead well placed, and in the chest with the cushions there are five pieces of hangings, which her Ladyship hath sent. Upon the hangings I have put the letter I last mentioned with a ring in it, which the postmaster sent me, as unwilling to promise its security. I waited upon Mr Crew yesterday, who told me he thought your Honour might shortly have occasion for that £300 which I paid him the last week, and consequently advised me to forbear endorsing it, for avoiding its crossing out again, or too great a trouble in procuring such a sum otherways. This I have done, till I hear further to the contrary from yourself, and have taken a single acquittance for the money. My Lady Pickering will write fully concerning the hangings, as also what hath passed in the Committee, by this post. The Parliament it's said hath renewed their lease, but for what time is not known. The capital dispute *An anima*

---

[1] Mountagu's sons Edward and Sidney.
[2] John Lambert.

(gubernatoris) debet generari vel creari[3] hath lately warmed a great deal of breath there, and to be feared some blood too, not one openly abetting *Generation* but the graver of those two your Honour may remember present at Sir William Petty's magnetic experiments.

Pagan-ffisher[4] hath a solemn speech prepared for the 16th current the day of his Highness' inauguration, to be spoken in the Cockpit one Tuesday next, and distrusting by his rhetoric he should loose the name of the Poet mendicant, he hath fitted a song, which Mr Hingston hath set for six voices, with symphonies between each Stanza for as many instruments the first of which (being at a practice at Mr Hingston's chamber I remember) runs thus

Funde flores, thura crema	['Pour flowers, burn incense,
Omne sit laetitiae thema	Let there be a theme of joy,
Facessat quicquid est amari	Let all bitterness and torment cease,
Tuba sonet et tormentum	Let the trumpet sound.
Grande fiat argumentum	The strength of the unconquered Oliver
Invicti virtus Olivari	will be the great proof.']

My Lord, your honour's dutiful servant
SAM. PEPYS

Pepys's letter to his master of 8 January 1657 shows how the young man's position was bringing him into direct personal contact with some of the most conspicuous and important members of the government. He had had another piece of good fortune during 1656. George Downing, now one of the four Tellers of the Receipt of the Exchequer seems to have made the young Pepys a clerk in his office around this time. It was not mere chance. Downing was behind the Exhibition to Cambridge awarded Pepys when he was at St Paul's School.

4. SAMUEL PEPYS TO EDWARD MOUNTAGU

For the Right Honourable
General Mountagu. At Hinchingbrooke
Huntingdon

8 January 1657

MY LORD

I have spoke with Colonel Ingoldsby who tells me that he hath an order (but not of his own procuring) whereby Mr Trafford and he are joined in the seeing so many loads of wood laid out for such a use. If there be anything against your Honour's privileges he desires your pardon, being himself the least concerned in it. But I since met casually with one who had formerly attended your Honour about something concerning wallwood, and purposely taking occasion to ask what he knew concerning such a business, he told me he believes it to be a trick of Sir Henry Mildmay, and that the order is obscurely got from Drury House and reported to be

---

[3] This refers to the debate about whether the Protectorate should be a hereditary or elective office. It means 'Whether the soul of the protectorate must be procreated or elected'.
[4] Payne Fisher.

his Highnesses: this week he will tell me more of it. However I shall take care that no lops be taken away, nor trees till your Honour have a particular accompt of the authority they pretend to act by, which I am informed is very unwarrantable.

I have sent this week fifty yards of bays as good as can be bought for that use, though of the same price, as the rest was. The house through the speaker's[5] indisposition is adjourned till Monday. Mr Feake (who with Sir H. Vane are lately set at liberty) the last Sunday fell a preaching out of a window towards the Street, protesting he as little knew how he came out as for what he was cast into prison, and when (after many extravagancies) the city Marshall from my Lord Mayor would have silenced him, he replied, that that Spirit which warranted him to speak was above Mr Protector's command, and therefore much more Mr Mayor's.

My Lord

Your Honour's dutiful servant

SAMUEL PEPYS

This curious letter of 5 December 1657 ends with the usual news from the political front, but opens with what was obviously a very delicate subject. Since 10 October 1656 Pepys was living with his wife but the text seems to suggest that Pepys had acted in such a way as to lead a maid to assume he wanted to commit an indiscretion with her. But letters later in the sequence describe how Pepys had been trying to find out what she was up to, discovering that in fact the maid had had few duties, and had been eating out at a victualling house where she had come into contact with men and engaged in an illicit marriage. However, given Pepys's candid confessions in the pages of the Diary about his inclination freely to indulge in sexual liaisons, solicited or otherwise, with almost any woman who took his fancy, especially servants, it seems more than likely that whatever misdemeanour this unnamed maid had committed, Pepys had very likely tried his luck with her.

Pepys also seems to have made allegations about his cousin Mark Alcock to defend himself for allowing the situation to arise, for which he now apologizes. If the maid was a victim, then she was to be a victim again – Mountagu had evidently instructed Pepys to sack her. In the series of letters that follows Pepys's concern that he might have compromised his patron's support gives rise to palpable panic.

Pepys's private life was certainly not as settled as he would have liked it to be. Elizabeth Pepys suffered from a number of ailments that affected her ability to enjoy normal sexual relations. These included what has been identified as dysmenorrhoea, characterized by uterine cramps during menstruation. This contributed to their frequent quarrels, recorded throughout the Diary, though Pepys was liable to become infuriated by anything, from her cooking to what he regarded as her extravagance. For a while in the late 1650s they were certainly estranged. Pepys disliked recalling the experience, calling them 'our old differences, which I hate to have remembered' (Diary 4 July 1664). He was also particularly unsettled by the thought that anyone else should know about such things. On 9 January 1663 he destroyed, amongst other documents, a letter she had written a couple of months previously to him about her unhappiness 'vexed' at the thought it might be 'met with and read by others'.

---

[5] William Lenthall.

5. SAMUEL PEPYS TO EDWARD MOUNTAGU

For My Honoured Lord
General Mountagu at Hinchingbrooke
Leave this at Huntingdon

5 December 1657

MY LORD

My Thursday's letter to Mr Barnwell mentioned my receipt of the £417 as also Mr Barton's lodging here since this late business of the maid, which I am glad to understand by Roger [Pepys] is your Honour's pleasure. As for my privity to her marriage, if no duty to yourself, a tenderness to my credit (as to my employment) obligeth me to avoid such actions which (like this) renders it so questionable. But I shall submit your opinion of my honesty in this, to that which Mr Barton and Roger shall inform you of from her own mouth. If the rendering me suspicious to the maid, and charging her to lock me from any room but my chamber, moved me to speak anything in an ill sense concerning my cousin Mark [Alcock], I desire it may be valued as my zeal to acquit myself, rather than prejudice him. For the weekdays I have not yet, nor for the future on Sundays shall I be more forth at night, though this was not past seven a clock, as my she-cousin Alcock[6] knows who supped with us at my father's. Your commands concerning her removal I shall obey.

Captain Clerke with his humblest service hath presented you, with six goodly planks of cedar, I gratified the men that brought it, and paid their expenses. As for your goods in the *Centurion* the westerly wind hath kept them out, so that the vessel came not to Woolwich till today. The things will come to me on Monday, and the horse delivered to Roger. Captain Guy hath his order, and I suppose his money. He hath waited at Woolwich these five days about these things, and will bring the horse hither on Monday. For news there is only, my Lord Whitelocke's being made Viscount Henley, and Colonel Hewson knighted, and that Mr Downing is to go resident into Holland.

Your Honour's in all duty
SAMUEL PEPYS

The issue concerning the maid continued. It seems that Mountagu's mother-in-law had taken charge of dealing with her, despite coping with the death of her eldest son Edward. With these matters covered Pepys goes on to provide one of his brilliant vignettes of the age: the sight of Oliver Cromwell making his henchmen dress up as Catholic priests, using captured vestments, for entertainment.

6. SAMUEL PEPYS TO EDWARD MOUNTAGU

For My Honoured Lord
General Mountagu at Hinchingbrooke
To be left at Huntingdon

8 December 1657

MY LORD

The things are come from onboard, and one of the boxes shall come this week to Hinchingbrooke and the rest kept till further order. The horse Roger purposeth to set

---

[6] Presumably Mark Alcock's wife.

out with tomorrow. I desire to know your pleasure concerning the Cedar. I was this day at Mr Crew's, where I find all in health, but sad for Mr Edward's death. Mrs Crew will soon acquaint me concerning the maid heretofore proferred to my Lady, till when I think it not best to let this maid know of her sudden going away; but I shall have a care to look over the inventory and goods. Sir Gilbert Pickering went out of town this morning. This week I shall also send razors, and battledoors for the children. Some talk there is of a plot, but I believe it is merely raised upon the late discovery of so many Jesuit-priests, whose copes and other popish vestments the Protector yesterday made some of his gentlemen put on to the causing of abundance of mirth.

My Lord
Your Lordship's dutiful servant
SAMUEL PEPYS

7. SAMUEL PEPYS TO EDWARD MOUNTAGU

For the Honourable General
Mountagu at Hinchingbrooke
Leave this at Huntingdon

22 December 1657

MY LORD

I was this morning removing the cedar into the back-entry when your Lordship's commands came to me, and I find it just of a length to receive it. The cup (I have formerly mentioned in a letter) I have in my hands, and expect your directions therein. The children's halts and ratteene for my Lady I sent the last week, and hope you have received it. I shall this week send your Honour some bottles of Rhenish wine from Captain Holland, who had attended on you himself had not his wife's lying-in prevented him. As for my cousin Mark if any unjust complaint of mine hath occasioned your Honour's displeasure against him, I heartily beg the same ill to my self, and shall observe your directions at his coming hither. The maid from Mrs Ann Crew I expect tomorrow or next day. In the interim I shall venture to acquaint your Honour that I am too evidently convinced that Sarah's and this maid's miscarriage hath risen from want of employment at home, and especially from their victualling abroad, under pretence of which four hours at least in a day was excused for their being abroad, and from thence at cook's shops comes their acquaintance with these fellows. To prevent this (from the time I perceived it) I have allowed this maid very plentifully for my diet for twenty weeks, and I am sure have thereby hindered many ill consequences, which in so short a time her liberty had in part occasioned, and your Honour lately sensible of. Your directions to give the next maid convenient allowance, encouraged me to this liberty of proposing it to your Honour that (if you think it fit) she shall diet as well as myself and my wife for four shillings a week, and by that means the disrepute of a maid's going to a victualling house, and neglect of your Honour's own doors will be prevented. I humbly mention this to your Honour upon confidence that it will be received as I intend it, viz. free from any other ends than your Honour's commodity. As for mourning, it will be next week before it will be done.[7] I shall wait upon my Lady Strickland tomorrow concerning the coat and follow her directions therein.

---

[7] For Edward Crew.

As for news, he that sees the strictness used for stopping that free passage of strangers through Whitehall, and the Ceremony used in passing the presence-Chamber, will say Sir Gilbert Pickering is a perfect Lord Chamberlain and who meets Colonel Jones with a white staff in his hand will acknowledge him as perfect a Controller. Mr Maidstone is Cofferer, and Mr Waterhouse Master of the Green Cloth. My Lord Laurence's eldest son is dead of the smallpox lately at his father's lodgings, which occasions my Lady Claypoole a circuit to Whitehall. There is an ambassador (rather drove than) come from Florida, forced by the Spaniard's rigour to an address to his Highness, but more by the calamity of shipwreck to the miserable condition of his coming, his Highness being necessitated to give him clothes. He is a Moor, and (by the perishing of his interpreter) cannot be understood. He was yesterday at Whitehall, and was received courteously there.

My Lord, your Honour's dutiful servant
SAM. PEPYS

8. SAMUEL PEPYS TO EDWARD MOUNTAGU

26 December 1657

MY LORD

This week your Honour I hope hath received five-dozen of bottles of Rhenish wine from Captain Holland. In my last by Tuesday post I gave you an account concerning the cup, cedar and mourning. On Thursday night there came a woman from Mrs Ann Crew, whom I received. But before I said anything to her concerning the house, she began and asked me if I knew what her work must be. I told her I supposed Mrs Crew had acquainted her with that; she told me, no. Whereupon I told her what had been the office of them that had been before her. She answered, she never had been used to make fires, wash rooms, or cloths, secure, or do anything like that, and that she expected only to take charge of the goods and oversee other maids, as a housekeeper. I answered I knew nothing to the contrary but that her work was to be as theirs that had been in her place before, but that if your intentions were otherwise, Mrs Crew could best advertise her. So she lodged here that night, and desired to be excused from undertaking anything, till she had advised again with Mrs Crew. Whereupon the next morn she went away and since I have not heard of her.

My cousin Mark is here, for how long I know not, but your commands concerning him I shall follow. Only it troubles me to hear, what your Lordship's apprehensions are concerning me (if his report may be credited). The loss of your Honour's good word I am too sure will prove as much my undoing, as hitherto it hath been my best friend. But as I was ignorant of this late passage, so I see little cause by anything I find yet to doubt of giving your Honour a good account of the goods in the house, and my care in keeping them so. My Lady Strickland returns her service to yourself and my Lady, and hath instructed me in that business, but it's necessary I should know what kind of coat for the bigness it should be.

Sir William Wheeler continues still ill of the gout and desired me to deliver his letter to the Commissioners for N[ew] buildings, which I shall do the next sitting. Your £250 at the Exchequer I have taken up for the last Quarter, for there is much fear of a stop there to the payment of salaries as there is at the Excise Office, and elsewhere. Mr Crew (with whom I spoke this afternoon) is in health and hath directed me to go to one Captain Cotes, who came over with Mr Edward from

Mardike, and is believed to have many things of Mr Edward's, which I am to endeavour a recovery of, and shall do it.

My Lord
Your honour's dutiful servant
SAMUEL PEPYS

The year 1658 was a critical one for Samuel Pepys. He felt he had no choice but to risk everything. The pain in his bladder had become unbearable. His father placed him in contact with a neighbour, the surgeon Thomas Hollier. Hollier and a colleague, a doctor called Joyliffe, agreed to operate on him. The occasion was 26 March 1658 and the operation was at least a qualified success. Pepys recovered, almost certainly because it was his good luck to have been operated on with instruments that were still clean enough not to cause a fatal infection. Some subsequent patients of Hollier's were not so lucky and several died. Pepys kept his stone, a solidified lump of uric acid weighing about 56 grams (2 oz), and celebrated his deliverance annually thereafter, though it is plain from references in the Diary and the correspondence to discomfort, and his nephew's account of the post-mortem that followed his death in 1703, that Pepys was never really free of the affliction.

Pepys is not known ever to have fathered a child by anyone. It is generally believed that the surgery was responsible for permanent sterility, though Pepys was never aware of this. Either way there was no pregnancy for Elizabeth Pepys before that date so it is possible either or both of them were infertile anyway. Indeed, throughout some of December 1659 a hiatus in his wife's menstrual cycle led him to hope that she might be pregnant.

It was also a momentous year for England. The third and last Parliament of the Protectorate sat, but Cromwell dissolved it after only sixteen days and then ruled on his own until his death on 3 September 1658. He was succeeded by his son Richard, and was buried in the manner of a monarch in Westminster Abbey, complete with a crown, orb and sceptre. By 22 April 1659 Richard Cromwell had dissolved his Parliament. By 7 May the Rump Parliament was restored and within a few days it had coerced Richard Cromwell into abdicating. In October the Army expelled the Rump. Pepys now updated Mountagu on the tide of events.

9. SAMUEL PEPYS TO EDWARD MOUNTAGU

For the Right Honorable the
Lord General Mountagu at Hinchingbrooke. Huntingdon.

20 October 1659

MY LORD
The Commissioners of the Great Seal their Commissions determined the last night. The Judges have been at their several Courts to assign the term and 'tis expected they will all sit the time of their Commissions, which I think is to the 20th of November next.

Sir Henry Vane, Salwey, Whitelocke, Sir James Harrington and Lord Warriston are five chosen to manage the civil power; Fleetwood, Lambert, Berry, Desborough and Sydenham are five chosen to the martial power but I do not hear they have acted anything yet, though sat these three days.

Concerning the accounts I have enclosed a paper.

Sir Arthur [Haselrig] and Morley are gone into the Country.

I find many of your officers desirous to have your Lordship to their colonel again and intend to move for it. I have by Mrs Crew's and my Lady Wright's directions been with Scott, who is to wait upon them anon concerning the business.

Answers are waited for out of Scotland and Ireland, which (they say) hinders the army's declaring what they intend. I have adventured to send your Lordship the enclosed pamphlets for your diversion.

Your Lordship's dutiful Servant
SAM. PEPYS

10. SAMUEL PEPYS TO EDWARD MOUNTAGU

22 October 1659

MY LORD

I have (not without much importunity) got Mr Scott to go speak with Mrs Crew. All that hath yet been done in the business is to know his demands which is a hundred pounds for his skill and pains in the cure, which he hopes to effect in three months. My Lady Wright intends suddenly to enquire the manner and rate of his entertainment from the friends of some of his patients. Both the ladies did consult the lessening of that expense and the avoiding of some worse inconveniences which will attend her lodging at his house, and to that end spoke to me concerning mine as being near to him (which I would most willingly wish might be thought serviceable to her) but he insists upon her being at his, because of her often dressing, and his practice too so great, as that he never stirs abroad to any. My Lady Wright will be speedy in her enquiry and so acquaint your Lordship with her determinations and Mrs Crew's herein.

Hitherto there hath been a mixed council (some or other of the Parliamenters still sitting amongst them) but all things are hatched at the Admiralty chamber, where the Army-officers sit. They determined last night of this list to make up the council. People talk now very boldly of the resolution the Kings of France and Spain have taken to assist the King of Scots, and that an envoy is expected with their proposals to us concerning him.

My Lord
Your Lordship's dutiful servant
S. PEPYS

I sent an account of the bills this week by Beard.

In this letter to Mountagu on 3 December 1659, Pepys recounts the fate of a Portuguese Jew called Ferdinando the Merchant, who had died after being operated on by the same surgeon as himself.

11. SAMUEL PEPYS TO EDWARD MOUNTAGU

For the right Honourable
General Mountagu at Hinchingbrooke. Huntingdon.

3 December 1659

MY LORD

I wrote to your Lordship by the carrier, and since that received your Lordship's of the 29 of November with one to Mr Andrews. I received a while since the remainder of the dollars, which I was to have of Mr Creed viz. 118 Rix Dollars, and the next day delivered them to Mr Shepley. Concerning the forest lands I had advised (by your Lordship's commands) with Mr Walker, servant to my Lord Lambert, but the parliament being so suddenly broke up, before the act for the Forests was finished, there is a stop at present to all the business concerning them; and for the bonds your Lordship remanded them from my cousin Thomas Pepys and to my best remembrance delivered them to Major Hart, in whose hands I believe they are now. I expect to hear from Captain Goffe the next week about the Regiment arrears.

Nothing more yet from the North. Yesterday there was a general alarm to our soldiery from London, so that the City was strictly guarded all night, occasioned by the apprentices' petition delivered to the Lord Mayor of that import, that a rising was expected last night, and many indeed have been the affronts offered from the apprentices to the Redcoats of late. Late last night was likewise a proclamation made up and down the town, to prohibit the contriving or subscribing any such petitions or papers for the future. The Quaker,[8] I mentioned in my letter this week, was arrested in an action of £4000 by some of the King's servants to whom the statues were formerly assigned for £2000 debts, and was bailed by his fellow Quaker, my Lord Pembroke.

My Lord
Your Lordship's dutiful Servant,
S. PEPYS

Being this morning (for observation sake) at the Jewish synagogue in London I heard many lamentations made by Portugal Jews for the death of Ferdinando the Merchant, who was lately cut (by the same hand with myself) of the Stone.

The expulsion of the Rump and the military coups were not popular. Riots began to break out. By 26 December the protests resulted in the recall of the Rump Parliament. Pepys witnessed much of the disorder, which he described as an unprecedented 'so universal a fear and despair'.

12. SAMUEL PEPYS TO EDWARD MOUNTAGU

For the Honourable General
Mountagu at Hinchingbrooke. Huntingdon.

6 December 1659

MY LORD

Yesterday's fray in London will most likely make a great noise in the Country, and deservedly, as being the soonest began the hottest in the pursuit and the quietest in the close of any we have hitherto known. In the morning a Common council being met, some young men in the name of the City apprentices presented their petition (much talked of, of late, and which the Committee of Safety set out a proclamation against) to the Lord Mayor and Common Council. This meeting of the youth was interpreted as a forerunner of an insurrection, and to prevent that, the soldiers were all (horse and foot) drawn into the City, which the apprentices by another mistake thought to be done on purpose to prevent the delivery of their petition. Hence arose jealousies on both sides so far, that the shops throughout London were shut up, the soldiers as they marched were hooted at all along the streets, and where any straggled from the whole body, the boys flung stones, tiles, turnips &c at [them] with all the affronts they could give them, some they disarmed and kicked, others abused the horses with stones and rubbish they flung at them; and when Colonel

---

[8] Not identified.

Hewson came in the head of his Regiment they shouted all along 'a Cobbler a Cobbler'; in some places the apprentices would get a football (it being a hard frost) and drive it among the soldiers on purpose, and they either darst not (or prudently would not) interrupt them; in fine, many soldiers were hurt with stones, and one I see was very near having his brains knocked out with a brickbat flung from the top of an house at him. On the other side, the soldiers proclaimed the proclamation against any subscriptions, which the boys shouted at in contempt, which some could not bear but let fly their muskets and killed in several places (whereof I see one in Cornhill shot through the head) six or seven and several wounded.

About four of the city trained bands were up, but nothing passed between the soldiers and them but sour looks. Towards evening the Mayor sent six aldermen and six common council to desire the remanding of the soldiers out and they would undertake the quieting of the City, which was not then granted, so the soldiers took possession of the gates all night, but by morning they were withdrawn out of the City (having only pulled down the gates at Temple Bar) and all now quiet as ever. Portsmouth stands out for certain, Morley is there, and Haselrig and Walton are believed to be gone that way.

Your Lordship's dutiful servant
S. PEPYS

I left Mrs Jem well just now.

13. SAMUEL PEPYS TO EDWARD MOUNTAGU

8 December 1659

MY LORD

I wrote to your Lordship by Saturday post (which letter your Lordship this week mentions not the receipt of) giving you an account of Mr Creed's payment of the remaining dollars due upon the bill and my delivering them the next day to Mr Sheply. Also concerning my writing to Captain Goffe by Major Hart's advice about the Regiment money, to which I hope for an answer this week. For Sir H. Crooke's money and the ballast there hath not any been accounted for yet for the last half year, but when my Lord Whitelocke moves for his share of that of Sir H. Crooke's, I shall not neglect to look after your Lordship's.

As for Mrs Jemimah I have spoke to Mr Scott, who hath promised all expedition, and that more particularly to her than many of his patients, some of whom have been five or six weeks at his house, and are yet no forwarder than Mrs Jem, for her bodice were tried on yesterday and be says shall be fitted against the next week. I have been solicitous to him and her concerning it and I doubt not, they will speedily provide for the child's cure.

I wrote (though a little too late) by Tuesday post concerning Monday's broil in London, which letter will come along with this. Since then the news is confirmed concerning Portsmouth (where Morley, Haselrig, Walton, Fagg, and Wallop are got): also the Isle of Wight have declared with them for certain; Plymouth is expected to do the same, and from Colchester it is said they have declared and are in arms for a Parliament. The greatest fear at Whitehall is what Lawson (now in the Downs) will do, some of whose ships I am assured from the Treasurer of the Navy are fallen in with Portsmouth. It is said that Haselrig hath set sail himself for Scotland, and that the more suspected because nothing hath come thence this Sevennight. Five troops and as many foot Companies were sent from hence on

Tuesday to Portsmouth, but cannot be thought able to do anything, for the Militia thereabouts are made sure to Morley.

The present posture of the City is very dangerous, who I believe will never be quiet till the soldiers have absolutely quitted the town. These circumstances (my Lord) may give your Lordship the best guess of the City's condition viz. the Coroner's inquest upon the death of those that were slain on Monday have given it in murder and place it upon Colonel Hewson, who gave his soldiers order to fire. The Grand Jury at the Sessions this week in the Old Bailey desired of my Lord Mayor that the soldiers might be removed out of the town, who answering that he knew not well with the safety of the City how to do it, they offered in open Court to indict their officers and undertake to bring them before his Lordship. Upon Tuesday last the Committee of Safety sent their desire for the Lord Mayor, Sheriffs and Aldermen to give them a meeting at Whitehall at night. The aldermen did so (but the Lord Mayor and Sheriffs would not). My Lord Whitelocke made a speech excusing the entrance of the soldiers into the City on Monday last, as having received intelligence that some ill design was intended against the City, and what was done was in defence to the City; and in the close of his speech offered the Recorder a Commission to try the Middlesex causes (as was customary). The Recorder thanked him, and let him know that for London causes the City Charter gave him a sufficient commission, and for Middlesex he darst not do what the Judges would not unless he could tell him from whom and in whose name he could lawfully give such a Commission. One passage more I shall add, that in the common council house upon the reading of the prentices' petition, Brandrith stood up and inveighed highly against the insolence of the boys to meddle in such businesses, whereupon he was hissed down by the whole Council and answered by Wilde the Recorder, who particularly defended the whole petition with a general applause. This is the present fate of the City, who are informed how the army have sent in granados to Paul's and the Tower to fire the City upon an extremity (which is certain) and I am confident will not rest but in the chasing away of the soldiers out of town. My Lord

Your lordship's dutiful servant

S. P.

14. SAMUEL PEPYS TO EDWARD MOUNTAGU

For the Honourable General
Mountagu at Hinchingbrooke Huntingdon

8 December 1659

MY LORD

I wrote today more largely by the carrier, though so late that I had not time to read over what I had wrote. Since noon I am informed Plymouth town and castle, and Colchester have declared for a parliament and that Morley, Haselrig, and Walton are gone by sea from Portsmouth to Scotland leaving that place to Whettam, Fagg, and Wallop, who are said to be very well prepared. Berkshire is upon the point of rising, and the City every hour express a greater dissatisfaction than before, and what by the pulling down of Temple Bar gates, sending hand-granados to Paul's, Sion College and other places are exasperated beyond hope of a reconciliation. Never was there (my Lord) so universal a fear and despair as now.

Your lordship's dutiful servant

S. P.

Upon the payment of the £1000 to Sir H. Wright, he desired that whereas he was indebted to your Lordship for one half year, and at Christmas there is another ½ year due) we would take the whole £60 at Christmas, which will be payable within this fortnight.

15. SAMUEL PEPYS TO EDWARD MOUNTAGU

For the Honourable General Mountagu
at Hinchingbrooke. Huntingdon

15 December 1659
Lincoln's Inn Fields

MY LORD

This morning proclamation was made for a Parliament and the City (as if satisfied therewith) have commanded all men to be quiet and forbear farther violence. I have done as your Lordship commanded me concerning the letter, but not delivered it, your excuse of ignorance of the affair (it being but for matter of debate) not being thought full enough. Wherefore it is advised that another may be speedily sent wherein your Lordship may own the same kindness from – as you do in this, and that your distemper at the time of the receiving of the letter, and the so sudden deciding of that question (wherein they desired your advice) now by this proclamation, be made your excuse. My Lord

Your lordship's dutiful servant
S. PEPYS

Mr Crew (if your Lordship contradicts it not) intends to send for Mr Edward to his house at Christmas.

In between these two letters Pepys commenced his Diary on 1 January 1660, aware that he had a ringside seat to history. Apart from a few minor breaks it continues until 31 May 1669. During this period we have more information about Pepys and his circle than at any other time in his life, but the Diary is by no means a complete record of his daily affairs. He does refer to sending this letter, but not the news that Mountagu's lodgings were being coveted by others or Lady Jemimah's fears of smallpox.

16. SAMUEL PEPYS TO EDWARD MOUNTAGU

For the Honourable the Lord
General Mountagu at Hinchingbrooke Huntingdon.

12 January 1660

MY LORD

There was one sent to me this morning from Sir Anthony Cooper to let me know that several were putting in for your Lordship's lodgings, and that he did desire to know your intentions concerning them, whether to keep them or part with them. If the last, then he doth intend to put in for them; but if you have any desire to continue them, he will wholly desist from any such endeavours of his own and be instrumental to hinder those of others, who are about the getting of them. I purpose anon to wait on him, and have in the interim promised to write to your Lordship and that I hoped by the next post to have something from you concerning the business.

My Lord, Mrs Jemimah presents her humble duty to your Lordship and my Lady, and bids me say, and so I think her, to be in as good health as ever she was. But whether the heat of her bodice (or what else the Dr cannot tell) hath disturbed her natural temper; she hath some pimples rise in her body, which my Lady Wright and her maid say is the smallpox. Dr Bates on Monday last said the contrary, but barely that it was heat But my Lord if it be, she hath none in the face at all, and for her health she was last night as well and merry as ever I knew her, and hath not yet had the least pain or sickness imaginable since they appeared, which is six days since. The house is not yet up, wherefore by the post I shall write again.

My Lord, Your lordship's dutiful servant
S. PEPYS

I wrote on Tuesday night last by the post.

Over the next few months Pepys's life changed immeasurably. His connection to Mountagu meant that he was invited to join the fleet as his secretary during the momentous voyage to bring Charles II back to England. On 23 March 1660 he boarded the *Swiftsure*. On 3 May the commanders and officers of the fleet in a council of war voted to accept the King's offer of grace to everyone that came over to him within forty days. Pepys drew up the vote and circulated it amongst the ships, and landed at Dover on 25 May in the company of the King.

This shorthand draft letter of 27 June 1660, transcribed here for the first time, is exceptionally rare as a surviving letter from Pepys of this period. On 26 June he recorded in the Diary that 'I met with Mr Throgmorton, a merchant … who did give me five pieces of gold for to do him a small piece of service about a convoy to Bilb[a]o, which I did.' Several later letters record Pepys's assertion that he could not be bought. The letter proves this was not wholly true, though the same day he declined a £500 bribe to turn down the post of Clerk of the Acts.

17. SAMUEL PEPYS TO CAPTAIN MOOTHAM

To Captain Mootham, commander of the Foresight, *Captain [Thomas] Bun commander of the* Essex, *or which of these Vice-Admiral Lawson shall appoint convoy to Bilbao*

Whitehall, 27 June 1660

SIR

I am to advise you in your passage into the Bay of Biscay that you are to forbear to surprise, block or molest any of the Spanish boats or vessels which you shall meet with there. It was not thought proper to insert this in your instructions, wherefore you are desired to observe it as if it had. I am directed to give you private advice hereof and rest,

Your loving friend and humble servant
S. PEPYS   SECRETARY

Two days later Pepys was appointed Clerk of the Acts, collecting his warrant for the post from the Duke of York. The personal loyalty Pepys would owe to the Duke of York, and then as James II, would also be one of the most defining and decisive aspects of his professional life.

2 Clerk of the Acts – the Diary Years: 1660–9

PEPYS'S TIME as Clerk of the Acts at the Navy Office established him. It happens largely to coincide with the years in which he wrote his Diary, which provides us with a wholly unparalleled means with which to scrutinize the Restoration government of Charles II as it faced the trials of rebuilding the political structure of the country, the Plague, the Great Fire and the Second Dutch War. There is no equivalent period in history until modern times where we are so well equipped to follow events in such a dramatically personal way. Pepys had a ringside seat to history. He knew this, and his relentless drive to record everything that happened between 1660 and 1669 makes the personalities of his world as vivid in literary form as if they were characters in a popular television drama.

As he gained increasing control over the administration at the Navy Office, Pepys became the focal point in a sea of paperwork. His meticulous approach to recording the daily events in his Diary was only one part of his routine. He dealt with vast quantities of incoming and outgoing correspondence, as well as compiling minutes and memoranda of meetings. These papers he accumulated, filed and occasionally weeded. Much of this is lost. As mentioned in the Introduction, some retained correspondence – presumably a copybook – referred to in the Diary on 6 June 1661 is not extant. Some letters have survived apart from those in the State Papers and circulate either on the open market or have found their way to libraries. On 24 July 1995, for example, several shorthand drafts or copies of letters sent by Pepys on 26–27 June 1660 were sold at Sotheby's. These all help explain why the available main body of correspondence from this period does not begin until 1664–5.

The letters that do survive substantiate many of the episodes recounted in the Diary, but Pepys only ever recorded selected events in its pages. Much is omitted from its pages, despite the popular impression that it is a comprehensive record of every day. The letters show that much else was going on in Pepys's life. They do not fill out all the gaps, not least because not all the letters survive. But they do expand enormously on the information in the Diary. The letters in this chapter feature a vast range of personalities and events and range from Pepys's family business to the humiliating indignities suffered by a Navy crippled for want of cash while trying to fight an international war. They also include the consequences of Pepys's flexible morality. Quite capable of criticizing his colleagues for their inefficiency and corruption, Pepys also wrote a letter on behalf of a ship's carpenter called William Bagwell. Those familiar with the Diary will know that for several years Pepys enjoyed the sexual favours of Mrs Bagwell in return for her husband's promotion; she would return to haunt him twenty years later. The Pepys in the letters of the 1660s and early 1670s is in every respect the Pepys in the Diary.

The availability of the Diary makes it possible to analyse the letters in a rather more detailed way than is possible with the rest of the correspondence. Wherever possible the commentary takes this into account. There is no doubt that several books could easily be compiled that dealt only with the surviving correspondence of the Diary years. However, much of the ensuing correspondence is taken up with the detailed business of the Navy, especially the chronic problems of its finances. Although of technical interest to scholars, these letters make less compelling reading for the layman. Some of these letters have been included but since the content is often similar, protracted and very detailed, most have been omitted in favour of including letters that deal with personal issues and interests.

This previously unpublished letter, preserved in the National Archives, is a fairly routine letter of news from a 36-gun ship called the *Sapphire*, then commanded by Captain Robert Clay. It contains the all too familiar complaints about a lack of supplies, but also includes congratulations to Pepys on his promotion to Clerk of the Acts. The manuscript is difficult to read in places and some words are uncertain.

18. CAPTAIN ROBERT CLAY TO SAMUEL PEPYS

Sapphire in Plymouth Sound
20 August 1660

HONOURED SIR

I have not had opportunity since I was at Lisbon to tender you with my service. At this time (encouraged by your freedom then) have presumed to do it; and to congratulate your entrance into the business you have better been to, in the office.

Give me leave to acquaint you (who I may have some occasion to trouble; yet should be as glad to serve) that one frigate is very foul, beyond others of this squadron, which I am much ashamed of, and there is no supply to be had for nought.

If your favour should be extended towards my supply of tallow(?) at Portsmouth I should endeavour (as I have occasion) to touch there for the same, being unwilling to disburse more money, until I can see satisfaction for what hath already been.

Sir, if I might be of any use to you in this part, your commands should find a faithful observation and performance, by him who desires to continue a friendship(?) [...][1] in you and remain

Your obliged affectionate friend and servant
ROBERT CLAY

Between 1661 and 1662 Edward Mountagu, now the Earl of Sandwich, was at sea. On 25 August he and Admiral Sir John Lawson bombarded Algiers in an effort to suppress pirates affecting English trade. Pepys was of course unaware of the action when he wrote this letter. Pepys instead mentions Tangier. In May 1661 Charles II had announced his intention to marry Catherine of Braganza. Negotiating the marriage was one of the reasons Mountagu was away. Tangier was to be part of the dowry brought by the new queen, and England took possession of it in January 1662. Mountagu brought Catherine into Portsmouth on 14 May 1662.

The scarcity of money Pepys refers to was occasioned by the decrepit state of the silver hammered coinage, much of which was clipped down, making nonsense of a system in which silver and gold denominations had to contain their denominational value in bullion. Hoarding, and export of coin to the Continental bullion market, compounded the problem.

---

[1] The manuscript is badly smudged here.

19. SAMUEL PEPYS TO EDWARD MOUNTAGU, EARL OF SANDWICH

29 August 1661

MY LORD

We have been under very great doubts concerning your Lordship's well-being, till your letters of the 22 and 28 of July from Alicante eased us, and from them we have reason to hope you have ere this been and dispatched at Algiers, and now upon return thence. The several I have writ (though I fear few yet have reached your Lordship's hands) have as well as I could informed your Lordship with what hath occurred most worth your notice; of which the latest hath been my Uncle the Captain's death, and disposal of what he had to my father and me (though with many cautions); the illness and recovery of my Lord Hinchingbrooke and his setting out this week toward France; and lastly my Lady's happy delivery of a young lady.[2]

The present season is generally sickly both here and in the country, even to a contagion or very near it. Among whom the known Dr Fuller (of the *Holy War*) is dead. All but Church-matters are very quiet; and them especially in Scotland make great noise, the common-prayer book being (they say) openly refused.

Money still scarce; of which evil the court, city, Navy (and your Lordship's own wardrobe concernments) do much labour.

The fleet however waits the King's commands to sail, but through want of tidings from Portugal matters are not ready at court, nor can we guess when they will; especially, if they go on to send preparations to Tangier (as 'tis said) by this fleet, I cannot think it can be this three weeks.

Hinchingbrooke-matters proceed I hope to your Lordship's contentment. Mr Edward Mountagu[3] is busy in his preparations for Portugal, though I fear the allowance from the King is much less than your Lordship expected. With daily prayers for your Lordship's health (in which I never was so anxious as now) I humbly bid your Lordship Adieu, and am

Your Lordship's most obedient and dutiful servant
SAMUEL PEPYS

Throughout this book letters have been selected that reflect Pepys's various family interests. This next letter is from his father, John Pepys, and concerns business affairs on the property at Brampton, which John Pepys had inherited from his brother Robert in 1661, and problems about the will. However, John Pepys also expresses concern about his son's health. This goes unmentioned in the Diary at the time though Pepys described being in agony on 14 May 1664 (Diary). Pepys visited his parents in Brampton 14–15 October and dealt with some of the affairs mentioned in this letter (see the Diary).

[2] The 'Captain' is Robert Pepys. Jemimah, Countess of Sandwich, gave birth to her youngest daughter and child, Catherine, in August 1661.
[3] Edward Mountagu (1635–95), a cousin of the Earl of Sandwich.

20. JOHN PEPYS SENIOR TO SAMUEL PEPYS[4]

10 July 1664

DEAR SON

You will find by the enclosed that the foul-mouthed doctor is resolved to be troublesome. It was with the consent of his brother, Mr Roger, for with Mr Phillips that brought me this letter, they got a promise from him to be for them before they told him against whom it was. And sent the note to him afterward and Doctor Thomas's(?) note that he had under your brother's hand for £10 but no seal to it. He did acknowledge to me and your brother John that it was but £8 that was due to him and there was 19 shillings and 6d was in your brother's book which was due to him of that £8. I was with Mr Phillips this morning and he showed me the note for the £10, and I see no seal to it, and I told him there should be no need of troubling a baly [bailiff?] to serve the leet.

Therefore pray good child let there be something done in it. Neither can I know how an new inventory can be made the goods is so dispersed. If you have added the money which is 24 shillings for the three shirts and 40 shillings for the cloth, and a letter case. I can but take my oath – as I have done already – that I have made a true inventory of all things that was his.

I hope you have received my last letter with the [receipt] enclosed under Tom's hands for an acknowledgment that the goods were mine with the other paper which was writ not a quarter of a year before he died where in he wished I would make an assignment of my goods over to him. Now, in answer to your last I have spoken to Will Stancks and he will sift out Steven Wilson and Fox what was due when your uncle died. He is afeared that Fox hath paid your uncle. I wished W. Stancks to let him know if he pleads, that he had no right to it tell he was admitted to it. And for Ashton Stancks cannot tell what it should be for that there should be money due from him for the close.

There was an acre that belonged to an other man that your uncle never agreed for but thinking he might have it at any time yielded to pay 8 shillings a year till he had concluded for it. And so your uncle set trees and dichet(?) and set a quick-set as far as that acre went. He that owned it being dead it is letten to another and he hath taken it to his one use. It was the land that the haycock stood on. Stancks got the gate removed when I was at London last, so Price's money is not to be paid till Michaelmas or the next court that we give up our right to him in the land, for the £39 which is yet due to us from Piggot do not know what security we are like to have from him for it more than we have all ready. We must endeavour to make sale of so much as is left for so much as is left unpaid.

I do not yet understand how it is that is to give satisfaction for the none payment of [rent] from the time that it should be paid as for Barton business there is seven rods of that land your uncle had of old Barton which is worth a matter of £15 or £16 to be sold, these and so much more as mad it up £14 or £16 a year was given to old Barton and his wife and to the heir male of them to after they're deceased. This was given four years before the owner died, [and] when he died he gave all the rest of his estate to old Barton. If we cannot find any writing that Barton was engaged to your

---

[4] The original letter is replete with erratic phonetic spellings, a virtual absence of punctuation or paragraphing, and little use of upper-case letters for names. The text here has therefore required substantial modification to all these to make it coherent.

uncle for to clear this, if we cold find anything then we could take a course with the old man. If we cannot, if the old man die it comes to the young man and we cannot hinder him. Mr Narborow hath a good part of this land and hath sold it to Price and Price hath the benefit of it this year. It is thought he refuses to pay Mr Narborow till he hath cleared this thing, I desired he would act for us as well as himself and according to the valuation of ours we would contribute toward the charges, you will do very well to write to him and at your uncle while you may know how to have your letter conveyed. Not receiving a letter by York makes me fear there is some hindrance of my daughter's coming next week, if there be I shall be very sorry for it for I should be very glad to see her hear as soon as can be.

Dear child I am very much troubled what my lord's apothecaries fear is of you – that you have an ulcer growing in your kidneys. For God's sake let me beg of you that you will have Mr Hollier's advice and some able doctor of his acquaintance with as much speed as you can and to beg a blessing from the Lord that your life may be preserved for what a sad condition should your poor old father and mother be in if the Lord should take you before us.

I shall be very glad if any lines come to Will Stanck today for our business requires his speedy assistance. This with mine and your mother's very kindly be presented to you both with your sister's service I rest who shall ever be

Your very loving father

JOHN PEPYS

The legal disputes over Robert Pepys's will dragged on for years, largely thanks to the objections raised by his brother Thomas.[5] The following letter is endorsed 'W. Coventry's answers to me about the Watermen for Chatham, *Victory* and *Dragon*, convoy for Tangier victualling(?) at Plymouth'. Unfortunately, the two letters Pepys had sent have not survived. The context was that on 5 October the King and the Duke of York had travelled to Portsmouth to oversee the equipping of a squadron of warships to be commanded by Prince Rupert. In May protests had been made to the Dutch about £0.8 million-worth of losses by English merchants at the hands of the Dutch. However, war for the moment was held at bay.

21. WILLIAM COVENTRY TO SAMUEL PEPYS

12 October 1664

SIR

This morning brings me two of yours. Commissioner Pett wrote to me also about the watermen in which I will move his Royal Highness.

Also the repairs of the *Victory* I suppose you have satisfied of the resolution of repairing her, however that had been resolved the *Dragon* ought to be dispatched with all speed. Pray write him to that purpose.

The *Dover* designed for convoy from Plymouth wants nothing from his Royal Highness God sending her a fair wind she may go – the money being on board.

I shall acquaint his Royal Highness with the other convoy required. I shall be very glad to see the flag business at safety(?). I confess it troubles me to see complaints from commanders for such petty things.

I had last night a letter from Mr Gauden which only enclosed a list of the victuals now on board. The letter is the enclosed which is all I had or expect.

---

[5] See Latham and Matthews, X, 320–1.

Your second letter hath nothing to answer but the kindness of it in which I will never be in arrear to you being with great truth Sir

Your affectionate most humble servant
W. COVENTRY

Pepys's *Navy White Book* contains a variety of memoranda, jottings and other documents. He also included references to some letters, which discuss the contents but which are not true copies. Here Pepys discovers to his astonishment that the recommended dimensions of a fifth-rate ship were unknown to Peter Pett, Master-shipwright at Chatham 1664–7.

22. COMMISSIONER PETER PETT TO SAMUEL PEPYS

April 4. 1665, Commissioner Peter Pett owns himself to seek about his dimensions of a 5th-rate ship.

Being in great haste about the contracting for the building of ships – I wrote to Commissioner Pett for his opinion as to the dimensions of a 4th- and 5th-rate. He keeps it a great while in hand, and returns me my copy of a 4th-rate that I have sent him of an old contract, with his opinion thereon. And afterward, I writing to him about the 5th-rate, he answers me in his letter, April 4 – which is among my papers no. 29, that he is at a very great loss as to the determining the main dimensions of a 5th-rate ship – which is very strange. And though he promised me, however, his opinion by the next, he then instead of an answer sends me word that it will be fit to advise with the shipwrights who is to build them, and therefore he will come up to town on purpose. Which methinks is a strange thing, that such as he should at this time of day be to seek in this matter.

In March 1665 the Second Dutch War, which had been brewing for months, finally broke out when the Dutch captured a Swedish ship carrying masts for the Royal Navy. It was not news Charles II wanted to hear. He had been trying to avoid war, anticipating the ruinous expense it would entail. The 'business of money' became one of the principal subjects of Pepys's correspondence.

23. SAMUEL PEPYS TO WILLIAM COVENTRY

15 April 1665

SIR

Now as to the business of money, what I have to acquaint you with is this. That finding our credit every day lessen, and prices thereby to rise upon us, and that upon notice thereof taken to the Treasurer he was come to give us no other reply but 'go to my Lord Treasurer[6] and try what you can do, for I can get no more money,' I thought it necessary to draw up a state of the present charge of the Navy and what probably it will be till November next, by which time some ships likely will be brought in. This having done and offered to the Board, they concurred with me in tendering it to the Lord Treasurer, which we did according to the copy thereof here enclosed, concerning which (because it would be too long to give you a rationale of

---

[6] Treasurer: George Carteret; Lord Treasurer: Thomas Wriothesley, Earl of Southampton.

every branch of it) I shall once for all assure you I have not knowingly magnified one sum in it beyond what I did see full reason to estimate it. The charge to November from Lady Day last amounts unto £1,015,948, and the weekly sum of what thereof ought to be readily paid comes to £23,865 per week, wherein neither have we included anything for the charge of the twenty ships more ordered to be taken up.

At hearing of this, my Lord Treasurer gave us no answer but signs of amazement and discontent, with many protestations that this money in nature is not to be found, nor anything farther than what he had already allotted for the Navy, and with this uncomfortable answer dismissed us.

I must confess I was grieved at heart to see to what pass at this rate we were likely soon to come, considering the arrears already of wages to seamen and the yards, the value of materials to be bought and difficulty of getting some of them even with money, as timber and plank and hemp (for the last of which we were forced this day to give Harrington 55s per ton to keep our hands employed at Chatham), as also cordage and canvas, the supplies the victuals must have, the consumption of the little, stores we have in the building of new ships, and the impossible repairs of our old ones after an engagement. These, I say, and other considerations (which every day gives occasion to) made me propose to the Board (not without great offence somewhere) that we should obtain a solemn hearing before the King, or whom his Majesty should refer us to, which by the Duke of Albemarle's mediation was procured to my Lord Chancellor,[7] Lord Treasurer, and himself, which ended in a silent dissatisfaction on all hands without any appearance of a possibility of compliance in my Lord Treasurer to support us, but plain declarations of the contrary, in which state we were a second time left and still remain, saving that we this day understand that the King will have no more new ships contracted for, nor any of the twenty hired which were last ordered. Which how little it will lighten our load you will easily see, and as easily judge what must be looked for without a miracle. . .

S. P.

'At noon dined at home; and to my office, very busy – till past one, Lord's Day, in the morning, writing letters to the fleet and elsewhere' (Diary 20–21 May 1665).

24. SAMUEL PEPYS TO WILLIAM COVENTRY

20 May 1665

... Whatever the success shall be (which God make the best), I must without flattery say the whole world bears testimony to your endeavours and their effects, which for themselves and our great Master's sake that is adventured with them, I will not fear (for whatever other reason there may be for it) but God will bless.

And not to be silent in my own bad case, where (without arrogance) my pains exceed any of my neighbours, and for all that shall not want as great a share of blame upon any miscarriage, I can safely say that were or could the imperfections of this Office in the dispatch of ships, etc., be greater than they are, or had the hire of my labour been £10,000 per annum, I could not be possessed of a more hearty

---

[7] Edward Hyde, Earl of Clarendon.

intentness in the early and late pursuance of my duty herein than I have been hitherto, and would you have it demonstrated, take it then in your own merry mathematics. I have heard no music but on Sunday these six months. ...

S. P.

25. SAMUEL PEPYS TO THE EARL OF SANDWICH

27 May 1665

...The absence of all my fellow-Officers obligeth me to such attendance that I come to the knowledge of nothing acceptable to your Lordship. For I am sure the want of money, men, materials, and meat will sound but ill, yet is the truest news I can send your Lordship, as living in the noise of nothing else. Which makes me sorrowfully apprehensive what at the best can be the issue of your first engagement when (to be open to your Lordship) I cannot foresee you can in any time be in condition (without a miracle) for a second. God of his mercy preserve your Lordship through what difficulties are now before you. ...

S. P.

26. THE EARL OF SANDWICH TO SAMUEL PEPYS

Off Harwich
29 May 1665

MR PEPYS

I think I am to return you thanks for two letters, one concerning Sir John Lawson's affair, concerning which I pray suffer me to add this entreaty, that you effect what he desires as much as possible. I shall receive great content when I find by him that you do so.

I thank you for your care in providing the things I wrote for; I have the same prospect of affaires you have, and perhaps yet more disadvantageous. Yet what God brings upon us must be run through with as much indifference and industry as we can, and I trust he will make the successes better than we look for.

We daily expect to meet the Dutch, being now lifting up our anchors to be under sail early in the morning, bound for Sou[thwo]ld Bay; and after a little stop there, to get our men and necessaries from Harwich, then into the sea to look the enemy out. God send the next account you have may be to all our comforts.

I am, etc., SANDWICH

While the fleet was out Pepys discovered Peter Pett was criticizing him. Pett complained that the contract for masts with Sir William Warren (which Pepys had encouraged acceptance of) was a poor deal. Pepys wrote a pointed letter, itemizing its advantages for the Navy in a matter-of-fact fashion that anticipated how he would deal with the far more serious allegations made against him in later years.

27. SAMUEL PEPYS TO COMMISSIONER PETER PETT

16 June 1665

SIR

You will by another from the Board this night (if you be at Chatham) receive tomorrow his Royal Highness' resolution touching the *Sovereign*, which it is expected should be out in a very little time, and thereto your promised assistance is desired.

In answer to yours of the 12th, which I received on Wednesday, I must own myself much surprised to find so severe a reflection upon the whole Board in the business of masts, as if they, contrary to your frequent advice, had committed some such heinous neglect in the contracting with one man for our supply of masts that it needed a public declaration of your incense thereon.

What I have to say is this:

1. That to this hour I never heard you, either publicly or privately, oppose this contract or offer any better or other, saving one with Mr Shorter, which he upon treaty did voluntarily decline. This I affirm and appeal to the memory of the Board as to what you have at any time discoursed hereon at the table.

2. That at the time of the making this contract, Mr Wood and others were summoned, but none would entertain our supply. Mr Wood declaring he would fetch no more till he had sold what he had here.

3. That no contract appearing in my books for fifteen years backward (so well as things were done then) equals this in cheapness and other circumstances of advantage to the King.

4. That it was made deliberately, and by His Royal Highness' particular approbation, as well as full advice of the Board, and upon this one consideration, his Royal Highness did proceed to prefer this method of contracting at that juncture, that it were fit to have some person to depend upon, and for the rest that might be brought to market, we were never a whit the further from buying them, besides the serving ourselves at a pinch with what were ready here, and which accordingly we have at this time bought viz., Mr Wood's parcel of forty masts.

Lastly. I have this further to vindicate the Board with, that as you never did propose any other way so I am ready to make good, that at the time and since, no English merchant but Sir W. Warren was, and has been, able to serve us with that quantity and sort of masts as he has done upon that contract, and therefore no contrary advice of yours (if you had given any) could have been of use to us.

You will please to pardon this unusual style, it being upon a matter extraordinary and in defence of the whole Board against a very untimely and, I think, unjust a charge, as in truth I know not one thing whereon more of their care, and with better success, has at any time been exercised than this, though it answer not all our wants.

I remain, Sir, Your very humble servant
SAMUEL PEPYS

Meanwhile, out at sea Sandwich's optimism had been well-founded. Within a few days he was to lead the defeat of the Dutch at the Battle of Lowestoft on 3 June 1665 in spite of the fact that his ship was shot up so badly it was 'pierced like a colander', as John Evelyn called it in his description of the death of Sandwich in the Battle of Sole (Southwold) Bay in the Third Dutch War (Diary 31 May 1672). Pepys of course wrote to congratulate his patron when he heard the news.

28. SAMUEL PEPYS TO THE EARL OF SANDWICH

17 June 1665

MY LORD
Finding your Lordship not come up with the Duke (which I hoped for), I dare not omit my duty of congratulating your safety, and honour gained in the late action, which I am not only well informed his Royal Highness doth everywhere give to your

Lordship, but am a witness with what ingenuity Mr Coventry doth your Lordship right both public and private, as well respecting your counsels as your personal performances, which God hath hitherto, and I trust will for ever bless.

Sir John Lawson is at Greenwich, and was visited by the King this day. His wound, it seems, doth well for what appears, but his fever, thrush, and hiccup are symptoms the physicians do greatly apprehend, and speak doubtfully of him for. I greatly long to kiss your Lordship's hand. . . .

Unfortunately for Sandwich the praise apparently heaped on him by the Duke of York and William Coventry did not last. On 23 June he came to see Pepys to express his outrage that Coventry's formal account of the battle virtually omitted Sandwich's part and passed almost all the credit on to Prince Rupert who had 'hardly a shot in his side' and the Duke of York who spent most of the engagement 'out of gun-shot' (Diary 23 June 1665). Pepys defended Coventry, believing that the journalist and pamphleteer Sir Roger L'Estrange had actually been responsible for publishing the account. It did no good. On 25 October 1665 Sandwich told Pepys that thanks to this, he and Coventry were 'declared enemies'.

29. SAMUEL PEPYS TO WILLIAM COVENTRY

Navy Office
1 July 1665

SIR

I am very much unsatisfied in my setting out with the ill tidings I must begin my correspondence with you this voyage, but though the matter will be unwelcome, yet fearing the want of your advice upon it may render it worse, I judge it necessary to trouble you therewith. The enclosed will tell it you better than any other words can. What the consequence of such a practice as this may be, for workmen (be their provocation never so great as this at Portsmouth I doubt is) to combine in a desertion of his Majesty's service, I am very unable to foretell, and do as little see how the present difficulty will be removed, the Treasurer's instruments here leaving us utterly unsatisfied therein till the Treasurer return to town.

This so unpleasing subject I could willingly lay aside, but every day administering fresh occasions of thinking of it, it is but necessary to give you a little share of what passes.

This morning, upon a pressing demand from Commissioner Pett for 1000 yards of kersies, we sent for Mr Medowes, who declaring to us that the debt we owe him for that commodity arises to above £2000, and part thereof in bills of twelve months standing, and that he could not with any security to himself proceed to trust us farther unless we would add to his price 18d per pound for what he should sell us, that thereby he might be in capacity of raising money from the goldsmiths, which he then knew he could of course compass and otherwise not; he pressed it publicly and with such absoluteness to the Board that (not knowing where else to be trusted) we were obliged to undertake for the getting him ready payment for this parcel or give him what he demanded in his price. I leave this to be reflected on at your leisure ...

S. P.

30. SAMUEL PEPYS TO WILLIAM COVENTRY

8 July 1665

SIR

It is my opinion that it would be of use, if you should think so fit, that his Royal Highness would be pleased to bestow his command upon us with some earnestness for the looking betimes into the state of our stores, before the necessities of the fleet put us upon those extremities which I am sure otherwise we shall if ever they come to engage again; and I am afraid from the little forecast which the best of us is guilty of, especially at a time when no man will sell without a promise of ready money, and the answers we both take and give to that question are generally very unpleasing; I say, I am afraid we shall easily be inclined to drive off the providing ourselves with stores till our wants grow greater and our capacity of buying less. . . .

S. P.

31. COLONEL THOMAS MIDDLETON TO SAMUEL PEPYS

July 25. 1665. Commissioner Middleton about the charge of all that is done in the King's yard above what the same thing is done for by private men. How little right the King hath from juries, especially where the King's officers are to be witnesses in the case.

He says thus: 'But this I observe in these two vessels (namely, the two sloops now newly built there, one by the King at Portsmouth, the other at Emsworth by the great), and I beg of you to mind it (for I have taken special notice of it – that this vessel built at Portsmouth shall cost the King full as much (I am apt to believe very much more) barely in the workmanship than the King payeth for the *Emsworth sloop* being wholly fitted. The *Emsworth* not having above five men at any time to work on her, and sometimes not above two or three, and was built in as little time or less than this hath or will be, and we have had seldom less than 10, 12, to 20 and 30 on this here; and from thence ariseth this, judge you. I am confident we can do as much as other men, but matters must be as they may. A greater experiment in point of labour cannot be, being both of one length and breadth, some difference in the depth, which is not considerable; and may this be amended and, shall it not be, I cannot help it.'

In the same letter: 'We have had at Winchester a gaol-delivery. Three [prisoners?] have lain there 18 months. The Grand Jury found the bill Ignoramus, albeit the King's goods found in the house, which was 5 cwt of white yarn, stolen the day after it was spun. Another was quitted, albeit the ropes found were some new, some of them, and by the master ropemaker affirmed to be laid by him not three months before stolen. But I thank God one was burnt in the hand, another whipped, and that was but for small faults. But the witness against him doth not belong to the King's yard; for the truth is, we that are the King's servants here are of so good nature one to another, that we are loath to hinder any poor man, albeit to cheat or steal, or what else it be, so 'ere he is a poor man and he hath helped me to steal, and why should I be a witness against him? It will ruin his wife and children, which is an act of cruelty. Besides, he may do as much for me hereafter, or it may be can do it now; and according as I order him, so I may expect the like from him; for in faith, Sir, I believe we are all k[naves]. I pray God make us better, for I protest to

God we are ashamed of nothing, of neither theft nor idleness: yet it is to be amended.'

By the late summer of 1665 the Plague was raging through London. Pepys had last seen Sir William Coventry at Hampton Court on 23 July, where he had mused on the difficulties of remaining familiar with a friend who had become 'great'.

32. SAMUEL PEPYS TO WILLIAM COVENTRY

5 August 1665

SIR

Partly from the uncertainty of finding of you, and partly from an unwillingness to interrupt your ease unnecessarily, I have hitherto forborne the troubling you with any account of our matters here, which what with the absence of the fleet and the general silence that the present disease puts upon all business, have not been very great since my parting with you at Hampton Court ...

I have been a good while alone here, the rest having to one place or other provided for themselves out of town. The truth is, few but ticketeers and people of very ordinary errands now come hither, merchants and all persons of better rank with whom we have to deal for provisions and otherwise having left the town; so that I think it will be necessary with respect to them that we remove to some place to which they may be invited to come to us, such as Greenwich or the like. Be pleased to let his Royal Highness's pleasure be signified herein; for though the removal of my particular papers and business be I think impracticable, and so do purpose myself to trust God Almighty and stay in town, yet I would be glad that we might have some place appointed where my fellow-Officers and those we have to do with may think it safe to continue their meeting, without which the King's business in a little time will be at a very great stand. . . .

S. P.

Since the Earl of Sandwich remained at sea with the fleet, Pepys took it upon himself to continue supplying news. Sandwich's daughter Jemimah had just married Philip Carteret, son of Sir George. The reason the King was at Salisbury was the Plague, the whole court having moved there on 27 July.

33. SAMUEL PEPYS TO THE EARL OF SANDWICH

Navy Office
7 August 1665

MAY IT PLEASE YOUR LORDSHIP

Your Lordship will see by the different dates of the enclosed, that it hath been want only of opportunity of sending which hath kept your Lordship so long from hearing how matters have gone relating to your family in general as well as those particularly to my Lady Jemimah, since your Lordship's departure.

I will prevent as little as I can the informations your Lordship will gather from the enclosed, and content myself to tell your Lordship generally, That after a fortnight's acquaintance between the young people their marriage was completed on Monday August 31. Present Sir G. Carteret, his Lady, and my Lady Slanning on that side, with my Lord Crew, Lady Sandwich, Lady Wright and all her family on your Lordship's and is the only occurrence of my life I ever met with, begun, proceeded on and finished with the same uninterrupted excess of satisfaction to all parties.

Upon Thursday the 3rd instant my Lady Jemimah and her Bridegroom set out from Dagenhams towards Scotts Hall in Kent, and were met by Sir George Carteret and his Lady at Chatham where I parted with them the next day, they onwards to Scotts Hall, I back to London.

About ten days since I received a letter from Paris from my Lord Hinchingbrooke intimating his readiness to return and thereupon I sent a ship of thirty-six guns to fetch him over from Calais, which took him in on the 3rd instant and (having signified to him my Lady his mother's direction to that purpose at the earnest invitation of Sir George and his Lady) he landed at Dover the same day, to meet his sister and all the rest of that good company the next at Scotts Hall.

The King and Queen keep their court at Salisbury, whether Sir George Carteret is shortly to go, and intends to carry my Lord Hinchingbrooke with him by my Lord Crew and Lady Sandwich's approbation and it's likely may (as matters show themselves from my Lord Hawley when he comes thither) go with him further westward.

Dagenhams hath been the scene of most of this work since the first interview, not without great charge to my Lady Wright, but most generously borne by her.

I have neglected nothing in my power that would contribute to the well speedying of this business, and do assure your Lordship that from all I have observed from my first bringing the two lovers together to my seeing the business ended, as also from the behaviour of Sir George Carteret and his Lady through the whole, I cannot but congratulate your Lordship with the content and usefulness this alliance will certainly be of to your Lordship and your family.

Yet (my Lord) considering Sir George as a man, and so mortal; as a Treasurer and so liable with his whole estate to answer accounts, wherein perhaps himself (through the muchness of his other affairs) is least conversant; and lastly, as one of great gettings and so subject to proportionable envy, I do humbly advise your Lordship that you would think fit to quicken the settlement of the money matter on both sides as soon as may be; which by his private discourse (wherein he hath been very open to me) I find he desires not should lie long undone, telling me in what readiness and in what manner he stands prepared to do his part towards the purchase, when it shall be demanded of him.

The Duke of York with his train is gone towards York, there to spend the season, the Duke of Albemarle acting the Admiral in his absence.

The *Sovereign* is not yet out of the river but will in few days.

It was freshly and confidently reported yesterday that De Ruyter is come home with his whole fleet and I fear it is true.

As to the state of the City as to health 3000 and odd died of all diseases the last week and of them 2010 of the Plague which is now more or less got into most corners of the kingdom.

The first vessel coming towards your Lordship from the river will bring your Lordship some plague-water, and perfume from my Lady Carteret.

With continued prayers for your Lordship's health and good successes I remain

May it please your Lordship

Your Lordship's ever obedient servant

S. PEPYS

One of Pepys's most frequent correspondents throughout the Second Dutch War was John Evelyn, in his capacity as a Commissioner of Sick and Wounded Seamen and Prisoners of War. Although a large number of letters from Evelyn to Pepys survive, rather fewer from Pepys to Evelyn are known. This example was preserved in the Evelyn archive. Since no copy or draft of it exists in any of the collections of Pepys correspondence, perhaps because none was ever made, it is a reminder that many of the letters written and sent by Pepys must now be lost.

34. SAMUEL PEPYS TO JOHN EVELYN

Navy Office
9 August 1665

SIR

I am once more to trouble you with my old question concerning the provision made for the sick and wounded seamen in Ireland, for that a charge is and hath for a good while been running on at Kinsale in expectation of payment from this office; which we have yet no authority to make nor is it fit the care of it should be put upon persons so little at leisure to look after it as the Officers of the Navy; besides that, I have been told, that it hath been by the King and Council left to the Lord Lieutenant of Ireland to give directions in. I beseech you Sir what advice you can give me in any part hereof, be pleased to let me receive, for that what is disbursed must soon or late be paid some where, and the longer it's left unsettled 'tis likely the King will be so much the more sufferer.

Sir I have looked after when you would think fit (in pursuance of our last discourse and Sir William Coventry's advice) to intimate at what ports, and what number of recovered men are ready to be called for, That so as we have ships in the way they may be directed to take them in. I remain

Your affectionate and most humble servant
S. PEPYS

During the Plague public affairs took second place, not least because of the King's withdrawal to Salisbury with the whole court. News had arrived on 19 August of an unsuccessful attempt to attack Dutch East Indiamen off Bergen that had cost the lives of several commanders, including a cousin of Sandwich's, though no ships were lost. These and other distractions meant that Pepys got behind with his work, which he tried to rectify on 25 August.

35. SAMUEL PEPYS TO WILLIAM COVENTRY

25 August 1665

… Little till now occurring to give occasion of writing to you, I forbore to tell you of my receipt of yours of the 14th, wherein nothing commanded answer more than the return of my thanks for the large share you give me of your good wishes, which (I bless God) I yet have the benefit of, though the sickness in general thickens upon us, and particularly upon our neighbourhood. You, Sir, took your turn at the sword; I must not therefore grudge to take mine at the pestilence.

S. P.

Despite the miscarriage at Bergen, the fleet had had to set sail once again in spite of the fact that there had been no time to restock the ships properly.

36. THE EARL OF SANDWICH TO SAMUEL PEPYS

Under sail wind at West 30 August 1665
(Excuse my haste, the Duke of Albemarle hath a list of the fleet)

MR PEPYS

Having not heard from you of diverse days, it was very good news to me to receive your letters, for I was in fear for you of the infection.

We have hastily hurried in what provisions we had by us, and without staying for more, or for any other supply of men, we are now got under sail. I believe we have near fifteen days drink in the fleet, and our actual condition will be much as it is stated in the account you sent me, but not so if we had continued at whole allowance and been full manned.

I have written largely of all particulars to none but my brother, Sir George Carteret, with whom I wish you to correspond. There be many things necessary for present care against the fleet's return; I pray use your best care for them.

God send you good news of us, and that at my return I may find your family and my other friends in health and prosperity.

I am, &c., SANDWICH

Pepys wrote to Lady Carteret with news of the Plague in London, including the worrying information that it might have spread downriver to Greenwich.

37. SAMUEL PEPYS TO ELIZABETH, LADY CARTERET

Woolwich
4 September 1665

DEAR MADAM

Your Ladyship will not (I hope) imagine I expected to be provoked by letters from you to think of the duty I ought and should long since have paid your Ladyship by mine, had it been fit for me (during my indispensable attendance alone in the city) to have ventured the affrighting you with anything from thence. But now that by the dispatch of the fleet I am at liberty to retire wholly to Woolwich, where I have been purging my inkhorn and papers these six days, your Ladyship shall find no further cause to reproach me for my silence. And in amends for what's past, let me conjure you (Madam) to believe that no day has passed since my last kissing your hands without my most interested wishes for your health and the uninterrupted prosperity of your Ladyship and family.

I took care for the present disposal of what were enclosed in your Ladyship's to me; and, in answer to that to Dagenhams, return these from my Lady Wright, who, in hers to myself, gives assurance of my Lord Hinchingbrooke's being got up, and the health of the rest of her family.

My Lord Sandwich is gone to sea, with a noble fleet, in want of nothing but a certainty of meeting the enemy. My best Lady Sandwich, with the flock at Hinchingbrooke, was, by my last letters, very well.

The absence of the Court and emptiness of the city takes away all occasion of news, save only such melancholy stories as would rather sadden than find your Ladyship any divertisement in the hearing; I having stayed in the city till above 7400 died in one week, and of them above 6000 of the plague, and little noise heard day or night but tolling of bells; till I could walk Lombard Street, and not meet twenty persons from one end to the other, and not fifty upon the Exchange; till whole families (ten and twelve together) have been swept away; till my very physician (Dr Burnet), who undertook to secure me against any infection (having survived the month of his own being shut up) died himself of the plague: till the nights, (though much lengthened) are grown too short to conceal the burials of those that died the day before, people being thereby constrained to borrow daylight for that service. Lastly, till I could find neither meat nor drink safe, the butcheries being everywhere visited, my brewer's house shut up, and my baker, with his whole family, dead of the plague.

Yet (Madam) through God's blessing, and the good humours begot in my attendance upon our late Amours, your poor servant is in a perfect state of health, as well as resolution of employing it as your Ladyship and family shall find work for it. How Deptford stands, your Ladyship is, I doubt not informed from nearer hands.

Greenwich begins apace to be sickly; but we are, by the command of the King, taking all the care we can to prevent its growth; and meeting to that purpose yesterday, after sermon, with the town officers, many doleful informations were brought us, and, among others, this which I shall trouble your Ladyship with the telling. Complaint was brought us against one in the town for receiving into his house a child newly brought from an infected house in London. Upon inquiry, we found that it was the child of a very able citizen in Gracechurch Street, who, having lost already all the rest of his children, and himself and wife being shut up and in despair of escaping, implored only the liberty of using the means for the saving of this only babe, which with difficulty was allowed, and they suffered to deliver it, stripped naked, out at a window into the arms of a friend, who, shifting it into fresh clothes, conveyed it thus to Greenwich, where, upon this information from Alderman Hooker, we suffer it to remain.

This I tell your Ladyship as one instance of the miserable straits our poor neighbours are reduced to.

But (Madam) I'll go no further in this disagreeable discourse hoping (from the coolness of the last seven or eight days) my next may bring you a more welcome accompt of the lessening of the disease, which God say Amen to.

Dear Madam, do me right to my good Lady Slanning, in telling her that I have sent and sent again to Mr Porter's lodging (who is in the country) for an answer to my letter about her Ladyship's business, but am yet unable to give her any accompt of it.

My wife joins with me in ten thousand happy wishes to the young couple, and as many humble services to your Ladyship and them, my Lady Slanning, Lady Scott, and Mr Sidney, whose return to Scotts Hall (if not burthensome to your Ladyship) will, I am sure, be as full of content to him as it will ever be of joy and honour to me to be esteemed,

Dearest Madam,
Your ladyship's most affectionate and obedient servant,
SAMUEL PEPYS

The shortage of money did not only compromise the Navy's efforts to fight the war. It also handicapped the Commissioners of Sick and Wounded Seamen and Prisoners of War, who found themselves with mounting numbers of men on their charge but without the resources to deal with them.

This letter from John Evelyn reports the problems in trying to guard the prisoners of war, and also the financial handicap he was trying to operate under. The references to Oxford relate to the fact that the King was headed to Oxford, which he reached on the 25th, and that Parliament was meeting at Oxford to avoid the Plague. 'Leeds' is Leeds Castle in Kent.

38. JOHN EVELYN TO SAMUEL PEPYS

For Samuel Pepys Esqr
One of the Principal Officers of His Majesty's Navy at Greenwich

Sayes Court
23 September 1665

SIR

There are diverse miserably sick prisoners at Woolwich, especially in this bearer's ship. If they could be conveyed down to our fly-boats before Gravesend, our chirurgeon there might look after them; and they have also a guard; but you know I am prohibited relieving any at Woolwich, even of our own men. They might be, I suppose, at Erith; but how shall we (when recovered) secure them from running away? At Gravesend we are forced to make stay of one of the fly-boats on purpose, for the numerous sick prisoners which we could not march with their fellows to Leeds; therefore I beseech you order them by some means or other to be sent (viz. the sick only) to those vessels at Gravesend, where there will be care taken for them.

Sir, Since I saw you yesterday, comes notice to me that of the £5000 I was to touch by promise this week from Mr Kingdome by order of my Lord Ashley, no less then £3000 of it is diverted for other purposes from Oxford. Consider with indignation, the misery, and confusion all will be in at Chatham, and Gravesend, where I was threatened to have our sick all exposed, if by Thursday next I do not send them £2000; and in what a condition our prisoners at Leeds, are like to be. If my Lord of Albemarle (to whom I am now hailing) do not this day help me by an high hand, dreadful will be the consequences, and I will leave you to consider, at whose doors, this dealing at Oxon is to be laid; I am almost in despair, so you will pardon the passion of Sir,

Your most faithful servant
J EVELYN

Despite this appeal, there was no improvement in the problems. Meanwhile, the issue of prize-goods and their legitimate sale by those allocated a portion was covered by a strict protocol, with the crown taking precedence. Two Dutch East Indiamen had been captured, and Sandwich 'did under his hand give Cocke and me his Certificate of our bargains, and giving us full power of disposal of what have so bought' (Diary 1 October 1665). Unfortunately, the protocols had not been observed and Pepys would soon find himself embroiled in a controversy.

39. THE EARL OF SANDWICH TO SAMUEL PEPYS

On board the *Prince-Royal*
At the Buoy of the Nore
1 October 1665

THESE are to certify all whom it may concern that Mr Samuel Pepys hath bought of some of the flag-officers of his Majesty's fleet several parcels of spices, silks and other goods taken out of the two East India prizes by Order, which goods he is fully authorised to dispose of as he shall think fit, he paying his Majesty's Customs due thereupon. And all his Majesty's Officers of the Customs and Prizes are hereby required to suffer the said Mr Pepys quietly to enjoy and dispose of the said goods accordingly. Witness my hand the day and year above-said

SANDWICH

Pepys had to listen to the 'lamentable moan of the poor seamen that lie starving in the streets for lack of money' (Diary 7 October 1665). This distressed him, especially when the seamen heaped abuse on him and other naval officials, but he saw no connection with his own profiteering, perhaps because the problem was so established. On 27 March 1662 he describes how the unpaid crew of the *Guernsey* had been forced to borrow money at ruinous interest rates. In 1665 Pepys was more preoccupied with reforming the naval victualling, and recommended the appointment of a surveyor-general to oversee the private contractors in order to bring to an end the constant shortfalls in supplies. He was also concerned about the claims for supplies for seamen no longer on the ship, or who were now on other ships and being claimed for twice. He heard from the Duke of Albemarle on 11 or 12 October that his ideas had been accepted in a letter that, although short, is now barely legible thanks to fading, and a minute insertion.

40. THE DUKE OF ALBEMARLE TO SAMUEL PEPYS

To Samuel Pepys Esq Clerk of the Acts
to his Majesty's Navy at Greenwich

Cock-pit 11 October 1665

SIR

I have received an account from Sir William Coventry that your proposition for the victualler is approved of by his Majesty. I desire therefore you will be thinking of four fit men to take an account of the provisions in each port, and the number (and to send me an account of it) of men that may send for his Highness's [...]ation. The victualler has orders to go on to provide provisions for thirty thousand men at least. I remain

Your very assured friend and servant
ALBEMARLE

41. SAMUEL PEPYS TO SIR WILLIAM COVENTRY

14 October 1665

SIR

I give you many thanks for your letter of the 11th, and in the first place have run over again with Mr Gauden the account of his great excess in this year's deliveries, wherein as to matter of fact I am not much unsatisfied in the justness of his computation, but do rather acquiesce therein, and rely on the truth of that which you have thought on to be the occasion thereof; which you will yourself be more confirmed in when I have told you that having lately sent down Mr Hayter (among others) to muster some of the ships in the river (directing him purposely thereto for the discovery of what practices he could in this part of the pursers' trade), he tells me that he himself did not meet with less than 100 born to that day and called at that time by the purser at the muster who had been put on shore two, three, four months ago, nay, some in January last; and further that he found some of these men when recovered have been received on board another ship (as supernumeraries) for their passage to their own, and therein continued a month or two in victuals and wages, while at the same time they have remained in both upon the purser's book of their own ship. Now the remedy you propose, as it is undoubtedly the best, and indeed the only one to be wished, so I have made it my business this day to visit Mr Evelyn in this afternoon to see in what order his accounts (with respect to our designs) are kept; beyond expectation I find that if the rest of his companions take the same course he doth, they will save the King a very considerable sum in the remedy they will give us to this very evil, for Mr Evelyn (to instance in one port) showed me his account of Gravesend, where for every penny he demands allowance for, and for every sick man he hath had under his care, he shows you all you can wish for in columns, of which I have here for your satisfaction enclosed an example, which I dare say you will say with me he deserves great thanks for. I have since wrote to him to cause transcripts of these accounts to be sent us, and hope our people will see the King have the benefit of it in the payment of ships and adjustment with pursers, and will send to Sir W. Doyly, etc., for theirs.

Sir, I am most glad to find my proposal about victualling so well accepted, and upon second thoughts am confirmed that if proper persons be set at work and those that will set their hearts upon the executing it painfully, the victualling business may be managed to such a degree of satisfaction as shall give life to all the other works of the fleet. The Duke hath commanded me to go on in proposing what is necessary for the putting this in execution, which as much as I can till his Majesty's and Royal Highness's pleasure is further known I have done, and shall forbear troubling you with from myself because it will better come to you from his Grace. Pray let as little loss of time be suffered herein as you can.

You shall have the estimate for the victualling the next post, it being now done, but I must send it to Erith to be signed. God be thanked for what the Parliament hath given, and send it well paid, and we to do our parts in husbanding of it. I pray for the continuance of your health and with strictest faithfulness am and will ever be

Your most humble and affectionate servant

S. P.

I have enclosed you an accompt of what masts we have already loaden in each ship at Gothenburg their intrinsic value is worth near £20,000 but their politic at this time 20 times as much for I know not what we shall do without them. Here is also an accompt from Scotland from Mr Pett our timber merchant there. Pray consider the post ... and give me your advice in it.

The affair of the prize goods from two Dutch East Indiamen suddenly bubbled up into a scandal. On 1 October Sandwich had sent Pepys a certificate to confirm his legitimate ownership of those he had bought and the right to dispose of them (see no. 39). It appears that the two ships had been apparently ransacked without any reference to Sandwich in the first instance. The king had issued an order 'to examine most severely all that had been done in the taking out any, with or without order, without respect to my Lord Sandwich at all ... I do find that extreme ill use was made of my Lord's order, for they did toss and tumble and spoil and break things in hold, to a great loss and shame, to come at the fine goods.' Sandwich was outraged at any accusation he might have behaved less than honourably and wrote to Pepys accordingly. Since he had indeed been implicated, and even arranged for some of the cargo to start their journey to his home, he was being disingenuous. By 16 October Pepys had received this letter, 'I having received letters from my Lord Sandwich today, speaking very high about the prize goods, that he would have us to fear nobody ... which doth comfort us' (Diary).

42. THE EARL OF SANDWICH TO SAMUEL PEPYS

14 October 1665

MR PEPYS

Your letter of so late a date as the 12th instant makes me somewhat wonder that before that time order was not given to clear all that was disposed by my direction. The King hath confirmed it and given me order to distribute these very proportions to the flag-officer; for that you are to own the possession of them with confidence and if anybody have taken security of them upon seizure, remand security in my name and return their answer, carry it high and own nothing of baseness or dishonour, but rather intimate that I shall know also have done me indignities. Thank my Lord Brouncker and Sir John Mennes for civilities and tell them I expect not less in reality for I have befriended them. And that I shall very ungratefully hear the news of base examinations upon any action of mine. What is more to be said in this matter is better referred to a fit occasion. I am

Your affectionate friend and servant

SANDWICH

Pepys discovered that the two prize ships seized had probably been grossly over-valued, and that by reducing this Sandwich could be seen to have had rather less from them. Since the untrustworthy merchant George Cocke was responsible for the reassessed value, it is unlikely to have been as correct as Pepys suggests.

43. SAMUEL PEPYS TO THE EARL OF SANDWICH

25 November 1665

MY LORD

In obedience to your Lordship's of the 23rd I shall look after the business of William Howe and give you the clearest and speediest account I can of it.

The Duke of Albemarle is coming to Oxford and sets out I hear on Tuesday next. I judge it not impertinent to tell your Lordship that upon late discoursing with him about the proceed of these two prizes, which I told him I believed would be between £200,000–300,000, I remember he replied that the embezzlement must needs have been great, for that their cargoes cost £400,000 in India. I have since reflected upon this and judging it a fresh way of diminishing what is due to your Lordship from what these ships at this necessitous time do really produce, by magnifying what they first cost in India. I have made enquiry what the value of the ships is reckoned to have been in India and do find, and by such authority as your Lordship if necessary may make use of it, that the cargoes of all thirteen ships cost not above £350,000, at most under £400,000, this Captain Cocke assures me.

Your Lordship's money shall be ready at a day's warning, but though I can without, yet it would be convenient to have the Vice-Chamberlain's consent to my paying Captain Cocke's bill out of the money I am receiving for the office. I desire your Lordship to move the Vice-Chamberlain in his next letter to give me a word or two to that purpose. The bill is £948. My Lord

Your Lordship's most obedient servant

S. P.

I have wrote myself to the Vice-Chamberlain, about Captain Cocke's bill.

Prize goods aside, the question of money to fund the Navy and efficient victualling had become the most important issue of the day. It had been a constant theme throughout the year and was already an issue beforehand. As a result of his efforts Pepys was appointed Surveyor-General of the Victualling on 27 October 1665. But Pepys, like everyone else, expected to profit from his position. Parliament had voted more funds to the Navy to fight the war but it made little or no difference since actually raising the money would take time. For the present the Navy was in debt to almost (if not all) its suppliers, in some cases for goods stretching back over more than two years. On 31 October 1665 Pepys closed his Diary thus:

> Want of money in the Navy puts everything out of order. Men grow mutinous. And nobody here to mind the business of the Navy but myself. At least, Sir W. Batten for the few days he hath been here doth nothing. I in great hopes of my place of Surveyor-General of the Victualling which will bring me £300 per annum.

44. SAMUEL PEPYS TO SIR WILLIAM COVENTRY

17 February 1666

SIR

Give me leave to trouble you with two or three small notes. Something I have newly heard from Harwich, tending to what we met with the other day about Portsmouth, makes me think it expedient his Royal Highness would command us to forbid his officers at the yards to become members of the Corporations adjoining. Is it meant the builder of a third-rate shall have his goblet as big as he of a second? If not, please to ascertain the difference to the rates; the value of the plate given to the *Royal Katherine* was £20. Pray let us have the Duke's order for our paying the last year's three muster-masters as the former muster-master hath been. I think verily it might be useful that it were ordered by his Royal Highness what was mentioned and approved of before him at Hampton Court, that no captain's wages should be paid, by imprest or otherwise, before his ship was paid, and he had given an account of his performance of his Royal Highness's Instructions in any point [that] should be enquired into by this Board. It would, I think, conduce to the making him more jealous of his own actions and his officers' over whom he is appointed to keep a check, whose miscarriage[s] appear not till the end of the voyage: example, this day's passage of the purser of the *Exchange Merchant, cum multis aliis*.

But, Sir, shall we let this year go away too without some amendment settled in the business of pursers, after we have advanced so far, (at least) further than ever before, in having the evils of our present practices thoroughly laid open to us? Or is it that the frauds practicable in the expense of £425,800 (for so much this year's estimate of the victualling comes to, and £638,700 the wages) are not worthy our preventing, when in the single ship above mentioned, a merchantman, whose complement of men was but 170, and continued in sea victuals but 6 months, and notwithstanding the complaint all the last year that the merchantmen were not ⅔ manned, (besides the late assertion in defence of the present method, viz. that the excess in number of men at one time is levelled by a shortness at another, which will not be found true in one ship in ten through the fleet), when, I say, in this one ship, besides all the other cheats we are told of, we find 9000 supernumeraries a day above her complement? I cannot dissemble my sense of this neglect of ours, for upon my word it wrings me hard to observe what a dust our penny wisdom will raise now and then, while we can permit the King to suffer under our pound follies, to the hazarding of the whole service (as the state of the fleet from embezzlement and from shortness in victuals in August last too well informed us), and those amongst us best able to lead will neither do that nor follow others in their endeavours to rectify them. Give me leave now to entreat that whereas my Lord Brouncker, Sir John Mennes, Sir William Batten, and Sir William Penn did under their hands promise to the Duke of Albemarle to give his Grace their opinion and advice touching this affair in writing, you would by a word from his Royal Highness put them in mind of what was undertaken, appointing a time for it to be brought in, and if done, I question not but out of that, and what is already before us, something will be collected that will be very useful. If not, I have done. . . .

S. P.

Anthony Deane, at this time master-shipwright at Harwich, became one of Pepys's oldest friends, and as a result were both accused of passing naval secrets to France during the Popish Plot of 1679. In 1666 their relationship was not so close.

45. SAMUEL PEPYS TO ANTHONY DEANE

8 March 1666

SIR

I have received your desires about the piece of plate and bespoke a flagon for you, which as soon as it is done you shall hear of.

For the other part of your letter, I will not dissemble with you because I love you. I am wholly dissatisfied in your proceedings about Mr Browne and Mr Wheeler.

For the first, you know you were the first man gave me notice of it, and directed me to Wheeler for further information, yet notwithstanding, I have seen a letter of yours to Browne, produced at the Board, wherein you clear him of all guilt, taking it upon yourself notwithstanding Browne himself did confess to us all that which was the occasion of turning him out. But, which is worst of all, it will be proved you have called Wheeler 'informing rogue', notwithstanding what I said before, you yourself was the first man occasioned the discovery, and which I reckoned a very good service of you.

As for Wheeler's case, he was but newly certified for by you to be a fit man for the place, and since well reported of. Now, all of a sudden, he must be made an idle fellow, an informing rogue, and one fit to be undone, under pretence that his servant was taken with two pieces of slit deal valued by Captain Taylor at sixpence.

The man is to me a stranger, and one for whom Mr Waith (who you tell me is his friend) nor any person else ever spoke one good word besides yourself and Commissioner Taylor, who at this day gives a very good character of him. But as much a stranger as he is, I will not to my power see him suffer for well doing.

Mr Deane, I do bear you still good respect, and (though it may be you do not now think that worth keeping) I should he glad to have reason to continue it to you. But upon my word, I have not spared to tell the Board my opinion about this business, as you will shortly see by a letter we have wrote to Commissioner Taylor. Wherein I have been very free concerning you, and shall be more so if ever I meet with the like occasion. The only kindness I have shown you in it is, that I have not acquainted Sir William Coventry with any part of it, and desire you will give no second occasion of doing it.

You know this hath formerly been my manner of dealing with others, therefore cannot wonder upon the like case to find me the same man to you, to whom notwithstanding I wish very well. . . .

46. SAMUEL PEPYS TO CAPTAIN SILAS TAYLOR

13 March 1666

SIR

In answer to yours of the 8th, I must needs confess to you I did always think, what you therein confess, that you were very suddenly fallen into a faction upon your first coming, and though it was in company with him to whom perhaps I bear as much good will at least as to any other in the yard, yet I was scandalized at it and am still, and to tell you the truth, I did never think there lay so much disobedience or undecency in Wheeler's words to you as in yours touching the Commissioner, which led me to invite the Board to be the less severe with him in reference to his misbehaviour.

I have been very free in telling Mr Deane my mind, and believe it will not be unadvisable for him to avoid giving the Board or me occasion to do the same again.

As to yourself, I bear you very real friendship, and that which both hath and shall be useful to you if occasion comes, but I must advise you to apply yourself first to the full mastering of your own business, and then it will be time enough to employ your observation on other men's, it being no graceful alteration in you that in so little time you should contract a friendship with an equal to the vilifying of a superior officer (and both strangers), and in a little while after that, magnify the latter as you do now and quarrel with the former. I doubt not but the business you were entered newly upon would have found you better exercise for the time, discourse, and thoughts this must have required.

I am much a stranger at Harwich, so cannot so well understand what you propose about storehouses, etc, as you desire. But be confident I will, when it comes to be discoursed, promote what appears of most use to his Majesty, wherein if you may also have your accommodation I shall receive somewhat the more satisfaction.

S. P.

The giving of gifts was often utilized as a means of easing one's way into a job. It was also a normal expression of respect. Pepys was anxious not to be seen to be susceptible to bribes. Nevertheless, here he accepts a gift from Anthony Deane but is at pains to stress such gestures will not defray his 'dissatisfaction' at anything deserving his disapproval. It was a theme he returned to later when offered a bribe in December 1678 (see Letter no. 120).

47. SAMUEL PEPYS TO ANTHONY DEANE

5 May 1666

SIR

I have received a book, and letter along with it, from yourself. The book, which you send me as a present, I do at your desire accept of and give you my thanks for, and the rather for that I am sure you know me so well as not to think I can be tempted by that or anything else to let fall my dissatisfaction, when taken upon such grounds as I declared in my late letter I had done that concerning you. I am sorry to find what I then feared prove so true, that now that league contracted so suddenly with a newcomer, to the dishonouring of the Commissioner and disordering of the yard, is broken, and you left (how justly I know not) to be the subject on which all the miscarriages of the place is laid by them both. What it was that first occasioned my singling you out for my friendship you well know, and so long as the same virtues of diligence and good husbandry remain, I will not fail to continue the good offices I ever did you, but truly when they shall be questioned, I shall not dare to be your advocate.

I am heartily glad to understand the good proof of your ship, and will rejoice to hear her sailing quality answer to the rest of her good parts. It is not from my late discontent that you have not received your piece of plate, for as I did my part in the getting it granted you so I have a good while since provided it, but want of money hath kept me from fetching it from the goldsmith. But now I am promised the money, I purpose you shall not be long without it.

The pains you took about calculating the *Royal Katherine*'s draught of water before she was launched I have laid up carefully, and shall be very glad to have the same, in the manner you propose in your letter, about the *Rupert,* which pray send me, because it is a thing of extraordinary practice and speaks more than what I usually find other builders pretend to; it would be of use to you to send me up a certificate from the master of her that her draught of water was so marked out to them before the 169 tons of shot, guns, etc, were put on board.

It is very likely what you desire may be granted about leave to be present at the King and Duke's being on board the *Rupert.*

S. P.

There is no avoiding the fact that Pepys was to some extent a hypocrite. He may have refuted the blatant offer of bribes and he certainly never grew as rich as some other public officials, but he willingly accepted gifts that could be passed off as just that. Pepys was possibly relatively unusual in also willingly receiving sexual favours from the wives of men keen to see their husbands promoted to an appropriate station in life. Perhaps his self-righteous response to anything that smelled of a possible bribe was his way of overcoming any residual sense of guilt. As far as the Navy's financial affairs were concerned, it was now time to go to the top.

48. SAMUEL PEPYS AND THE NAVY BOARD TO THE DUKE OF YORK

The Navy Office
12 May 1666

Though it be our great grief to find ourselves necessitated so often to trouble your Royal Highness with the repetition of our want of money, yet such are the disadvantages his Majesty's Service lies under by that want, and such too is the daily growth of those disadvantages, that we dare not but make our tenderness of your Royal Highness's trouble give way to our general duty to his Majesty, in laying our condition yet once more before your Royal Highness; it being now become such as would require a speedy redress did it suffer under no other evil than the loss of so great a part of our time as it occasions, at a season so full of exercise for the whole. For such are our debts, and the clamour arising from them, that not less than half our time is busied either in discoursing with and answering those who come to demand payment for what is past, or reasoning with others as to method of payment before they will be induced to treat with us for any service or commodity for the time to come.

But, may it please your Royal Highness, his Majesty suffers not only under that loss, but the expense of his treasure also increased by the excessive rates we are forced to give for everything his service wants, the merchant resolving to save himself in the uncertainty of his payment by the greatness of his price; while the constant occasions we have for a long lime had of exhausting our stores without capacity of giving them proportionable supplies, necessitates us to look out for and embrace almost any bargains we can procure, though at rates ourselves know to be very excessive.

We could trouble your Royal Highness with too many instances of this, but in a matter so unpleasing we shall particularize but in one, and that of very late date, viz.:—

A hemp-merchant (that from £60 first demanded had fallen to £58, and at last was prevailed with to accept £57 per ton), being reproached by us that a private person had very lately bought of the same goods at £49 10s he immediately replied that he would thankfully exchange the price he had then agreed with us for of £57 for £49 to be paid by ready money, which is 16 per cent, difference.

We conceive it likewise no slight evidence either of our want of money or the ill effects of it, that in his Majesty's yards, where the constancy of the employment used to make it matter for petition to be employed there, it is now so far from being such as to be reckoned a punishment, so as the workmen are frequently found to neglect and loiter therein in design only to provoke us to discharge them.

But there is a circumstance behind wherein this want of money appears as injurious to his Majesty as in any yet mentioned and that is our inability to execute your Royal Highness's late orders for paying in course, an expedient calculated (and with just hopes of success) for bettering our credits under this dearth of money, while every merchant should be secured in having equal right done to him in his payment to what any other hath had. But so far have we been from a power of acquitting ourselves in the conformity we ought to have paid to these your Royal Highness's instructions or giving the merchant opportunity of understanding his benefit therein, that we have not been enabled to satisfy the debts due before the time your Royal Highness's said instructions were to take place from, but contrarily, have been put to great shifts for small sums wherewith oftentimes to make an hundred or a ten pound payment, even in cases the most pressing, as your Royal Highness (by the weekly troubles you have for a good while had from us) doth too well understand.

Now, may it please your Royal Highness, having gone thus far in the mention of the consequences of this lack of money, we shall humbly lay before you something that may serve to the giving your Royal Highness some measure of that lack, and thereby also inform you in the reasonableness of the demand we shall presently come to propose for a supply.

Your Royal Highness may be pleased to remember that in a letter of the 6th of February last we did, for the same ends of right-informing your Royal Highness and therein also acquitting ourselves, largely lay before you, not only the sum necessarily to be supplied for the then pressing payments, but also that for the enabling us to go through this year's service it would be necessary that the weekly sum of £24,979 should be provided for the current expense of this Office, besides what should be necessary for payment of seamen's wages, the victualler, the sick and wounded, and widows and orphans.

That we did not at that time make any lavish demand we appeal to our books since, and shall always be prepared to satisfy your Royal Highness and my Lord Treasurer that it was no more than what actually hath been our expense since the first of January. What our supplies of money have been since that time (being 19 weeks) have not exceeded (besides what hath been paid in sea wages and to the Victualler) £5,300 a week.

What then our growing debt is, how much our credit must be impaired thereby what his Majesty will unavoidably suffer in the excess of prices, how much his service will be obstructed here and everywhere else, and lastly, what the debt of the Navy will be at the close of the year after twelve month's increase of 35,000 men's wages, besides the remains of the last year from the first of August, we do hereby humbly beseech your Royal Highness may be timelily considered; and that in the meantime you would be pleased to mediate with his Majesty that some effectual and speedy provision may be made for the raising wherewith:

	£
To enable us to pay what bills remain at this day unsatisfied, computed at	120,000
To discharge the debt due to the workmen in the several yards	47,000
	167,000

And for the supplying us with a constant weekly payment of £20,000 towards the current expenses above mentioned.

If this can be obtained, we might hope in some time to recover the lost credit of this Office, and carry on the service thereof with husbandry and dispatch.

But if this sum of £167,000 cannot be raised, and that it be only expected the service should be gone through with under the same disadvantages to itself and the King's treasure as for some time it hath been, we conceive the bare weekly sum of £20,000 may enable us to do that. But without this weekly supply, we do in all humility hold it our duty to declare to your Royal Highness that we do no apprehend the utmost of our endeavours (which shall never be wanting) will suffice to preserve his Majesty's service from a speedy and dangerous disappointment.[8]

BROUNCKER   W COVENTRY   W BATTEN
W. PENN   T. HERVEY   S. PEPYS

Memorandum. That for the informing myself in the weekly supplies of money this Office hath had since January last, I proposed the following question to my Lord Brouncker, who had particularly concerned himself in examining the Treasurer's weekly returns.

Q. What our supplies of money since January the first (being 19 weeks) hath amounted unto per week, excluding what hath been paid in seamen's wages, and to the victualler and the yards?

To which his Lordship under his hand returned me this answer:

A. There hath not been paid (besides the assignments upon the Chamber of London) above £5,258 per week, and those assignments included not above £9,045 per week, and but £16,293 per week all manner of ways, excepting only what hath been bought or assigned upon the Act. But this hath brought us to be vastly more in debt than we were January the first, 1665–6.

S. P.

By 1666 the problems had got worse. In January France declared war on England and Denmark entered an alliance with the Dutch against England. An inconclusive engagement in June off the Downs between the English fleet under the Duke of Albemarle and Prince Rupert, and the Dutch, led to both fleets withdrawing to refit. In the middle of all this, Pepys wrote to Prince Rupert's secretary in what would be just one of many letters concerning his brother-in-law's career.

49. SAMUEL PEPYS TO JAMES HAYES

7 July 1666

SIR

My last trouble to you is that of recommending to your favour a young man and brother-in-law of mine, his name Balthazar St Michel, muster-master of the Rear-Admiral squadron of the Blue. His Grace[9] hath been pleased to give him much of his countenance for the little diligence he hath observed in him in his place, which I hope he will improve. I know not whether he hath had the honour of being known to his Highness,[10] but my request to you for him is that you will give him leave, in any matter relating to his employ, to make his address to you for your advice and assistance. . . .

S. P.

Pepys worked late into the night on 24 July 1666, preparing a report on the improved state of victualling for the Duke of York. He was particularly pleased that two fleets had been

---

[8] A further letter followed on 14 July 1666 that listed details of some of the costs faced, and the impossibility of obtaining supplies without the ready money to pay for them. Published by Tanner, 1929, 137ff.

[9] George Monck, Duke of Albemarle.

[10] Prince Rupert, whom James Hayes served as secretary.

despatched, far better equipped than their predecessors. On the morning of 25 July he made a fair copy of his report for the Duke and read it through with Sir William Coventry. He was unable to get hold of the Duke until 26 July but then 'I did read my declaration of the proceedings of the victualling action this year'.

The Duke of York responded by saying that 'it was a good account, and that the business of the victualling was in a much better condition than it was the last year – which did much joy me, being said in the company of my fellows, by which I shall be able with confidence to demand my salary, and the rest of the sub-Surveyors' (Diary 26 July 1666). However, there were other problems still afoot with paying the men who were serving on the ships.

50. SAMUEL PEPYS TO THE DUKE OF YORK

The Navy Office
25 July 1666

Your Royal Highness having (for prevention of the many and dangerous difficulties his Majesty's Service was found subjected to the last year from the frequent want of victuals in the fleet and the unreadiness of our stores in the dispatch of supplies) instituted surveyors in the several victualling-ports, and been pleased to place upon myself the inspection and improvement of their several returns in order to the obtaining a constant and ready understanding of the general condition of the victualling-affair, I do in all humility hold it my duty to lay shortly before your Royal Highness what hath been the state of that action hitherto this year.

Two fleets have been provided for; the former in such plenty as will be found chargeable to the King through the necessary waste made of great quantities of beer, occasioned through want of room in the holds of many ships for the receipt of wounded men; the latter (though conceived the greatest ever yet set forth) dispatched without one day's loss of time, or the least complaint from the fleet or trouble to this Office (more than the releasing of men pressed out of the victualling-vessels), and lastly, with a sufficiency to complete the whole fleet with 4 months' provisions to determine the 3rd of October next, so far at least towards it as any commander or purser would own themselves capable of receiving; and that with such satisfaction to the Generals that they thought fit (notwithstanding the heat of the season and the supposed number of supernumeraries) to send back above 200 tons of beer above ten days before the departure of the fleet, and leave near 200 tons more (besides considerable quantities of dry provisions) upon the place at the time of their sailing.

Want of necessary advice of the certain quantity of provisions wasted the last engagement, and the numbers of men borne then and now (there being but one division of the nine from which we have to this day received any muster-books), disables me from knowing the just expense of the fleet; but if the excess of supernumeraries do not mislead in computing the consumption, nor the impresting of men out of the victuallers prevent us hereafter in the transportation of our provisions, I find no reason (may it please your Royal Highness) to fear but the remaining service of the year will be answered with the same readiness as that which is past.

Lastly, if your Royal Highness shall be pleased to command from me an account how far the year's declaration is expended and what remains unserved, either of the whole or in any particular part, I am and shall be always prepared to give your Royal

Highness satisfaction therein, or whom else that you shall be pleased to refer that enquiry to

S. PEPYS

It was 29 July when news arrived that four days earlier Albemarle's fleet had defeated the Dutch. But, despite the improvement in the state of victualling the Navy that Pepys so proudly recorded in July, the problems were very far from over. On 19 October 1666 the Navy Board confronted the Duke of York with the unpalatable fact that the ships could not go to sea without vital supplies, and those supplies could not be had without money to pay for them. They presented him with this before he could demand an explanation for why the fleet had not gone out. The Duke of York, to Pepys's relief, said that he could not see how they could do anything without at least £20,000 and would see the King about it. Pepys then mused on the more attractive prospect of retreating to Brampton and serving the nation from the peace and solitude of a country seat. Meanwhile Pepys wrote to Sir William Penn to record the meeting and tell him that unpaid seamen were beginning to cause riots.

51. SAMUEL PEPYS TO SIR WILLIAM PENN

19 October 1666

SIR

The occasion of this is to tell you that upon some disorderliness among the seamen in town this day at the pay, and their number without great care being as likely to increase as it is to be feared the occasion of their dissatisfaction is (namely, want of money), I was commanded by the Duke of York, in presence of our brethren, to signify this to you, and his pleasure thereupon that as much care as can be may be used to keep the seamen from coming up to town, and that no companies may be sent up (as we had determined) till you have advice that we are ready with money for their payment.

Then as to broom and reed, which without some money in hand Mr Swan hath declared he will not give us any further credit for, I demanded but £200 and the like sums for some other supplies necessary to be sent you; and the Vice-Chamberlain declared before the Duke that if £50 or £60 would do us any good he would strain for it, but for such a sum as £200 he could not compass it.

Upon which I did, with as much plainness as I think could be worded, pray the Duke not to expect any further service from us, for we should but abuse and betray him and the King's service if we should seem capable of being longer able to execute any of his orders.

The Duke showed great resentment of what was said, and promised to deliver it as plainly to the King, and so we broke up without hopes (at least, any assurance) of giving you any further help hence. With which melancholy story I take leave.

S. P.

Needless to say, with the Great Fire of London little more than a month in the past, Charles II had many other things on his mind. The mounting cost of the war meant that peace was now being sought, with Sweden acting as intermediary. Another substantial letter to the Duke of York from the Navy Board followed on 17 November 1666. It explained that although the Navy Board had accepted in the letter of 12 May 1666 a weekly supply of £20,000, they had not been receiving even as much as £3000. It went on to point out that

£179,793 would be needed to equip the fleet in 1667 and pay for new ships being constructed, and that other money would be needed to help offset the existing debt of £934,000. The following January Sir William Coventry resigned his position as Commissioner 'which I believe he hath done upon good grounds of security to himself, from all the blame which must attend our office next year'.[11]

52. SAMUEL PEPYS TO SIR WILLIAM COVENTRY

10 January 1667

SIR

Though ill tidings are become so familiar to this Office as to have lost their wonder, if not their other usual effects, yet I cannot be silent at that my Lord Brouncker brought me yesterday concerning your withdrawing your assistance and protection from us by quitting your relation to this place. What little temptation you had to continue with us, I am too well acquainted, nevertheless you will give him who so well also knows the effects of your coming hither, leave to be apprehensive of what may follow your leaving us ...

S. P.

Pepys always believed Sir William Batten to be corrupt, though if so he was probably no more corrupt than anyone else in his sort of position, including Pepys himself. The point of contention here is the Chatham Chest. It was notoriously mismanaged, with the funds often being appropriated to cover other expenses. Pepys was a member of the commission established in November 1660 to resolve the problems. Batten, who was Master of the Chest, was regarded as one of the principal culprits, but was not the only problem. Evelyn wrote to Pepys on 12 October 1665 to describe how sick and wounded seamen were slipping down from London hospitals to Chatham to collect their gratuities, which they promptly spent on getting drunk once back in London, thereby causing disorder and inhibiting their recovery. Evelyn was particularly outraged at the abuse of the fund by seamen who were already in receipt of a pension. After Sir William Batten's death later the same year the true nature of his appropriations emerged (see Letter no. 63).

53. SAMUEL PEPYS TO THE GOVERNORS OF THE CHEST

2 February 1667

... As for the business of Sir William Batten's account, I must say it is one of the most extraordinary things that I have met with in all my life from a man of honour, viz., that after so many demands thereof both public and private by myself and others, with his so often promising it and fixing on precise times for its delivery, affirming it to be ready, he should for so many years avoid the giving it in, when within that time he hath been several times sick even to despair of recovery, and at the same hour knew himself possessed of the poor's money in such a manner as not (in case of death) to leave his executors chargeable therewith by anything under his hand; though nevertheless I do not doubt but we shall be able to prove what he hath, or should have, better perhaps than is apprehended. I have not spared to say this to himself, so do not write it to you in any secrecy; for contrarily, I shall repeat it to him shortly once more, and in such a manner as becomes my duty and faithfulness

[11] The letter of 17 November is published by Tanner 1929, no. 110. For Coventry see the Diary 9 January 1667.

to the poor for whom I am concerned and will see right done to, let who will be offended. . . .

William Bagwell was a ship's carpenter in the dockyard at Deptford. He had the good fortune to be married to a woman who was not only attractive to Pepys, but also prepared to offer Pepys sexual favours in return for her husband's advancement. The couple had first solicited Pepys's help on 7 August 1663. Pepys's interest was immediate and resolved 'to know his [Bagwell's] wife a little better'.

Mrs Bagwell was probably Judith Campion, whose marriage to a William Bagwell was recorded at St Botolph Bishopsgate on 26 September 1658. She has not previously been identified. Pepys first seduced her in an alehouse beyond Moorfields on 15 November 1664 but it was not until 20 February 1665 that he agreed to write to Sandwich to ask for her husband's promotion to a better ship. It is implicit from the various accounts of their assignations in the Diary that Bagwell and his family allowed the meetings to continue, presumably because of the advantage his promotion would bring them. Pepys had been with Mrs Bagwell on 1 February 1665, just a few days before Pepys composed this letter to further Bagwell's interests. The information in the Diary, and the nature of the letter, show perfectly how uninhibited Pepys was in exploiting his position in order to indulge himself at a personal level. Needless to say, Elizabeth Pepys knew nothing of the liaisons that continued on and off over nearly four years.

54. SAMUEL PEPYS TO SIR WILLIAM COVENTRY

6 February 1667

SIR

The bearer is Bagwell, for whom I have once received your favour in his present employment in the *Providence,* and assure you would not appear to solicit for any advancement for him, were I not upon enquiry well satisfied in his activeness, care, and sobriety in his former and present employment. Mr Deane, from his former knowledge and late information concerning him, does approve, and is desirous of him, if you shall think fit, for the carpentry of the new ship he is building, wherein if you are not already pre-engaged, I do also add my request, and do believe you will find him a man in whose deportment you will be well satisfied. My confidence in this makes me appear in his behalf, which I therefore hope you will pardon.

S. P.

The letter was apparently successful. Pepys went back to see Mrs Bagwell on 4 March 1667, had a sexual encounter with her and then sent for her husband in order to discuss his new job. Pepys had obtained him a position in charge of a new ship now being built at Harwich, the third-rate *Rupert.* Unfortunately for Pepys, Mrs Bagwell was then away for almost a year in Harwich with her husband. It seems to have brought the affair almost to an end but after failing to find her back home on 15 January he slept with her again on 2 June 1668. It was the last time there is any record of the affair. But the Bagwell issue did not go away. Nearly twenty years later, when Pepys was the exalted Secretary of the Admiralty, Mrs Bagwell was still soliciting Pepys's help for her husband's career (see Letter no. 172).

Although naval financial business continued to occupy Pepys, he also had time for other diversions. On Thursday 7 February he had just finished a conversation with his brother John about the latter's impending trip to Brampton when John fell over and knocked himself out. This put Pepys into a 'great fright'. John gradually recovered during the rest of the day and Pepys decided to let John travel. He gave him money for books, himself, and the journey and a 'letter to my Lady Sandwich for him to carry, I having not writ to her a great while' (Diary 7 February 1667). The letter includes the memorable observations that the ruins caused by the Great Fire had made it difficult to keep in touch with events at Whitehall and Westminster, on the side of the city, and that it was the ladies at court who really ruled the country, despite spending longer in bed than anyone else.

55. SAMUEL PEPYS TO JEMIMAH, COUNTESS OF SANDWICH

7 February 1667

MADAM

Your Ladyship being now so supplied from the court itself, I have been doubtful of offering your Ladyship anything of news from this end of the town, which the late fire hath removed almost as far from court as Hinchingbrooke is. However, Madam, having directed my brother, at his return to my father, to attend your Ladyship with the tender of my wife's and my most humble services, I shall adventure to let them come, accompanied with the best account of matters under my view.

The Parliament rises this day, or tomorrow, having with much difficulty given the King a sum really too little, yet by them thought enough, if not too much, for his occasions. However, better thus much given, and they parted, than to have had them sit longer to have increased the discontents which were already come to great height between the court and the country factions.

Our enemies are busy in their preparations, and bold, having begun the year with the unhappy taking of a very good frigate of ours, the *St Patrick*, of about fifty guns, built but the last year. The news of her loss came to us but yesterday morning.

We are in our preparations as backward as want of money and stores can render us, but do hope that what the Parliament hath given us will, in a little time, better our condition; yet not so, I assure your Ladyship, as to give me any cause to be sorry for my Lord's being abroad, but contrarily to wish his continuance there some time longer; although, should he return tomorrow, his Lordship would find the world give him another look than when he left us, the last year's work having sufficiently distinguished between man and man.

Who commands the fleet this year is not yet known, but, for aught I see, there is no great striving likely to be for it, the Prince not being in condition of health, and the Duke of Albemarle, as I hear, declaring his not going. Whoever goes, I pray God give him more success than I can, without presumption, hope he will find.

This, Madam, is what occurs to me in our sea affairs; and as for court matters, your Ladyship having them from other hands, I shall not meddle with them more than to say, that they seem to me just that they have always been, — that ladies lie longest in bed, and govern all when they are up.

The Vice-Chamberlain's[12] concerns are all in very good condition; and his family (wherein I reckon my Lady Jemimah) in good health, and still in love. So God preserve your Ladyship!

May it please your Ladyship, Your Ladyship's most obedient servant,

S PEPYS

Our humble service to my Lady Pickering we beg, and to the rest of the ladies

---

[12] Sir George Carteret. Jemimah Mountagu had married his son Philip in 1665.

This pleasant social letter was an interlude in the Navy's financial crisis. Promises of money had been totally unfulfilled, leading to the ludicrous situation in which a ship could not be built because there were no bolts to be had, and even the lead for a furnace could not be funded. The damage was more deep-seated since the letter points out that the credibility of the Navy Board was being eroded by its inability to pay for anything, while other goods in store like whale oil were being sold off for less than the Navy had paid for them.

56. SAMUEL PEPYS AND THE NAVY BOARD TO THE DUKE OF YORK

The Navy Office
31 March 1667

IT IS WITH utmost regret that we are forced to give your Royal Highness such disquiet as we have for a long time together done in the matter of money; especially after our having so lately, by letter of the 23rd of February last and our personal address to his Majesty and yourself at my Lord Treasurer's the 14th instant, declared our condition, and the necessity of our being supplied with £40,000 per week until the £500,000 (concluded at the same time by his Majesty necessary to be provided for us) should be completed. But that which occasions this so speedy return of our complaint to your Royal Highness is, that of that small sum of thirty and odd thousand pounds said to be allotted out of the Poll Bill for this Office, and to have been in readiness for our disposal five weeks since (and which accordingly was then distributed by us by particular assignments as his Majesty's service most required) not one penny is yet paid. Insomuch that we have not only missed of the reparation we expected to have gotten to our credits by this ready sum, but have put ourselves further backward (we fear irrecoverably) in the esteem of those few whom our promises (built on the presumption of this money) had once more prevailed with to trust us a little farther.

As this practice of ours (may it please your Royal Highness) of persuading persons to the parting with their goods on promise of money (when at the same time we are conscious of our incapacity to perform them) is in itself both scandalous and grievous to us, so the considering of how ill consequence it is to his Majesty's service in general, though it may speed us for one single pinch, enforceth us humbly to crave your Royal Highness's pardon that we beg to be relieved therein by more certain supplies of money. For that your Royal Highness may see by fresh instances the success of such our forced dealings and the posture his Majesty's affairs are at this day in, be pleased to know that the dispatch of the ships, both in this River, at Portsmouth, Harwich, and more particularly the chain and boats at Chatham and the furnishing Sir Jeremy Smith's fleet with ketches, are at this day at (or next to) an utter stand for want of money.

And to be yet more clear, we crave leave to communicate to your Royal Highness some such particulars as we dare not mention but to yourself, namely, that we have not credit left us for procuring lead for covering of a furnace, but have been forced to melt our very weights to answer that occasion with. For want of broom we are reduced at this day to the emptying of our tar-cask for the getting their staves for firing, and in our want of rosin for graving of ships are put to the paying them with pitch, and to boil up tar ourselves even for the supplying that occasion with pitch. Oil we have been lately forced to give £33 per ton for, and would yet be glad to have a farther supply thereof at the same price, while his Majesty's own was sold at

Plymouth for £20 and £22, after our repeated desires and a promise of a supply of fifty tons thereof for his own use. The smith's works everywhere fail us, and at Harwich particularly not a bolt to be had for the new ship,[13] the smith's shop there having been wholly shut up this week.

Our regard to your Royal Highness's trouble, and knowledge of the sense your Royal Highness already hath of this our ill state, is the reason of our adding no more; but our want of relief (after so many addresses) giving us reason to fear lest our difficulties may not have appeared to others so great as they indeed are and we from time to time have represented them, we durst not but lay before your Royal Highness these few, and do therefore in most humble manner implore your Royal Highness's pardon for the same, and the considering of some instant means of removing these present, and preventing the yet greater evils which the want thereof must inevitably draw upon us.

BROUNCKER   J MENNES   W BATTEN
W. PENN   S. PEPYS

The following letters were read to the Duke of York on 3 April 1667 and were recorded by Pepys in the order given here. Unlike the more general complaints issued by the Navy Board to the Duke, it highlighted the personal crises occasioned by the failure to finance the Navy properly. Commissioner Thomas Middleton tells of an oar-maker, himself unpaid, being chased by his timber supplier for payment and how Middleton had had to pawn his own plate to pay for oil.

57. COMMISSIONER THOMAS MIDDLETON TO SAMUEL PEPYS

31 March 1667

Just now is with me a poor oar-maker crying and wringing his hands for money, and desires to be a labourer in the yard to keep him from being arrested, for that he tells me he dareth not go home to his wife any more, for he shall be carried to jail by his timber-merchant; which request of his I granted, and is now entered a labourer, albeit the King oweth him for oars near £300. But I thank you that you do mind it, and will relieve me as soon as you can.

This morning came a boat loaden with broom into the harbour. Mr Lucas the shipwright would have bought it, but considering we have six ships to clean and not one broom faggot nor which way else to do it, I seized on the boat of broom and brought her to the yard and is unloaden, the poor man lamenting that he had no money to buy more and was in debt for that, and I having but poor £11 14s 6d in my custody, was forced to pay him for his broom out of that stock I had to buy me victuals. The sum comes to £8 15s, so I have left to supply me £2 9s 6d, which will not find food for my family at the outside above six months.

Oil we have not above 1½ hogshead, which is but convenient for our caulkers and ropemakers. By the wheel of Fortune I met with two men that had four hogsheads of whale oil; £32 I bought it for; tomorrow it will be brought into stores. I was in hope to have received my quarter's salary, out of which I intended to have paid for it and to have given myself a recruit for some time, but Mr Salmon cannot pay me because

---

[13] Presumably the *Rupert*, the ship Pepys had obtained a position for William Bagwell in building (see the letter of 6 February 1667).

he wants money to pay the men in ships ready to sail, so now must be forced to pawn that little plate that I have for money to pay for the oil, and I thank God I have as much plate as will fetch so much money, for I had rather drink in a horning cup than that the King's ships should stay here for want of anything that I have in my possession that may give them dispatch.

On 7 April Middleton wrote again. This time he announced that he had pulled down a chimney at the yard so that a ship's furnaces and hearth could be constructed. This, he felt, was the only option available since there was no cash with to buy bricks. Commissioner John Taylor had also written to describe an even more wretched scenario at Harwich.

58. COMMISSIONER JOHN TAYLOR TO SAMUEL PEPYS

30 March 1667

The carpenters were marching to London, but by persuasion are turned back. They will live upon the spoil and grow uncontrollable, if not supplied with money. It troubles me to see the service suffer thus; it's more profitable to give 20 per cent, for money. Yesterday and this day comes some and say they can go no further for want of board wages, can get no victuals. Clerk of the Cheque and others tells me of several labourers and carpenters dead for want of diet and nourishment. I do this out of conscience to lay it before you. We compel them to work; it's most just to provide that they may have a livelihood, or to suffer them to get it elsewhere till money come. I leave it all to consideration.

Taylor was well aware of how things operated in the Navy. Pepys recorded on 15 December 1663 that 'Captain Taylor hath not been observed to pay me any money, he bringing it in a handkercher to my office, which nobody observed, and left it with me so'.[14] This was at a time when Taylor was working as a private shipwright at Wapping. The money had arisen because the Navy had hired a ship of Taylor's to transport goods to Tangier. His bill was £278 15s. Pepys had £30 but Taylor offered him another £6 and Pepys recorded 'I am loath to have it said that I ever did it' (Diary 11 December 1663). The truth is that Pepys was content to receive gratuities like this if he could conceal the fact. It is perfectly clear that Pepys's morality was as flexible as everyone else's. The curiosity is that, given his analyses of the Navy's financial problems, he did not associate his behaviour with those issues.

On 11 June 1667 the Second Dutch War reached its climax in a humiliating debacle. A Dutch fleet under De Ruyter entered the Medway, ignoring what Evelyn called the 'trifling forts' (Diary 24 June 1667), and for the loss of two of their ships sank six English vessels and captured the *Royal Charles*. The Dutch sailed over a chain across the river, intended to protect the fleet. On 11 June Pepys wrote to Sir William Coventry to describe Dutch activity further up the Thames. On 1 July he wrote to Lord Brouncker to discuss what had happened to the protective chain. Peace, which had been under negotiation since March 1666, had now become essential. The debt problems had become insurmountable and the Dutch blockade of Newcastle colliers in 1666 had shown how susceptible England was with the Royal Navy in its current state. The articles were agreed at Breda, but were not settled until 25 July following the arrival of another Dutch force in the Thames a couple of days before.

[14] NWB, p. 8.

59. Samuel Pepys to Sir William Coventry

11 June 1667

SIR

I went down, as our letter told you, to Woolwich, in order to the dispatch of the *Golden Hind,* which finding not yet come thither, I conferred with the officers about having hands, etc, ready against her coming, and so went down to Grays and took care for her coming up this tide, which she is, and will be gone in hand with early in the morning.

Having some of the tide of ebb left, I bestowed it in going down to Gravesend, where I found them at some ease, the Dutch being fallen down again this noon, and by the report of a small Ostend man-of-war (come up while I was there) they were below the Nore when he met them. They took from him three ships which he came convoy to from Ostend. They are commanded by Van Gent, and in number 26 men-of-war and four fireships. Some poor houses and stacks they have burned in Candy Marsh, and a house or two at Lee, but were thence repelled by the country.

The offal of some muttons drove up the river the last flood shows what they had been doing. Most of their fleet came as high as Shell Haven about a mile below the Hope, and 2 or 3 to within the Hope; some of them judged to have 60 or 70 guns apiece.

During my being at Gravesend I heard distinctly great guns play below, and at my coming away Sir William Jennings and the commanders were going on board by the Duke of Albemarle's order to bring up their ships and place them in a line thwart the River between the forts.

I met several vessels in my going down loaden with the goods of the people of Gravesend. Such was their fright. . . .

60. Samuel Pepys to Lord Brouncker

Navy Office
1 July 1667

The disturbance I gave your Lordship so late last night was too great to admit of my troubling you than with anything that was not purely public. But I cannot now forbear to tell your Lordship that neither by my own view, nor by any of the few I met with yesterday at Chatham, could I be fully informed whereabouts the chain is broke, or whether indeed the chain be at all broke, I must confess I was surprised to find any of it there, it having been the town talk that the Dutch had taken it away with them. But finding it there, and it not being obvious to me that it was broke, I have (perhaps impertinently) been thinking that either it may have rendered at the end where the crane stood to haul it taut, or that the floats which supported it in the middle may have been forced under water with the weight of the ships over-pressing it, in the latter of which I can the less satisfy myself, because the same tautness could not keep it (I think) at the water's edge both at high and low water.

The fatality of our miscarriage in this one matter will easily excuse our endeavouring to trace the method of it, and me (I hope) in begging your Lordship's favour therein, who I believe have taken the best account of it. *Quaere* whether we had ever tried it with any of our own ships?

[Postscript.] Sir John Mennes (it's feared) will hardly survive a day.[15]

---

[15] Mennes lived on until 1671.

By 1666 the Earl of Sandwich had been sent as ambassador to Spain. Despite his success in the Battle of Lowestoft in 1665, the scandal over the prize-goods and a refusal to make his fleet brave storms to engage the Dutch, meant that he lost favour. His job was to settle the war between Spain and Portugal, which he accomplished. Pepys wrote to tell him what had been going on, including how scapegoats were being sought for England's performance in the Second Dutch War. Pepys had a good idea of where the finger would be pointed.

61. SAMUEL PEPYS TO THE EARL OF SANDWICH

Navy Office
7 October 1667

MAY IT PLEASE YOUR LORDSHIP

Though your Lordship's silence (by Mr Sheeres) touching the receipt of either of those letters I have been bold to address to your Lordship since your leaving England, denies me the satisfaction of knowing that they reached your Lordship's hands, yet I am unwilling, without more certainty, to take upon myself the shame, as well as affliction, which it were fit I should, did I know that your Lordship had them not. And yet I must acknowledge, my Lord, that this is but the third, having no desire of disquieting your Lordship with bad news; and the times affording not one passage fit to be called good, from the hour I had the honour to see your Lordship last, to that of publishing of your Lordship's articles of peace with Spain: for, besides them, nothing that I know of, of public management, hath found so much as common excuse, much less the universal acceptance (which this hath done) in all this time.

The bearer, Mr Sheeres, will leave little untold your Lordship, either of what hath passed, or what is at present expected; so that I hold it not fit for me to offer at the troubling your Lordship with what you will have more particularly from him, but content myself with the giving your Lordship this general representation of matters as they now stand with us, namely:

That after a war chargeably and unsuccessfully managed, as well as unsatisfactorily concluded, the Parliament (who parted last upon jealous terms) is come together again this week, with as great an inclination on their side (as is believed) to inquire into faults, as the King is also said to be resolved on his to give way to their examining and correcting them. But their work, as it is thought, will be the less, by the late removal of my Lord Chancellor; an act wherein I cannot inform your Lordship more, touching the grounds of it, than that its doing is generally imputed to reasons delivered the King by Sir William Coventry (who I know do not spare to assert the requisiteness of it), with the concurrence at first of his Royal Highness, though afterward it proved not so pleasing to him, but that he is said to have endeavoured the preventing it when it was gone too far.

The matters that take up most men's observations at present are the proceedings of the Commissioners of the Treasury, whose tax, and a great one it is to provide it, is to provide for the paying of the fleet and the other navy debts. To which end they are reduced to the seeing all ways of raising and saving monies. Towards the latter of which they are likely to make a good step by the reductions of charge they seem to design through all the parts of the kingdom's expense, from which, they are likely to contract from particular persons much envy; but I do not see but the generality are not only well contented with their proceedings, but look upon them as persons proper to redeem the nation by the right administration of its treasury. And that which increases their hopes is, the countenance given them by the King in cases where powerful solicitations have not been wanting to oppose them.

Among these commissioners Sir William Coventry seems the principal, as he is at this time, I think, in almost everything else; though, since the Chancellor's fall, he hath parted with his relation to the Duke of York. And I must confess my observations on all his proceedings will not suffer me to think otherwise of him than (what I have always professed to your Lordship) as of a man of no less justice and severity in general, and of no inclinations of disservice to your Lordship in particular; as I see confirmed by some late instances, which I have communicated to my Lord Crew, and others of your Lordship's friends. Nor hath the Vice-Chamberlain any reason to conclude longer that the opposition he hath formerly met with from him sprung from any singular ill-will of his to him; my Lord Anglesey, his successor, having already felt more effects of his unkindness (if it must be termed so), in the loss of his having the payment of the victualler, than ever the Vice-Chamberlain did in all his time. This I thought requisite to say upon this matter, from my opinion of how great value it would be to your Lordship to have a better understanding with this gentleman, especially in the condition to which fortune, or rather his abilities, have raised him.

The same discourse I am bold to take opportunity of preaching to my Lord Crew and Mr Vice-Chamberlain, to whom I am not forgetful to communicate whatever I can judge of use to your Lordship, and receive the like from them; and particularly do at present contribute what I can towards forwarding your Lordship's return home, (which were certainly much to be wished on behalf of your Lordship and family), or the obtaining certainer supplies of money than ever your Lordship hath of late had, or the present state of the Treasury will, without great solicitations I fear, prompt the Commissioners to the settling of. Towards which, however, and everything else relating to your Lordship's service, I beg the continuance of your Lordship's belief that I will ever be as industrious as faithful.

The enclosed I am desired by the writer to give cover to your Lordship; and shall add of my own concerning him, that I am so well informed of his civil and commendable manner of employing his time (as a student in Gray's Inn) that I believe your Lordship will be inclined, at your return, to receive him into your favour again. My conclusion shall be (as it ought) my wishes of constant prosperity to your Lordship, and the tender of my utmost services in all that may conduce thereto, as being,   May it please your Lordship

Your Lordship's most obedient and faithful servant

S. PEPYS

Pepys's relationship with Anthony Deane continued to improve. The letter of 14 December 1667 is in stark contrast to the rebuke sent on 9 March 1666. Pepys is delighted with the launching of a new ship, the third-rate *Resolution*, at Harwich.

62. SAMUEL PEPYS TO ANTHONY DEANE

14 December 1667

SIR

I could not sooner congratulate you in the safe launching of your new ship and the satisfaction you receive in her condition and beauty, as well as the further proof you have in this ship received of your art in foretelling her draught of water light, and I will not fail to watch how she answers your calculation in her draught of water when fitted and manned, victualled, and furnished for sea with guns, etc.

I have had a fine plat[16] prepared some time for you to spend your leisure upon as soon as I can find opportunity of sending it you.

I did not doubt but to have got your mind satisfied about your piece of plate, to have had it a dish as you desire, but upon proposing it to the Board they say that the custom in all cases of this nature hath always been to have it a bowl or some drinking-vessel, with design at the drinking his Majesty's and Lord Admiral's health at the launching of the ships, and that it is not convenient to alter an old practice. So that you must be contented to think of some drinking-vessel, of what fashion you please, and it shall be provided for you.

S. P.

On 2 February 1667 Pepys had written to the Governors of the Chatham Chest to raise the thorny issue of Sir William Batten's management of the finances, intended for the benefit of sick and wounded seamen. On 5 October 1667 Batten had died suddenly after two days' sickness. As Batten's affairs were tied up, so the reality of what had been going on emerged. He had taken on the administration of the Chest purportedly as an act of goodwill, but had siphoned off £500 for himself over and above legitimate expenses.

63. LORD BROUNCKER AND SAMUEL PEPYS TO GOVERNORS OF THE CHEST

6 February 1668

This is to convey to you an account lately delivered to us for your use by direction of my Lady Batten, administratrix of Sir William Batten, containing, as the title declares, an account of the money by him received upon the extraordinary Chest, and how the same hath by him been expended; touching which in general we do, in pursuance of the trust incumbent on us as Supervisors of the Chest for the present year, give it you as our opinion that it will be requisite that you commit it to some able hand forthwith to examine the said account as to the truth of the charge and the justifiableness of his discharge, wherein what assistance we can by any authority of ours, or any accounts or papers lodging with us, give him we shall readily do it, and unless you know any person more proper, we hold Mr Burroughs very able to do it, and by his present relation to the service of the Chest more concerned to attend it than any other.

Next, we think ourselves obliged to take notice of two particulars demanded in the account which we can by no means think reasonable in the demanders nor justifiable for us to allow, namely the 6d per pound demanded by the paymaster amounting to £112, and £500 by Sir W. Batten himself in consideration of his pains. We are sorry this seeming ill office was left to us to do after the death of Sir W. Batten, but you well knowing what endeavours were used by us in his lifetime to the obtaining a state of this account, and how he to the time of his death did avoid the giving of the same, we doubt not but we shall be held excusable by all the world in our not making these exceptions sooner. We shall not disagree to the allowing Sir

---

[16] The meaning here is probably a map or chart.

William Batten whatever charges shall appear to have been occasioned to him by this work, and therefore we except not against the other allowance demanded by him on that score; but for this reward of £500 to himself, we do again declare ourselves totally unsatisfied therewith, it being a work taken upon him with profession during his whole life of doing it in charity for the Chest, without any the least intimation in all his discourses of anything of profit expected by him for the same; wherefore unless you can inform us in anything (not appearing to us) for the rendering this demand reasonable, we desire that both it and the £112, to the paymaster may be expunged, or left to the Lord High Admiral to determine in.

In early 1668 the Earl of Sandwich completed his term as ambassador to Spain and set sail for home. On 27 September Pepys heard that his patron's ship, the *Greenwich*, had reached Mount's Bay in Cornwall several days before. Sidney Mountagu, Sandwich's second son, had left the ship and travelled ahead to London, meeting Pepys to tell him that his father needed money immediately. Pepys sent Sidney to Portsmouth with a loan of £500 (on which he, incidentally, charged 6 per cent interest). He had already lent Lady Sandwich £100 in 1668. The reason was that the posting had been financially ruinous to Sandwich, with his pay now severely in arrears. Pepys made no entries in his Diary for the last two days of September and the first ten of October. This letter fills out some of that gap.

64. SAMUEL PEPYS TO THE EARL OF SANDWICH

29 September 1668

MAY IT PLEASE YOUR LORDSHIP

Just now are arrived the tidings of your Lordship's safe arrival at Portsmouth, which I beg your Lordship to believe me to receive with that welcomeness which is due to whatever, by the greatest obligations of duty and gratitude, I ought most to be concerned for. I am not without hopes of getting leave to wait upon your Lordship before you reach London; therefore shall spare the troubling your Lordship with any other present matters, than that being yesterday made acquainted by my Lord of Hinchingbrooke, and Mr Sidney Mountagu, with the straits they found themselves under of providing a sum of money for the answering your Lordship's present occasions; and, being unwilling your Lordship should want what part thereof I could by any shift supply, I undertook, for the present, furnishing your Lordship with £500; and not knowing what present use thereof your Lordship might have at Portsmouth, nor what conveniencies my Lord of Hinchingbrooke might have of a speedy remitting any thither, I acquainted his Lordship this night, that I would take care for your Lordship's being furnished with £200 there; which I have done by the enclosed bill to Mr Salisbury, not only for that sum, but that your Lordship might be the less straitened, for the whole £500 though the more your Lordship leaves to receive here, the better it would suit with my occasions to comply therewith.

I shall need not to say anything particularly touching the healthful state of your Lordship's family, believing that that will be abundantly told your Lordship by others. The freshest Court news is, that Sir John Trevor was this day sworn Secretary of State in the room of Sir William Morice, and Prince Rupert invested in the Constableship of Windsor Castle; both purchased: the former for £8000 and latter for £3500.

The King and Queen are at this time at supper at my Lady Carteret's. Tomorrow morning his Majesty and the Duke of York set out for a month's progress towards Norfolk and Suffolk.

I have written to Mr Deane, his Majesty's shipwright at Portsmouth, an ingenious as well as a sober man, to attend your Lordship, for the receiving your commands, and anything wherein he may be serviceable to your Lordship during your stay there, who I know will readily embrace them. So, with the tenders of my most humble duty to your Lordship, I take my leave.

May it please your Lordship,

Your lordship's most obedient and faithful servant,

S. P.

The ill state of my eyes has not allowed me to read or write thus much for several months, but by the help of another's, which, I hope, will excuse me to your Lordship, in my not appearing with my own hand here.

The money and letter reached Sandwich on 30 September, much to his relief. He recorded that it was 'absolutely necessary for my occasions and no more'.[17] Pepys's problems with his eyesight, which he mentions here, led him to conclude he was going blind and occasioned the end of his Diary on 31 May 1669. This is probably why the Diary was not written up for 29 September to 10 October. On 24 October he tried 'Tubes for Eyes', designed by a Mr Shotgrave of the Royal Society, 'so that mine are better'. He of course never went blind and was probably suffering from the normal onset of long-sightedness (hypermetropia), which makes close work difficult. This is common for people in their forties, but Pepys had perhaps made things worse by his long hours of paperwork well into the evening and night on numerous occasions.

Regardless of his vision difficulties Pepys was already enormously appreciative of art, especially drawings and engravings, and remained a lifelong collector. In this letter he expresses his admiration for a drawing of the new ship *Resolution* which he has had framed. The 'great work' mentioned in the letter was Deane's *Doctrine of Naval Architecture*, published in 1670.

65. SAMUEL PEPYS TO ANTHONY DEANE

Navy Office

24 October 1668

SIR

My draught of the *Resolution* being now finished adorns my closet, so as I think there is not so grateful a draught in any man's possession as this is, and you will probably think so when I have told you that, besides your own labour upon it, I have paid Mr Walker £7, Fletcher £3, and the framemaker £3 more, for their parts therein. The truth is, I am very proud of it, and do therefore return you my most hearty thanks once more for your share in it, which exceeds all the rest, though I am afraid you will not think I value your pains therein as I ought to do when I have told you that I have bespoke a pair of boards upon which I must engage you to give me the draught of the new ship you are now upon, which I ask not only out of my general design to furnish myself with a draught of one ship of each rate, but out of a particular desire of having this, wherein (whatever the additional mystery of Sir Laurence Van Heemskirke shall contribute to her quality) I do not doubt but what

---

[17] Noted in the Diary, vol. IX (1668–9), 321, n. 3

the judgment of all that have looked upon her now upon the stocks do say, she will be found as complete a piece of naval architecture as we have ever yet seen.

My end in this collection of draughts is calculated so much for common benefit as well as for the preserving the honour due to the masters of your quality and such as shall arrive at eminence therein, as that I will not doubt your excusing the freedom I take of offering you the new trouble which you are to expect from me as soon as my boards are done. In the meantime, I give you thanks from the hopes I receive from you of your advancement in the great work you wrote of, wishing I could give you any assistance therein; but pray forget not to bestow a little of your leisure and thoughts upon that subject, on which you have already given me a sheet or two ...

Will Hewer would eventually become so loyal and long-lasting a friend of Pepys's that he lived with Pepys from 1677 on and was an executor his will. He served as a clerk and manservant under Pepys from the 1660s. On 8 December Commissioner Thomas Middleton accused Hewer of corruption involving the stores at Chatham. It was not the first time such an accusation had been made. On 23 May 1664 Sir John Mennes alleged that Hewer had organized a double payment for something, helping himself to one of the payments. Pepys was appalled in 1664 and now again in 1668. An almighty row between him and Middleton blew up in the Navy Office. Pepys then composed this letter to the then storekeeper at Chatham, Thomas Wilson, who Pepys had in fact seen about the issue in person the very same day as the letter was written at The Pope's Head tavern in London. One of the abiding mysteries about Will Hewer was the substantial wealth he had accumulated in later life. This has never been resolved and perhaps Mennes and Middleton were closer to the truth than Pepys was ever willing, or able, to acknowledge.

66. SAMUEL PEPYS TO THOMAS WILSON

11 December 1668

SIR

There is lately come to my notice a suspicion in some of our Board touching one of my clerks William Hewer, his being concerned in some undue practices relating to the serving in of kerseys and cottons into his Majesty's stores at Chatham by one Coleby. The continued experience I have for eight years had of his diligence and faithfulness will not easily admit of my suspecting him, nor of his being traduced by others; as on the other hand the ground which is alleged for this suspicion is such as I shall not acquit him as to this particular either in my own judgment or expect he should stand clear in the judgment of others till I am satisfied therein from yourself, by copies of those many letters with which he is said to have pressed you for the making out bills for those goods. Which therefore I desire you to send me by the next post, with an account of the time between the measuring of the goods and the date of the bill, with what other circumstances you can help me to for the proving of his guilt, it being alleged that his importunities to you by letter upon letter were such as did apparently demonstrate a fraud therein. I desire you by no means to withhold any light from me that should inform me in this matter; for as I shall give him my utmost protection while he is innocent, so I'll be found the forwardest of the Board in the promoting of his punishment when he shall be found blameable.

S. P.

The letter survives as a copy in Pepys's copybook, written out by Hewer. By 15 December no evidence had been found to substantiate Middleton's allegations. Hewer and Pepys then worked on a letter to answer Middleton, which they finished the following day. Pepys took the opportunity to throw in a few points of his own 'which I should otherwise have wanted an opportunity of saying'. On 18 December the Navy Board threw out Middleton's allegations and he was forced to burn the letter in which he had made them. Middleton was forgiven and they 'fell to talk of other stories'. The bonhomie was not matched at home. Pepys went home to face his outraged wife who had heard gossip that had caused her to believe he had resumed his affair with Deb Willet. The affair with Deb Willet is one of the most dramatic sub-plots in the Diary and had almost destroyed Pepys's marriage when Elizabeth Pepys caught him with her in a compromising position on 25 October 1668. The gossip was untrue, and Pepys managed to convince her of that.

67. SAMUEL PEPYS TO ANTHONY DEANE

3 February 1669

SIR

In answer to yours of the 31st of the last, I give you many thanks for what you give me hopes of receiving from you about not only a draught of the *Nonsuch* but also of the several parts of ships in general, which I am so far unwilling to occasion any stop to the dispatch of, as to desire that nothing that I desire [d] of you in my last should employ any of your thoughts or time, unless without inconvenience you could do that of the *Nonsuch's* draught. ...

But I am particularly satisfied in that instance which you give us of the ill consequence of our bad payments, its being a circumstance indeed which does in some manner surmount all that we have yet met with, namely, that the badness of our payments have long since discouraged all the timber merchants in your country but one from dealing with us, viz., Mr Cole, whose stock being greater than the rest, made not only him better able to trust us, and better acquainted, as well as thereby less discouraged, with the former delays met with in his procurement of payments, but put us under a necessity of making him amends for the same by being reduced, for want of other merchants, to the accepting of his goods for the most part at his own price; I find (I say) this further evil attending it, that at this time, when we are under an assurance of ready money to pay for all we buy, no man but Mr Cole has made any provision for materials fit for the King's service, and by that means we are left, even with ready money, under the same want of choice, and consequently under a no less liableness to the being imposed upon in the price (besides the insufficiency even of all his stock of goods at present to be had) than we were under the worst condition of our credits before. A mischief ruinous to his Majesty, and not to be prevented without further proof of the amendments of our payments than (notwithstanding what at present we make a hard shift to do) I can yet see any good grounds of hoping for. God send I may find myself mistaken.

S. P.

[Postscript.] Since my signing of this, yours of the 2nd instant is come to my hand, wherein I find cause to give you double thanks for your care about my draught, wherein I find all the reason that may be for my choosing the way you have pitched upon, and shall therefore send down my draught of the *Resolution* whenever you would have me, being willing to keep it in its place till then for the sake of the place where it hangs. All I have to add is, that I shall be unwilling to have the painter lose

so much of his time and pains in my particular work, and therefore desire you to order it so as I did at Chatham, that I may pay him for it when it is done. But above all this, pray remember to draw the ship by the same scale as the *Resolution* was.

68. SAMUEL PEPYS TO ANTHONY DEANE

4 February 1669

SIR

Besides what I have already wrote to you by this post, give me leave to trouble you with three or four questions of desiring satisfaction in, and would be glad to receive from you at your leisure your thoughts concerning them, viz.,

1. Wherein principally the advantage consists of having wet docks, and what objections of any kind are to be made against them? A proposition having been lately started of having one made in each of the King's yards, to which I would be glad to be furnished with what from your experience thereof, both at home and abroad, you are able to say thereto.

2. What is to be said in defence of the Dutch their practice, and I think the French also, of making the captains of their ships victuallers? This being also propounded for our imitation here, and that not only as to victuals but that the captains also should indent for all boatswain's and carpenter's stores, and you having this (if I mistake not) among your late notes to be considered of, I desire that you will think of it and give me your opinion about it.

3. How far in your experience you find that commendation true touching English oak above oak of any other growth, touching its receiving of a shot with less shivering. And whether it be true what I hear said, that the galleon hulk at Portsmouth which was built of cedar is found to have endured wet and dry as well as our vessels built of oak. Which last will be of use to me in something which I have lately met with touching the different duration of the several sorts of timber. . . .

69. SAMUEL PEPYS TO ANTHONY DEANE

25 February 1669

SIR

I have received, and return you very many thanks for, your painful letter of the 16th instant in answer to mine touching of a fit method of distinguishing the several rates of his Majesty's ships; wherein you have furnished me with many substantial considerations relating not only to that but other circumstances of essential importance to the improvement of his Majesty's Royal Navy. You may be confident I shall not omit to lay not only this particular matter before his Royal Highness but your general industry and study to promote his Majesty's advantage in matters of the Navy, and especially in these, which fall within your proper function and observation; and you may be assured I shall in this endeavour to represent the same to his Highness in such manner as may procure and confirm that opinion in his Highness which is due to one so studious of his Highness's honour as you are ...

Let me also know what I shall answer to them that would justify the weight of our guns aloft by saying that one of them will do the service of two below by how much they may be employed with better aim, and by reason of the smoke's being blown away be discharged twice for once in those between decks; and consequently the greater as well as readier execution. Besides that I remember I have heard it observed that it is not so much choice as necessity which make[s] the Dutch carry lighter guns aloft, forasmuch as not only their ships are weaker and much higher carved, and therefore much less able to bear in foul weather the great weight aloft which ours may, but being built more floaty than ours do necessarily roll more and consequently strain more upon the nails, and so are forced to content themselves with guns aloft of less service and force against the hull of an enemy's ship, though it be confessed they may when near do as much upon the rigging and sails of an enemy as greater.

One thing more let me also observe to you, that though it be very manifest that the Dutch have the advantage you speak of in the height of their carriages, yet they have this disadvantage which we are freed from by the lowness of ours: that their guns are much more subject in time of service to overset, as well as to strain more upon the ship's side.

These little notes I thought fit to trouble you with, that if you find any force in them you may give me your information upon them.

I have received yours of the 21st, and am taking care to send down the plat(e).

As for the *Nonsuch*, I am not at all doubtful of her being found abundantly sufficient for the doing of you right that built her, but that she should ever earn Sir Laurence van Heemskirke the reward expected from the King, I meet with nobody that has faith enough to look for it.

But I will not fail to give you the first intimation I receive of Sir Jeremy Smith's report of her. But pray excuse me that I am forced once more to ask you what piece of plate you pitch upon for her, I having at last got an assurance of money of the Treasurer's to pay for it, and therefore would presently put it in doing, but I dare not rely upon my memory for the form you pitched upon, though I think it was a flagon.

Sir John Mennes, Comptroller of the Navy 1661–71, had been a naval officer under Charles I and the Commonwealth. Thanks to his considerable reputation, had he never been promoted to the Comptrollership no-one would have ever doubted his ability to fill the post. Once in position he proved he was entirely unsuited to such a demanding job. In 1667 he had been compelled to allow Brouncker and Penn to do his work for him. Pepys was greatly unsatisfied with a man he once referred to as 'old coxcomb' (Diary 23 May 1663) and this letter to Brouncker in March 1669 confronts the need to dismiss Mennes. The issue of sacking Mennes had surfaced several times in 1668 (for example 25 March) but no mention of the affair or this letter is made in the Diary for March 1669. In fact Pepys did not doubt Mennes' integrity and cited this in his defence in January 1670 before Charles II and the Privy Council, even though Pepys had made it clear he considered Mennes' shortcomings to be a significant failing in the Navy Board's management.

70. SAMUEL PEPYS TO LORD BROUNCKER

11 March 1669

Though the thanks I received from all but your Lordship for my late endeavours of helping the Board to a right knowledge of the posture wherein they stand in relation to their discharge before the Commissioners of Accounts, were such as might well put an end to the care I have so long unprofitably undergone on the behalf of others; yet so much is his Majesty's service and the joint honour of the Board interested in our giving satisfaction to the said Commissioners, that I cannot think any care too much that may conduce towards it, and therefore have adventured in the enclosed to give Sir John Mennes occasion of being farther displeased with me.

My intent in troubling your Lordship with it is, that if upon perusal your Lordship find no cause of correcting it, it may be communicated and seconded by your Lordship, whose authority with him I have good reason to believe will render it the more operative and less offensive.

The truth is, my Lord, the ill success of my so many endeavours with his Royal Highness, Mr Wren, and Sir John Mennes himself (to some of which your Lordship hath been both privy and assisting) of getting him without prejudice eased of an office wherein his infirmities render his continuance unsafe to his Majesty as well as burdensome to the Board, makes me the more willing by my advice and help to supply the want of his removal by making his stay as little to be repented as I can. Wherein I am sure your Lordship will also readily concur, and consequently excuse the trouble given you on this subject.

What I have to add is, that partly from this weakness in Sir John Mennes, partly from the imperfect answers from Sir George Carteret and the Surveyor without any at all from my Lord of Anglesey, and partly from the several books and papers said to have been already delivered in to the Commissioners of Accounts by Sir John Mennes, etc., which were to have constituted part of our general answer to the said Commissioners, I do very much doubt whether this Office will ever be able to give them any laudable reply; and therefore do humbly offer it to your Lordship to consider what is advisable for the Board in general to do for its justification in a case where I cannot but think it too much that the honour of the whole should be sacrificed to the failures of some particular members.

In the meantime I shall by my daily representations and all other means do my part to quicken the Board in what lies before them to do, and therein being sure of your Lordship's furtherance, Remain. . . .

The Diary ends on 31 May 1669. Pepys believed his eyesight was failing and felt he could not go on, since he would have to rely on clerks and other assistants to write for him. There is no escaping the fact that the rest of his life, and that of all his associates, is incomparably less vivid as a result. From now on we have only the letters through which to watch Samuel Pepys mature, and grow old. In short we have to see him in the same way as we see almost every other historical figure – from the image he presented to everyone else and not the one he intended only for himself. The rest of the year 1669 would bring him unexpected tragedy, and before long Pepys was to find that administering the financial and practical problems of the Restoration Navy had earned him enemies in high places.

3 Clerk of the Acts – after the Diary: 1669–73

AFTER THE DIARY years, the rest of Pepys's life would take him through the final fifteen years of Charles II's reign and the high drama of the Popish Plot, the short and turbulent rule of James II, the Glorious Revolution, the sole reign of William III and on into the first year of the reign of Anne. For the moment though, Pepys was still a 'rising man' and this chapter takes us to the point when he became Secretary of the Admiralty a year after the outbreak of the Third Dutch War in March 1672. Along the way he faced his first really serious crisis when he found himself a scapegoat for the Navy's problems during the Second Dutch War.

Pepys had designs on entering Parliament. Sir Robert Brooke was MP for Aldeburgh in Suffolk when he died suddenly in a bathing accident in France in 1669. Captain Thomas Elliott was a bailiff at Aldeburgh and Pepys wrote to him in an effort to have himself selected as a candidate in the ensuing by-election. Ever one to take advantage of influential contacts, Pepys went straight to the top and secured the support of the Duke of York.

71. SAMUEL PEPYS TO CAPTAIN THOMAS ELLIOT

Aldeburgh
1 July 1669

CAPTAIN ELLIOT

Upon the late arrival of the news of Sir Robert Brookes's death who served as one of the Burgesses for the Town of Aldeburgh, his Royal Highness was pleased upon considerations of his own to command me to endeavour after the procurement of the election of myself into this vacancy; an honour which I should not of myself have pretended to, as among other reasons so in particular from my being wholly a stranger to that Corporation. But his Royal Highness having been thus pleased to think upon me in it, with a resolution of engaging his whole interest in the accomplishing of it, I think it my duty to obey him therein, and in order thereto to direct my first applications to yourself, whom his Royal Highness is pleased to pitch upon as one of whose endeavours in the promoting of all his desire his Highness rests most assured, and in an especial manner relies upon your capacity and influence for doing the same in this particular.

The enclosed will deliver you his Highness's mind under his own hand, and more particularly by another from Mr Wren to which I must be referred, having never yet had the good fortune of serving you in anything that might oblige you to the exercise of your interest and kindness on my behalf. But as your favour herein will be very acceptable to his Royal Highness, so will it engage not only myself singly but the whole body of this Office upon all future occasions to express their sense of your kindness shown to one of its members; besides that, if his Highness's desire herein do succeed, I do not despair of having opportunity of showing myself a faithful and useful servant to the Corporation.

I shall not think it needful to offer you any advice touching the method of your proceedings, but submit the whole to your prudence. Which I pray you to believe that I will see you fully and thankfully reimbursed for what charges shall attend the same, and pray that you will please to give me a speedy account of your thoughts and advice, how his Royal Highness's influence, or any other recommendations, may be most advantageously employed and directed for the obtaining of these our desires.

This is all the trouble you shall at present receive from your most affectionate friend and humble servant,

S. P.

ENCLS

THE DUKE OF YORK TO THE TOWN OF ALDEBURGH IN SUFFOLK

16 July 1669

GENTLEMEN

Being informed of the death of Sir Robert Brookes, who served in Parliament as one of the Burgesses of your Corporation, I recommend to your favour in your future election Samuel Pepys, Esquire, one of the Commissioners of the Navy, who besides his general qualifications for that trust will, I assure myself, be found on all occasions a useful servant to your town. And what kindness he shall receive from you in this matter I shall esteem as a testimony of your respect to me.

I am, your loving friend, JAMES.

In spite of his impressive sponsor, Pepys was unsuccessful and was not selected as a candidate. In the autumn of 1669 Pepys and his wife Elizabeth made a long-planned trip to France, together with her brother Balthazar St Michel. Little is known about the journey. On 21 August John Evelyn, who had travelled in France in the 1640s, wrote him a lengthy guide to the sights on offer and included some introductions. The Pepyses must have left shortly afterwards. They returned home on or around 20 October, a date Pepys gives in his Brooke House Journal.[1] Elizabeth Pepys was already seriously unwell, having been taken sick in Flanders. In spite of this vastly more pressing priority, Pepys wrote to Evelyn on 2 November to offer his profuse apologies for failing to pay Evelyn a visit to thank him.

72. SAMUEL PEPYS TO JOHN EVELYN

Navy Office
2 November 1669

SIR

I beg you to believe that I would not have been ten days returned into England without waiting on you, had it not pleased God to afflict me by the sickness of my wife, who, from the first day of her coming back into London, hath lain under a fever so severe as at this hour to render her recovery desperate. Which affliction hath very much unfitted me for those acts of civility and respect which, amongst the first of my friends, I should have paid to yourself, as he to whom singly I owe the much greater part of the satisfaction I have met with in my late voyage. Next to you, I have my acknowledgements to make to Sir Samuel Tuke; to whom (when in a condition

[1] NWB, p. 334. Evelyn's letter is published in PF A28.

of doing it) I shall beg your introducing me, for the owning of my obligations to him on the like behalf. But Sir, I beg you heartily to dispense with the ceremony, till I am better qualified for paying it; and in the meantime receive the enclosed, which I should with much more satisfaction have delivered with my own hands.

I am, Sir,

Your most obliged and obedient servant,

S. PEPYS

I most humbly kiss your ladies hands, and pray my service be presented to Sir Richard Browne.

The situation was indeed desperate. Elizabeth Pepys died a little over a week later on 10 November. She was buried at St Olave's, Hart Street, on 13 November and lies there still. Pepys commissioned a portrait bust of her, which remains on display in the church. John Evelyn attended the funeral though he merely mentions the fact in his diary, and provides no description of the occasion.

In spite of the personal devastation he felt, Pepys had finally to confront the findings of the Parliamentary Committee for Accounts, which had been established along with the Committee for Miscarriages to investigate why the Second Dutch War had gone so badly. Established in 1667, it met at Brooke House, and became known as the Brooke House Committee. Pepys faced the Committee for Accounts in early 1668 with considerable trepidation, since the question of the prize goods had resurfaced and so had the uncomfortable issue of gifts made to members of the Navy Board in return for appointments. Unfortunately, men whose own corruption had led to their being sacked now took their revenge. James Carkesse was a clerk in the Navy Office sacked in 1666 for corruption, but through influential friends he had been reappointed. He therefore took the opportunity to denounce Pepys, Penn and Batten for paying the crew of a privateer, the *Flying Greyhound*, in their ownership, rather than the Navy's sailors. It seems this is what had happened, so Pepys had good cause to be worried and, moreover, Carkesse was not the only accuser.

On 5 March 1668 Pepys faced the House of Commons to answer the Committee's report. In spite of the 'dissatisfaction of the House' Pepys's reply was a triumph with some people considering it the finest speech to have been heard in Parliament for generations. The following day he enjoyed further congratulations, with the Duke of York announcing, 'Mr Pepys, I am very glad of your success yesterday.' Unfortunately for Pepys the matter did not end there. When he returned from France in October 1669 the Committee presented him with eighteen accusations. The rest of the year involved him in the meticulous construction of his defence for the conduct of the war, which he then presented to the Committee in hearings that lasted throughout January and February 1670. During this time Pepys wrote to the Brooke House Commissioners and to the King to defend himself.

73. SAMUEL PEPYS TO THE BROOKE HOUSE COMMISSIONERS

Navy Office
6 January 1670

MY LORDS AND GENTLEMEN

Your Lordships' silence to what I (now some weeks since) presented you with relating to the common defence of this Office, joined with what hath lately come to my notice touching your acceptance of separate answers on the same subject from some particular members thereof, leads me to the thinking it seasonable for me to put into your Lordships' hands something of what may hereafter come more amply to you in right to myself. The distinct duty of whose place as Clerk of the Acts being not to be denied to have shared in the increase of trouble occasioned by a war, equal (at least) to that of any of my fellows, especially those of them who, standing charged with little of the active, were at more leisure to attend only the consultive part of the Office, I cannot conceive any person conversant in the business thereof will scruple to allow the well executing my single share thereinfor a task sufficient to exercise the best industry of one man, without the additional charge of an accountableness for the reasons and actions of others.

To give your Lordships therefore a summary account of the method wherein I have in my particular place endeavoured to discharge my duty to his Majesty, both in the diligence of my attendance on it, the effects of my performance of it, and uprightness in both, give me leave to say:

First – That for what respects my diligence: as no concernments relating to my private fortune, pleasure or health did at any time (even under the terror of the Plague itself) divide me one day and night from my attendance on the business of my place, so was I never absent at any public meeting of this Board but upon the especial commands of the Lord High Admiral, and that not thrice during the whole three years of the war. To which let me add that in my endeavours after a full performance of my duty I have neither made distinction of days between those of rest and others, nor of hours between them of day and night, being less acquainted during the whole war with the closing my day's work before midnight than after it.

And that your Lordships may not conceive this to arise from any vain assumption of what may be grounded more upon the inability of others to disprove than my own capacity to justify, such have ever been my apprehensions both of the duty and importance of my just attendance on his Majesty's service that among the many thousands under whose observation my employment must have placed me, I challenge any man to assign one day from my first admission to this service in July 1660 to the determination of the war August 1667 (being a complete apprenticeship) of which I am not at this day able upon oath to give an account of the particular manner of my employing the same.

Secondly – That although this resignation of my whole time and strength to the service of his Majesty might in other cases be admitted for the equallest method of rating my performances, and albeit that other, by which alone your Lordships seem inclined to measure the same, namely the exactness of their conformity to and compliance with the ancient Instructions of the Lord High Admiral, calculated for a time of peace and small action, will not (I conceive) either in the reason, practicableness or intention thereof be upon examination insisted upon as such during a war, yet to the end that when your Lordships shall find me reasonably urging the same in behalf of the Board in general, you may not apprehend me interested in the behalf of that argument from any use I have to make of it in reference to my particular, to whom the meanest article of a Navy Officer's duty ever seemed of too much moment to be left unexecuted without the communication of it and the reasons thereof to the Lord High Admiral, let it not be thought ostentation for me to own the result of my humble labours in his Majesty's service by pretending to the having strictly answered every part of those Instructions incumbent on myself; and that in such method as to be willing to submit the same (while under the most tumultuous difficulties of a war) to be compared with and censured by what can be found of most methodical in any of my predecessors during the most leisurely time of peace, though (to say more) your Lordships shall at the same time find the work of my place to have exceeded by little less than a tenfold proportion that of my predecessors in the busiest time of their war. Wherein your Lordships are humbly referred to the written evidences of both, now extant.

And yet, that after having thus acquitted myself in my particular duty I may not be found unmindful of what your Lordships seem to expect from each member in the justification of the acts of the whole, I shall take upon me further to say that though the fullness of my proper employment may (I doubt not) be reasonably offered in defence of my necessary concurrence with others in matters foreign thereto, yet forasmuch as through the frequent absences of my fellow Officers during the late war (and that sometimes for weeks together) hundreds of letters and warrants have for the dispatch of his Majesty's service been necessarily issued under my single hand and advice, I shall alone undertake for every such act, without the support of any defence for the possible imperfections thereof, deducible from my want of their advice, who stood equally obliged to an attendance with me on the same.

Nay further, forasmuch as though in the quality of my employment it hath in an especial manner been esteemed my part to subscribe to the determinations of the Board, it may have so happened that my advice has nevertheless taken place in matters where one only of my fellow Officers may with myself have been present at the debates, I am contented also to stand personally accountable for every such act of this Office vouched but by one hand more than my own; leaving to your Lordships the considering how far you will expect the like from me in cases where I shall be found subscribing only to the resolutions of a greater number, and those either by the nature or leisure of their proper places more concerned for and better instructed to guide the Board then and justify it now in the reasonableness of the same.

Thirdly – That as I expect not that either my diligence or best performances should be held worthy owning otherwise than as they are accompanied with integrity to my master and fair dealing towards those whom his service hath led me to have to do with, so I do with good assurance desire the whole world to allege one instance to the prejudice of the same, having the comfort of being able to affirm that my conscience in its strictest retrospections charges me not with any wilful declension from my duty, either in the faithfulness of my deportment therein, or care of rendering it the least expenseful to his Majesty – the execution of my place (under the utmost pressures of the war and the necessary increase of charge attending it) being to be found of less cost to his Majesty by one half than any other branch of the work of this Office, or what (by the necessary latitude given me with the rest of my fellows on that behalf) I might without censure have rendered my own to have been, and thereby not only gratified myself with a greater leisure of attending my private concernments, but prevented that untimely ruin of my eyes by the constancy of their night services during the war, which renders the remainder of my life of much less content or use to me than can be supplied by any other satisfaction than what flows from the consideration of that duty to his Majesty to which I sacrificed them.

And as to my behaviour towards others in reference to those gratifications which both practice and the quality of my place might justify an expectation and acceptance of, when (by the direction of the Lord High Admiral or the Board) employed in matters of lawful favour to private men, especially while the trust and burden of my place falling short of none of my fellows, no other reason than the consideration of such advantages incident thereto has been ever assigned for that difference of encouragement current amongst us by which the wages of the Clerk of the Acts stands inferior not only to what attends the lowest of his fellow Officers but to the avowed profits of some of their servants, I shall with the same openness and truth wherewith your Lordships have in every other matter (relating no less to myself than others) found me ready to assist your inquiries humbly say:

First – That from the first hour of my serving his Majesty in this employment I did never to this day directly or indirectly demand or express any expectation of fee, gratuity or reward from any person for any service therein by me done or to be done them.

Secondly – That no gratuity, though voluntarily offered, hath ever met with my acceptance where I found not the affair to which it did relate accompanied with the doing right or advantage to his Majesty.

Thirdly – That the sums wherein I stand at this day in disburse on occasions wholly relative to the execution of my said employment during the war, and which (amounting to above £400) my fellow Officers have in their respective places either not at all known, or been reimbursed the same from his Majesty, do far exceed whatever profits have accrued to me from my said employment within that whole time.

Fourthly – Lastly, that I have in this place been in general so little solicitous in the study of my private fortune as to own with fullest and most humble thankfulness the favour and bounties of his Majesty to me under my low endeavours therein; though in exchange for near ten years' service, and those the most valuable of my life for such improvements, I find not my estate at this day bettered by one thousand pounds from all the profits, salary or other advantages arising from my said employment beyond what it was known to be at my admission thereto.

Into the truth of all which I do not only invite but pray your Lordships to exercise your strictest inquisitions; being ready to justify the same not only by oath but by a double retribution of every penny or pennyworth of advantage I shall be found to have received either in manner or value different from what I have here declared.

Which leaving with your Lordships as an appendix in my own right to what you have already received from me on behalf of the Board in general, and submitting both to your disposal, I remain,

My Lords and Gentlemen,
Your Lordships' most humble and most faithful servant
S. PEPYS

74. SAMUEL PEPYS TO CHARLES II

Navy Office
8 January 1670

SIR

Your Majesty's having been pleased with one hand to receive what has been offered you in charge against the Officers of your Navy, I cannot without offence to your justice doubt your vouchsafing me the other, for what in most humble manner I come to tender your Majesty in their and my own behalf, being a duplicate of what hath lately gone from me in answer to the observations of the Commissioners of Accounts.

In which, as I have aimed at the doing all (fair) right to my fellow Officers, so has it not been without regard also to the honour of your Majesty's service, which seems not a little interested in the removal of what at this day meets (as I apprehend) with too easy an admission, namely that the different issues of the former and later war with the Dutch are chiefly chargeable on the different degrees of method and good husbandry exercised then and now by the managers of this Office.

Not but those acting in the former have [not] left us many things worthy imitation, and which I have not only borne witness to in my particular practice, but may one day have opportunity of doing it by a more solemn representation of them, as such, both to your Majesty and the public.

But because better success did attend them than it has pleased God to allow us, that therefore this success must (to the depreciating all that comes after them) be necessarily referred to some transcendency in their methods, while the whole style of the transactions of that time demonstrate a principle, as in other things so in those of the Navy, wholly incompatible with that of forms; as having neither directed themselves by the ancient Instructions of the Lord High Admiral (now urged to our prejudice) nor bound themselves up by any other of their own. Nay, when neither in the balancing storekeepers' accounts, frequency of their surveys, tenderness in granting or regularity in clearing imprests, use of tickets or infallibility in their examinations, uninterestedness of their contacts or lowness of their prices, or any other of those circumstances wherein your Majesty's present Officers are deemed most peccant, they will be found to outdo or in many of them even to come up to what hath been arrived at under your Majesty's government. This (I say) seems a concession so injurious to the honour thereof as in faithfulness thereto I durst not in my following discourse permit to pass unreflected on.

Especially when I consider not only the issue of what's past, wherein (as it will ever be in actions like this, while managed but by men and subject to disappointments from plague, fire, etc., neither to be foreseen nor obviated) so many real failures must inevitably be looked for as shall not need to be aggravated by the suggestion of others, which indeed are not; but [are] the fatal effects of any miscalculations of the means designed for securing your Majesty's better success to come.

To which mistake I cannot see what can contribute more than an assignment of our present miscarriages to the want of what our predecessors under all their successes were no greater masters of than we; but so much the contrary, that whoever shall have opportunity of taking the same leisurely view of the management of that time which my employment under your Majesty has led me to will easily concur that there appears not anything in the whole conduct of that age to which (under God) their success can be more duly attributed than a steady pursuit of all means conducing thereto, both in preference and exclusion to all impediments arising from considerations either of thrift or method.

Of which, and what else my best observations upon the managements and events of these two great actions, together with the collections which by your Majesty's command I have at my late being abroad made on the same subject relating to our neighbours, may have furnished me with, improvable to your Majesty's future

service, neither my common duty as a subject nor especial obligations as the eldest
(though otherwise the least worthy) of your Majesty's servants enjoying at this day
the honour of that name in this Office will suffer me to want, much less to let slip, a
more fit occasion of exposing to that gracious censure with which your Majesty hath
ever been pleased to encourage the humble offers of, Royal Sir,

Your Majesty's most loyal, most obedient and faithful
subject and servant
S. PEPYS

The Committee fizzled out after February 1670. As Pepys said, there was no 'end to be
foreseen of it; while answers being given to satisfaction to this day's objection, that
satisfaction shall never be owned but in lieu a new race of objections shall be started ... So
this matter and the whole business of these Observations ended'.[2]

With the Brooke House Committee out of the way, Pepys returned to more personal
business. This letter from Pepys to Thomas Elliot provides us with some idea of the impact
Elizabeth Pepys's death had had on her husband. However, we know from a codicil to
Pepys's will added in May 1703 that his relationship with Mary Skinner, who became his
housekeeper and apparently his common-law wife, had begun thirty-three years earlier –
that is, in or around 1670.

The letter also thanks Elliot for his assistance in Pepys's attempt to be selected as
Parliamentary candidate for Aldeburgh. It seems a faction in Aldeburgh, led by a Mr Duke
and Captain Shipman, had opposed Pepys's ambitions and as a result insulted the Duke of
York. This was an inevitable matter of concern to Pepys too, since he was loyal to the
King's brother and remained so when James succeeded in 1685 with drastic consequences
for Pepys when James was deposed in 1688.

75. SAMUEL PEPYS TO CAPTAIN THOMAS ELLIOT

3 March 1670

CAPTAIN ELLIOT

I beg you earnestly to believe that nothing but the sorrow and distraction I have been
in by the death of my wife, increased by the suddenness with which it pleased God
to surprise me therewith, after a voyage so full of health and content, could have
forced me to so long a neglect of my private concernments; this being, I do assure
you, the very first day that my affliction, together with my daily attendance on other
public occasions of his Majesty's, has suffered me to apply myself to the
considering any part of my private concernments; among which, that of my doing
right to you is no small particular: and therefore, as your charity will, I hope, excuse
me for my not doing it sooner, so I pray you to accept now, as late as it is, my hearty
thanks for your multiplied kindness in my late affair at Aldeburgh; and in particular,
your courteous providing of your own house for my reception, had I come down; the
entertainment you were also pleased to prepare for me, together with your other
great pains and charges in the preserving that interest which you had gained, in
reference to his Royal Highness's and my Lord Howard's desire on my behalf: in all
which I can give you good assurance, that not only his Royal Highness retains a
thankful memory of your endeavours to serve him, but I shall take upon me the
preserving it so with him, that it may be useful to you when you shall have any
occasion for asking his favour. The like I dare promise you from my Lord Howard,

---

[2] Brooke House Papers in NWB, pp. 432–3.

when he shall return; and both from them and myself make this kindness of yours, and the rest of those gentlemen of the town who were pleased to concur with you, as advantageous both to yourself and them, and to the Corporation also, as if the business had succeeded to the best of our wishes: and this I assure you, whether I shall ever hereafter have the honour of serving them in Parliament or not, having no reason to receive anything with dissatisfaction in this whole matter, saving the particular disrespect which our noble master, the Duke of York, suffered from the beginning to the end, from Mr Duke and Captain Shipman, who, I doubt not, may meet with a time of seeing their error therein. But I am extremely ashamed to find myself so much outdone by you in kindness, by your not suffering me to know the expense which this business has occasioned you; which I again entreat you to let me do, esteeming your pains, without that of your charge, an obligation greater than I can foresee opportunity of requiting, though I shall by no means omit to endeavour it. So with a repetition of my hearty acknowledgments of all your kindness, with my service to yourself and lady, and all my worthy friends about you,

I remain, your obliged friend and humble servant,

S. P.

In that letter to Elliot, Pepys makes it clear how ashamed he was Elliot had gone to expense on his behalf. Pepys was extremely conscious of patronage and how the game was played. It was, after all, exactly how he had come to be where he was at the time. He had now reached a position where he was a source of patronage himself. One of Pepys's greatest virtues was his unfailing sense of loyalty to his own extended family. In this letter Pepys writes to John Evelyn's father-in-law, Sir Richard Browne. Browne had been Charles II's envoy to the French court during the Interregnum. Naturally, Pepys had come to know him through Evelyn but also in Browne's involvement with Trinity House.

London's Trinity House had begun life as a guild of seamen. By the seventeenth century it had become responsible for navigational aids around the coast, such as lights and buoys. Trinity House provided pilots and supervised the certification of sailing masters. It worked closely with the Navy Board, and Pepys, like most of his colleagues, was a member. In fact, Sandwich had been made Master of Trinity House in 1661. Sir Richard Browne donated land to Trinity House to build almshouses at Deptford in 1671, and would himself become Master from 1672–3. Pepys, having heard that the clerk of Trinity House was dead, took the opportunity to recommend his brother John on the basis of his 'sobriety, diligence, and education'. Pepys, who had secured referees from other influential sources including the Duke of York, was of course playing the game. His private opinion of John Pepys was not quite the same. 'I fear he will never make a good speaker – nor, I fear, any general good scholar' but 'he seems sober, and that pleases me' (Diary 17 October 1666). In 1667 he had considered sending John to Cambridge and making him go into the church. The plans came to nothing and evidently the Trinity House vacancy, Pepys decided, was the opportunity he had been waiting for. He dashed off a letter to Browne, and also sent one to John insisting that he make himself available for interview the following week.

76. SAMUEL PEPYS TO SIR RICHARD BROWNE

Navy Office
26 March 1670

HONOURED SIR

I have a sudden occasion offered me of asking your friendship, as well as a full assurance that I shall. 'Tis this: Mr Ascew, Clerk of Trinity House, is dead. I have a

brother of my own (John Pepys), whose relation to me could not tempt me to thi
motion, were it not that his sobriety, diligence, and education, (being a scholar, and
think in every respect qualified for the employment in a very different proportion t
what Mr Ascew's education could render him), doth lead me to think it a service t
the Corporation to offer him to them. I aim not so much at the salary for him, as th
opportunity, by this means, of introducing him to that unit of business for which
have for some time designed him. He is about thirty years of age, unmarried; his lif
that of a scholar's, as having resided in the University till, having past three or fou
years Master of Arts, I called him thence some time since to my own tuition, an
that acquaintance with business which my trade could lead him to. Now, Sir
knowing your influence upon the Society of Trinity House, I pray you so far to trus
my report in this matter, as to think it worthy of your countenance by a word or tw
between this and Wednesday next, either to the body of that house, or such member
of it as you think may be most operative, in conjunction with that assistance whicl
your recommendation shall receive from my Lord Sandwich, Lord Craven, and m
brethren of this office, who have promised me to concern themselves thoroughly i
this matter, besides a letter which his Royal Highness was pleased to give me on th
same behalf.

   Your particular favour herein shall be owned with all possible expressions o
thankfulness by

Your obedient Servant,

S. PEPYS

77. SAMUEL PEPYS TO JOHN PEPYS JUNIOR

26 March 1670

BROTHER

Something hath offered itself which may prove of advantage to you, that makes i
necessary for me to have you here on Tuesday night next. It is an employment intc
which some or other must be elected on Wednesday morning. If my endeavours fo
you succeed it will be a good provision for you. If it do not, it is very well worth a
journey to attempt it.

   I am sensible this may be inconvenient to my Brother Jackson; but I hope some
way or other may be found to put off the meeting on his business for a few days. For
whither this succeeds or not, you shall be at liberty in a few days to return for a little
time. Therefore pray fail not to be here on Tuesday night next. I beg my father's
blessing and rest

Your loving brother

S. PEPYS

The efforts were successful. John Pepys became clerk at Trinity House. In 1673 he was
made joint-Clerk of the Acts in the Navy Office with one of Pepys's former clerks, Tom
Hayter. His new job diverted him from Trinity House and at his death in 1677 Pepys had to
pay £300 to Trinity House to settle his brother's accounts.

Pepys's evolving relationship with Anthony Deane meant that when he learned Deane was
making unauthorized experiments in shipbuilding technology, he now chided him in a more
restrained fashion than a few years before (Letter no. 45).

78. SAMUEL PEPYS TO ANTHONY DEANE

2 May 1670

SIR

I have yours of the 28th of the last with the enclosed particulars relating to the Office of the Ordnance, and shall in that, as well as in what respects our own Office, endeavour to procure you all the satisfaction and with what speed I possibly can, being very desirous to give you all the ease and furtherance within my reach towards the great work you are upon.

But there happens a particular which, though I believe in itself it signifies but little, yet in the noise which some people are disposed to raise upon it, seems to be designed to do you a greater prejudice than is fit for me to permit without giving you notice of it. It is that you have of your own head, without precedent, as well as without the advice, or so much as the privity, of this Board or the Commissioner upon the place, presumed to lay aside the old secure practice of fastening your beams in your new ships with standards and knees, and in the room thereof taken upon you to do it with iron. An experiment which they would represent as the more extravagant, as being made upon a ship of such value as that you are now building.

Whether you have done this for dispatch, husbandry, or any other convenience, or reduced to it by necessity, I shall not enquire. But the complaint has reached as far as the King and Duke; in whose presence hearing the matter urged, and that not without some expressions of dissatisfaction in them, I took liberty to say that I doubted not but that if the matter were in fact true, you would be able to give them a reasonable account of your proceedings therein, and therefore prayed that they would suspend their censure concerning it till I had wrote and received your answer about it; which his Majesty and Royal Highness readily granted me. I desire that you will draw up such an answer speedily to this matter, directing it either to the Board or me, grounded upon mine to you, for the satisfaction of his Royal Highness and them, and let it be so as may be fit for me to show to the King and Duke.

The matter I believe springs from Mr Steventon, his name having been used in it; but as I am confident your understanding, so I do not doubt but your care on his Majesty's behalf and prudence on your own is such as cannot have misled you to the doing anything in this matter beyond your ability to justify, and therefore am not in any pain for you, though I shall always have a regard to the preservation of your esteem with his Majesty and his Royal Highness, and therefore wish myself armed to do you right in this particular. . . .

Deane defended himself strongly in a letter of 5 May 1670,[3] arguing that his use of iron was far more suitable for securing beams. He went as far as to say that building more 'great ships' would be impossible without them. This convinced Charles II, and Deane's unauthorized innovations were permitted.

Pepys's family responsibilities also included his brother-in-law, Balthazar St Michel. 'Brother Balty' remained an issue for the rest of Pepys's life. He was a comic figure, but with Pepys's patronage his naval career was reasonably successful. He reciprocated Pepys's generosity with his own brand of loyalty, which extended to securing evidence to discredit Pepys's accusers in 1679. Meanwhile, in 1666 Pepys had found him a job as muster-master on the *Henry*. The job involved maintaining records of personnel, and he handled it

---

[3] MS Rawl A179.f.179.

satisfactorily, so that by 1670 he was promoted to muster-master at Deal. Several other post
followed but in this letter Balthazar is bringing Pepys up to date with muster administratio
and news from the coast about the movements of a Dutch vessel. 'Mr Coulmer' is unknown
The letter illustrates Balthazar's excitable and narcissistic personality.

79. BALTHAZAR ST MICHEL TO SAMUEL PEPYS

For his Majesty's Service.
*To the Honourable Samuel Pepys Esquire at the Navy Office
in Seething Lane, these. London.*

Dea
11 June 1670

HONOURED SIR

This comes humbly to acquaint you that yesterday sailed out of the Downs the
Falcon and *Speedwell* (bound for the River Thames), and that I have a perfec
muster-book from the Purser of the *Falcon* now, who brought it me ashore
according to promise and I am a preparing them to be sent to your office within thi
two days which I hope will be time enough for the ships before they be paid off.

Yesterday there came into the Downs a Dutch pleasure boat with a pennant above
her anchent which when I saw (walking upon the beach with Mr Coulmer) I said to
Mr Coulmer, 'let you and I go on board her, and see what she doth here'. So we
went and found on board two or three brave gallants amongst whom (as he said) the
Dutch ambassador's brother whose pleasure boat this was. He kindly entertained u
with a bottle of wine, and told us he came for pleasure to see all along the coast
saying he had been at Dover, and that after he had been ashore at Deale, he would go
to Sandwich, from thence to, and through all the creeks and view Sheerness, and
Chatham and then to London; and would if he could (he said) sail his boat for £100
with any of the King's pleasure boats. I having nothing more of news to present you
with, (with all our most humble duties: respects, and services to you) I remain

Your Most faithful and obedient servant

B ST MICHEL

Pepys seems to have fallen out with the Swedish ambassador in late 1670. The disagreemen
was bad enough for the possibility of a 'challenge' between the two men. Duels were a
serious matter. In 1662 a Colonel Giles Rawlins was killed in a duel, and Pepys hoped i
would lead to 'good laws against it' (Diary 19 August). Sweden had mediated in the peace
negotiations that brought about the end of the Second Dutch War as part of the efforts to
organize an anti-French coalition. Since Charles II was in debt to Louis XIV for Frencl
support during the Interregnum and in other more practical ways, and the English also
resented the terms of the peace, the relationship with Dutch and Swedish representative
was necessarily liable to some tension. It is possible that Pepys's loyalty to the crown lec
him to express a partisan view, or to take offence on behalf of Charles II. In June 1670
Charles II had signed the Treaty of Dover with Louis XIV. This secured for Charles two
ports on the mouth of the Scheldt but in a secret version of the same treaty he and the Duke
of York agreed to convert to Catholicism and eventually to restore Catholicism to England
Charles II, unlike the Duke of York, kept his own conversion secret. Lord Arlington
secretary of state 1662–74, encouraged this and was himself converted to Catholicism on hi
own deathbed in 1685. However, there is no clue in this letter from Matthew Wren
secretary to the Duke of York, of what the row was about.

80. Matthew Wren to Samuel Pepys

9 November 1670

SIR

His Majesty having accidentally heard of some dispute between you and the Resident of Sweden, to prevent any further inconvenience that may happen, has by my Lord Arlington Principal Secretary of State signified his Pleasure to me, to require you neither to send any challenge to the said Resident of Sweden, nor to accept of any from him; But that as soon as you receive this you immediately attend the Lord Arlington.

I am, your most humble Servant
M Wren

Unfortunately we have no idea what the outcome of the incident was. Pepys seems to have avoided ever making the challenge, which is not wholly surprising as there is no evidence at all to suggest he had any proficiency or interest in the use of weapons himself, though on 2 February 1662 he had started wearing a sword 'as the manner now among gentlemen is'.

The Third Dutch War started in March 1672. Thanks to the secret provisions of the Treaty of Dover, Charles II was obliged to help Louis XIV against Holland. The English and French navies fought the Dutch at Sole Bay on 28 May 1672. The engagement was inconclusive and involved some unfortunate losses. The French lost Rear-Admiral des Rabesnières-Treillebois, who was buried at Rochester on 4 June. John Evelyn was one of the pall-bearers and helped organize the ceremony. He was once again serving as a Commissioner for Sick and Wounded Seamen and Prisoners of War in Kent and in regular correspondence with Pepys. The death of the Earl of Sandwich in the battle was also a personal tragedy for Pepys and John Evelyn who called him a 'a true noble man'.[4]

The Duke of York's secretary, Matthew Wren, was wounded in the battle. There seems to have been some hope that Pepys would succeed him in the post. Pepys wrote to Balthazar St Michel who had clearly expressed his 'hopes' for Pepys, probably for this promotion. In fact Pepys was never offered the job, and here he warns his brother-in-law not to rely too much on what he can do for him. Balthazar's present employment was still as muster-master at Deal.

81. Samuel Pepys to Balthazar St Michel

22 June 1672

BROTHER BALTY

I came last night home from the fleet, where I have spent about five days. I thank God I am well, saving some little disorder an uneasy lodging for so many nights hath given me.

At my coming back I find a very kind letter from yourself for which I am your debtor, and also for your last, wherein you take notice of some of the world's late discourses, and your hopes nevertheless concerning me, the success whereof what ever it may be; I cannot but advise you to make this use of it, that even diligence and integrity itself is not always defence enough against censure, nor can be while envy remains in the world, and that therefore you are by all honest improvements of your time to provide against a day where possibly I in my place may not be able to help you, nor you in yours be able to help yourself.

---

[4] Evelyn's diary 31 May 1672.

I tell you this out of a very serious reflection upon what you may very possibly find my condition to prove; and to show you the more that I am not without apprehensions of that sort, I have laboured now within a day or two to get that from the Duke for you, which I have respited for so many years to look after, least i should fall out of my power to procure it, I mean his Royal Highness's Commission to you for your present employment. Wherein I do both desire and charge you to behalf [= behave?] yourself so, that your own merit (if possible) may continue you in that, which the endeavour of your friends have by God's blessing brought you into. I say not this with so much a seeming melancholy, as if I would have you lay aside your expectations of good success, but to caution you against the worst effects of bad. A doctrine which I the rather press upon you from the trouble that it in some degree gives me, that I no sooner learnt it myself.

So with my blessing to my Godson and love and service to all. I remain

Your very affectionate brother and servant

S. P.

82. BALTHAZAR ST MICHEL TO SAMUEL PEPYS

To the Honourable Samuel Pepys Esquire at the
Navy Office in Seething Lane. These London.

Deal
14 August 1672

HONOURED SIR

You daily and hourly so comble me with (not only expressions but also) deeds of your worthiness, and goodness, as well to myself, as the rest of your most devoted humble creatures here, that I am (as well as my poor drooping mother, whose continual illness since the death of my father, gives me but little hopes she will survive him long (only but to be something longer a living witness of your dearness to her poor childe, your late dear consort, my beloved sister) by that your noble, worthy, and kind expressions and promises to be still her benefactor, for which she hath only (saith she) the capacity left her, to bless God for your prosperity, and to continue still her prayers to the almighty God, to power upon you, and yours multitude of heavenly blessings; these Sir are her own expressions, and I am sure from the very bottom of her heart and soul) I am then Sir as I said confuted in myself how I may ever strive to deserve, the least of those your many-fold, gracious, good, kind, fatherly, and dear (not only expressions) but effects which I for ever shall own.

Well, Sir since I fear it will never lie in my power to serve you as I ought (without devoting my life and fortunes at your feet be pleased to accept, and command both upon all occasions which you will find, with so much zeal still; for you, and your cause, that never man living, will ever be named more grateful (as I am in duty bound) to your favours and more zealous for your concerns, and interest; then him who is proud to be, Sir, your most faithful and obedient humble servant

B ST MICHEL

Little Samuel (who speaks now very prettily) desires to have his most humble duty presented to his most honoured uncle, and godfather, which please to accept from your most humble little disciple.

This day the *Dragon* is come into the Downs which tomorrow God willing I intend to muster. Pray present my most kind and Humble service to my cousin John Pepys.

B. ST M

Knowing that Pepys was keen to enter Parliament, the Duke of York recommended him to Henry Howard, Baron Howard of Castle Rising since 1669, as a possible candidate for the seat at Castle Rising. This letter arrived from Henry Savile, Groom of the Bedchamber to the Duke of York, with the news.

83. HENRY SAVILE TO SAMUEL PEPYS

For his honoured friend Samuel Pepys Esquire
Clerk of the Acts of his Majesty's Navy
at the Navy Office in Seething Lane London with care.

Burlington Bay *Prince*
14 August 1672

SIR

His Royal Highness has commanded me to write to you to send away with all possible dispatch to Southwold Bay the shallop that he ordered should be made for Monsieur le Comte D'Estrées, that he may have it ready for him when we are there where we shall be in a very little time if his Highness's resolutions are not prevented by ill weather or some other unavoidable accidents.

He has further ordered me to acquaint you that upon a report we have here that Sir Robert Paston is to be called to the House of Lords. He spoke to my Lord Harry Howard that you might be Burgess of Rising, which his Lordship has very willingly consented to both out of obedience to the Duke's commands and out of kindness to you, and therefore it will be your part to watch Sir Robert's promotion and inquire into the truth of it and acquaint my Lord H. Howard with it; I hope you have received the letter I sent you by the Duke's command to assure you of the care he will take in your own private affair which he mentioned to you the last time you were with him, I heartily wish that during the short time of my being in office some opportunity would happen of showing you with how much truth I am Sir

Your most faithful humble Servant

HENRY SAVILE

The Castle Rising seat was expected to fall vacant when Sir Robert Paston entered the House of Lords, then anticipated imminently. Pepys composed this obsequious letter of thanks to Howard believing he was Howard's only choice. Pepys enclosed it with a letter of his to Sir William Coventry and asked the latter to hand it on.

84. SAMUEL PEPYS TO LORD HENRY HOWARD

20 August 1672

MY LORD

Having by his Royal Highness's appointment understood his Highness's recommending me with success to your Lordship for the Burgess-ship of Rising, upon the expected removal of Sir Robert Paston to the House of Lords, I hold it m duty to make this my humble and thankful acknowledgement of it to your Lordship Not that I dare imagine your Lordship's favour to me therein arises from any othe consideration than that of my being a humble creature of his Royal Highness; bu that the assurance I have of his Highness's devoting me to your service no less thai favour, together with a due sense of my former obligations on the like occasion te your Lordship, makes it [a] duty in me to tender your Lordship my most humbl thanks and faithful engagement of employing the capacity your Lordship shal herein give me, to the particular use and services of the Houses of Norfolk and o that country whereto so many advantages both of honour and protection have arisei from your noble person, by whom I shall ever be ambitious of being conducted ane commanded, as becomes

My Lord
Your Lordship's most obedient servant
S. PEPYS

Pepys was rather premature. Paston gave up his seat in August 1673 when he was createe Viscount Yarmouth. He did not enter the House of Lords until 1679 when he became Earl o Yarmouth, though ironically Henry Howard did as Earl of Norwich (in 1677 he became the sixth Duke of Norfolk). It turned out that Henry Howard had already been associated witl two other candidates. Thomas Povey wrote to Pepys to explain what was going on and alse to point out the simmering resentment in the 'country' (= 'county') at the prospect of a stranger representing them.

85. THOMAS POVEY TO SAMUEL PEPYS

31 August 1672

SIR

I had this morning full discourse with the Lord Howard, who was telling me how he finds himself oppressed with his prerogative of recommending on elections: and how he stands engaged to the King for Sir Francis North, to the Duchess of Cleveland for Sir John Trevor (her council and feoffee), and to the Duke for you telling me by what circumstances the Duke attacked him: and I find not that he hath any hesitation in the complying with the Duke on your behalf; though he be in much distraction how he shall accommodate the other two persons. The present expedient is the putting what interests and force he can for the getting the solicitor elected at [King's] Lynn. Yet in what particular he conflicts with a great dilemma; because Cook, a youth of the principal estate in Norfolk, stands at Lynn, and his Lordship is tender of giving him an opposition there, because the gent, of the country do already murmur at his disposing those places, upon which he hath a full and particular influence, upon strangers and courtiers, neglecting gentlemen of the country, who hold themselves disobliged thereby; and are more reasonably, perhaps, dissatisfied, that he concerns himself at Lynn, also, where he ought to leave them to a free competition, without concerning himself.

I took no notice that I had heard anything of his concession to the Duke: but my advice is, that you go on Monday to give him a visit at Arundel House, where I am sure you will not find him: but you are to see the porter, to write down your name, and not forget the acquainting his Lordship that you were to wait on him. He goes on Monday into Surrey, to return on Tuesday; and perhaps to go with the King on

Wednesday to the Fleet, where he will receive your letter. It is not doubted but Sir Robert will have his promised title, though I cannot yet hear that anything is yet done in it. I shall inquire somewhat more closely, and you shall receive what can be collected by, Sir,

T. POVEY

Pepys cannot have received Povey's letter by the time he replied to Savile on 2 September. He clearly believed the way was still open for him to stand at Castle Rising the moment Paston was promoted to the Lords.

86. SAMUEL PEPYS TO HENRY SAVILE

Navy Office
2 September 1672

SIR

I am surprised with the coming back to my hand of a packet directed to you so long ago as you will find by its date to Burlington Bay, occasioned (I suppose) by the fleet's departure thence, and its being handed from place to place after you. However (as late as it is) I am glad I understood its miscarriage, least I might otherwise have continued longer under an unbecoming silence to you, with regard to the matter both of it and yours to which it was in answer, and for which I do now repeat to you my most faithful acknowledgement.

I have newly come to understand my Lord Howard being in town, and endeavoured, but without success to kiss his hands but shall attempt it again. However, least by the strictness of my attendance here I may be prevented therein as much by his lordship's sudden leaving the town, as I was by the lateness of my knowledge of his coming to it, I beg you to present his lordship with the enclosed and to do me the needful favours (whereof yourself are the best judge) both towards his Royal Highness and my Lord, for the rendering effectual to me the honour and favour they have been pleased to propound me.

Sir Robert Paston's promotion is by all taken as certain, though the forms for it are not yet passed.

As for business, you will please to be referred to the packet that accompanies this from the board, which shall ease you of further trouble from my particular, more than the taking my most unfeigned acknowledgements of your favour to

Honoured Sir
Your most humble and faithful servant
S. P.

Paston's eventual promotion to the Lords in 1673 made Pepys's candidature possible once more (see Letter no. 92). In the meantime, Pepys returned to normal business with Henry Savile. This letter clarified the conditions that needed to be met for compensation to be payable if a seaman was killed.

87. SAMUEL PEPYS TO HENRY SAVILE

17 September 1672

SIR

Enclosed are the accompts his Royal Highness expects from me for the use of th
Comte D'Estrées, viz., one of the gratuities given by the King to the relations o
persons slain in his service at sea. Concerning which I shall not need to observ
anything further, than that by Persons Slain is meant, Slain in Fight. Loss of Life b
Accidents, such as fall into the hold or otherwise out of Fight, being not therei
provided for, nor is there any provision elsewhere made for such cases.

The other contains the relief, which out of the general contribution of sixpenc
per man a month out of each man's wages, every seaman maimed (whether in Figh
or otherwise) on board any of his Majesty's ships is entitled to, distinguished in th
value hereof according to the quality of the maim, and paid by select person
annually chosen out of the standing officers of the Navy by the title of Governors o
the Chest at Chatham, to whom for this use the Treasurer of the Navy is from time t
time accomptable for the sixpences before mentioned, by him collected out of eacl
seaman's pay.

This Sir is all I have to trouble you with at present saving the acknowledgemen
of all my late obligations to you, and the profession of being

Your most affectionate humble servant

S. P.

In a letter to Colonel Middleton, Pepys enclosed another note, asking for help for a M
Clerke, injured probably in the Battle of Sole Bay on 28 May 1672, and possibly the
husband of Pepys's Greenwich landlady in the winter of 1665 to 1666.

88. SAMUEL PEPYS TO COLONEL THOMAS MIDDLETON

17 September 1672

SIR

These are only to acquaint you, that by several express commands from his Majesty
the enclosed ought to want no possible care in its dispatch to him; it being intended
(as I suppose) for the use of the Comte D'Estrées who has some days since taken
leave of the country and is expected will sail away at the first opportunity.

I send it to you open, to the end you may please after perusal to call for Mr
Gregory, and give order, that his part being dispatched, a conveyance may be
immediately provided for Mr Savile.

So with tenders of my best respects and service, I remain

Your affectionate humble servant

S. P.

SIR

I have already troubled by an express this afternoon, about another matter. These are
only to tell you, that there will shortly come before you at the Chest table an
unfortunate poor friend of mine (one Mr Clerke) who hath lost his arm onboard the
Mountague, Captain Darcy commanding, in the late engagement. I ask no partiality
on his behalf, but pray that he may not want any reasonable kindness you and my

friends of that board can show him in his dispatch and relief; which I shall be indebted to you and them for and remain
Your truly affectionate friend and servant
S. P.

'Short Allowance' was money credited to seamen when provisions were short. The potential for corruption is plain from the reference to how the purser was supposed to pay this himself from his own pocket when he was able to do so. James Southerne, then a clerk in the Admiralty, had clearly written to Pepys to clarify what the rates were, what the form was, and to ask for financial assistance to pay the Short Allowances owing. Pepys says he has ordered up some of the new farthings. Copper farthings and halfpennies first went into production in this year of 1672, and were intended to make official small change more readily available in preference to the tokens which were being widely made by merchants. The new copper coins were only legal tender up to a value of sixpence. The £300 suggested here would have amounted to 288,000 coins weighing 1.67 tons.

89. SAMUEL PEPYS TO JAMES SOUTHERNE

Navy Office
17 September 1672

MR SOUTHERNE

In answer to your letter of the 14th, the rate his Majesty pays to seamen for Short-Allowance at 6 to 4, is twopence per diem, it being not the practice of the Navy to put seamen to any broken proportion of victuals, nor hath the King ever paid (to the best of my memory) any other sort of Short Allowance than that of 6 to 4 of all sorts of provisions, drink excepted. Where seamen indeed (as they sometimes are) shall be at Short Allowance of beer, also there the King hath paid after the rate of a halfpenny a day more. Where it hath happened that any particular sort of provision falls short, there the purser generally makes it good to him by money or otherwise in specie. One thing more I am to add, that many times where the purser is able he pays to[?] the company out of his own purse what is due to them for their Short Allowance, which I think no unfit to hint to you, that you may be satisfied before you pay the same to any ship, that the purser has not done it before.

I have acquainted the Board with what you propose touching your being supplied with two or three hundred pounds in new farthings, who approving very well thereof, have wrote to Sir Thomas Osborne to provide and send you the same with what speed he can, which I hope will come to you before it be too late for your use. These with my particular respects to yourself, and like to Mr Billop are all this present needful, from
Your very affectionate friend and servant
S. P.

In 1673 Pepys was introduced by his friend Thomas Hill to a musician called Cesare Morelli. Pepys decided to act as Morelli's patron. That Morelli was a Catholic was not apparently considered to be a serious issue, though it would become one for Pepys during the Popish Plot of 1679 (see Letters nos. 116 and 117).

The 'misfortune' which Hill refers to in the second paragraph of the letter is the fact that on 29 June 1673 the Navy Office in Seething Lane had been destroyed by fire. Ironically, this part of the City had escaped the Great Fire of 1666. Pepys had now had to move to Winchester Street.

This letter is also one of the first to allude to the convivial and intimate social circle that would dominate much of the rest of Pepys's life. The 'excellent ladies' are Pepys's friends Elizabeth, Lady Mordaunt, and 'her sister Johnson', later (or perhaps by now) 'Mrs Steward' (see Letter no. 230). The letter was in fact dated 14 April since it was sent from the Continent, where the Gregorian calendar was 10 days ahead. Great Britain did not convert until September 1752. The dates given for every letter in this book are by English reckoning in the 1600s, regardless of the date on the actual letter.

90. THOMAS HILL TO SAMUEL PEPYS

Lisbon 4/14 April 1673

MY WORTHY FRIEND

Next to the letters from those excellent ladies, we both admire, I never received any with so much ravishing delight at yours of the 10th of October. Little did I think that the curse I cast on you in drollery, should take place in good earnest for, certainly nothing less than love is able to inspire such noble expressions as yours when you discourse of those persons; who, if any can, deserve them all. But less you could not do in justice, for they are desperately in love with you, and sigh out their passions so charmingly, that I find strange alterations in myself, and 'tis hard to conclude, whether to envy, or pity you. Your enjoyments in their conversation, can nowhere else be found; and theirs is so great, when you entertain them, that they all acknowledge your humour the best in the whole world. Long may you enjoy these happinesses, which I should envy in my King, if he were so fortunate, but not in my friend. Your expressions of kindness for me are such that I shall always admire, but can never answer that task I have desired the ladies to undertake, which they may do, being as much assured of my respects for you, as for themselves.

I do most unwillingly mention that misfortune happening lately to your house being unable to say anything suitably, upon so sad an occasion, and less able to declare my concerns for you but, I assure you, my affliction was proportionable to that friendship you are pleased to bestow on me.

Whilst this thought is in my mind, it may be unseasonable to mention one enjoyment I have here, but I beg license to tell you, that we have a little consort among us, which gives us entertainment. We have five hands for viols, and violins, three of us, use both, and all, except one, the viol, but the want of music in this country obliges us to play over, and over again, some few things I brought from home accidentally, which wears off the relish, so that we are forced to go a-begging to our friends, as I do to you, that if you have anything new, you would bestow it on us and because Mr Monteage (accountant to Messrs Houblons) intends to present me some things, it may be fit to compare compositions, that they be not duplicates.

Mentioning music puts me in mind to acquaint you, that here is a young man, borne in Flanders, but bred at Rome, who has a most admirable voice, and sings rarely to his theorba, and with great skill. This young man lives with a nobleman, upon a very mean salary, and having been formerly in England, most passionately desires to return thither again. If either yourself, or any friend be desirous to favour an ingenious person, I know none more deserving than he. He speaks Latin, Italian, French, and Spanish, and 'tis ten thousand pities to let him live here among people, who will see no virtue but their own; if I were going home, I should entertain him myself, for besides his Parts, he is a very ingenious, and which is more, a very good, and discreet young man.

I have received the whole library you bestow on me for which I give you humble thanks, when the ships are dispatched I shall have time to read a little. Pray present my services to all your kindred, and if the King, and my aunt Maskelyne, afford you a minute, oblige me with a letter. I most affectionately embrace you and remain

Dear Sir

Your very faithful and most humble Servant

THO. HILL

The little note enclosed, is a receipt for a few Gammons, and some of our Hunns water, which I have ordered to be got aboard the Queen's frigate. Pray do me the favor to accept these trifles.

Shortly afterwards Pepys's time as Clerk of the Acts came to an end. The last thirteen years had been a decisive time in his life. He had proceeded from modest clerical status to that of a prominent individual who had played a major role in managing the basis of England's power: the Royal Navy. He had even been called before Parliament to defend himself and the Navy Office. Meanwhile he had lost two key individuals: his wife and the Earl of Sandwich. Now Pepys was increasingly the man of status and source of patronage in his own right. But storm clouds were brewing on the horizon. The Third Dutch War was under way, challenging England's ability to defend itself against what was then the greatest naval power in the world. Failure or any other shortcomings in these difficult times would expose Pepys to his enemies and those of the King. The ugly face of religious bigotry was becoming increasingly exploited as the means by which England's power politics were fought, and Pepys's loyalties meant he was in a dangerous position.

Pepys's Whitehall. William Morgan's map, created in 1682, shows a number of places that played an important part in Pepys's life. Axe Yard, where he lived in 1660 before moving to the Navy Office in the City, is just off King Street (modern Whitehall) opposite the Privy Garden in Whitehall Palace. Derby House, where he moved as Secretary of the Admiralty, is below the Privy Garden on the banks of the Thames. At the upper right is York Stairs, a few yards from York Buildings in Buckingham Street where he spent much of his later life.

4 Secretary of the Admiralty: 1673–9

IN JUNE 1673 Pepys was made Secretary of the Admiralty. His brother John Pepys, and Tom Hayter, succeeded him as joint-Clerks of the Acts. The appointment came in the aftermath of the Test Act of March that year, which obliged the Duke of York as a Catholic to resign as Lord High Admiral. The time was the middle of the Third Dutch War, which had begun in early 1672. In 1673 there were several inconclusive engagements that carried on throughout the summer but Pepys's promotion came at a time when negotiations for peace started. The war ended in February 1674 with the Treaty of Westminster and coincided with the time Pepys moved to the Admiralty Office at Derby House.

By 4 November 1673 Pepys had fulfilled his ambitions to enter Parliament by being elected MP for Castle Rising, Norfolk. But his candidature had been tainted by allegations that he was a Catholic, and the issue rose again in January 1674. The Earl of Shaftesbury now led the anti-Court faction, which utilized any means to smear its opponents. Since an allegation of Popery was the easiest means to blacken a man's reputation and that of his associates, Pepys's election became a conveniently topical target. Soon afterwards his enemies alleged that Pepys was not qualified to sit in Parliament because he was a Papist. Lord Henry Howard, a member of England's most senior Catholic family, supported Pepys's candidature. Shaftesbury claimed that he had seen an altar and a crucifix at Pepys's home. There were all sorts of political sub-texts involved and although Pepys successfully defended himself before a Parliamentary committee the mud had been thrown and it stuck. In 1678 when the Popish Plot erupted, Pepys's association with the Duke of York made it inevitable he would be accused of being implicated in some way.

91. SIR WILLIAM COVENTRY TO SAMUEL PEPYS

Minster Lovell
25 June 1673

SIR

You may reasonably imagine when you see a letter from me that it is to congratulate your new employment, which I persuade myself you will as easily believe me to rejoice at, as any man whatsoever; and should have acquiesced in that persuasion, without giving you the trouble of telling you so, had I not been solicited by a servant of mine, to entreat your favour to a brother of his, whose name is Robert Krewstub; my servant tells me, he hath during this and the last war been employed as steward in the Navy, his ambition is to become a purser, of which he doubts not to make his capacity evident, and to give good security, I know you, and the place you execute, too well to think it fit for me to recommend an unfit man to you, but if he appear fit for it, I do very seriously entreat your favour to him. I am very unlikely ever to make you a return, unless you have occasion to keep a running horse at Burford, in which case I offer you my diligence to overlook him, therefore you have it in your power

to lay an obligation upon me, without the least prospect of interest to sully it. I wis!
all you oblige may be as much as myself (and if so you will be happier than some o
your predecessors).

Sir

Your affectionate humble servant

W. COVENTRY

By August 1673 the way was open once more for Pepys to be the Parliamentary candidate a
Castle Rising. Since there were only about fifty voters, this provides a good indication o·
how much these elections were formalities rather than anything approximating to a
democratic process. Pepys wrote to Henry Howard on 7 August 1673 and then again on the
14th to tell him about the promotion and to lobby for his selection.[1] This time Howar·
accepted that Pepys had the support of the King and his brother.

92. LORD HENRY HOWARD TO SAMUEL PEPYS

15 August 1673

SIR

I received yours yesterday, after my return from Rising, where my chief business
was to secure your service, as I had long since proposed and engaged to his Royal
Highness; for soon as I heard of Sir Robert Paston's promotion, I needed no fresh
commands to spur me to serve one I honour so much.

I believe, 'ere this, Mr May has told you from me I was about it; and you may
depend upon it as done, though unluckily the Mayor (a perfect creature I could
depend upon) dying, will put us to a little trouble extraordinary; but I think 'tis so
well provided for since I was there, as nothing can start to disturb it, with all which I
beg of you to acquaint his Royal Highness. And as soon as the house sits next, if
your colleague, Sir J. Trevor, (for whom it is most proper), desire the writ to choose,
I ask no more charge or trouble from you but on all occasions to be freely
commanded as, sir,

Your most affectionate humble servant

NORFOLK, EARL MARSHAL

Pepys was elected as MP for Castle Rising in November 1673, with a turn-out of thirty-six
voters, twenty-nine of whom voted for him. It was a hollow and ominous victory. Not only
had it cost Pepys around £700, but also since Henry Howard was a Catholic it opened the
way for Pepys's enemies to accuse him of being a Catholic too, helped by Pepys's
association with the Duke of York.

The Third Dutch War reprised familiar problems, almost entirely based on the limited or
non-existent financial resources made available. In this letter Pepys responds to one from
John Evelyn, who was evidently finding great difficulty in securing supplies and billets for
the sick and wounded seamen, and prisoners of war, in his care as a Commissioner for them.
This had caused Evelyn endless frustration in the days of the Second Dutch War thanks to
the chronic shortage of funds. Nothing, it seems, had changed. Only the end of the new war
the following month would provide any relief.

[1] Tanner 1929, 273–4.

93. SAMUEL PEPYS TO JOHN EVELYN

Derby House
23 January 1674

SIR

Before I durst think it fit for me to write anything to Deal to the effect you desired, I thought it expedient to satisfy myself from my brother as particularly as I could, whether the refractoriness of the persons he complains of might not arise either from the pressure of the arrears due to them for charges past, or apprehension (by the example of their neighbours) of the uncertainty of their being better used for what is to come. And as I foresaw, I do find from him, that this is the ground of that unwillingness with which the poor people there, do receive any new burdens by the putting upon them as any fresh numbers of sick men from the Fleet, which being so, and led thereto from the reason of the thing, no less then from the captiousness of the time wherein we now are, I am of opinion, that it is neither fit with regard to the honour of his Majesty's Service, nor the safety of any of us his servants, that anything like severity or threats should be used upon any of the persons complained of, without good advice and express order, either from his Majesty or those of his ministers who are better able, both to advise and justify, what shall be fit to be determined concerning them. Therefore let me advise you, not to expect or to depend upon any single interposition from me in the matter; but consider whether it may not be more advisable, both with regard to yourself and the efficacy of it to the King's Service, that you make a representation of the matter to his Majesty or my Lords of the Council, and receive their directions for your further proceedings. In which as far as any solicitation of mine can be either useful to the thing, or grateful to you, you shall command

Your most affectionate humble Servant
S. PEPYS

In spite of his faults, Balthazar St Michel could occasionally be useful. Since the allegations made about Pepys also affected his sister's reputation, Balthazar wrote a letter of support to refute any suggestion of Pepys having Catholic leanings. Pepys endorsed the letter: 'Brother Balty's letter to me giving an account of the fortune of his family, particularly done for clearing the imputation laid on me in Parliament for the turning his sister from a Protestant to a Catholic'.

94. BALTHAZAR ST MICHEL TO SAMUEL PEPYS

Deal
8 February 1674

HONOURED SIR

In answer to yours of last night, which I received this morning at 8 of the clock, I wonder indeed, that you, whose life and conversation, hath been ever known to be a firm Protestant, should now be called in question, of being a papist. But, Sir, malice and envy will still oppress the best of men; wherefore, Sir, to the hazard of my life I will prove (if occasion be) with my sword in my hand (since it hath touched so near of the memory of my dear sister) that your competitor is a false liar in his thought, as to your having ever an altar in your house, or that my dear sister ever since she had the honour to be your wife, or to her death had the least thoughts of popery, this I know, by my not only often conversation with her myself, but in my presence on time, I remember, she having some discourse with my father, concerning your life and conversation, as well fortunes.

This was his speech with her, that amongst the greatest of the happinesses he enjoyed in his mind, was that she had by matching with you, not only wedded wisdom, but also one who by it, he hoped in Christ would quite blow out, those foolish, popish thoughts, she might in her more tender years have had of popery, these (to the best of my memory) were his very words; to which her reply was (kissing his eyes, which she loved dearly), 'dear father', said she, 'though in my tender years I was, by my low fortune in this world deluded to popery by the fonde-didly(?) thereof, I have now a man to my husband so wise, and one to religious in the Protestant religion (joined with my riper years which give me more understanding) to ever suffer my thought to bend that way any more.'

But Sir, I have given you too much trouble with one thing. Now to what you desire as to the knowledge how, and when, the popish fancies were first put in my poor dear sister's head, which (to the best of my memory) in every point I shall declare to you. First my father, son to the High-Shreeve of Boge [Baugé?] (in Anjou in France) a papist and all his family, in which religion, also my father was bred, and continued in, till he was 21 years, at which time, (he being then in the German service) turned Protestant, and without troubling you with the rest of his life there, till he returned to France, I shall only say that he did so, where he found his father dead, having given all he had (hearing of my father's being turned Huguenot as he termed it) in marriage with his Daughter (my father's only sister) so that my father, being disinherited of all for his religion['s] sake, had nothing left but his sword and friends, to prefer him in the world, though an uncle of my father's a Chanoine of Paris who loved [him] so well, that he promised to make him his heir and give him 20,000 *livres Tournois* which is about £20,000 sterling, if he would but go to mass again, but all (to this dear man who lived and died a saintly life) nor anything could shake his resolutions of continuance in the true Protestant cause.

At last fortune in this world seemed to smile one him again, he being (us you knew sir) a Gentleman, extremely well-bred, got him the friends (together with his name and quality being of a very good house in France) to prefer him, when the match was concluded, between his Majesty Charles I of blessed memory, and the Daughter of France to be of her retinue, in the place of one of her gentleman carvers, so he came over with her Majesty, but long had he not continued here in her service, but the clouds of his misfortunes (as to the loss of his place) frowned on him again, being took notice of by some of the friars that he came not to mass, was by it immediately known in he what he was viz. a very strong and firm Protestant, so that the Queen dismissed him [from] his employment, he having in discourse and controversy of religion struck a friar.

Well, (as I said before and as your Honour knew) he being a man not only extreme handsome, but also of mighty winning courtly parts, went for Ireland where he soon by it won the affection of my mother, daughter to Sir Fancis Kingsmall and then late widow to an Irish esquire, so my father, after he had married her, though much to the dislike of her friends (my Lord Moore &c) with what moneys they could then raise being £1500, intended for France again (with his wife, my mother) to endeavour by law (to recover if possible some part of his father's estate,) with his sister; but in his procedure, having turned the moneys he had into goods marchandable for France, at sea he and goods were all took by the Dunkirkers, and he also prisoner some months, so that he and my Mother were again to begin the World, but he, being bred to nothing but the sword; that was his recourse, and by it had in his time many very honourable commissions both in France, Holland and Germany as well as England. He for some time settled himself upon that little he had in Devonshire at a place called Bideford, where, and thereabouts my sister and we all were born.

Sir, my small age at those times hinders my giving you so exact accompt as I would wish; how that, at last my father, mother and family went for France again, neither can I tell on what accompt only at first I remember that he carried a company of foot under his command by order of England, to assist the French against the Spaniard in the taking of Dunkirk, and Arras which was about the year 1648 or 9 neither any further acompt can I say we went to Paris about, but that my father (at last) grew full of whimsies,[2] and propositions, (of perpetual motions etc) to kings, princes, and others, which soaked his pocket, and brought all our family so low (by his not minding anything else spending all he had or had got and getting no other employment to bring in more) of nothing more, and my mother (for fear of her children's want) brought into extreme troubles.

At last she was persuaded by some deluding papists, namely Madam Trouson, a rich councillor's wife, Mr Duplesis a rich advocate of the Parliament, with many others pretended devouts, that if my mother with her children would get [away] from her husband my father, that damned troublesome Huguenot (as they called him) they would provide for all of us namely my mother, sister and self by allowing her a considerable allowance fitting a gentlewoman of her quality, give a round sum of moneys and make my sister a nun, and myself page to the Pope's Nuncio, (by which I might since I have thought on it [be] either a Cardinal, or a Bardash) then at Paris resident; in order to these persuasions, my Mother agrees, appoints the day and however, when exactly, came two coaches on of Madam Trouson aforesaid, and the other of Mr Duplecy and Madam Trouson in hers carries mother and sister away as swift as lightening for fear of my father's interest and furies, and puts them both into the Nouvelle Catholique of Women, and I in M. Duplecy's conveyed to that of Garçons.

At last my dear sister being extreme handsome was deluded into the nunneries of the Ursulines (all this about her 12th or 13th year of age) where she was received with gladness, thinking to have her there sure enough it being the strictest nunneries in all Paris, but she was not there long I mean not twelve days 'ere my father by some stratagem or other, I know not well how, got her out, and us all, he having been almost distracted about it (poor dear man) but in fine he got us all for England again, where after some time we had the Honour to be related to you by my dear sister's match, which was of extreme content to my father, that his dear child had another firm Protestant protector, and guide. Truly sir, I believe (that could I remember or that of my mother who by her absence from my house at this present, for health sake I can have no accompt of) that never man for religion in these later ages hath suffered what my father hath, and now sir I do declare from my very soul, and am extremely well satisfied that you kept my dear sister in the true protestant Religion till her death.

I am your honour's most obedient humble servant,

B. St Michel

---

[2] MS: 'wheemsis'.

On 10 February 1674 Pepys was confronted in Parliament by Sir Robert Thomas, who claimed that a 'Person of Quality' had seen an altar and crucifix at Pepys's lodgings. Pepys of course denied this. Sir William Coventry then led the demands that the identity of Pepys's accusers be made known. The Earl of Shaftesbury was named. A committee made up of Coventry, William Garraway and Sir Thomas Meres was appointed to go and see Shaftesbury. In the meantime, Shaftesbury wrote to Meres, a copy of which Pepys retained amongst his papers.

95. THE EARL OF SHAFTESBURY TO SIR THOMAS MERES

Exeter House
10 February 1674
SIR

That there might be no mistake I thought best to put my answer in writing for those questions yourself, Sir William Coventry, and Mr Garroway were pleased to propose to me this morning from the House of Commons, which is that I never designed to be a witness against any man for what I either hear or saw, and therefore do not take so great notice of the things enquired of as to be able to remember them so clearly as is requisite to do in a testimony upon honour or oath and to so great and honourable a body as the House of Commons, it being some years and distance since I was at Mr Pepys's lodgings. Only that particular of an oath is so signal that I must have remembered it had I done any such thing which I am sure I do not. This I desire you to communicate with for Sir William Coventry and Mr Garroway to be delivered as my answer for the House of Commons, it being the same I gave this morning. I am Sir

Your most humble servant
SHAFTESBURY

Having thus stated he was in no position to make an oath about something so long ago, Shaftesbury denied to the committee (at which Pepys was present) having seen an altar though he conceded he had seen something resembling a crucifix. He patronized Pepys, with all the complacent superiority and arrogance of his social rank. Pepys was infuriated by the manner in which Shaftesbury had circulated a highly damaging allegation that he then equivocated about. Pepys tried to secure a personal interview with Shaftesbury. This was refused, so he wrote to his accuser.

96. SAMUEL PEPYS TO THE EARL OF SHAFTESBURY

15 February 1674
MY LORD,

I shall rest upon your Lordship's nobleness for the expressing my taking this way of supplying what your Lordship thought not fit to admit me to do yesterday by word of mouth; namely, the observing to your Lordship the injurious consequence of that ambiguity, under which (for reasons best known to your Lordship) you have been pleased to couch your late answers to the Questions brought you from the House of Commons, touching your having declared to some of its members (said to be ready to justify it) your having seen an Altar with a Crucifix erected upon it at my lodgings.

Concerning which, as I must take leave of asserting my being in no wise [= ways] chargeable with either, so while your Lordship would yourself seem to acquit me of the former (as a thing too signal, if seen, to have been forgotten) you are pleased nevertheless (though with a voluntary unbespeaking of any credit to your testimony therein) to own some imperfect impressions sticking with you (and thereby giving grounds to some doubtful suggestions in others) touching the latter, I mean, the Crucifix; which cannot (I presume) be held a thing less signal than the Altar, as being of a figure not so much akin to any other object as an Altar is to every table that stands against a wall, differing only (I think) in furniture.

With all the earnestness therefore that can become, and may be forgiven one used as I am, I do both desire and conjure your Lordship by all that is honourable in itself and just towards me, to perfect your recollections so far as to give the House (in what method you shall think fit) a categorical answer one way or t'other tomorrow morning in this business of the Crucifix. Which whether it be Aye or No, I do hereby declare I will hold myself equally (and but equally) obliged to your Lordship for it; as being one who has always directed myself in my duty both towards God and my Master, with such open blamelessness, as not to leave either my security or good name therein to depend upon the single Aye or No of any one, friend or enemy. Which plainness in a circumstance of this moment to me, I doubt not but after the twenty years observances I have paid your Lordship on all other occasions, you will be pleased to take in good part from, My Lord,

Your Lordship's most obedient servant,

S. PEPYS

On 16 February Pepys defended himself in the Commons, describing his conscientious observation of Protestant worship. In the end no vote was taken and Pepys was allowed to take his seat but it had been a damaging experience that would return to him. He also had to confront a private accusation of (effectively) fraud. Thomas Povey wrote several letters to draw Pepys's attention to an agreement they had made in 1665 to share the profits of the Tangier Treasurership. According to Povey, in a letter of 16 February 1674 Pepys had continued to insist that he had made no money apart from the salary.[3] It seems that Povey had some basis for the claim though Pepys replied in an outraged tone at the idea he had defrauded Povey. He later sent Povey fifty guineas but the matter remained unresolved. A further letter followed in which Povey expressed his hope that his 'satisfaction' was imminent, but he raised another matter that suggested that he still did not trust Pepys.

97. THOMAS POVEY TO SAMUEL PEPYS

3 April 1674

SIR

Hoping that you are preparing the whole accounts for, that the satisfaction I have pressed is not far off. I importune you not further in that particular.

I do at this time make a request to you, which will seem as hard a thing in you to deny, as anything I have resented. Which is that what money you have yet to return to Tangier by bills, may be done by a person whom I shall propose upon such terms

---

[3] Quoted from by Bryant ii, 117–18.

as you have agreed upon the last returns. For your security he shall be one as of unquestionable credit as one you have dealt with, and as satisfactory to the Commissioners. I desire your ready answers, this matter requiring little consideration, being indifferent to you (for you would have me believe so) but will be a convenience to me, who in many considerations, ought not to be held impertinent in intermeding in these affairs and particularly in this wherein your compliance will be some sort of respect to

Sir your servant

THO. POVEY

In these trying times for Pepys, there was still the opportunity for pleasant experiences. In late 1673 his friend, the merchant Thomas Hill, had told Pepys about a remarkable musician of his acquaintance, Cesare Morelli.[4] Now Morelli needed a new patron, which had unforeseen consequences for Pepys during the Popish Plot.

98. THOMAS HILL TO SAMUEL PEPYS

Lisbon

27 September/7 October 1674

SIR

This letter I suppose, may come opportunely to welcome you from France if our ladies prevailed with you to accompany them thither, as I hear they endeavored but I conclude the voyage was deferred, for no other reason, but that I perceived no motion unusual in my heart, which I should most certainly have done, when you, and the good company put your feet ashore upon the Continent where I am. Be it as 'twill, I wish you all much health and happiness, and so much to myself, (and that's enough in all conscience) that I may live to see you once again.

I formerly acquainted you that here was a virtuoso, exceedingly desirous to wait upon you and by what I understood by your letter to Captain Jenifer, you were willing he should have embarked on the *Saudades* what then hindered was, that the Marquis, (whom he served,) was not only loath to part with him, but kept him filled with such hopes, by frequent promises of good preferment, that the young man was not unwilling to attend upon his fortune. But, as all things contribute, not only to your honour, and advantage, but to your gusto also, this Marquis is lately dead, and by that means has left this ingenious person free, to enjoy a better fortune in your service. So if you please, he is ready to wait upon you, if you yet continue in your former resolution, which I desire to know as speedily as may be with convenience. I am certain you will like his voice, and his manner of singing is *alia Italiana di tutta perfettione*. I beg of you, not to let my recommendation engage you to the least inconvenience, for that would exceedingly trouble me. But if you are willing, as I am sure you are, to favor ingenuity and virtue, I think you cannot find a fitter object. Pray give my service to the ladies, for by this indirect conveyance, I shall not write to them. I kiss your hands and am Sir

Your most faithful and most obliged servant,

THO HILL

The person I have been speaking of is now with me, and presents you his service by the enclosed.

---

[4] In a letter of 4/14 April 1673, printed by Howarth, no. 40.

99. SAMUEL PEPYS TO THOMAS HILL

Winchester Street
21 November 1674

DEAR MR HILL

The forwardness of your *Saudades* in her fittings for Lisbon had so prepossessed me, that overlooking all other ways of conveyance, 'tis but just now that I am here told, that (if I will use it presently) I may have opportunity of writing to you from this house, which I dare not lose; though all the use which (for my eyes, that for this last week have been more than usually out of order) I can now make of it is, to tell you that your last (whose date I ha'n't about me) I have received, and is most acceptable to me in what relates to the gentleman's service you so kindly tempt me with; and concerning which I have only one thing by way of preface to note to you; namely, that nothing which has yet or may further happen towards the rendering me more conspicuous in the world, has led or can ever lead to the admitting any alteration in the little methods of my private way of living; as having not in my nature anymore aversion to sordidness than I have to pomp, and in particular that sort of it which consists in the length and trouble of such a train (I mean of servants for state only) as the different humour of some and greater quality of others do sometimes call for.

Which being premised, for the setting right the young man's expectations in reference to that part, I come now to tell you, that if you conceive that my silent and unencumbered guise of life will sort with him, and that £30 a year certain, (to be increased as you shall direct, or at my courtesy upon proof of his service,) with his lodging and entertainment, will invite him to come to me, he shall not only on his part be welcome, and possibly find me not the most uneasy to be lived with, but myself on mine also shall (I am apt to believe) find in him a servant not of less real use to me by his languages, in reading, writing, translating and other offices depending thereon, than satisfaction to my sense in his excellent qualifications in music, in which my utmost luxury still lies, and is likely to remain so. Give me leave, therefore, without mixing one word either of the ladies, news, our travels, loves, or aught else, (which are to be left to Captain Jenifer) to refer to you the doing whatever you shall think advisable for us both in this matter, assuring you that if I find him answering the sober part of the character you give him, I shall cherish him with a great deal of pleasure, and esteem your friendship in directing him to me, as the most obliging and satisfactory courtesy I could, at this time, have begged of you, it being what for some time I have been laying out for, without expectation of compassing it in any degree so fully to my wish as this you have found out for me. For which I send you a large heartful of thanks, and forced by my eyes, bid you good-bye, referring you for more to the *Saudades,*

Your most affectionate and faithful humble servant
S. P.

The *Saudades* shall give him passage. But if any earlier conveyance happen, it shall be the welcomer to me, if as convenient to him

100. THOMAS HILL TO SAMUEL PEPYS

Lisbon 21 June/1 July 1675

SIR

Although my indisposition, when your admirable picture arrived here, prevented my returning you earlier thanks for so extraordinary a favour, yet this delay has not diminished that just sense I have of so great a kindness. The picture is beyond praise, but causes admiration in all that see it its so stately, and magnificent a posture, and hits so naturally your proportion, and the noble air of your face, that I remain immoveable before it, hours together. I know not how to thank you for so great a kindness nor do I see any possibility of requital but this I assure you, if I die here he bequeath it to you, or rather restore it, and if I carry it off it shall always be at your disposal.

I am in great expectation to hear how you approve of my choice in your servant Cesare Morelli it would be exceeding satisfactory to me to hear, that you like his manner of singing. I think its well his ability of performing at sight the most difficult Part, is to be valued, and I have seldom met with any Person that exceeds him. I recommended to him to study the theorba, which will be of great use, but that depends upon the spare hours you please to allow him. I expect to hear a ravishing choir of your voice, joined with our ladies by what I foresee, I shall allow you time enough to study, for as yet I have no prospect of leaving this place but, whether I stay, or go, I shall be for ever Sir

Your most faithful and obliged humble servant

THO. HILL

A number of routine letters were exchanged by Pepys and his brother-in-law in 1674–5. This example illustrates the importance that Pepys attached to expressions of loyalty to Charles II and the Duke of York, gestures which reinforced his image in the eyes of his enemies.

101. SAMUEL PEPYS TO BALTHAZAR ST MICHEL

Mr St Michel at Deal

Derby House
6 July 1675

BROTHER BALTY

This comes only to thank you for your letter of 29th June, which I met with at my return home from Portsmouth last night. You did very well in attending his Majesty and the Duke, and making them the little present of the lamb and fish you mention, the King having need enough of it (I believe) before he got on shore at the Isle of Wight.

Pray take care for the immediate conveying of the enclosed letters to the ships in the Downs, which is all at present from

Your very affectionate Brother to serve you

S. P.

One of the great issues of the moment in 1674 and 1675 was the state of the fleet. Pepys and Deane clamoured for the resources to restore it. At least twenty ships needed to be rebuilt, but even with that done the Royal Navy was unable to match the Dutch or French navies.

The Dutch Navy was at that date three times larger and around forty new ships would be needed to compete with it. Despite this, there was plenty of opposition to Pepys's extravagant plans. In July 1675 Charles II inspected the fleet including Deane's newly launched ship, the *Royal James*, and two yachts built by Deane for Louis XIV. He was particularly impressed by the yachts, which shortly afterwards Deane took to France along with Will Hewer. Hewer wrote to Pepys to let him know how things were going and his excitement at the sights.

102. WILL HEWER TO SAMUEL PEPYS

from Monsieur Deimast's House in Paris
12/22 August 1675

SIR

Since our arrival in France, I have given you the trouble of two letters: one from Havre de Grace and the other from Roan, hoping they both found you in good health, since which praised be God, Sir Anthony Deane and Company are well arrived at Paris and do all continue in very good health presenting their most humble service and respects to you. We arrived here upon Monday the 16th instant about noon and in our way we met with one of the yachts upon the road which is safe in the Canal, and this day by the care and industry of Sir Anthony Deane the other will be in, he having spent Friday and Saturday in giving direction touching her carriage which has not only facilitated her dispatch by doing that in a day and ½ which the French were four days about, but done that for 500 crowns[5] which the other cost for carrying to the Canal upwards of 1300 crowns.

Sir Anthony hath been so taken up about the yachts since our arrival here that we have as yet seen only the King's house and garden at the Versailles, the place called the Gobelins where the King employs the year round several artificers to work for him as painters, stone-cutters, makers of hangings, silversmiths and a hundred more sort of artificers.[6] The Gardens at the Louvre and St Germain but not the houses in regard we could not then get tickets, my Lord Colbert's house and garden at a place called Shoone two leagues from Paris, and several gentlemen's houses out of town where Sir Anthony has been nobly and extraordinarily treated, besides there is one appointed on purpose to attend and defray all his charges during his stay here. I shall not take up your time in troubling you with the particulars of what we have seen, which is all so fine and magnificent, that as I never in my life saw the like, so I do believe there cannot in the whole world be anything that is finer, but more particularly the King's house and garden at the Versailles.

The King went to Fontainebleau the same day we got hither but his return is expected upon Saturday. And now the yachts being in the canal, the Treasurer-general for the Navy affairs is directed to attend upon Sir Anthony to Fontainebleau where, it is said we shall see a very stately house and garden.

As to his journey to Toulon and Marseilles he is not yet come to any resolution, in regard he knows not when he shall have his dispatch from hence. Besides if the person directed to attend upon him should receive the like orders to defray his charges out of France after his having taken his leave of the King, my Lord Colbert

---

[5] £125, equal to at least £8,000–12,000 today.
[6] See Evelyn's diary 4 October 1683.

and Mons Seignelay, it is fit to consider then whether it would be convenient for him to go. I confess I am of opinion that they do defray his charges here on purpose to prevent his going which every body is enquiring about, however if my Lord Colbert or Lord Marquis de Seignelay shall prompt him to it, and that he finds he can compass it within the time limited then he doth resolve to go. And since I am no like ever to have such an opportunity, and finding myself very well I do purpose unless you shall command the contrary to accompany him.

So with tenders of my most humble duty, wishing for the continuance of your health and prosperity I remain

Honoured Sir

Your ever faithful and most obedient servant

WM. HEWER

Unfortunately, the trip was to provide more ammunition for Pepys's enemies, who alleged that its sole purpose was to hand over naval secrets to Louis XIV. That October Pepys made an important speech to Parliament: since 1660 the building of 90 new vessels meant the Royal Navy now had 150 ships in far better condition than the 157 in existence at the Restoration. This explained where the £400,000 spent on the Navy annually had gone, but the key issue was that England's enemies had more ships. Parliament agreed to build twenty new ships of forty guns or more.

This next letter concerns the privileges seamen enjoyed of being exempted from imprisonment while on his Majesty's service. Balthazar St Michel had intervened to protect a seaman called Bowles pursued by a Mr Lodge.

103. SAMUEL PEPYS TO BALTHAZAR ST MICHEL

Mr St Michel at Deal

13 August 1675

BROTHER BALTY

I have received your letter of the 9th instant, though by my being out of town not so soon as you might have expected; however, soon enough in reference to the matter of it, there being nothing wherein my Lords of the Admiralty receive less satisfaction than in that of being applied to for protection for seamen and others, under pretence of their employment in the Navy, from being arrested, and consequently from being obliged to do right to their creditors. A privilege which indeed his Majesty's service does give, but such a one as ought to be used with great gentleness, and principally (if not only) in time of war or other great action, and not in peace, when plenty of men may be had to answer all his Majesty's occasions without robbing of the gaols. Upon which account it is that my Lords have at no time entered into any consideration of the particular rights of man and man; but upon application made by any person for leave to arrest any officer or seaman in his Majesty's service, their course is, to give that officer or seaman twelve days to satisfy their creditors or show their Lordships good reason why they should not deliver him up to the law. Upon failure whereof, my Lords have never yet denied liberty to any plaintiff, after leave thus asked, to take his remedy at law, which will certainly, if Mr Lodge insist upon it, be granted him in this case of his, though probably my Lords will demand satisfaction from him for his arresting a seaman in his Majesty's pay without leave.

But I must tell you in the first place, I do by no means approve of your concerning yourself in anything of this kind, the privilege that a seaman has being a matter that the King's honour only and his service ought to be concerned in, and not any private man's; besides, I do not think it for your credit that it should be thought you cannot find men enough to man a boat without obliging his Majesty's service to a dependence upon such persons as are not masters of their own liberty. To which, when all is done, let me add that a man being employed in the King's service at day-wages, not constantly, and too, not under any certain muster, will not be reputed such a relation to the King's service as will give him protection from it; and that I fear is the case of the person you are concerned for. But whether it be or no, pray, for the time to come, keep your own credit to depend upon yourself and not the good or ill deportment of other people. As for the present case I have written to Mr Lodge as much as is fit for me to write, a copy whereof I enclose to you; which when I have received his answer to, I shall be able to say more to the business; but till then cannot. Which is all at present from

Your affectionate Brother to serve you

S. P.

The Lodge and Bowles affair continues with Letter no. 105. Meanwhile this curious letter arrived in the late summer of 1675. Nothing is known about its sender, Johan Gibbon, but he apparently knew a woman who knew the Sandwich family. She had heard that a female ghost had appeared during a musical party attended by Pepys, and told Gibbon. Gibbon was clearly fascinated by the subject and he accosted Pepys in the street. Pepys must have been unsettled by the experience, since the letter opens with an apology. The letter is endorsed 'One Mr Gibbon to SP about the vision appearing (to Mr Mallard) at his playing by night on the viol'. Thomas Mallard was a musician on Sandwich's staff. Pepys describes a similar evening on 21 December 1662 when in Sandwich's presence they enjoyed a 'great store of good Musique'. However, the subject of 'second sight' was an interest of Pepys's and it features in the correspondence of his retirement years.

104. JOHAN GIBBON TO SAMUEL PEPYS

These for Samuel Pepys Esquire
One of his Majesty's principal officers
and Commissioners of the Navy per *a servant*

27 August 1675

GOOD SIR

I pray pardon me, I am sorry I appeared so abruptly before you. I'll assure you a paper of the same nature with the enclosed, was left for you at the public office some 10 days since (as likewise for every one of the Commissioners). But Sir I am heartily glad of the miscarriage, for now I have an overture to request a favour by writing, that I should hardly have had confidence by word of mouth to have done, and in that I have much wanted my friend Mr Spenser.

Sir, a gentlewoman of my acquaintance, told me she had it for a great certainty from the family of the Montagues, that as you were one night playing late upon some musical instrument (together with your friends) there suddenly appeared a human feminine shape and vanished and after that sometime, walking in the study, you espied the appearing person demanded of her if at such a time she were not in such a place. She answered no but she dreamed she was and heard excellent music.

Sir, satisfaction is to you my humble request and if it be so, it confirms the opinions of the ancient Romans concerning their Genii and confutes those of the Sadducees and Epicure[an]s.

Your most humble servant,
JOHAN GIBBON

105. SAMUEL PEPYS TO BALTHAZAR ST MICHEL

29 August 1675

BROTHER BALTY

I have received yours of the 15th in answer to mine of the 13th instant touching the business of Lodge and Bowles, by which and what I have met with since from other hands, I find much more dissatisfaction in the matter, than I conceived, from your first representation of it, though even that gave me enough: For instead of its being a case of the common sort, I mean, that of Debtor and Creditor, (according to which apprehension of it, the whole style of my said answer of the 13th runs) I find it to be a business much less becoming you to be an interposer in, as being grounded upon a private squabble between those two persons, wherein whatever you tell me in yours of the 15th of Lodge's ill usage of Bowles his misbehaviour towards him by ill language, threats and personal assaults, besides an action first entered by him against Lodge which is still depending. One part of which yourself confess, I mean, his ill language, which of itself is enough to make it very unfit for you to become his or any man's Advocate in: For 'tis not to Lodge alone, but to all the world that you administer matter for the lessening you in your authority (which seems the great thing that touches you) while you shall pervert that authority of yours to uses it was never given you for. If Bowles had decently by petition resorted to my lords with his complaint of being without their leave arrested, and thereby interrupted in the execution of his duty to the King, or shall still, I don't doubt but (his relation to the King's service first appearing) my lords would in right to his Majesty, and not in complement to him call Mr Lodge to an account for the indignity done the King therein; and if a petition so prepared had been handed to my lords from you as the petitioner's next superior officer and no more, your concernment therein so far might have been well enough admitted.

But for you to embark yourself in the merits of the quarrel, mixing prejudices of your own in the matter, and this in favour of One who whilst he pleads the King's service for his not being arrestable, can find leisure from it to attend a suit against the said person by whom he would not be sued, is a piece of presumption, and can by no means excuse you; and the less by how much I may have any reason of thinking it grounded upon any reliance you may have of my supporting you in it, which you know how often I have advised you to avoid any thoughts of, as being, besides the injustice of it, too conscious of frailties of my own and the care due to myself under them, to take upon me the answering, and therefore much less the patronizing the faults or misbehaviours of others, especially where (as in your case) the nearness of relation suffices to make me a partaker in the blame, though never so much a stranger to the guilt or matter of it, as you know to how much trouble to me it did in the late case of the privateer.

In a word therefore I do conjure you whatever present reflection you think it may have upon you to let fall whatever concernments you shall have in this quarrel, and for the time to come reckon it the best means of preserving your authority to restrain the use of it, to causes honourable, and such as properly come within your cognizance, and no other; assuring you, that as in general I shall never interest myself in your defence while you do otherwise, so I know not what you can expect of friendship from me in the present case, more than the persuading of Mr Lodge to withdraw his action upon condition of Bowles's doing the like with mutual promises of peace on both sides. All which I pray you to take in good part from me, as proceeding from the truth of the love I bear you, and which shall never suffer you to be injured by any man, where anything within my power can right you. So I remain

Your truly affectionate Brother and Servant

S. P.

As MP for Castle Rising, Pepys had concerns for his constituency and more particularly when his generosity was ignored. He had offered £50 towards repairs of the church, but by the winter of 1675 nothing apparently had been done. The news came from one Thomas Pepys, who Pepys called his cousin but it is not now possible to know exactly who this Thomas was though he was probably the son of Pepys's uncle Thomas. Pepys wrote to the Mayor of Castle Rising to express his concern and to tell him that the money had been advanced to his cousin from whom it should be collected.

106. SAMUEL PEPYS TO ROBERT BULLER, MAYOR OF CASTLE RISING

11 December 1675

SIR

I was not a little troubled when I understood from my cousin Pepys of [King's] Lynn, at his late being here, that no advance had been then made in the work towards which I have long had a purpose of being a small contributor, and did in Easter Term last give him commission on my behalf to acquaint yourself and the rest of my worthy friends of your Corporation with the same, in the presenting you and them with the sum of £50 towards the repair of your Church. And the more for that at Mr Boulton's being in town about five or six weeks since, I had the opportunity of making known to him my readiness to pay that sum to whomever your Corporation should think fit to intrust with the receipt of it, promising him also to become a solicitor on the same behalf to Sir John Trevor; which I did in few days after, and received a courteous answer from him concerning it.

Since which having heard nothing from Mr Boulton, and being unwilling that the work should lie longer unbegun, my cousin Pepys has at my request taken the trouble of receiving from me that sum, and to undertake the answering the same to your Corporation for the religious use aforesaid, as soon and in such manner as you and they shall please to call for it from him. Which I pray you to accept in good part from me, as a small instance of the good will I bear to the place from whence I have received so much honour and favour, assuring you that however it came to pass that through Mr Offley's unreasonable competition the accomplishment of your kindness on my behalf was rendered of so unexpected a trouble to you and charge to myself, yet such was the proof I received of the general respect and favour of the Corporation, that I shall never forget the obligations I have to you and them for it by all the service I shall be able to do either to the Corporation in general or any particular member of it.

Which with the tender of my very humble service to yourself and all my worthy friends about you, I remain, their and your most obliged and faithful servant.

S. P.

Edward Homewood was a clerk in the Navy Office in 1663. He was probably the same man as the Mr Homewood to whom this letter was addressed. Pepys had a lifelong interest in art and sculpture, something that was encouraged by men like John Evelyn, and already calls it here as an 'addiction'. It seems to refer to the arrival of antiquities from the Sanctuary of Apollo at Delphi. Homewood's role is unknown, as is the fate of the antiquities mentioned.

107. SAMUEL PEPYS TO MR HOMEWOOD, CLERK OF THE SURVEY, CHATHAM

24 December 1675

SIR

I own myself much to blame that I have no sooner answered the kindness of your letter of the 20th of November, which pray place to the multitude of my businesses here, and take my kind thanks for it now; letting you also know that I shall very much esteem the relics you mention therein of Apollo's Temple, having a know[n] addiction to things of that kind, and shall therefore pray you to find passage for them up to me at your convenience, together with the account of the dimensions you speak of the great figure as it was measured at Delphos; which I shall take as an additional instance of your kindness.

S. P.

At some point in 1670 Samuel Pepys had come into contact with Mary Skinner, daughter of an Essex merchant called Daniel Skinner. Skinner and his wife Frances (née Corbet) seem to have originated in Egmond in Shropshire but presumably moved south. Mary was in fact brought up by her childless aunt Elizabeth, Lady Boteler, who lived in Hatfield but her real parents lived in London and were part of the congregation at Pepys's church of St Olave's, Hart Street. This is probably where Pepys first met Mary. She became his common-law wife but they never married. In 1670 she is likely to have been around 17. By 1676 we know she had been involved with Pepys for long enough for her parents to discover the liaison and to force a separation. The only source is a Latin letter from her elder brother, Daniel junior, who wrote to Pepys in a letter received on 5 July 1676.[7] A series of letters between Daniel and Pepys followed, largely concerned with the former's efforts to secure Pepys's support for his career.

On 9 November 1676 Daniel Skinner wrote at considerable length from Rotterdam to apologize for asking that Pepys advance him £10, since his efforts to secure a position in London had been unsuccessful, and for not waiting to see him in person. He then committed another misdemeanour. Having been offered a post as secretary in the embassy at Nijmegen, partly thanks to a good reference from Pepys, he had raced off to take the post without thanking Pepys face to face. Unfortunately, on arrival he found 'a very unkind letter' had arrived already from Sir Joseph Williamson concerning him. The 'unkind letter' drew attention to how the young Skinner had allowed state letters of John Milton (who had died in 1674), formerly in Williamson's possession, to be seen by an Amsterdam printer with a view to publishing them. The Amsterdam printer, Skinner claimed, went ahead without permission, producing an inferior edition. Skinner insisted he had no plans to publish but

---

[7] In Latin. The letter is printed by Howarth, no. 49.

was now being accused by Williamson of intending to do so. Skinner was now desperate for Pepys to write a letter to clear his name.

108. SAMUEL PEPYS TO DANIEL SKINNER

17 November 1676

SIR

I have received your letter of the 9/19[8] instant, and shall leave to another time what might be reasonable for me to say (notwithstanding the modesty of your excuse for it) touching your leaving England without bidding me adieu, upon an occasion wherein I had with so much design of friendship interested myself on your behalf to my Lord Ambassador, to whom I should never have thought it decent either for me or you to have let you gone without some fresh letters from me in acknowledgment of my obligation to him for his answer to my first (which I communicated to you) in your favour.

This only I shall take the liberty at present to say, that had you thought fit to have seen me and imparted to me then what necessity has driven you to do now, I am apt to believe you would never have needed the asking that office of friendship from me now which I have nevertheless heartily applied myself to the doing you, though without any present success. Know then that I no sooner received your letter but, in pursuance of the faithful friendship I bear you, I betook myself to the visiting Sir Joseph Williamson from whom I understood several interests to have been made to him, not only from my worthy friend your father but from my Lady Peterborough and others on your behalf, and had also opened to me by him many aggravating circumstances in your affair which you either forgot or thought fit to omit the mentioning to me. And yet I can assure you I do not see that what Sir J. W. has done or saith concerning you in the matter in question hath proceeded from anything else than a just regard to his Majesty's service, the duty of his place, and truly consistent with his utmost professions of kindness towards you, he at this day expressing to me (with a sincerity which I cannot doubt) not only a great esteem of your natural abilities and your studied acquirements, but a design of contributing what his favour could do towards the rendering the same under his patronage advantageous to you.

But, in short, I do not see but that notwithstanding what you say and what he has understood from Elzevir himself to have been done by you towards his satisfaction, such apprehensions do still remain in him of the possible impressions which Mr Milton and his writings may have wrought in you as that I do not find him to be to be prevailed with for the absolving you presently of the crime which this inadvertency of yours has exposed you to the suspicion of; and yet I can as little say that I can find the least cause of charging him with any more unkindness towards you than upon the like consideration I think I should myself have had towards my own brother in the same case ; my opinion also concurring with his, that some time must be suffered to pass before you can reasonably look to have this unfortunate concernment of yours with Mr Milton and his writings forgotten or your innocence therein so cleared as that you may recover Sir Joseph Williamson's fair opinion concerning it; wishing only that since you are abroad you could find yourself in a

---

[8] That letter is dated 9 November old style, 19th new. It is published by Howarth, no. 52, but is so long–winded it has been thought better to omit it in favour of a description of its contents on p. 116.

condition of passing so much time there and in France as might suffice for the making you master of the French and Dutch languages, which are with much more facility to be obtained abroad, and without which no man under any public character can, as the world goes, support himself in any public charge, either here or in any foreign court; and this I in a special manner do recommend to you, the rather from the consideration of the much greater difficulty and dissatisfaction it will be of for you to have them to learn when you should have them to use. Which, from several intimations which Sir Joseph Williamson was pleased to give me, I do in no wise [ways] doubt but you may have reasonable hopes of meeting with, so soon as some little time shall have cleared you of this unhappy jealousy, and your improvement of the said time shall qualify you by these languages for those employments for which your other learning and endowments have already so far prepared you. In which my endeavours of serving you then will I hope make some amends for that want of success which I have met with in my desires of doing it now. Which (among others) is one of the causes why I forbear at present to send any second letter to my Lord Ambassador touching this affair.

Excuse me that being at this time a little out of order, I make use of another's hand.

109. DANIEL SKINNER TO SAMUEL PEPYS

For Samuel Pepys Esquire Secretary to the Lords of the Admiralty, and One of the honourable members of the House of Commons. Present.

28 January 1677

MOST HONOURED AND MOST WORTHY SIR

Since my late and most unfortunate repulse at Nijmegen caused by the groundless and severe jealousies of Sir Joseph Willamson (for *invocato Deo*[9] never had I the least thought of prejudicing either King or State, being infinitely loyal to one and mighty zealous for the other, all the concerns that ever I had with Milton or his works being risen from a foolish yet a plausible ambition to learning) being at Rotterdam in expectation of returning into England, my father by his letters commanded me instantly to repair to France, there to retire privately and complete myself in the French tongue, which having no sooner done, arriving in France and being commodiously settled at Paris, I received a whole packet of letters from Holland, amongst the rest one from your most worthy self. A letter so beyond expression kind and favourable, so infinitely obliging, that I may safely declare you to be one of the worthiest most generous person[s] living. I see, Sir, my unhandsome departure out of England has not quite ruined the friendship and inclination that your noble breast entertains for me. And I'll assure you Sir, most ingeniously, that you shall never have any cause to repent of your placing so cordially your affection upon so unworthy a person as myself, intending at my return to England you to be the first person whose hand I shall desire to kiss, there to express in person the high value and esteem, and the grateful sense and acknowledgments I have of all your favours and kindnesses. I meeting with this worthy person Mr Tregonwell here accidentally at Paris, and rendering him all the services imaginable that I was capable of, I presumed so far as to convey a letter by him to you, who can give you Sir an account of the great industry diligence and pains that I use in attaining the French

[9] 'I swear to God'.

tongue, desiring no other character then what he can unfeignedly report of me, intending if you'll please to give me leave to salute you in French very speedily to give you some testimony of my advancements that I make here, hoping in six months' times to return to England with those advantages that few English gentlemen here make in twelve, and withal to be more deserving of yours and Sir Joseph Williamson's favours, whom Pray Sir let me beg of you to certify, that though 'twas his pleasure to shipwreck me in the very port of Nijmegen merely out of jealousy, I hope he will be so compassionate as to give me another vessel when I come to London, assure him also that as for Milton or his works or papers I have done withal, and indeed never had had to do with him, had not ambition to good literature made me covet his acquaintance. Pray tell him Sir that all his papers will be very suddenly in his hands as soon as the printer Elsevire at Amsterdam can find an opportunity of sending 'um over, and that I am here indefatigably studying the French tongue only to render myself more capable of serving him and your self, intending ever to gratefully acknowledge you for my Grand Patron

I am Sir
With all imaginable gratitude
Your most obliged and devoted servant

DANIEL SKINNER

Sir, if it be your pleasure to honour me with a word or two, or to command me any service here in France, you may please to direct so:
A moi, logé chez Madam Albert à la porte St Germain proche la fountain. À Paris.

Just as with his dead wife Elizabeth, Pepys's new choice of female companion in Mary Skinner had brought with it a host of familial obligations that would feature throughout the correspondence for years to come.

Perhaps with already an eye to posterity, Pepys subscribed towards the cost of new building work at his old college in Cambridge. Today the college houses his library, deposited there by his nephew John Jackson under the terms of Pepys's will.

110. DR HEZEKIAH BURTON TO SAMUEL PEPYS

Magdalene College
9 April 1677

SIR
The foundation of that building in our college to which you are pleased to contribute is now laid and they begin to want moneys to go with it. I have said enough to tell you my business which is to desire you will send yours to Mr William Potts, an apothecary, who lives at the Elephant and Castle near St Antholin's church in Queen Street, London, who is appointed Receiver in the City.

Sir, I would not have put you to so much trouble but that indispensable business has forced me.

Sir I am your most obliged and humble servant.

HEZE. BURTON

James Houblon was one of Pepys's closest friends and first appears in the Diary on 1 February 1665. They came together through business, but their personal relationship rapidly developed and lasted until Houblon died in 1700. Houblon's grandfather was a Huguenot merchant and this remained the family business. A wealthy man, Houblon used his commercial contacts and his eyes to act as a source of intelligence on a variety of issues that affected Pepys's professional interests. He wrote in an undisciplined and chaotic fashion, which he acknowledged himself. This letter seems to have accompanied some sort of rough map or chart that illustrated the location of countries and individuals most likely to cause England trouble. However, it also highlights how drunken carousing and other decadent activities were liable to compromise the Navy's ability to fight when it really mattered.

111. JAMES HOUBLON TO SAMUEL PEPYS

To the Honourable Sanuel Pepys Esquire
Secretary to the Navy. Derby House

3 May 1677

SIR

To be as good as my word to you I have here sent you a heap of rubbish, a thing composed according to my usual way of writing without method or order, however it's at your commands I did it and I should be glad out of such a confusion of matter you may extract wherewith to build that goodly frame intended by it, (the public good and the honour of the King, with a reasonable advantage to yourself), for the care and pains you are like to have to pursue and finish this work, that is here cut out for you and that which you (by seeing farther then I can) will find over and above necessary, and more to the purpose. I prophesy it will be vastly great especially in time of war so that you are like mightily to increase the number of the papers and never to be at rest.

The difficulties will be in procuring faithful and honest intelligencers and such who will have the wit to prevent the danger of a rope. But being we are now in a stark calm of peace, 'twill be a good time to begin with them that they may learn how to behave themselves when they will be more useful, instructions will be very needful for them according to the several places where they are and to what particular points they ought to apply their industry to.

Holland and France are likeliest to be the chief stages where the greatest actions – will be as to us and from whence we may fear the greatest mischief as to the body of the state; next, Spanish privateers who of all Christians are the most dangerous to the English trade by reason of the extent of their dominions: Ostend etc, all the Biscay and Galicia ports and the coast of Spain within and without the straits, the Islands of Majorca and Minorca etc, the coasts of Sicily and Naples and Gulf of Venice, next them the Turks within and without the straits and the less dangerous are the northern princes of Sweden and Denmark, who can only be auxiliaries to the French or Dutch.

I send it, Sir, rough as I drew it not thinking my foolish conceptions worth the writing fair, but my hopes are you will lick it into a better form for the view of those you intend it, who I hope will have the grace to see that there is great reason, to make the Secretary of the Admiralty's office valuable to the person that enjoys it and that as his care and industry and the means to enable him to be truly serviceable to the King and Kingdom will require a considerable yearly allowance, so they will be liberal in the settling it, that he may be really above those petty advantages and sneaking perquisites your predecessors did stoop to and which you have to your hurt rejected though the King and the Kingdom hath had the benefit of it, for that ever since the several officers and commanders have been under better discipline and more fear to offend, and I hope will be more kept to their duty by such a light as this intelligence when once established will give you when you will be enabled to tell them first in private of their offences and forewarn them of the like and upon a second commission to get them and I know very well that herein will lie all the difficulty for that most of the rascally officers of the fleet have powerful friends to intercede for them, so that without drawing the envy and malice of great persons upon you under whom these vermin shroud themselves you cannot presently rid your hands and the fleet of them but I know your great wisdom is such as backed with your great interest with the King and the Duke, that what by counselling and threatening some, by making others exemplary, by letting the friends of those best supported know their errors, by degrees insinuating the faults of the incorrigible to the King and Duke and other good methods, best known to you because you have practiced them you will at last do the great work which all honest men would rejoice in that is that the management of the King's fleet in all particulars may be executed by sober, discreet and diligent persons and men of business and that all drinking, swearing, and gaming, and expensive and sumptuous eating may be banished the fleet and particularly that the King's ships may not be made bawdyhouses nor the captains publicly carry and entertain their whores on board as some of them have formerly done and that from port to port in the Mediterranean to the great scandal of our religion and government both amongst Turks, Jews and Christians. But it's time to give you no further trouble. For God's sake impute this fit of zeal to the love I bear to the service of my country and to the earnest desires I have to see the King's navy a protection to the nation and a terror to our enemies, which without a strict discipline and real sobriety in officers and seamen it can never be.

If you think it worthwhile I'll wait upon you and talk further about this foolish paper of mine that is of the ways to putt it in practice, which is a thing that must ripen by degrees. I am

Sir
Your most humble servant
J. HOUBLON

Pepys's office brought with it the trappings of status, including a barge that he used to journey up and down the Thames. Here Pepys wants a cabin ('house') built on the barge, but fears it will affect its appearance. He therefore speculates if he might justifiably obtain a new barge. The addressee is Phineas Pett, master-shipwright at Woolwich.

112. SAMUEL PEPYS TO MR PHINEAS PETT

Derby House
22 June 1677

SIR

I have by your late invitation sent you down my boat, in order to her being a little cleaned, and to the giving you the offer of a little further trouble about her, which is the desiring you to consider whether there may be any great inconvenience, or that the charge will be very great, in having a house built upon her, as a barge, to be either fixed or moveable, for I am told that such things have been done to barges; and to tell you the truth, though I have done all I can in fitting my oiled cloth to my iron bails, yet I find it troublesome in the opening and shutting, as the weather being cold, hot, or wet requires, and yet carries as much wind-taut as a house. Not but that it may be very possible there may be nevertheless objections against building of a house upon her, and particularly that she being in her build broad and short, I fear a house may make her appear yet much shorter, and so may render her shape less agreeable to the eye; wherefore I do leave it entirely to you to judge whether it may be convenient to have the thing done or not, or whether possibly I may not, without any loss to his Majesty, obtain from the Officers of the Navy another boat to be built for me more barge-shapen in exchange for this. Against which proposition also I have nevertheless this to object, that the summer will be most of it gone before I shall get it done to have any use of it. And I know not also whether that would be so good a boat to answer my occasions of being carried below bridge, though it may be better for above; but I leave the whole entirely to you to consider and to give me your opinion in a word or two before you go about doing anything to her; because if you are of advice to have a house built upon her, I would be glad to offer you some thoughts of mine as to the manner of it, and particularly in reference to the windows, which I would propose unto you to slide up and down in grooves, as your glasses in coaches do, as being safer, closer, and more handy than the hanging them upon hinges.

[Postscript.] If the largeness of the house to answer her present bails be any considerable objection to it because of the shortness, I should be well contented to have it made somewhat less, by its being shortened cither abaft or before, so as there may remain good room for six persons.

Pepys's ambitions for a well-appointed barge came back to haunt him. When he fell in May 1679, accused of complicity in the Popish Plot, various other allegations of corruption were circulated. In a scurrilous pamphlet called *Hue and Cry*, scorn was poured on Pepys's modest origins as the son of a tailor, his extravagant carriage and his barge fitted out with 'damask curtains and cushions'.[10]

George, Lord Berkeley, was an old acquaintance of Pepys's and also a Fellow of the Royal Society with an interest in mechanical design. It appears that Pepys had helped a man called Mr Bonithan, but later learned that Lord Berkeley's daughter-in-law Elizabeth had accused him of being less than supportive when Mr Bonithan was passed over for a command, in favour of a Lieutenant Beele. Pepys defends himself by pointing out what he did for Mr Bonithan, while at the same time recognizing Bonithan's shortcomings. According to Braybrooke, who originally published the letter, it was accompanied by 'the Report of the Navy Commissioners, certifying Mr Bonithan's insufficiency and Mr Beele's competency to manage a ship'. Berkeley immediately responded to Pepys's hurt feelings to apologize for the misunderstanding, and to reassure Pepys of the high regard in which he held him.

113. SAMUEL PEPYS TO GEORGE, LORD BERKELEY

Derby House
22 February 1678

MY LORD

I am greatly owing to your Lordship for your last favour at St John's, and did, till now, reckon myself under no less a debt to my Ladies for the honour at the same

[10] The pamphlet is quoted in Tanner 1925, 240–1.

time done me, in their commands touching Mr Bonithan. But, my Lord, I have lately had the misfortune of being undeceived in the latter, by coming to know the severity with which some of my Ladies are pleased to discourse of me in relation thereto. I assure your Lordship, I was so big with the satisfaction of having an opportunity given me by my Ladies at once of obliging them, paying a small respect to you, and doing a good office to a deserving gentleman, that I did not let one day pass before I had bespoke and obtained his Majesty's and Royal Highness's promise of favour in Mr Bonithan's behalf and was so far afterwards from failing him in my further assistances with Captain Trevanion and others, that I took early care to secure him a lieutenancy, by a commission actually signed for him by the king, in the ship *Stavereene*, relying upon the character Captain Trevanion had given me of his capacity to abide the examination, established by the King, upon the promotion of lieutenants; which was not only the most I should have done in the case of a brother, but more than ever I did in any man's case before, or, for his sake, do think I shall ever do again.

True it is, my Lord, that when, upon his examination by the officers of the Navy, he was found not so fully qualified for the office of lieutenant as was requisite, I did with all respect, and to his seeming satisfaction, advise him to pass a little longer time in the condition he was then in, under a stricter application of himself to the practice of navigation. And, in pursuance of my duty to the King, I did acquaint him also with Mr Bonithan's present unreadiness; and had, therefore, a command given me for conferring the commission prepared for him upon another, who, upon examination, at the same time with Mr Bonithan, was found better qualified for it.

As to what I understand my Ladies are pleased to entertain themselves and others with, to my reproach, as if money had been wanting in the case, it is a reproach lost upon me, my Lord, who am known to be so far from needing any purgation in the point of selling places, as never to have taken so much as my fee for a commission or warrant to any one officer in the navy, within the whole time, now near twenty years, that I have had the honour of serving his Majesty therein – a self-denial at this day so little in fashion, and yet so chargeable to maintain, that I take no pride, and as little pleasure in the mentioning it, further than it happily falls in here to my defence against the mistake the Ladies seem disposed to arraign me by on this occasion. Besides that in the particular case of this gentleman, Lieutenant Beele, who enjoys the commission designed for Mr Bonithan, he is one whose face I never saw either before or since the time of his receiving it, nor know one friend he has in the world to whom he owes this benefit, other than the King's justice and his own modest merit: which, having said, it remains only that I assure your Lordship what I have so said, is not calculated with any *regard to,* much less any repining at, the usage the Ladies are pleased to show me in this affair, for 'tis fit I bear it, but to acquit myself to your Lordship in my demeanor towards them, as becomes their and, my Lord,

Your Lordship's most obedient servant,
S. P.

114. GEORGE, LORD BERKELEY TO SAMUEL PEPYS

Berkeley House
23 February 1678

GOOD MR PEPYS

Though I thank you for the favour of your letter yet I confess myself both much surprised and troubled to receive a letter from you upon such an occasion [and] so is my wife who professes herself wholly innocent of any crime of charging you in thought word or deed and hopes you will do her that right to believe so of her. My daughter Berkeley says she expressed some trouble that the friend she recommended had not success and that she was told the commissioners of the Navy did report they had given the same recommendations of the person she proposed as they did of him that was accepted of for the lieutenant's place which my daughter supposing to be true wondered the more. He lost the preferment but by the copies enclosed in yours, it appears her Ladyship was very much misinformed, as for Mrs Henrietta[11] she is extremely troubled in saying anything that gave you offence and though she did not in the least intend it yet she begs your pardon and now my good friend. Though I am not under an accusation and therefore need not say anything to vindicate myself yet give me leave upon this occasion to assure you that there is no person has a better opinion of you than myself, nor is more sensible of your particular civilities to me which I should be very glad to make a return of when in my power to serve you, and give me leave to add further without flattery to you and with great sincerity that I believe our gracious master his Majesty is so fortunate in employing you in his service that If he should lose you it would be very difficult for his Majesty to find a successor so well qualified in all respects for his service if we consider both your integrity, vast abilities, industry and zealous affections for his service; and if his Majesty were asked the question I will hold ten to one his Majesty declares himself of my opinion so will I believe all that truly know you more especially our fellow traders that are so often conversant with you and obliged by you. This is asserted as a great truth by, Sir,

Your very affectionate and hearty friend and servant
BERKELEY

The Popish Plot erupted on 14 August 1678 when Dr Israel Tonge showed papers to Thomas Osborne, Earl of Danby and Lord High Treasurer, purporting to show that there was a Jesuit plot to assassinate Charles II. On 6 September Tonge and his co-accuser, Titus Oates, swore an oath that their claims were true before Sir Edmund Berry Godfrey. Various denunciations followed, but on 17 October Godfrey was found murdered. The hysteria mounted and on 25 October a royal proclamation was issued ordering any Catholic who refused to attend Protestant church services to go at least ten miles from London and Westminster. On 30 October the Commons accepted the existence of the Popish Plot. During the weeks and months of panic that followed, Pepys found himself implicated. But first the religious affiliation of a musician in his service became an issue.

Cesare Morelli was the singer and musician, educated in Rome but born in Flanders, first drawn to Pepys's attention in 1673 by Thomas Hill (Letters nos. 90 and 98). Morelli had been in service with a nobleman but the latter's death in 1674 meant that Hill wrote once more, on 27 September that year, to ask if Pepys would take him. Pepys offered £30 per annum. Morelli was a Catholic and once in Pepys's service this had implications when the Popish Plot erupted. The proclamation that followed ordered Catholic recusants to leave London. Morelli went to Pepys for advice. Pepys sent Morelli to Houblon with the following letter, requesting that if Morelli could not be convinced to convert to Protestantism then perhaps Houblon could help make sure Morelli's connections with Pepys could be severed as soon as possible, although Pepys would help support Morelli. Given later allegations made about Pepys's Catholic sympathies, his reference to the 'villainous principles of these Jesuits' would have been useful evidence in his favour.

---

[11] Berkeley's youngest daughter.

115. SAMUEL PEPYS TO JAMES HOUBLON

2 November 1678

SIR

After thanks for your last night's favour, at my coming home Monsieur Morelli came to me himself to desire direction how he should behave himself in reference to what I had troubled you for your advice in, about his obeying the proclamation. Great pity it is that one so moderate as I take him to be in the business of his persuasion, and otherwise so sober and harmless, should come under any difficulties upon the account thereof, but the law ought and must be conformed to, and therefore I have taken the liberty, according to what I told you I would do at my leaving you tonight, of sending him to you, entreating you that if the late instances of the villainous principles of these Jesuits will not suffice to convince him of the error of that Church and prevail with him to come over to ours, which I would to God they would, you will think of some way how, with the help towards his sustenance which I will in charity allow him, he may dispose of himself so as his relation and residence with me may be removed within the time appointed by his Majesty's proclamation. I shall speedily wait on you for the result of your thoughts herein.

116. JAMES HOUBLON TO SAMUEL PEPYS

For Mr Secretary Pepys.   *These Derby House*

3 November 1678

SIR

I have discoursed [with] Monsieur Morelli and according to your desire have used all the arguments I could think of against the errors of the Romish Church und us an inducement to distrust the doctrines of that church have urged to him (though it is a wrong way of arguing) the wicked and intolerable policy and practice of its members for this thousand years I mean of the Pope and Cardinals and the several societies of the clergy in most countries who have made no scruple to trample upon the temporality (as well corporations as private persons,) and have used all violent and bloody means to maintain and increase their riches and dominion; to enable them to tyrannize over the souls and bodies of men but Sir I must tell you that I find Monsieur Morelli so resolved in his religion that it will be in vain to hope his conversion, only saith that he really believes that the governors of the Roman faith do use unlawful ways to compass their designs which he abhors but dares not abandon that Church for that. I am sorry Sir you have not your desires in seeing him a good protestant. As to the other point, of his necessary removing out of your house I have propounded to him going to Brentwood where he would be well used and upon moderate terms, but he rather inclines to go to Flanders, his native country, and humbly leaves himself upon your charity professing that of that allowance you have so honourably been pleased to make him what with clothes, living and other necessaries, he hath not been able to save one penny and I perceive hath not anything left.

He intends to embark for Antwerp by way of Ostend or Rotterdam, so if no yacht suddenly bound that way I'll speak to some skipper upon departure to take him in.

What you have farther to command me I entreat you freely to make use of

Sir, your most humble servant,

JAMES HOUBLON

117. SAMUEL PEPYS TO JAMES HOUBLON

4 November 1678

SIR

This comes pursuant to the liberty you gave me by your kind letter on Saturday of giving you the trouble of assisting Monsieur Morelli in the disposing of himself in obedience to his Majesty's proclamation, wherein as I am desirous to acquit myself in my duty as I ought to his Majesty's and the Parliament's commands, so I do fully concur with you in your opinion for his passing some further little time at least in England before he leaves it, upon the consideration you offer me of any misconstruction which may happen to be made if that care of mine in this matter which I chiefly aim at deserving well by, – I mean, in the readiness of my parting with one whose qualifications have rendered him the almost sole instrument of all the pleasure his Majesty's service leaves me any leisure or opportunity of enjoying, namely, his music, languages, and sobriety. Pray therefore let him retire to Brentwood as you so kindly propose, from whence he may easily be removed in order to his getting beyond sea to his own country when it shall be judged convenient. I beg you heartily to take this trouble in good part from me and doubt not your doing it, there being so much humanity and charity towards a helpless stranger concerned in it.

S. P.

118. CESARE MORELLI TO SAMUEL PEPYS

Brentwood
6 November 1678

SIR

After my most humble respects, I inform you of my arrival at Brentwood, Tuesday evening, at the house of a most obliging family. The situation I find very pleasant, the air is more pure than at London, and consequently favourable to my voice. This I hope to improve, without forgetting my lute. For my own satisfaction I would trust that your mind is more at ease than when we parted, for I am, indeed, so well aware of your afflictions, that, were the loss of my life necessary to your happiness, I would, with all my heart, offer you the sacrifice; though I can never return all your kindness. I am, Sir,

Your very humble, very affectionate, and very much obliged,

CESARE MORELLI

Pepys had to defend his relationship with Morelli on 20 May 1679 when he faced the House of Commons:

> As for Morelli; my leisure will not permit me to go abroad for diversion, and I sent abroad for a man of learning, and a good musician; a merchant, one Hill, sent me over Morelli. His qualifications are these: He is a thorough-bred scholar, and may be the greatest master of music of any we have. He came to Lisbon a page to a great man; and my friend, Thomas Hill, found him put there for me ... I have entertained myself harmlessly with him, singing with his lute, till twelve o'clock, when it was time to rest. At Lisbon he was thought so moderate a Catholic, that he was under some suspicion.[12]

---

[12] Grey's Debates of the House of Commons, quoted by Howarth, p. 73 n.1.

Meanwhile the Popish Plot placed the establishment on high alert. On 30 November Oates and a conman and opportunist called William Bedloe accused the Queen of being implicated in the Plot. Although clearly a step too far, the madness was far from over. Now Pepys became a potential suspect when Bedloe spotted another chance to profit from the hysteria. He claimed he had seen a clerk of Pepys's called Samuel Atkins standing by the body of Godfrey in Somerset House on 19 October, two days after the murder, and that Pepys had asked Atkins to find someone to help him murder Godfrey. Pepys was probably the intended target but as he was in Newmarket on 16 October he had a cast-iron alibi. It would have to be done by association, so Atkins was chosen. When he wrote to his sister Paulina on 5 December, Pepys was assembling an alibi for his clerk and thus his own defence.

119. SAMUEL PEPYS TO MRS PAULINA JACKSON

Derby House
5 December 1678

SISTER

This comes to thank you for your letter of the 26th of November and to give my father und you the satisfaction of knowing that I am (I bless God) in very good health, and in every other particular as well as it is possible for anyone in my place to be at a time when things seem in so ill a posture everywhere else, — I mean, with respect to the safety of his Majesty and the peace of his Government. In and for both which, as all good men ought, so I in particular by many obligations cannot but be concerned with great care and an anxiety of mind, but not without hopes that God Almighty will in due time dispel our fears and establish his Majesty and people once more in security of peace and religion and the enjoyment of the blessings attending them.

One misfortune there is indeed which has created me much trouble, namely, that by a most manifest contrivance one of my clerks (Atkins) has been accused and is now in custody as a party some way concerned in the death of Sir Edmund Berry Godfrey; which (though most untrue) cannot be thought to pass in the world at so jealous a time as this without some reflections upon me as his master, and on that score does occasion me not a little disquiet. But I thank God I have not only my innocence to satisfy myself with, but such an assurance of his also as that I make no question of his being able to acquit himself with advantage to him and infamy to his accusers; and that being done, the care which this accident occasions me will soon be over.

In the meantime, pray desire my father to give no way to any fears concerning me, for that I bless God I have lived so carefully in the discharge of my duty to the King my master and the laws I live under, both towards God and towards men, that I have not one unjust deed or thought to answer for, and consequently neither am myself, nor would pray him to be, under the least doubt or care what can befall me, it being of no use to any man in my place to think of supporting himself by any other means that has such an innocence as mine to rely on, and there, I bless God, lies my comfort, whatever befall me.

Which having said, I have nothing at present to add but to pray you to continue your care of my father all you can, and though through the muchness of my business I may fail you, pray do not you fail to let me know once a week how he and your family do. So with the tenders of my most humble duty to my father and kind love to yourself, etc., I remain,

Your most affectionate Brother

On 5 May 1666 Pepys had responded to a gift from Anthony Deane by stressing that he would not accept anything that amounted to a bribe, or which could be mistaken for one. He was being slightly disingenuous, since on 15 December 1663 he had indeed accepted a 'gift' concealed in a handkerchief. His acceptance of less readily traceable sexual favours from women, such as Mrs Bagwell, in return for advancing her husband was simply another form of bribery that Pepys chose not to recognize as such. Here once more he reiterates his public view on the subject of bribes, doubtless aware that at this time above all others he had to appear beyond reproach.

120. SAMUEL PEPYS TO MR TREVORS

Derby House
18 December 1678

SIR

I have your letter of the 12th instant, and could not have believed the method of my proceedings in the Navy could, after near twenty years' observation, be so ill understood by any one man therein as it seems to have been by you, when you would think any offer of money or any other argument can obtain anything from me that bare virtue cannot. But all the amends I shall take for the wrong you have done me in it is to let you remain under your mistake concerning
Your very loving friend
S. P.

As the winter progressed more accusations, denunciations and executions in the Popish Plot followed. Danby was impeached. Bedloe accused a silversmith called Prance of the murder of Godfrey. Prance accused Robert Green, Henry Berry and Lawrence Hill of the murder and then fell out with Bedloe over sharing out the £500 reward. Green, Berry and Hill were executed on 21 February. A month later Parliament voted that the £500 be paid to Bedloe. Since the Duke of York was a Catholic the question of the succession now arose. On 15 June a bill was introduced in Parliament to prevent James succeeding to the throne when Charles II died.

In the meantime Pepys had been elected MP for Harwich in March 1679. Now that his religious affiliations had been called into question he wrote to Captain Thomas Langley, then master of the packet boats at Harwich and its mayor in 1675. He referred to the allegations made by Shaftesbury in 1673–4 when the latter supported the efforts to invalidate Pepys's election victory at Castle Rising in 1673 on the ground that Pepys was a secret Catholic. The letter is a firm and explicit declaration of Pepys's Protestancy.

121. SAMUEL PEPYS TO CAPTAIN THOMAS LANGLEY

Derby House
6 March 1679

SIR

Your late journey into Suffolk for the assisting of Mr Allin's election, and mine into Kent upon it like occasion, has prevented my earlier acknowledging to you both the kindnesses I received from you when I was at Harwich and the letters you have sent me since my return thence. For the former of which, as well those which concerned my election in general as what respect you showed me in your particular house, I return both you and Mrs Langley my most hearty thanks, assuring you of my taking all occasions of answering the same by whatever service I shall be able to do you nd your family, nor shall be less solicitous to acquit myself as I ought to do to the whole body of the Corporation of Harwich and every member of it in return for the extraordinary expressions of their good will which I have so lately received the benefit of from them. And this I entreat you to communicate, with my most humble services, to Mr Mayor and the rest of my worthy friends the gentlemen of the town, as you shall have opportunity for it.

For what you write touching the discourses you have met with in your neighbourhood about the election Harwich has made in their choice of Sir Anthony Deane and me, as if he were an Atheist and myself a Papist, I take the suggestions which any shall make of that kind to be so foolish as well as malicious that I shall not give myself the trouble to say or you to read more in answer thereto than this, viz., that as to Sir A. Deane, whoever knows him as well as our friends of Harwich and I do, knows that he has too much wit to be an Atheist, it being the fool only that Solomon tells us says in his heart, There is no God.[13] And as for my being a Papist, let them examine but the entries in our Parliament books, upon occasion of a controversy some time since happening between a great Lord and myself upon that subject, and they shall find such a trial and proof of my Protestancy as I doubt no private man in England can show but myself upon record in Parliament.

And this (I say) is all I shall think now necessary to urge between you and I in defence of my partner and myself and justification of Harwich's choice of us for their servants. But if you do in the least apprehend that what has been said on this occasion to our prejudice has made any impressions upon any other of our friends in the Corporation, to the shaking them in the good opinions they had conceived of us in this particular of religion as well as in other things, I do hold it a point so considerable that though we are already possessed of the benefit of the Corporation's kindness in their choice of us, yet I am of opinion, and believe Sir Anthony Deane will be of the same mind with me, that we ought to be as much concerned for the giving the Corporation satisfaction therein now, as we should have done had the doubt been raised before our election, and therefore I entreat you in your next to be very open with me whether you think there be any in the whole number of our electors, from Mr Mayor downwards, who has the least scruple remaining with him touching our devotion towards God Almighty, for if so, I shall (in the absence of Sir Anthony Deane) undertake for both that we will remove it by such evidences of our faith and doctrine, conformable to the true Protestant doctrine and worship of the Church of England, as shall leave no ground for any Corporation in England (upon comparing elections with respect to religion) to reproach Harwich with the choice of her Burgesses.

Your most faithful friend to serve you,

S. P.

It was essential for Pepys to drum up as much support as possible. In this letter to the Duke of York, Pepys swears his loyalty and looks forward to the imminent arrival home of Sir John Narbrough, an old friend and supporter of his. He suggests the possibility that a transfer from the Secretaryship of the Admiralty into the Commission of the Admiralty might help solve the current difficulties. Given the mood in London James was then in Brussels, having moved there at the King's request at the end of February. He had to be

---

[3] In Psalm 53, verse 1, it is David who says, 'The fool hath said in his heart, there is no God', referring to the corruption of a natural man.

temporarily recalled when Charles II fell ill in August 1679, but after that crisis was over h was made High Commissioner in Scotland, not returning to England until 1682. It was mark of how weak Charles II was. There was little prospect of any practical support fo Pepys from the crown, if even the heir to the throne had had to leave the country.

122. SAMUEL PEPYS TO THE DUKE OF YORK

Derby Hous
6 May 167?

MAY IT PLEASE YOUR ROYAL HIGHNESS

I acknowledge with all humility and thankfulness the honour of your Highness' letters of the 24th and 25th of the last, and do with equal grief and shame observ how much your Highness's solicitude (even at this distance) for the security of thi kingdom against the power of France does exceed all that we ourselves have ye expressed upon that subject, otherwise than by a general but unactive restlessnes under our apprehensions of the danger, but without any alteration made since you Royal Highness's departure in the state of our ships or coasts, other than what i consequential to their having lain so much longer neglected.

Sir John Narbrough, Admiral and Commander-in-chief in the Mediterranean, ha been occupied in crushing the Algerine corsairs. Sir John Narbrough's last letter were of the 7/17 of March from Alacant, where having newly met with hi Majesty's orders for his coming home (after a short visit to Algiers), he therein tol me he would accordingly proceed thence forthwith to Port-Mahon [Minorca] for th settling some matters in that place, and from thence to Algiers; so as to be at Tangie (in his way homeward) about the 7th of April. Since which, though we have wholl wanted advice from him, yet by a letter I have seen from a slave at Algiers of the 1 of April, it appears that he came before that town the 25th departed the 29th March after having sent two of his captains ashore to treat a peace, but without effect; thi only is added by the slave, that had Sir John Narbrough stayed one day more in th Road, those of Algiers had certainly made a peace with him, that government havin afterwards (it seems) expressed some trouble that it was not done. By whicl calculation of time we may now from day to day expect his being here.

I have remembered your Highness's command in reference to Captain Lloyd' being appointed one of the Newfoundland convoys, which his Majesty has bee pleased to agree to, in company with Captain Talbot in the *Mary Rose,* Captai Priestman in the *Antelope,* and Captain Kempthorne in the *Dover,* and will take car that Mr Hickman be entertained as a volunteer with Captain Lloyd.

How his Majesty has been pleased (among his other great changes) to dispose o the Admiralty by a new Commission to these gentlemen, viz., Sir Henry Capel, M Dan. Finch, Sir Thomas Ley, Sir Thomas Meres, Mr Vaughan, Sir Humphre Winch, and Mr Hales of Kent, your Highness (I doubt not) has many days sinc known; nor shall I think it becoming me to interpose any thoughts of mine touchin his Majesty's choice therein, more than that (for his and his service's sake) I coul wish his naval action to be for time such as might allow these worthy gentleme opportunity of being informed in the work of their great office before they be urge to much execution in it.

And this I am the bolder in wishing, since their having taken upon themselves th performance of that branch of the Admiral's task which his Majesty was pleased, fo the ease of his last Commissioners, to reserve the trouble of to himself, namely, th issuing all sailing instructions to his fleet and ships, his Majesty having, at the instance of these gentlemen, put that part also in their hands, together with the granting of all offices in the Navy, in the same manner as it has at any time been exercised by the Lords Admirals of England.

For what concerns my own particular, your Highness was pleased to foretell me, at your going hence what I was soon after to look for; and it is come to pass. For, whether I will or no, a Papist I must be, because favoured by your Royal Highness, and found endeavouring on all fitting occasions to express in the best manner I can the duty and gratitude due to your Highness from me. But how injuriously soever some would make those just endeavours of mine towards your Highness inconsistent with Protestancy, neither they, nor any ill usage I can receive from them for it, shall (by the grace of God) make me any more quit the one than I suspect your Royal Highness will ever take offence at my perseverance in the t'other.

His Majesty indeed is pleased to express a much more favourable opinion of me and my slender qualifications for his service than I dare own any right to, and (us an instance thereof) has not spared to tell me how much weight he is pleased to place upon my experience in the Navy for supplying, by my Secretaryship, what his present choice of Commissioners may possibly *be* found less perfect in. Nor shall I think it becoming me to dispute the giving his Majesty my service on whatever terms he shall think fit to require it from me.

But as your Royal Highness well knows how far I had not long since made it my humble motion, and pressed it upon your favour, that after almost twenty years' continued drudgery in the Navy, to the rendering myself almost blind, and otherwise disabled in health to support it much longer, his Majesty would be pleased to take the residue of my small service by admitting me into the Commission of the Admiralty, so truly (Sir) I have now upon other considerations purely relative to his service made the same motion to the King upon occasion of this change. For if I was truly conscious of being become less able to bear the fatigue of my office any longer under a Commission that had many members of it competently furnished for its execution, besides the easy and helpful recourse I at all times had to his Majesty himself and your Royal Highness in matters needing it (and those, as old a navy-man as I am, not a few), how much less fit ought I to think myself to go through this task when not only stripped of all those helps but (to say no worse) charged with a new piece of duty, and that not a little one, of informing those who should inform and are to command me, and I remain accountable for all the ill success that should attend my obeying those commands, though possibly differing from my own advice? Besides, however fairly some of these gentlemen seem disposed towards my continuance in this Secretaryship, yet that compliance of theirs I well know to be grounded upon some opinion they have of the necessariness of my service to them till they have obtained a stock of knowledge of their own, and then, Farewell. But others there be with whom, your Royal Highness knows, (what converts soever they are now to be thought), I have for many years lived in a constant state of war, they censuring and I defending the managements of the Navy, and with such success on the Navy's side as to have always met with too great an appearance of his Majesty's well-accepting my humble endeavours therein, that (however our conjunction may now succeed in reference to his Majesty's service) I should promise any satisfaction to myself from them; especially upon terms so unequal as that of my being brought down to be a servant to them whom the dignity of the trust I have so long had the honour of serving his Majesty in might (I hope) be thought to have set me upon a level with.

Whereto I have humbly to add, what some have not spared publicly to let fly in opposition to my continuance in this office, namely, that so long as Mr Pepys should be there his Royal Highness remains in effect Admiral. In which, though they do me a much greater honour than either I deserve or their malignity designs me, yet, Sir, I cannot but so far consider the importance of having all rubs removed which may either be of impediment to the happy going on of this great part of the King's service or give any unnecessary occasions of keeping alive the jealousies touching your Royal Highness, that if his Majesty may as well secure to himself the full use of my service, and your Highness receive no less content from my being in the Commission than in my present post (which you were pleased, upon my former motion to that purpose, to express your well-liking of), I see no inconvenience (but to myself) likely to arise from his Majesty's giving them the satisfaction of his withdrawing me from this invidious Secretaryship, I being for these reasons not only contented to submit to, but desire it, and shall be most ready to give my assistance in this Commission with the same faithfulness and industry (though not with the same fullness of private satisfaction) wherewith I ought and should were your Royal Highness yourself at the head of it.

Which having said, I make it my humble prayer to your Royal Highness to interpret with your usual justice my deliberations upon this subject, pardoning ought that shall happen not to find your full liking, as being designed most entirely for the benefit of his Majesty's service.

But if it shall be my better fortune to meet with your Royal Highness's approbation in what I have here humbly catered, I then make it my suit to your Highness that you will be pleased to consider how far it may be fit for your Highness to enforce from yourself this my humble proposal to his Majesty for my being transferred from the Secretaryship into the Commission; your Royal Highness well knowing that however bounteous you have always been to me in your frequent callings on me to the improvement of your favour to my benefit with his Majesty, I have never to this day done it to the obtaining sixpence from the Crown by any boon extraordinary beyond the plain allowance of my office, and not that neither yet, by much more than all I have else reserved in the world to depend upon, as your Highness was pleased to be informed from me by particulars (and from you, the King) just before your going.

So as while the sincerity of my wishes for the weal of his service prompts me to this voluntary divesting myself of my present employment, I should be in very ill condition to bear its not being made up to me by his Majesty's granting (for his service's sake, as well as in justice to your Royal Highness's mediation and his own promises in my favour) the latter part of my motion for his placing me in the Commission, or at least making some other provision for me, as one superannuated in his service.

Wherein nevertheless submitting myself still to your Royal Highness's disposal, and beseeching God Almighty to put some timely bounds to your misfortunes, whatever becomes of mine, I in all humility remain

May it please your Royal Highness
Your Royal Highness's most obedient
and dutiful servant
S. P.

The Duke of York wrote to Charles II to recommend that Pepys be offered a position as one of the Commissioners of the Admiralty.

23. THE DUKE OF YORK TO THE KING

Brussels
12/22 May 1679

I hope your Majesty will pardon me for writing to you in the behalf of an old servant of yours in the Navy that has long and faithfully served you; it is Mr Pepys, who now upon this change in the Admiralty is like to suffer without your Majesty's favour; and truly I think should he be quite laid aside I believe the service there would not be so well carried on, and those who are named to be Commissioners of the Admiralty, though in other affairs are very able men, yet must needs be very raw in that, and will want one amongst them that understands it. Therefore that I have humbly to offer to your Majesty in Mr Pepys's behalf is, that you will be pleased to add him to that Commission and let him be one of their number. Sure none can reasonably find fault with your Majesty's doing it for him when they consider his long service in the Navy and that you do it as a recompense to him for all his services, and besides I think it very necessary for your service always, and the easiest and less chargeable way of doing something for him that can be thought on, for, give me leave to say, your Majesty is bound to do something for him that has spent so many years in your service to your satisfaction. Pray, Sir, pardon me for being earnest in this affair; I can never help being so where I think your honour concerned, and I wish all your subjects were as true Englishmen and as dutiful and as loyal as I am and ever shall be

JAMES

In the end Pepys fell foul of those who had a vested interest in alleging any Catholic connection in government in others. They included the Duke of Buckingham and the Earl of Shaftesbury. Of course Shaftesbury had already played a part in trying to discredit Pepys after he was elected MP for Castle Rising in 1673.

The visit by Hewer and Anthony Deane to France in August 1675 provided an excuse to smear Pepys. Colonel John Scott, an international fraudster, was used by Pepys's enemies to claim he had evidence Deane had sold secret maps of English ports and the coastline to the French to facilitate a Catholic invasion. He was backed up by John James, once in Pepys's household but sacked for bedding a housekeeper. He had been discovered *in flagrante* by none other than Cesare Morelli. Unfortunately both Pepys and Deane had invested during the Third Dutch War in a privateer called the *Hunter*. Since the *Hunter*'s captain had found English ships easier to attack, this added a plausible charge of treason. On 28 April 1679 Pepys and Deane were called before the Parliamentary Committee of Naval Miscarriages. Manned by Pepys's enemies the Committee damned his career, interpreting his every action corrupt and intended to favour Catholics. On 20 May Pepys and Deane were committed to the custody of the Parliamentary Serjeant-at-Arms and on the 22nd they were sent to the Tower. Pepys set about organizing his affairs. One of the first jobs was to cancel his plans to take Henry Norwood's house at Parson's Green. He also commenced a journal to record the proceedings against him.[14]

---

[14] 'King's Bench Journal', 20 May 1679–30 June 1680. Printed by Knighton 2004, 42–104.

124. SAMUEL PEPYS TO COLONEL HENRY NORWOOD

Tower
30 May 1679

SIR

I must beg you to forgive me, if my unwillingness to forego the pleasure I had proposed to myself from your intended kindness at Parson's Green has kept me too long from owning to you the incapacity, which I at length fear this my unexpected restraint and the consequences of it will lay me under, of taking the benefit of your favour therein; and therefore (though with infinite regret) do send this to signify to you my most thankful resignment of it back to you, that you may be at ease to bestow it upon somebody more fortunate in his liberty of enjoying it, though none is more sensible of the obligation to you from it, than shall be

Your most humble servant
S. PEPYS

125. COLONEL HENRY NORWOOD TO SAMUEL PEPYS

Parsons Green
2 June 1679

SIR

On Saturday I received your discharge of the little cell (which shall ever be at your devotion) and that with no small trouble to see you otherwise divertised from the use of it at present by the most unreasonable occasion in the world. I hope 'ere this comes to your hands, you will have weathered that storm which Satan-Scott has so unskilfully conjured to alarm you; and I make no doubt but your virtues will so improve this affliction to your spiritual as well as to your secular advantage that in the same time you rejoice in your tribulation, you will open those eyes to behold your innocency with shame and confusion upon themselves, who have been so vile promoters of this marked piece of malice towards you. I am at the point of leaving this place and do expect by the first to hear you are disentangled of this vexation, I wish everything may succeed as you desire as being most truly

Your most assured faithful servant
H. NORWOOD

My humble Service to Sir Anthony Deane

Pepys then started compiling the necessary evidence to discredit his accusers. Part of the crucial case Pepys hoped to mount against them was a denial from the Marquis de Seignelay that Hewer and Deane had ever handed over any secret papers to him. The addressee of this letter is uncertain but it clearly was a reply to a letter from the Continent sent by a supporter because it refers to the Gregorian calendar. The original manuscript is dated 5/15 June 1679 and refers to a letter of the 10th. This letter is preserved amongst the manuscripts of Thomas Tanner at the Bodleian Library but since Tanner was only five years old in 1679 he clearly cannot be the addressee. It may very well have been to John Brisbane, then secretary to the English embassy in Paris and engaged in helping Pepys amass the evidence against Scott.

126. SAMUEL PEPYS TO JOHN BRISBANE?

The Tower
5/15 June 1679

SIR

This comes to acknowledge most thankfully my receipt of yours of the 10ᵗʰ instant [N(ew) St(yle)?] and extraordinary instance you therein give me of your goodwill to my particular, no less than of your general justice and tenderness to all under my misfortune. The effects whereof I shall patiently wait for, in expectation of Monsieur de Seignelay's return; and ever own the obligation my innocence (whereto you are in your just opinion of it so friendly) receives from you on this so unhappy occasion, remaining

Sir
Your most faithful and
obedient servant
S. PEPYS

Despite the inherent dangers in any Catholic association, Pepys wrote this letter to express his loyalty to the Duke of York.

127. SAMUEL PEPYS TO THE DUKE OF YORK

The Tower
9 June 1679

MAY IT PLEASE YOUR ROYAL HIGHNESS

I should not have thought it in any wise [=ways] becoming me to trouble your Royal Highness with the notice of anything relating to the present difficulties I lie under, otherwise than as they serve for the necessary excuse of my no earlier owning the favour of your Royal Highness's by Captain Sanders,[15] which found me in the custody under which I with Sir Anthony Deane do now remain, upon no less suggestions than those of Popery, Felony, Piracy, and Treason, but so grounded as to render it hard for me to tell your Highness which of the two enjoys the greater pleasure, whether Mr Harbord in public from the contemplation of the conquest his malice has obtained over me, or I in private from what my innocence tells me I shall some time or other (if any justice may be hoped for) obtain against him. Hardships however I do and shall contentedly suffer, and the more in that I had the honour of having my duty to your Highness assigned for the real cause of what my adversaries are pleased artificially to pretend of Popery and other like chimaeras for. Begging your Royal Highness to believe, that as your Royal Highness shall never receive any dishonour from the favour you have been observed to incline to towards me, so neither shall any of the hard usages which the malignity of some or want of information in others can subject me to, render me either less zealous in my duty and allegiance to my Royal Master, or less forward in the payment of that gratitude which even that Protestancy of mine the world would be thought so doubtful of, exacts from me towards your Highness, and shall have it to the last point of my fortune and life.

---

[15] P's letter of 6 May 1679 to the Duke of York had been carried across the Channel by a Captain Sanders.

For what concerns your Royal Highness's particular goodness to me in your late letter to his Majesty, the condition I am in puts it out of my power to apply it to my benefit, but not so as to make me anything doubtful of the fruits of it in his Majesty's justice so soon as the justice I am waiting for from lower hands shall put me into a capacity of asking it. Towards which referring your Royal Highness in all humility to Sir John Worden for some particulars wherein your present aid and direction may be of instant benefit to me under my present misfortune, I pray God protect your and her Royal Highness and am, May it please your Royal Highness,

Your Royal Highness's most obedient and
ever most dutiful servant, S. P.

Pepys's immediate priority was clearing his name. But he found that some of those who had depended on his generosity in the past still took it for granted he could help them. Far from being able to oblige, Pepys was now in debt himself.

128. EDMUND D'OYLY TO SAMUEL PEPYS

10 June 1679

SIR

Requests of this sort should not be made without a preamble, which I hope your friendship will excuse my want of ability to perform. When I came from Flanders I was in hopes to have received a legacy of a thousand pound which was left me by my good mother, but I find I must stay two terms longer for it, my present occasions oblige me to beg the favour of you to lend me fifty pounds for six months to secure which I will give you a bond to repay it within that time, and for fear of accidents I will also give you a note to Sir Allen Apsley to pay to your order out of my Michaelmas quarterly payment £28 and at Christmas the remainder (in case it should not be repaid before) your excusing this trouble will bee a great obligation to

Sir, Your faithful friend and humble servant,
EDMUND D'OYLY

129. SAMUEL PEPYS TO EDMUND D'OYLY

The Tower
10 June 1679

SIR

I protest to you, my being sent hither was so sudden, that I have been forced to be beholden to my friends for £100 to pay my fees and defray my expenses here, and must be constrained to do the like for more, before I shall (in the state my affairs are) be able to repay the former. So as I will not lessen the credit of this real excuse for my [not] answering your desire, by adding anything that is artificial, which, I assure you, I would in no kind do, were I in a capacity of serving you, as being with all sincerity,

Your most affectionate, and humble servant,
S. PEPYS

Pepys and Deane were released on bail of £30,000 in July 1679. Pepys then went to live with Will Hewer at York Buildings. It would be almost another year before the case against them was dropped. A key player in Pepys's efforts to rubbish Colonel Scott's claims about Pepys's supposed passing of naval secrets to France was his brother-in-law, Balthazar St Michel. Numerous letters dating from 1679 and into 1680 record how Balthazar travelled to France on Pepys's behalf, locating the French officers cited by Scott, who could testify to the falseness of the allegations. The letters to St Michel in the following selection are therefore merely examples from the many available. Pepys was sceptical about any evidence that looked too promising. One incident involved Scott's whereabouts. The witnesses said one thing, but paperwork said something else. On 9 October 1679 Pepys warned Balthazar 'to be most slow to believe what we most wish should be true; considering what the consequences would have been of such a mistake as this should we have gone along in it to my trial, to the blemishing every other part of our evidences'.

In this earlier letter Pepys is anxious that Balthazar avoids Catholic witnesses as far as possible. Indeed, a Catholic witness was clearly almost worse than having no witness at all, though in the end this proved unavoidable. But anti-Catholicism could also be exploited since Pepys had heard that even Colonel Scott had posed as a Catholic when it suited him.

130. SAMUEL PEPYS TO BALTHAZAR ST MICHEL

28 July 1679

BROTHER

I kindly thank you for yours of the 21st and 22nd instant, and the great instances they give me of your diligence in my concerns, praying you to go on with your purpose of obtaining Madame Pellissary's and her family's attestation in all the particulars depending touching Mr Scott, and to let it be as particular as you can, and vouched per as many of her family great and small (besides herself) as you may. I being willing that this be done only before a notary as you are advised for her Ladyship's ease though if more shall be hereafter judged necessary I may come again to her to desire more, I shall not (I hope) need to repeat anything of the particulars to be mentioned in the attestation my former letters having been very plain therein.

Nor am I against your having a copy of so much of Mr Pellissary's inventory as concern the charts, globes and maps, though I must pray you to remember that the things of that kind which Scott mentions to have been sent to him from the Marquis de Seignelay were not for him to keep by him, but to be sent by him to Captain La Piogerie So as I am not to expect to find them remaining among the *meubles* [= chattels] of Mr Pellissary.

Another thing I must pray you to note in what I already heretofore wrote you which is, that it imports me mightily to make as little use as I can of any Papists for my witnesses, and that therefore if a Protestant can be got, of which you may consider, it will be of much more benefit and security to me than to depend upon the evidence of a Papist such as I take our worthy friend Mr Pelletier to be, though a man of the utmost integrity, and one to whom I am infinitely bound for his generous offer of coming into England, on my behalf and I pray you to return him my most humble thanks accordingly, but such is the captiousness of our age against anything that is not Protestant.

I have at length spoken with Mr Brisbane, but cannot be ready to give you my opinion touching your applications to Monsieur De Seignelay at present but I presume I shall make use of Monsieur De Ruvigny about it and write to you in it by the post on Monday the 4th August I being obliged to go out of town for so long tomorrow.

Heartily grieved I am for Mr Trenchepain's sickness whose recovery I pray for, and beg you to present him with my most humble services and the like to Mr Pelletier.

Pray pursue your getting of Mr Le Goux's evidence as particularly as you can in the points you mention. My sister[16] and her family were well last night, and full glad I am that you are so, hoping that one post or two more will put an end to your absence from home.

Lastly, pray find out what you can of Scott's ever having been in the King of France's service where he has heretofore bragged of his having been a Major-General under the prime of Condé after his having deserted the Holland's service, and endeavour also to learn any instances of his having been or pretended to be of the Church of Rome as I am told he has to one of the English nunneries in Paris about the year 1673 and was very civilly treated by them and others on that account, as I doubt not but you may upon enquiry (if you could find out any of his haunts) discover.

So being driven to make use of my own eyes in writing this, I bid you heartily adieu, and am

Your truly loving brother to serve you

S. P.

This letter to Cesare Morelli, written by Pepys from the Tower of London, is a mixture of business and pleasure. Much of the text is taken up with music but Pepys began by asking Morelli to compile any information he could to refute allegations that he, Morelli, was a Catholic priest.

131. SAMUEL PEPYS TO CESARE MORELLI

The Tower

25 September 1679

SIR

Though I was very well satisfied, at my return from Windsor, to find you gone back to Burntwood, according to your resolution before my departure, yet I found myself disappointed thereby in two or three particulars in which I did design to discourse with you before your going; whereof one was, to advise you to make a recollection in your memory of the several places and conditions in which you have spent your time for some years past, so as to be able to contradict anything that may happen to be suggested by those who have maliciously invented the story of your being a priest; for I do expect that those who have the wickedness to begin that lie, will not forbear to assert it as often as they shall judge it apropos to do me and you mischief with; and that undoubtedly they will do when I shall come to my trial upon the business which Scott has so falsely charged me with; and therefore, pray make it your business to recollect and consider how to discover the truth in that particular, and give me a short account thereof, for my private satisfaction, as soon as you can.

Next, I would have seen you furnished with some wine (as you desired) before your going, and shall do it still, in case you have not already done it yourself; which if you have, let me know what it cost, that I may reimburse you.

---

[16] Balthazar's wife, Esther.

I would have also informed myself touching the condition you are now in as to your entertainment, and whether you want anything towards it of that which you have to expect from me, to the end I may supply you therewith,

Also, I would have consulted with you about the use of the table which you have given me for the guitar; for the little knowledge in music which I have, never was of more use to me than it is now, under the molestations of mind which I have at this time, more than ordinary, to contend with; and therefore I would be glad to improve that little knowledge as far as I could, to the making myself capable, by the help of your table, of playing a *basse continue*; which I would not despair of doing, in a tolerable degree, after you shall have made me master of that table. In confidence of which, since, upon some other considerations it is not so convenient for me at this time to see you here, I do design to come and spend one day with you where you are, to receive your instructions therein, so soon as you shall have finished those other matters, which I now come (in the last place) to commit to your care, viz.

First. To transcribe anew into the blank ruled paper, which I now send you, all those several pieces which accompany the same, to the end that when they are all in paper of the same size, I may bind them up all neatly in one book, and not be troubled with so many several papers (and those of several sizes) as I now am. And in the transcribing thereof I shall desire you to observe these few directions, viz.

1. To do it in as legible a letter and note as you can for the ease of my eyes.
2. To take care that the words do stand as just under their proper notes as may be, out of the same regard to the ease of my eyes.
3. To begin every several piece upon a particular paper, and upon the left side of the sheet when it is opened, according as you have done in your song, *No no 'tis in vain,* that I may have as much in view at once as I can before I am obliged to turn over the leaf.
4. To observe very strictly to make the bottom of every leaf on the right hand to end with their quadrins, that I may not be subject to turn over the leaf in the middle of a passage, which gives a very troublesome interruption to the music.
5. Not to oblige yourself, as heretofore, to divide the notes of the *Basse continue* to the notes in the upper part, but to preserve the notes whole, as they use to be in a *Basse continue;* the method which you lately taught me of pinching the base not requiring the breaking of the notes thereof, which I was obliged to, when I played it by way of battery.
6. Lastly, to take care in transcribing of these pieces, never to go beyond the red line, for as much as that renders it impossible to cut the edge of the paper conformable to the book in which they lire to be bound, besides the spoiling the beauty and order of the transcription, as you see in the first side of the *World's a bubble.* And the same caution I am to give you against writing anything too much above or below the top or bottom of the leaf for the same reason, as in your song, *No no 'tis in vain.*

Secondly. In case you have not lost the anthems which I remember I sent you to show you the manner of the *basse continue,* which I then was used to, I desire they may be transcribed also, as the rest of the things arc: to be which I send you. 3dly. You are to observe that in transcribing the enclosed anthem, *Laudate Dominum,* there are three little symphonies numbered 1. 2. 3., which are severally to be played before the respective parts of the said anthem numbered in like manner 1. 2. 3.

Lastly, I do herein send you an English anthem lately made by Dr Blow, Master of our King's Music, which I desire you to accommodate with a bass to the guitar, and in transcribing the same, to observe to leave out the two staves which are left blank in my copy in the chorus for two in our parts.

All which I recommend to your care to see dispatched as soon as you can, I having nothing remaining in my hands to practice upon, but the *Lamentations of Jereemias.*

One thing indeed there is more, which I would be glad to have set to the guitar, viz. your French song, where are these words, *Les plus lourds Animaux.* Which, with wishing good health to you, is all at present from

Your most affectionate friend,
S. P.

On 23 October Pepys went to court, hoping he would be given a date for his trial. No date was forthcoming, since no-one offered any case for the prosecution. Pepys wrote to Mrs Skinner to tell her about this. Judging by later correspondence, and the content of this letter, this must be Mrs Frances Skinner, Mary's mother and sister-in-law to Sir Francis Boteler.

132. SAMUEL PEPYS TO MRS [FRANCES?] SKINNER

24 October 1679

MADAM

The principal errand of this is to inquire after your health, with Sir Francis Boteler's and my Lady's, to whom pray tender my most faithful and humble services.

But with all, it comes to give you this short account of my own affairs, which now seems to be as much too good as it was before the contrary. For at my appearance yesterday in court, (being the first day of the term,) instead of obtaining a day for my trial, (which was the only favour I had to beg,) I found nobody to be heard of to prosecute me, my accuser being withdrawn, (or at least absconding,) and Mr Harbord, my old prosecutor, not appearing. So as all I could have was to be continued in the state I am in, till the end of the term, in expectation of what my adversaries may offer towards prosecution within that time. From whence my friends, indeed, please themselves with an opinion of my being then discharged; and, by the course of the court, I am told I ought to be so, in case my adversaries continue silent. But then (which is an evil equal to any I have sustained) my being discharged in that manner, without a trial, leaves me liable to the same vexation again, whenever the same malignity of my enemies shall meet with the like juncture of state circumstances, to prompt them to my mischief.

However, my stock of sufferance is still good (I thank God), and it would do wrong to my innocence, if it were not. Therefore look not upon me as one to be condoled, but only wish me some more grateful occasion for being in *good humour* than this of the incapacity of my enemies to put me into *bad.*

I am, Madam, Your most humble servant,
S. PEPYS

By early 1680 John James, Pepys's former butler sacked for bedding a housekeeper and who had had his revenge by making allegations to support the case against his former master, was dying. Pepys wrote to Thomas Povey, who had served as Treasurer for Tangier before him, in the hope of securing a deathbed confession to add to the arsenal of evidence he was amassing to clear his name.

133. SAMUEL PEPYS TO THOMAS POVEY

Ash-Wednesday Night
25 February 1680

SIR

An occasion offers itself wherein you may exercise that kindness which you have sometimes exchanged with me; and it is this. You may, I doubt not, have heard that one James,[2] who had some time been my servant, has been made use of as my accuser. He is now upon his sickbed, and, as I am told, near the point of death, and has declared himself inclined to ease his conscience of something wherein I may be nearly concerned, with a particular willingness to open himself to you, whom he says he has known and observed during his serving the Duke of Buckingham and me. You may please, therefore, in charity to me as well as to the dying man, to give him a visit tomorrow morning, when I shall appoint one to conduct you to his lodging. It may be you may hesitate herein, because of the friendship which I no less know you to have with Mr Harbord than you know him to have of ill will against me, and of the effects of it under which I still remain, of being held obnoxious to others, to whom you bear great reverence. But that makes me the rather to importune you to the taking this trouble upon you, because your candour is such, that, with a fair and equal indifferency, you will hear and represent what that dying man shall relate to you, who, it is likely, will reveal nothing at this hour but truth; and it is truth only, and the God thereof, to which I appeal, and which will, I hope, vindicate my reputation, and free me from the misunderstandings which I find many ingenuous and worthy persons have had of me, from their being seduced by the false testimonies which have engained and improved to my disadvantage, even to the hazard of my life and estate, and no less to the disturbing of the Government, than to the raising injurious reflections upon those public trusts in which I have (much to your knowledge) carried myself diligently, and (I am sure) faithfully. And in this I the rather take the liberty of opening myself thus freely and amply to you upon this occasion, because I would move you the more strongly, to take upon you this just and charitable office, so much importing others, as well as

Your most humble servant
S. PEPYS

134. SAMUEL PEPYS TO BALTHAZAR ST MICHEL

8 March 1680

BROTHER

I have received yours of the 6th instant from Dover, where I am very glad to find you and our friends well arrived to whom I pray you to repay once more my most humble service, and thanks, being very sorry on their score, as well as my own, and yours for the hindrance they meet with to their passage through the crossness of the wind; praying you to use as much good husbandry in it, as you can, and to make all the use you are able of your stay there to get information in the business I wrote you about from the several gentlemen I named to you, taking the advice of Mr Joyne concerning the maps and what else Mr Nephew can remember, that he saw upon the opening of Scott's baggage. Enquire also of his demeanour whilst in custody, and the letter which Mr Bastinck wrote me word, he wrote to my Lord Shaftsbury from prison, and whither he ever let fall any threats or words concerning me.

As to your stay there, or coming away I confess I am loath you should leave them there. And yet if one wind should continue cross above a day or two longer I think you must of necessity get yourself excused by them. Of which I shall write to you again. And in the meantime it would not I suppose cost much for you to go over to Deal, and go on board the *Foresight* Captain Killigrew, and see the three receipts given by him to Captain Sanderson commander of the *Chariot* yacht, which sailed from hence on Saturday with Sir Palmes Fairborne and £8000 put in eight several boxes for the garrison of Tangier. And this will be a service to the King, and no great time spent in it. Which with my very humble service to all the gentlemen my friends of Dover is all at present from

Your truly affectionate brother to serve you

S. P.

John James repented of his malicious allegations before dying on about 20 March. With so much evidence available to refute the allegations, Pepys was able to consider others who needed help. Mrs Elizabeth Turner was the wife of Thomas Turner, storekeeper at Deptford dockyard from 1668–80 and before that clerk to the comptroller. Pepys thought Turner was a 'knave' but on 27 February 1680 Evelyn wrote to Pepys in Turner's defence.[17] It seems that someone had been promoted over Turner's head, despite having previously sworn he had no interest in any such post. Evelyn was 'in some passion on this account' and he seems to have convinced Pepys to take an interest in the family's distress. Mrs Turner is frequently mentioned in the Diary, and although Pepys thought her a gossip he seems to have been prepared to help in her husband's and son's careers as well as availing himself of her physical charms when it suited him. Either way, by 1680 and despite his own problems, he evidently felt able to do something for her.

135. SAMUEL PEPYS TO MRS TURNER OF DEPTFORD

York Buildings
24 March 1680

MADAM

I am extremely afflicted for that additional misfortune in your health which you this day tell me you lie under and to which I pray God give you an additional supply of patience. For what you desire of me in reference to Mr Turner, if the Duke make any stay in town, whereof I am yet ignorant (as being by a business extraordinary kept all this day to my chamber) I will not fail of seeking a speedy opportunity of accosting his Highness. If it be possible I may be able to do you and your family a just office in it, the hardship you suffer being such, as no man who knows your case can hear report of, without pity on your behalf, and reproach to the authors of it. In the meantime, I can assure you my Lord Brouncker is no less sensible of, and desirous of relieving you under it, than he who is

Your truly affectionate and faithful humble servant

S. P.

---

[17] PF C3.

A few days later Pepys wrote a very optimistic letter to his father, John Pepys senior. The nightmare was all but over. John Pepys had inherited a Brampton property from his brother Robert in 1661. When his wife Margaret, the diarist's mother, died in 1667 he moved in with his daughter Paulina (after 1668 Mrs John Jackson), living at Ellington and then at Brampton once more.

136. SAMUEL PEPYS TO JOHN PEPYS SENIOR

York Buildings
27 March 1680

SIR

It is long since I have expressed my duty to you, and truly every day has followed one another with some new occasion of care, so as that, though I have been in a great measure restored to the liberty of my person, my mind has continued still in thraldom, till now that it has pleased God, in a miraculous manner, to begin the work of my vindication by laying his hand upon James my butler, by a sickness whereof he is some days since dead, which led him to consider and repent of the wrongs he had done me in his accusing me in Parliament, which he has solemnly and publicly confessed upon the holy Sacrament, to the justifying of me and my family to all the world in that part of my accusation which relates to religion; and I question not but God Almighty will be no less just to me in what concerns the rest of my charge, which he knows to be no less false than this. In the meantime His Holy Name be praised for what he has done in this particular.

What I have to add is the letting you know that I am commanded to attend the King the next week at Newmarket, and, by the grace of God, will go and wait on you one day in my going or return, which I presume will be either Tuesday or Saturday next, I designing to set forth hence on Monday, and shall rather choose to call upon you in my going (which will be on Tuesday), for fear lest I should be commanded to accompany the court to London, where the King designs to be this day seven nights. In the meantime, trusting in God to find you in good health, and with my most humble duty presented to yourself, and my kind love to my brother and sister, and their family, I remain,

Sir, Your ever obedient son,

S. P.

À TRUE

NARRATIVE

OF THE

Horrid P L O T

AND

CONSPIRACY

OF THE

POPISH PARTY

Againſt the L I F E of

His Sacred Majeſty,

THE

GOVERNMENT,

AND THE

𝔓𝔯oteſtant Religion:

With a L I S T of ſuch N OBLEMEN, G ENTLEMEN,
and others, as were the C O N S P I R A T O R S :

And the H E A D - O F F I C E R S both Civil and
Military, that were to Effect it.

---

*Publiſhed by the Order of the Right Honourable the Lords Spiritual and
Temporal in* P A R L I A M E N T *Aſſembled.*

Humbly Preſented to His Moſt Excellent M A J E S T Y.

By *T I T V S O T E S*, D. D.

L O N D O N :
Printed for *Thomas Parkhurſt* , and *Thomas Cockerill* , at the Bible and Three
Crowns in *Cheapſide* near *Mercers Chappel,* and at the Three Legs
in the *Poultrey.* M DC LXXIX.

The Popish Plot. In this publication of 1679 Titus Oates laid out the damning evidence
concocted by Israel and Tonge and himself in 1678 for the existence of a Catholic
conspiracy to topple Charles II. The allegation that Pepys was involved created the greatest
crisis of his life.

5 Restored to Favour: 1680–9

THE YEAR 1680 was a turning point for Pepys. His brother-in-law John Jackson died in the late summer. His father died in the autumn and was buried on 4 October 1680. Pepys and Deane were released from bail at the end of February, but the prosecution stalled. Doubtless it had become known that Pepys had enough evidence to prove the allegations spurious. On 30 June 1680 the charges were dropped. He wrote to Mrs Skinner, probably Mary Skinner's mother, to announce the news.

137. SAMUEL PEPYS TO MRS [FRANCES?] SKINNER

1 July1680

MADAM

I would not omit giving you the knowledge of my having at last obtained what with as much reason I might have expected a year ago, I mean my full discharge from the bondage I have, from one villain's practice, so long lain under. However (as the world goes) justice ought to be welcome at any time, and so I receive it, with thanks to God Almighty, who might have respited this his goodness to me, till (as from all appearances I fear it) justice might have [been] yet less easy to come by. In which contemplation I cannot but own God's express indulgence to me in my deliverance, as late as it is; ascribing it not to my own innocence alone, but to the good wishes also of my friends, and in particular to those of your family and your own; which shall be ever answered with the best of mine, who am,

Madam, Your most faithful and humble servant,

S. P.

William Howe had been in the service of the Earl of Sandwich as a junior colleague of Pepys's. By 1680 he was a lawyer in Barbados, married to a god-daughter of Pepys's.[1] Pepys wrote to renew their friendship, asking Howe to help Mary Skinner's brother Daniel deal with some of their father's business affairs there.

138. SAMUEL PEPYS TO WILLIAM HOWE

To Mr Wm Howe at the Barbados

8 July 1680

SIR

'Tis long that I have been in arrears to you for your kind remembrances from the place where you now are. And the truth is, I am but just got clear from an encumbrance whereto public envy had exposed me, and which has (for a great while past) almost suppressed the remembrance of my friends, through the daily clamours of my enemies whose designs being levelled at the King my master they thought no surer aim could be taken at him than through his servants who stood nearest to him.

[1] Probably a Sarah Bartlet. She has not previously been identified. See pp. 261–2.

Among whom their malice having done me the honour of reckoning me one, they deemed me worthy to be first removed, though at the price of perjury. But God Almighty has, after being committed to the Tower, and lain more than a year under thirty thousand pounds' bail, been pleased to deliver me, and I am now restored to myself, with liberty of recollecting my obligations to my friends, and in particular to you, as well as my old friendship for you. Which because I would never have die, I take the opportunity of this young gentleman the bearer, son of a very honest and good friend of mine, a merchant of this city, to give you and your lady (my daughter) my humble services and blessings, to be divided, not between you two only, but among the lower members also of your family of which you have ere this (I hope) an ample number, and shall be glad (as you have opportunity) to be made certain of it; and of the continuance of your healths and good fortune. To which as none can be a better willer, so none shall be more ready to express it then myself, by anything within the power of

Your truly affectionate
and humble servant,
S. P.

This young man, Mr Skinner, comes to look after some occasions of his father in your island; in which, if by your advice you may be in anywise aidful to him, you will very much oblige me.

Dr John Turner, rector of Eynesbury, was an old friend of the Pepys family. Pepys had asked him to examine a Bible in his possession to see whether it contained texts by Sixtus V (1585–90) or Clement VIII (1592–1605). Sixtus V had produced a thoroughly corrupt version of the Vulgate Bible, which was withdrawn after his death because of the mistakes. Clement VIII produced a corrected version in 1592. Pepys's reply to Dr Turner's answer is an interesting insight into the perception of Catholics at the time, as well as also including news that his brother-in-law John Jackson was seriously ill. Jackson died soon afterwards. His sons Samuel and John junior became an important part of Pepys's plans for his estate.

139. SAMUEL PEPYS TO DR JOHN TURNER

London
3 September 1680

SIR

I am newly returned from a small journey to Essex, and find both your letters, of the 26th and 30th instant; of which, though the latter puts some stop to my present consideration of the former, yet I cannot nor ought to forbear the returning you my most faithful thanks for your extraordinary friendship, expressed upon the occasion of its contents. Which I must confess carry matters in it of very little satisfaction to me, unless it be that it would have been yet less satisfactory to have had my knowledge of it longer delayed. And since it has pleased God to put this sickness of my brother Jackson's in the way of my coming to any determination concerning it, I shall respite the offering you any new trouble on that subject till the event of that sickness appears; and at present only add my further thanks to you for the safe return of my Bible, wishing only that it had better answered your trouble of perusing it. Not but that, though its title at the beginning deceive us, the table at the end does make good that greater fallibility of the Popes, which we Protestants please ourselves with, from those different translations of Scripture exposed by Sixtus and Clement, with

the additional cheat of putting the title-page of one Pope to the text of the other. So, respectfully kissing your hands, I remain
Your obliged and most humble servant,
S. P.

The death of Pepys's father, and then the fatal illness of John Jackson senior, meant that Pepys had family business to attend to in Cambridgeshire in the autumn of 1680. Will Hewer wrote to Pepys to give news about developments in the final legal efforts to bring about an end to the Popish Plot with the trial of Catholic peers (Powys, Stafford, Arundel, Petre and Bellasis) arrested in 1678. He also had news of his own wife's sickness and that of Pepys's coachman.

140. WILL HEWER TO SAMUEL PEPYS

28 October 1680

HONOURED SIR
According to what I promised you by Tuesday post I did this day by the carrier send you Mr L'Estrange's case put in print which will at your leisure be very well worth the reading, with it I likewise sent you the votes of the house for yesterday; and enclosed you will receive a copy of what past this day, which is all the news discoursed of besides the confirmation of the accompt given about the success we had against the Moors at Tangier in regaining Pole fort and other places which the enemy were fortifying. There were very fine speeches made this day in the house by Sir H. Capel, Mr Harbord, and Mr Bennett, the first setting forth how all public offices of trust, especially in the Navy were filled with Papists, the other gentlemen seconded him, but after a little insisting upon that, and the present danger of the Plot, he did move that the house would presently fall upon the preparing themselves to bring the Lords to a trial, and setting a time within which all information relating to the Plot should be brought in, that so they may putt an end to the Plot, and get his Majesty's gracious and general pardon, which being not well relished by the house, the debate ceased, and Mr Bennett found them new work to discourse of which was more pleasing and agreeable to them. This is what is discoursed without doors.

Katherine is taken very ill and has kept her bed this two or three days, the coachman being not yet recovered though it is hoped he is some what better then he was. Sir Anthony Deane's business detains him yet in the country, though he longs to be in town, as I know you do, but business is not to be neglected, and if anything should happen that should make either of your company's necessary in town I shall not fail to advise you of it, in the meantime with presentation of my mother's and own humble service and respects to yourself and Madam Jackson, where I hope you have got safe thither though we have not heard of you as yet I remain
Your very faithful and most obedient servant
WM. HEWER

In this light-hearted letter to his friend James Houblon, Pepys pretends that his delay in returning to London has been occasioned by his failure to supply the Houblon household with gifts in return for what he owes for their support during his recent difficult times. The 'Patten in Southwark' could not be identified, but perhaps was a tavern or individual connected with the Pattenmakers' Company, chartered in 1670.

141. SAMUEL PEPYS TO JAMES HOUBLON

Brampton
14 November 1680

SIR

My last said I should be in town the beginning of this week; but (to tell you the truth) though there be no place (I thank God) where I dare not show my head, yet there is one where I am ashamed to show my face again till I have done something (that ought long since to have been done) for securing the remembrance of what I am owing there, though I can never hope to discharge it, and that is at a namesake's of yours in Winchester Street.

But don't mistake me, that his forgetfulness I am jealous of, and not my own; for it is no less possible for me, or just, to forget myself as him, without whom I am not sure I should, ere this, have been myself. But he, you must know, is one of so tender a memory, that there is no good deed of his own that will stick in it, for he shall do you twenty good offices before he will think them one; nay, and do them with more thanks than he will endure to take from him he does them to.

To supply which, I have bethought myself of fastening my picture (as a present) upon him, in hopes that, when he sees that, it will be out of his power not to recollect his errands on my score to Westminster Hall, his visit to the lions, his passings over the bridge to the Patten in Southwark, and a thousand other things which, by his goodwill, he would never come within the hearing of. Nay, in my conscience, if he knew this were the design of my present, he would turn his head a' one side every time he comes in sight on't.

And even, lest he should do so, I have been fain to think of an assistant device; and that is, to send a small bribe to every one of his family, to get them, in such a case, to be putting in some word or other as he passes by, to make him look upon it; as thus: – 'Was Mr Pepys in these clothes, father, when you used to go to the Tower to him ?' Or thus: – 'Lord, cousin, how hath this business of Scott altered my poor cousin Pepys since this was done!' Or thus: – 'What would I give for a plot, Jemmy, to get you laid by the heels, that I might see what this Mr Pepys would do for you'. With these helps, I don't doubt but it will do; at least so far as to stick an impression upon the young ones of what, in their father's right, (if he won't,) they may challenge from me as they shall grow big enough to make work for me, and find me become not too little to do them any.

I make it, therefore, my request, that by your hand these small mementos may be distributed to the end and use aforesaid. Upon notice whereof from Mr Hewer I shall appear in town again, and not sooner.

I am, dear Sir, Your most obliged
and most affectionate humble servant,
S. PEPYS

Will Hewer continued to take care of Pepys's affairs in London. In the two following letters Hewer updates Pepys on events in London, including Scotland's support for James's right of succession and the throwing out of the bill in the House of Commons intended to deprive him of that. Paulina Jackson seems to have become ill, further delaying Pepys's return, but Hewer has taken care of delivering Pepys's presents to the Houblons.

142. WILL HEWER TO SAMUEL PEPYS

For the honoured Samuel Pepys Esquire
At Brampton near Huntingdon

15 November 1680

SIR
By Saturday's post I wrote to you from Sir Anthony Deane's and being detained on business at that end of the town till it was to late to send to the post after I came home I could not send you the enclosed bill of fifty pounds which I paid here upon sight being tendered but upon Saturday last, and paid by Thomas in my absence, and not knowing what occasion you may have for the money before your leaving Brampton, I thought fit (rather then stay for the next post) to send David on purpose with it, hoping that he will be with you tomorrow morning.

I dined yesterday at my Lord Brouncker's, and supped at Mr Houblon from whom I had command to present you with all their services, and from the lady belonging to the former family I understand that the King has very lately received a letter from Scotland wherein the whole council, nobility, and gentry of that place returns the King their hearty thanks for the honour he has done them, in sparing his brother, and affording them his company; that they will with their lives and fortune stand by him and his brother in the maintaining of the just right of the succession.

Upon Friday last my Lord Mayor called a common-hall which ended in an address the city made to his Majesty carried up the said evening by the Mayor, wherein they numbly returned his Majesty their gracious thanks for the sitting of the Parliament and humbly prayed that they might sit, till the Plot was thoroughly found out, and the persons guilty brought to punishment. To which his Majesty contrary to everybody's expectation gave them this answer, that he did believe what they offered was out of a great deal of good will to him, but it being a matter not proper, nor in their sphere to meddle or concern themselves in, he did advise them to mind and look after the City concern, and not harken or follow the advice of those that wished neither well to him, nor them, if they did, they would find it would fall heavy on them.

On Saturday the speaker with the house attended his Majesty with an humble address as you will find by their votes, but his Majesty receiving it, without returning any answer thereto, makes us very melancholy for fear the Parliament may be prorogued, which at this time would generally be thought of very ill consequence to the public. Pray God direct and guide his Majesty and Parliament to the taking of such resolutions as may tend to the safety and preservation of our Government and the Protestant religion which has been, and is thought now to be in so great danger.

I hope your letter of this day will ascertain the day of your coming to town, and which way for Mr Houblon's family are very earnest to know, and against that time I am taking care to provide a mourning chariot for a month's time and shall meet you at Highgate with it, in regard it will be on many considerations (besides that of the respect you design to pay the deceased) fit for you to appear in here in town.

I shall not give you any further trouble now referring you to the printed narratives, which you will herewith receive from David, and tendering you the services and good wishes of all our family I remain

Your ever faithful and most obedient servant,

WM. HEWER

143. WILL HEWER TO SAMUEL PEPYS

16 November 1680

SIR

Since mine of yesterday morning by David, who I sent on purpose for the reasons therein expressed, I have received yours of the 14th with the enclosed for Mr Houblon, and have exactly complied with your commands in relation to the several presents designed to that family, and in the manner you directed it viz., by putting up the several things wrapped up in paper, and subscribed to each, in a box, leaving it with your own picture (carefully done up in a coarse cloth) early this morning at Mr Houblon's as from you, and two hours after I sent him your letter, and afterwards acquainted him myself upon the 'change with your determination touching your return to town, and whereas in my said letter I acquainted you that I did purpose to meet you at Highgate with a mourning chariot, I shall now endeavour to meet you at Barnet on Friday about 11 of the clock in the morning, but not with the mourning chariot in regard the ways are so bad.

I had not said anything before of the precise time of your return, to Mr Houblon, so as they were not at any trouble about it, and as to the regard you have, and which you so kindly mention in relation to myself, as I know nothing can make my life more uneasy to me, then your making any other place your home, while I have one, so I am sure, if it shall not be thought inconvenient for you (to which for your sake I shall always submit) your living with me, can't be any to me, assuring you whatever times shall come, nothing shall withhold me from making you and your concern, my own, while I live, and though the integrity and faithfulness wherewith his Majesty and the public have for so many years been served by us, may not at present protect and support us from malicious reports and calumnies of evil men, yet I am satisfied that God Almighty, who is always just, will make it up to us some other way to the shame of those who do now triumph over us, and I thank God, if I know my own heart, I am much more contented in my present condition, then I ever was in any.

I am heartily sorry to understand that your sister's ague continues so bad, being but an ill companion at this time of the year; and pray (upon the accompt of her illness) consider whether it may not be fit for you to leave Lorrain behind you for a little time with work for him to do, and though it may be some present inconvenience to you, yet in my opinion there may be that good use made of it, as may counterbalance it, but if not, you may have him up in two or three days in case you shall not find it necessary to return, he knowing nothing but that you do intend to be down again, there are many reasons which I shall satisfy you in about it, at our meeting, therefore you may so order it, as to leave him on your sister's illness and your intentions of returning, speedily.

Enclosed is a copy of the city's address to the King on Friday last, and of the Parliament's on Saturday of which I gave you a short accompt in mine by David who, I hope got well down to you with the Bill of Exchange of £50 I paid here for my Lady Bernard's use.

Yesterday the Bill against the Duke of York was carried up to the Lords by my Lord Russell and after several debates, (which held them till 11 of the clock at night) the Bill was cast out, there being 31 for and 63 against it, which has made many heavy hearts about it, and none but Almighty God knows what effects it will produce, this only I am informed of by Sir John Banks this morning that upon a motion made in the house by Sir John Hotham the Commons in great disorder adjourned till tomorrow morning without doing any business too day – pray God direct the King and them in their taking such resolutions as may tend as well to his honour and safety as the preservation of our religion and properties. Which is all the trouble I shall give you at present save the tenders of our most humble services and respects to yourself and sister remaining

Your most faithful and ever obedient servant

WM. HEWER

In 1680 Balthazar St Michel was sent out to Tangier to serve as muster-master and Surveyor of the Victualling. He had already postponed travelling out and even en route the complaining started. The whole experience gave vent to his volatile personality, which resulted in several letters that seem almost implausibly comic, were it not for the fact that the personality of Elizabeth Pepys, as described in the Diary, had so many similarities. This letter, garbled in places and apparently dictated from a sick bed, describes to Pepys the level of his misery, which he attributed to the corruption of the place and also a desire by Pepys's enemies to wreak revenge on him through Balthazar. When Pepys later sailed out to Tangier he made a far more detailed and professional report on the problems, rather than interpreting its defects as a personal insult as Balthazar characteristically did. Balthazar's real purpose was to tell Pepys about a post that had fallen vacant thanks to the death of a certain William Coleman, hoping he could be put up for the job. This does not appear to have happened and it would be another year before he came home, without leave.

144. BALTHAZAR ST MICHEL TO SAMUEL PEPYS

Gibraltar

21 April 1681

HONOURED SIR

Though my grievances, miseries, torments, and disencouragements hath been to such extremity, passing the expression of tongue, since my being in this part of the world, by not only my continual labour, and slavery occasioned by the severest injustice, cruelty and unkindness of fortunate fops; as in time will be manifestly made known by many here, as well as else where, besides great impositions wants, and miseries, endeavoured to be burthened on me, to my utter ruin all which to prevent, as well to my own I honour as friends, though I groan under: yet with the help of my God, I do not doubt but to labour through in despite of all malice.

Sir all these, with millions more of miseries, which I hourly suffer without rest or justice, as most commanders if they live to come home will acquaint you, is not comparable to the grief of spirit I have for your silence, and although they boldly dare tell me at this distance, and friendless helpless and moneyless, what were they Caesars they should not dare else where, that they only plague me thus, to be revenged of you; yet Sir though I have never for almost this twenty years past in his Majesty's service, which I have executed in all employments which by your favour I have been put upon, with uttermost diligence and honour eat my meat but with bitter-sauce, yet do I kiss that rod, and will still to my life's end obey, cherish, and love, my dear benefactor. Sir, it is not a quire of paper, can give you an exact state of my condition, nor the full height of the misery thereof. It may please only to suffice you that I say as the world and others will like wise join that if I stay longer here I shall be ten times worse ruined (if my life can bear the burthen out longer) then should I (as a castaway) have at home Newgate for the reward of my well serving my prince and honouring my friends, in all which that just God which I adore, I am sure will revenge my cause and those innocent ones which will by my ruin groan, and bring your dear Honour to a time to show ingrates their duties.

The chiefest occasion of my giving you trouble at this present, is to acquaint you that this day died in this road Captain William Coleman, late commander of his Majesty's ship the *James* galley, who during his life had besides that advantage of going abroad, by the Duke's only favour the place of Collector at Plymouth which being void by his death, if your goodness would be such as that immediately (this being the very first advice and no doubt but that speedy solicitations will follow) you would please to get from his Majesty, Duke or Lords of the Treasury, or whosoever's station else it is to grant it, that place for me it would not only (as formerly it was to Captain Coleman) be a part of a reward for my long and zealous service, but also a quiet and happy being in that cheap place for me and mine the remnant of my days, and God I hope will reward you for it, and I to the last of my blood acknowledge it. I have only to add, and repeat the praying you that not one minute's time may be deferred while if, by (as I said before) the speedy solicitations which will from all parts be made for the same, will baulk my hopes, and null your honour's endeavours but if one the contrary by your justice and kindness I may be so happy as to get it, you will have the prayers of all your humble little creatures that his divine Majesty give you in this world many happy days of prosperity, health, and welfare, and in that to come life eternal which is also the daily petitions to the Father of Heaven from Sir

Your honour's ever obedient and dutiful servant

B. St Michel

My most humble service to Mr Hewer's and family with the dearest love and blessing to mine.

B. St M

I being very sick in bed with the griefs and wants I suffer, in a strange place, without any credit, friendless and comfortless and reduced for the wants aforesaid to bread and water these six days past and sometimes (when I could have credit for it) a little raw milk till a friend of mine by chance, a captain of Tangier, namely Captain Trelaney happened to be here and lent me five pistoles and a Frenchman here five more, otherwise I might not have been in a condition to have given your honour any trouble at all; the reasons aforesaid and consequently my disability of writing hath occasioned my present making use of another hand

B. St M

I hope that dear Mr Hewer's kindness and friendship to me and the memory of yours and mine will not prevail with you or any others to my prejudice in favour of his uncle Blackborne but that with the same faithful assistance which I have ever received from him and his goodness he will rather join with you for my aid and with usual honour and kindness to me wards value true friendship and balance it equal with interest or blood which I most humbly pray you to beg of him on my behalf as I do from my very heart with humble request not doubting but that one day yet as I have more then any of his relations so shall I be in a condition some way, yet not known to make him sensible by some eminent service that he hath not befriended an ingrate.   B. M.

By the summer of 1681 Daniel Skinner, sent out to Barbados almost a year before, had reached Bridgetown where he was met by William Howe. Howe responded to Pepys's request to help Daniel Skinner in a letter that cannot have reached Pepys before well into 1682. Daniel Skinner had arrived safely but it seems the local contacts were not interested in any of the business propositions he brought with him from his father. Skinner therefore took the opportunity of passage to the island of Nevis to the northwest of Barbados.

45. WILLIAM HOWE TO SAMUEL PEPYS

For Samuel Pepys Esquire
at Mr William Hewer's house in York Buildings in the Strand

15 June 1681

HONOURED SIR

His excellency Sir Richard Dutton gave me the satisfaction of hearing of your welfare, with an intimation of your favours to me which makes me believe, if I should have any occasion to make use of him, that I should not want his friendship. Sir, the young gentleman Mr Skinner that was recommended to Mr Steed by his father, and by yourself to me; I met upon his arrival at the Bridgetown, and before my going out of town waited upon Mr Steed with him to know what acceptation Mr Skinner might have with him he being recommended] by his father to Mr Steed and for the solicitation of some interest that his father has here, which was formerly left to Mr Steed's care to manage. But finding him very unwilling to concern himself in it, or to countenance young Mr Skinner in any of his father's propositions; upon which I told Mr Steed that if he had no employment for him that I would take care of him; and in order to it I placed him with a friend of mine, an eminent practitioner of the law living in the Bridgetown upon liking; and that if he did not like his residence there, that he might be with me in the country; but because I would not have him live an idle life, and that he might be the better able to understand, and to solicit his father's business I thought it the best expedient; his father having sent no money to bear his own charges or to maintain a suit in law. Upon my coming to town a week after; (whether upon his own advice or Mr Steed's) I found he was gone to Nevis in a man-of-war that was bound from hence thither, and that Mr Steed had taken care with the captain for his passage; I am sure he could have no discouragement where he was, for he eat at the table with Mr Walley who married Sir John Yeaman's lady in this country and I directed him that if he liked not his residence he should give me an account of it; because I found him something soft in his disposition; I hear he is very well at Nevis and If I can do him any service either here, or where he is I shall for your sake do it. I was very glad to hear by Sir Richard Button that your charge was out of malice according to what you wrote me in your former; I hope we shall live to have the happiness to see you in England with our young offspring which is only a son and daughter alive thus with mine and my wife's humble duty to you and remain

Your affectionate humble servant
WILL. HOWE

Throughout 1681 and into 1682 feelings about the Popish Plot continued to run high. On 2 July 1681 Shaftesbury was sent to the Tower for high treason by attempting to force Charles II to accept the exclusion of the Duke of York from the succession, though the case against him foundered in the Old Bailey thanks to his supporters on the Grand Jury. On 14 August 1681 the Scottish parliament passed an act asserting that the right of succession to the throne of Scotland would not be affected by religion, and that no law could change the right to succeed through the bloodline. Titus Oates had lost his pension and was thrown out of Whitehall on 30 August. During this time Pepys considered withdrawing permanently from public life by retreating to Cambridge. He was encouraged to consider the position of Provost of King's College by his cousin Joseph Maryon, a fellow at Clare, since the incumbent, Sir Thomas Page, had just died. Maryon seems to have regarded the matter a highly urgent, and sent letters to London and Brampton.

146. JOSEPH MARYON TO SAMUEL PEPYS

To Samuel Pepys Esqr, at Mr Hewer's house
in York Buildings. Deliver with all possible speed

Cambridge
8 August 1681

HONOURED SIR

For fear my messenger to Brampton might not meet you there, I presume to acquaint you, that this night Sir Thomas Page died.

Hearing you say you would be content to live in a university, I thought it my duty to give you information of it – since your interest can command it. The preferment is seven hundred pounds per annum. You would, I am sure, be a man as acceptable as the King could present, not only to that college, but to the whole university. I humbly beg your pardon if I am too officious.

Sir, Your most humble servant
S. MARYON

The statutes require the person to be in deacon's orders, but the King can dispense with that.

Pepys replied, insisting his scholarly inadequacies made it impossible. Pepys had also discovered that his friend George Legge, agent to the Duke of York in London, had recommended his own former tutor (a Doctor Copplestone) for the position.

147. SAMUEL PEPYS TO JOSEPH MARYON

10 August 1681

SIR

I own, with infinite thanks, the kindness of yours of the 8th instant, and the trouble you gave yourself in your most obliging message to me at Brampton, from whence I have been a week returned. Your letter came to hand yesterday, in the evening of which another from you, on the same subject, was also communicated by my cousin Wynn Houblon, giving more instances of your friendship at once, and in one occasion, than would have sufficed another (though much more engaged to it than you have been, or, I fear, ever can be by me) for a whole life.

As to the matter proposed, I acknowledge it to be not only a most honourable one, but, to me in particular, (under the present inclination I have to retirement,) most agreeable; and I am apt to think my Royal Master, the King, wants not goodness more than enough, to bestow it on me, could I think myself as adequately fitted for that, as, in all its circumstances, it would suit with me. But, indeed, cousin

Maryon, I cannot be so self-partial as to pretend to it, there requiring a much greater stock of academic knowledge to the capacitating a man to fill this province, to which your too goodwill would advance me, than I am furnished with, or at this time of day, can with any industry ever hope to acquire.

Besides, however I might be induced (from a possibility of supplying, by some other way of usefulness to the College, what I should fall short of in knowledge) to embrace the proposition, in case I saw any other of no better or more rightful pretence than myself bidding for it, I cannot believe a foundation of that quality can be without a store of pretenders of its own breed, sufficient to put a just stop to the attempts of any foreigner. One of this kind, in particular, I have understood to be already proposed to the King by my worthy friend Mr Legge, *videlicet*, his tutor, whose name I don't at present remember; but he is said to be, both by education, standing, and learning, entitled beyond any competition, if merit have the determining, as God forbid but it should.

On which considerations I cannot persuade myself to interpose in this matter. Besides that, what I mentioned the other day, and you so kindly remember, concerning a disposition to retirement, I fear may not be so fully answered this way, as I intended in my mention of it; which was no less than a total seclusion from pomp and envy, as well as noise and care. This, I doubt, would give me no perfect exemption from either.

Take, therefore, in kind part, that I make no further use of your so extraordinary friendship, or rather fondness, on my behalf in this matter, than to wish myself worthy of it, and yet, that one more worthy may have it, and that one were you. And I will not doubt of living to see you possessed, though not of this, of something more worthy of you than what the University or Church have yet found for you. Nor, shall I enjoy my whole wish, if (in return for this your kindness to me) I find not myself some time or other in condition of being serviceable to you towards it.

I am, your obliged and most affectionate humble servant,

S. PEPYS

I am your debtor for your messenger to Brampton.

Pepys never made the move to a university, though ironically he is now forever linked with Cambridge. John Matthews was a schoolmaster and distant cousin of Pepys. He seems to have been charged with looking after the interests of Pepys's nephews, Samuel and John Jackson, after their father died in 1680 as well as other aspects of Pepys's business in and around Huntingdon. Within a year the boys were ragamuffins.

148. JOHN MATTHEWS TO SAMUEL PEPYS

These for the worshipful Samuel Pepys Esquire
at Mr Hewer's House in York Buildings near the Strand London

20 October 1681

SIR

That which puts me upon giving you the trouble of these lines is the great need which your kinsmen have of clothing, those which they wear being so bad, that I am almost ashamed they should be seen in them; wherefore I humbly entreat, that you would be pleased either to send them some, or give me your commands, and I will be both careful and frugal in providing for them: they are both (I bless God) in good health, continue good boys and observant of my commands, the youngest will infallibly make a scholar, the other (I question not) an honest well-tempered man; the utmost of my regards shall be toward them: you were pleased (when in the country) to speak of some single basses (which you had at London) proper for one voice, one or two of them obtained at your hands would add a greater weight to those many obligations which I already lie under, of being

Sir

Your devoted Servant

JOHN MATTHEWS

Your nephews present their duties.

My wife begs your acceptance of her humble service.

Receiving no reply, Matthews wrote again with more urgency on 6 November, this time eliciting a response from Pepys.

149. SAMUEL PEPYS TO JOHN MATTHEWS

12 November 1681

COUSIN MATTHEWS

I give you my very respectful thanks for yours of the 6th instant, and am no less sensible of your regards to, and care of my nephews, than glad of the characters you give them.

If it be indifferent to you to have your last quarter paid here, I will see it immediately done upon letting me know the hand I shall pay it to. But if not; I will find the first convenience I can for its being done in the country.

I take notice of your advice touching their wants of clothes, and am desirous of their being instantly supplied therewith. To which purpose, since you are contented to take the trouble of it, I shall entreat my cousin and you to consider what is necessary to be bought for them; not doubting your good management in the price thereof. Nor will you (I suppose) think it of any use to make them overfine (especially for winter) provided what you buy be such as will keep them warm and clean, and last well. The charge of which and of what other expenses you have been at for them, since my last waiting on you, I shall upon your sending me an account thereof, see instantly made good to you, my sister (though I thank God in a good state of recovery) not being yet fully in condition to take that care again upon herself.

I pay my cousin and you many thanks for your continued care of them, and the civilities I received myself from you both, when last in the country. I remember too my promise about some basses for a single voice. And will perform it some time the next week, by sending you a couple of short anthems to begin with which when you have you will from the proof of them, be better able to say what you would have the next to be, as to more or less difficult, whether English or Latin, serious or more gay: For I think I can accommodate you every way. Only the hand that ordinarily pricks for me, is not just now with me; and my own eyes being under some present indisposition will not suffer me to prick them myself now. But I doubt not of doing it the next week.

When I was last at Huntingdon I left (I doubt) a small thing unpaid for at Dr Fulwood's. As I remember it was an ounce of the Leaf of Asarum finely powdered. If it were so, pray do me the kindness to see it satisfied, and bespeak two ounces

nore of the same to be prepared for me, and sent up when done; putting it into your
>ther notes of disbursements which you shall have to send me. Which with the
enders of my very faithful respects to my cousin and yourself, and my kind loves to
ny nephews is all at present from
Your very humble servant
S. P.

Jn 11 March 1682 the Duke of York returned from his exile in Scotland. On 3 May he set
>ut on the frigate *Gloucester* at the head of a flotilla of vessels going to collect the Duchess
>f York. He urged Pepys to join him on the *Gloucester* and all Pepys's friends assumed he
lad accepted the invitation. On 5 May the *Gloucester* was wrecked on a sandbar called 'The
_emon and Oar' off the mouth of the Humber, thanks to a careless pilot.

The event nearly changed the course of history. Almost everyone on the *Gloucester* was
ost but thanks to the machinations of precedence, the Duke of York, his footman and his
log were saved. So also was John Churchill, later the Duke of Marlborough. It was taken
'or granted that Pepys had been lost too, so when news reached London that Pepys had
ictually sailed on one of the other vessels there was great relief.

Pepys's graphic description of the disaster makes it clear that thanks to the priority
>laced on saving the Duke of York, the opportunity to save other men was wasted. Although
Will Hewer accepted this as part of normal protocol, James Houblon was clearly far more
listurbed by it. The reference to Portugal Row means the street in which Pepys's special
friends and cousins by marriage, the sisters Lady Mordaunt and Mrs Steward, lived.

150. SAMUEL PEPYS TO WILL HEWER

Edinburgh
8 May 1682

MR HEWER

After having told you that the Duke is well, and then myself, I may safely take
notice to you of what will, I know, soon become the talk of the town, and be very
differently entertained by it. But be their constructions of it what the worse part of
them please, our solace must be that the Duke is well arrived here, though with a
greater loss in his train than we can yet make any just computation of, by reason of
the *Kitchin* yacht's not being yet coming; which of all the yachts had most
opportunity of saving men, as lying nearest and longest about the wreck of the
Gloucester, which struck upon the edge of the (Well, say some; Lemmon, say
others,) about five in the morning on Friday last, from an obstinate over-winning of
the pilot, in opposition to all the contrary opinions of Sir Jo. Berry, his master,
mates, Colonel Legge, the Duke himself, and several others, concurring
unanimously in our not being yet clear of the sands, and therefore advising for his
standing longer out to sea. The pilot is one Ayres, a man that has heretofore served
the Duke as pilot in the war, and in his voyage hither, and one greatly valued as such
by him. But this, however, is fallen out, and will, as it ought, be strictly inquired
into, the man being, as is said, saved, and (could it be regularly done) would be tried
and hanged here, for the nearer satisfaction of those great families of this kingdom,
who, it is feared, would be found the greatest sufferers in this calamity; and among
others my Lord Roxburgh (one of the flowers of this nobility) not yet heard of, nor
Mr Hyde my Lord Hyde's brother, and lieutenant of the ship; though Sir John Berry
is, and is very well spoken of by his Royal Highness, for his comportment in this
business, though unfortunate.

I told you, in a line by Mr Froud, that though I had abundant invitation to have gone on board the Duke, I chose rather, for room sake and accommodation, to keep to my yacht, where I had nobody but Sir Christopher Musgrave and our servants with me; the Master of the Ordnance being obliged, by his indispensable attendance on his Highness, to leave us.

Our fortune was, and the rest of the yachts, to be near the *Gloucester* when she strook; between which and her final sinking there passed not, I believe, a full hour the Duke and all about him being in bed, and, to show his security, the pilot himself till waking by her knocks.

The Duke himself, by the single care of Colonel Legge, was first sent off in a boat, with none but Mr Churchill in her, to prevent his being oppressed with men labouring their escapes; for two or three, however, did fling themselves after him into her, and my Lord President of Scotland by the Duke's advice endeavoured it but falling short, was taken up out of the water by him.

Mr Legge, then, looking after his own safety, got into a boat, and was received on board us with Captain Macdonell, Mr Fortry, one of the Duke's Bedchamber, and some poor men unknown. We also had the good fortune to take up Sir Charles Scarborough almost dead, and others spent with struggling in the water and cold; but were prevented in our doing so much good as we would, by our own boat's being easily sunk by our side, and her men with much difficulty saved.

Had this fallen out but two hours sooner in the morning, or the yachts at the usual distance they had all the time before been, the Duke himself and every soul had perished. Nor ought I to be less sensible of God's immediate mercy to myself, in directing me (contrary to my purpose at my first coming out, and the Duke's kind welcome to me when on board him in the river) to keep to the yacht. For many will I doubt, be found lost as well or better qualified for saving themselves by swimming and otherwise, than I might have been.

Captain Wyborne, in the *Happy Return*, was the only frigate near us, and she indeed in no less danger than the *Gloucester*; but taking quick notice of the other's mishaps, dropped presently her anchor, and is this morning with the *Kitchin* yachts come safe in harbour, and by her we now know that very many are lost; I judge about 200 men. But particulars are not yet fully known; only my Lord Roxburgh and Lord Hopton are certainly gone, and our young English Lord O'Brien.

The haste the express is going away in will not allow me to write to my Lord Brouncker now; but pray give him my most humble services, and communicate this to his Lordship, and the like to Crutched Friars, Winchester Street, and Portugal Row, as soon as you conveniently can, to remove any causeless care concerning me, giving my Lord Brouncker a hint at my thinking it very expedient in itself and regardful in him towards the Duke, that some enquiry be made into the care the Navy Office will be found to have used in providing for his safety and ship, with respect to the appointment of good and a sufficient number of pilots on this occasion; for I hear something muttered here about it, and it will not, I doubt, be judged enough for them to leave it to the Duke to take whom he pleased, or might possibly be otherwise advised to, without interposing some immediate care of their own in it, as I am sure was heretofore done in my time upon his going to sea. I do privately think it will be very well received by his Highness to hear of his Lordship's interesting himself of his own accord in this enquiry.

The Duchess is very well, and (saving the abatement given her in it by this disaster) under much joy from the Duke's kindness, and the errand he comes upon of fetching her home.

So, with my service to Clapham and everywhere else, I wish your family and self continuance of health, and am ever,

Most affectionately yours,

S. P.

151. WILL HEWER TO SAMUEL PEPYS

York Buildings
13 May 1682

HONOURED SIR

The welcomest news I ever received in my life was what you were pleased to honour me with by yours of the 8th inst. from Edinburgh, after the late misfortune to the *Gloucester*, concerning which we had some imperfect account on Wednesday morning about 11 of the clock, it coming from my Lord Canaway at Windsor to Sir Lyonell Jenkins's Office at Whitehall, where I was then waiting at the Treasury Chambers, and was not a little surprised at the report, which in less then an hour's time ran through the whole city, and was variously discoursed of, as people were affected and inclined, some would have it, that the Duke and all were lost, others that all were saved, and the ship only lost, but all generally concluded it to be a very unfortunate and unkind disaster, but the thoughts of the Duke's safety and our friends does very much ease our minds, and give us great satisfaction.

You can't imagine in what consternation all your friends in general were upon the report of your being cast away, but more especially those at Crutched Friars, Winchester Street, and Portugal Row, to whom I communicated your letter, which was matter of no small joy and satisfaction to them, they all join with me in returning God Almighty thanks for his great mercy in directing you in your passage as he did.

My Lord Brouncker, to whom I communicated your letter and command, was not a little glad to hear of your safety, returning you very kind thanks for your hints, which he will make use of.

The Commission omitted to be given Sir John Berry for holding a court-martial at his going out, is sent last night express, as I am informed.

They have been so disordered in Winchester Street, that I am commanded to tell you, they shall not be themselves till they see you, and the enclosed from Portugal Row will let you know how they do, all your friends in general giving you their very humble service, and heartily wish your safe return.

One accident has happened here the last week near in town to be lamented, viz. our friend Colonel Scott's being fled for killing a coachman, the coroner having found it wilful murder; means are using to buy off the widow who has three small children, but we are considering what to do to prevent it; Sir Anthony Deane being come to town.

The Officers of the Navy were directed by the Admiralty to go down this day to Chatham to make some further enquiries concerning the business of the wet dock, that matter being not yet adjusted, my Lord Finch having been very severe on Sir Phineas Pett, who bears up, and thinks nothing has been yet said to the prejudice of the reasons he gave against it.

Sir John Banks took very kindly my waiting on him with the account you gave, he having not met with any, that was so particular, and being to dine with my Lord Chancellor today, where Mr Seymour was to be, he did very much press me to give him an extract of your letter relating to the loss of the *Gloucester*, and the circumstances thereof, which I did do, leaving out all that related to yourself, and the hints to my Lord Brouncker.

Pray present my very humble service to Mr Legge, whose great prudence and regard towards the Duke's safety is very much spoken of to his great Honour by all that wish well to the Duke. I shall not offer at the giving you any further trouble at present, hoping my letter under cover to my Lady Peterborough met you at Edinburgh, but with all due respects and service remain

Your ever faithful and most obedient servant,

WM. HEWER

152. JAMES HOUBLON TO SAMUEL PEPYS

London

13 May 1682

SIR

Mr Hewer's bringing with him last night your letter of the 8th from Edinburgh was the most welcome alive to all your friends in my family for before that as you were numbered among the dead by almost all the city except myself and some others, so no arguments could work upon my women and girls to believe otherwise and though I assured them from Sir J Narbrough, Sir R Haddock, Mr Pett and others that you embarked in the *Katherine* Yacht, they had no faith and would have you with the Duke, for they were sure you loved him so well you could not be from him. You see and are like to be told so when you come home what your *Iter Boreale* hath cost us and what it is to leave us on that sudden as you did without either asking or for all that I know having our prayers, we were all so angry at your going.

You intend I hope to continue your resolutions to come home by land, which is much desired. For I think by this time you are convinced that a Scotch voyage with a ship especially of a great draught of water is more dangerous then to go to the Indies.

But now to come to the unfortunate wretches that have perished certainly it makes a great cry amongst the families in Scotland that have lost their relations as it doth here, and the circumstance of their loss is more aggravating then can be imagined, to be lost in broad daylight summer, and fair weather and with so much help about them is intolerable. Some think the Duke's heat and courage to save the ship, made him stay too long aboard and overlook the thoughts of saving the men who knew their desperate condition but would not (in good manners to him) provide for their safety while he stayed with them. Some lament the misfortune of princes in being prevented generally to make use of their own judgment in the choice of their officers but have them put upon them by the importunity and solicitation of others and they think this pilot one of that sort, though others think the contrary. But sure he was ignorant that did not know where he was when he had sailed so few leagues, but he is generally accused of being an obstinate man wilful and that is impatient of advice, then which qualities in a pilot there cannot be worse, God forgive him. But I cannot, that he should not have had either a yacht or a smaller ship ahead, sounding to know the certain depths while they were past those wretched sands for without the lead [weight] they could not well know they were so as neither seeing the land nor any beach, and again I cannot forgive the captains of the yachts and other ships that they should not be near at hand being broad day[light] and fair weather and knowing that they were not clear of the sands. But God would have it so and he leave off censuring and judging excuse it upon the score of my pity for so many brave men to perish in a moment.

I pray God fit us all and give us grace to fit ourselves for our last hours. I am sorry your land journey will not be pleasant to you for with all this wet the roads must needs be bad and after your journeys you cannot have evening walks for, in these parts we have not a dry place to set our feet on, so you have need of our prayers for your homeward journey which you shall be sure of. You will favour me with a line how you proceed and what are your stages and which the last night's lodging that if I can get leave of my cold and perpetual coughing I may come and meet you there or at your last dinner

I am Sir Your humble and obedient servant &c.

JAMES HOUBLON

You have services and Good wishes from everybody here.

As he made his way home Pepys found himself appalled by the behaviour of the Scots, despite the beauty of Glasgow. The reference to the 'business of the Rocker' concerned a possible position for Pepys's sister-in-law, Esther St Michel, and had been suggested by Will Hewer in a letter to Pepys of 4 May.[2]

153. SAMUEL PEPYS TO WILL HEWER

Berwick

19 May 1682

MR HEWER

I mightily thank you for yours of the 6th under my Lady Peterborough's cover. By which it appearing you had received mine of the 4th, your care would be over as to my particular safety, (under the misfortune of the *Gloucester*,) I having herein told you of my purpose to reside on board the *Catherine* yacht. Nevertheless, I failed not, by the very first express the Duke sent upon his arrival at Edinburgh, to tell it you more largely. And this also I sent also under Mr Froud's cover, hoping its coming to your hand for your fuller satisfaction, both as to myself and other matters.

Since then (the Duke being almost wholly taken up in settling public affairs before his leaving the kingdom) Mr Legge and I made the most of our time in visiting what was most considerable within reach there, and particularly Stirling, Lithgow, Hamilton, and Glasgow, which last is indeed a very extraordinary town for beauty and trade, much superior to anything to be seen in Scotland. But the truth is, there is so universal a rooted nastiness hangs about the person of every Scot, (man and woman,) that renders the finest show they can make, nauseous, even among those of the first quality.

'Tis nevertheless a thing very considerable the authority the Duke maintains with so much absoluteness, and yet gentleness here, to the rendering it morally impossible for any disquiet to arise in his Majesty's affairs in this kingdom. And truly, as their government seems to be founded upon some principles much more steady than those of ours, so their method of managing it in council (his Royal

Highness having been pleased to give me opportunity of being personally present at it with him two Council-days,) appears no less to exceed ours in the order, gravity and unanimity of their debates.

I mentioned the business of the Rocker to my Lady Peterborough, who was very ready to give me her advice and assistance, when there shall be opportunity for it Which she could not make any judgment till she comes to London, and sees how the old ones are disposed of. But she tells me, what is to be done must be by the hand of my Lady Hyde, and that she doubts some money it will cost, and not much; but, a her coming to town, she will be able to inform me more particularly, promising me her assistance in all she could towards it, if she found room for any; I not telling her who I designed the inquiry for.

Pray give Sir Anthony Deane my most humble service, and my poor lady, whose pain under the disorders of her family through sickness I do much condole, praying God to shorten it by a return of health. Let Sir Anthony Deane know that I lately took an opportunity to acquaint the Duke fully (Mr Legge being present) with his controversy with the Commissioners of the Admiralty who was infinitely pleased with the shameful and ridiculous proceedings of those Commissioners, and the advantage Sir A. Deane has taken of it, and will necessarily receive from it. Mr Legge also is no less gratified, not only from the mean esteem he has of them, but real value and consideration he expresses for him.

He gives you also his kind service, and, (though in the main, I find him a favourer of a wet-dock), yet is he convinced abundantly of the ignorance of those gentlemen both in relation to that and everything else, and particularly the points you mention in your letter, which I communicated to him.

I thank you for the news about the death of that insolent and mutinous lawyer [William] J[ones]. The Duke showed me a copy of Harbord's articles with Algiers But I cannot for my part imagine what the King will do with that about leaving our captives unredeemable.

Pray give my service and wishes of health to your mother, and all with her. The like for the ladies in Portugal Row, and Mr Houblon and his family.

I long to be at Newcastle, in hopes of meeting with some notice from you there of all your healths, I having desired it in my last, as I hope I shall afterwards at Scarborough and Hull, at each of which, Mr Legge's business will successively oblige him to call, and spend two days, as he has now done first here; from whence we shall sail this night or tomorrow morning; so as, (touching in our way at Holy Island to visit the castle,) to be at Newcastle on Sunday or Monday. According to which, the best calculation I can yet make of absence from you is fourteen days from hence; when, I trust, I shall see you in health, which God grant, and so Adieu.

Yours most affectionately

S. PEPYS

Pray give my Lord Brouncker and Lady Williams my most humble services, I having done it more largely to him by you in my last.

Having been less than impressed by the Scots, Pepys found on the journey home that he was equally unimpressed by how the Bishop of Durham, Nathaniel Crewe, lived, but for different reasons.

154. SAMUEL PEPYS TO WILL HEWER

Newcastle
26 May 1682

MR HEWER

Having by a former letter from Berwick owned and thanked you for yours by my Lady Peterborough, this comes to do the like for another of [the] 13th instant, which met at my arrival here three days since, and was most welcome to me, as bringing me both the satisfaction of understanding your healths, and the kind resentments you had upon the notice of mine. For which, after what is first due to God Almighty, I give all our friends, and particularly yourself, my most affectionate thanks.

Since my coming hither Mr Legge and I have made a step to Durham, where the Bishop seems to live more like a prince of this than a preacher of the other world, and shall today set out for Scarborough, where if I find none from you, pray let me meet a line or two at Hull, which is the last port we are to touch at in our way home; where I hope we shall in ten days have a safe meeting.

I am infinitely bound to my friend[s] in Portugal Row and Winchester Street for their thoughts of me, and the favour of their letters, which I will acknowledge to them myself from Scarborough, where we shall (God permitting it) be tomorrow. Sir Ralph Delavall's just now coming in and forcing us away to a seat of his some few miles from this place, where he will have us eat with him before we sail, interrupting me in my letter to them this post. Pray tell them therefore in the meantime (to stay their kind stomachs) that I thank them, love them, long to see them, and (having thus escaped [. . .]) will not now despair of living to serve them.

And this leads me to the tidings you give me of our friend Scott, whom God is pleased to take out of our hands into his own for justice; for should he prevail with the widow for her forgiveness (which yet, in some respects, I could wish might be prevented) there is the King's pardon behind, which I suppose he will not easily compass, unless by some confessions, which I am confident he is able to make, relating to the state as well as us, that might well enough atone for this his last villainy; nor do I doubt but, to save his own life, he will forget his trade, and tell truth, though to the hazard of the best trends he has; which pray let Sir Anthony Deane think of, and of putting in a caveat against his getting any pardon from court, if he should attempt it, till we are first heard; which, upon advising, I believe he and you will find the thing regular enough for us to do.

We daily long to hear of the Duke's arrival in the River.

Mr Legge gives you his service, which pray distribute among all our friends, and to yourself my most serious wishes of health and all that's good. Adieu.

Yours most affectionately
S. P.

The appeals to Pepys to wield his influence continued to come from friends and family alike. Although there had once been a breach between Pepys and Mary Skinner's parents, Daniel senior and Frances Skinner, that was long in the past. It seems that Mary's brother Peter had been purchased a maritime apprenticeship for £100, a considerable sum equivalent to at least £7000–10,000 today. Unfortunately, there had been little in the way of any training. Sir Thomas Grantham was a well-known naval commander of the day, but it appears he was planning to work the apprentices as 'common seamen'.

155. MRS FRANCES SKINNER TO SAMUEL PEPYS

25 April 168⁣3

HONOURED SIR

Let me earnestly entreat you to do me the favour and kindness as to speak to som⁣e persons of quality, to speak to Sir Thomas Grantham in my son's behalf. Mr Skinne⁣r five months ago bound his son to him and gave a hundred pounds with him. H⁣e promised Mr Skinner that he would be gone out by the 10th of March, he is not gon⁣e out yet and it is not known when he will go out, he has taken five apprentices mor⁣e beside my son, which if he had acquainted my husband there with he had never pu⁣t his son with him. We hear he intends to put them all as common seamen before th⁣e mast. We could have made a common seaman of him without given a hundre⁣d pounds. They are all ordinary men's sons that he has taken (except mine). I than⁣k God he is given to no ill vice nor never was. But had a great mind to go to sea. H⁣e writes and understands arithmetic very well. He has been these two months with Si⁣r Thomas Grantham and he has given him no business to do. My husband's intentio⁣n was that he should learn him the art of navigation and keep him to writing an⁣d differing in all his business, and that he might have a convenient cabin by himself t⁣o sleep and write in, and not be exposed to run up the mast and furl sail as a commo⁣n seaman. Good Sir do not fail me, but do it with a strong recommendation. I shoul⁣d be very glad to see you at my house

Sir, your servant

FRANCES SKINNER

Pepys evidently interceded on the young man's behalf. A letter of thanks from Peter Skinne⁣r was sent on about 29 November 1686 (Letter no. 168).

Tangier was a massive drain on England's resources by the 1680s. A substantial garriso⁣n was stationed there, and a huge amount of money had been poured into building a mole i⁣n the harbour. By 1683 it had been decided to destroy the mole and the fortifications, and pul⁣l out the population. Pepys was given two days' notice in August 1683, to take part in a⁣n expedition led by George Legge, now Lord Dartmouth, the purpose of which, for th⁣e moment, remained a secret even to him. He reached Tangier a little over five weeks later o⁣n 14 September 1683.

156. SAMUEL PEPYS TO JOHN EVELYN

Portsmouth

7 August 1683

SIR

Your kind summons of the 2nd instant has overtaken me here, where it cannot b⁣e more surprising to you to find me, than it is to me to find myself; the King'⁣s command (without any account of the reason of it) requiring my repair hither at les⁣s then eight and forty hours warning. Not but that I now, not only know, but am wel⁣l pleased with the errand; it being to accompany my Lord of Dartmouth (an⁣d therewith to have some service assigned me for his Majesty) in his presen⁣t expedition, with a very fair squadron of ships to Tangier.

What our work nevertheless is, I am not solicitous to learn, not forward to mak⁣e guesses at, it being handled by our masters as a secret. This only I am sure of, tha⁣t over and above the satisfaction of being thought fit for some use or other ('tis n⁣o matter what,) I shall go in a good ship, with a good fleet under a very worthy leader, in a conversation as delightful as companions of the first form in Divinity, Law, physic, and the usefullest parts of mathematics can render it, namely, Dr Ken, Dr Trumbull, Dr Lawrence, and Mr Sheeres; with additional pleasure of concerts (much above the ordinary) of voices, flutes, and violins; and to fillings (if anything can do't where Mr Evelyn is wanting) good humour, good cheer, good books, the company of my nearest friend Mr Hewer, and a reasonable prospect of being home again in less than two months. But, after all, Mr Evelyn is not here, who alone would have been all this, and without whom all this would be much less then it is, were it not that leaving him behind, I have something in reserve (and safe) to return to, wherewith to make-up whatever my best enquiries and gatherings from abroad, without his guidance shall, (as I am sure they must) prove defective in. With which, committing myself to your good wishes, as I do you and your excellent family to God Almighty's protection, I rest, Dear Sir,

Your most faithful and most obedient servant,

S. PEPYS

157. JAMES HOUBLON TO SAMUEL PEPYS

To the Honourable Samuel Pepys, Esq.
aboard the Grafton, *Portsmouth.*

London
11 August 1683

SIR

I fear this will find you at Portsmouth the winds, though calm today yet are contrary, But men-of-war with sloping tides will get to windward, I say, I fear you are still there for being this voyage is to be made, the sooner you go the sooner and safer will your return be. I hope the excellent company you have being all of them masters of Arts and Sciences, with the additional diversion of music of all sorts will divert your melancholy thoughts of leaving old England and some of your friends, those of this family are not a little proud that you should out of your great kindness to them form to yourself superstitious omens from your being forced to omit biding them Adieu in those forms your great civilities would have obliged you to have used upon this occasion. I beseech you: draw no uneasy thoughtfulness from hence for we will help you to drive away this thinking faculty about the success of the voyage by our most ardent prayers and wishes for your safe return and to confirms your faith in this point I am sure you'll believe these devotions of the major part of my tribe to be innocent and zealous and all of them sincere.

I am now with them all at the forest where we wished for your company and drank to your good voyage and communicating to them the kind expressions of your letter (for which and your great affection to us I remain infinitely obliged to you). They quickly showed by their grave looks how sensible they were of the truth and sincerity of your affection towards them and which you have so often made good to them by real obligations.

The letter I sent you for Mr Gough will not I believe deserve the tenth part of the thanks you bestow upon me for't, if you chance to call at Lisbon and it may for all that I know do the King service that you do so, here's a letter for my friend Mr Bulteel whom I am sure will count himself a very happy man to possess such a dear friend of mine at his house. You'll find that he knows you very well when he will tell you what he hath heard Mr Tho. Hill his partner say of you, you will also be extremely pleased to hear him give you an accompt of his friendship for him which certainly was most sincere. I doubt not but he will serve you to the utmost of his power during your stay there as will any of our masters if they are then in that port.

I am streitned for time being late that I cannot entertain you farther as I would with news we have this evening by our French and Dutch posts is that Vienna defends itself very well and mighty succours from Poland and other princes are drawing towards its relief. We hear the Queen of Portugal is dangerously sick that a great number of Jews are clapped up in the inquisition so possible you may see how these holy inquisitors propagate the Gospel by carbonading of Jews.

You have, Sir, the continuance of my prayers I embrace you and pray the great God to direct you and to be conservator of your health and happiness and am,

Sir,

Your most humble and obedient servant,

JAMES HOUBLON

Sir, let me have one line more from you per Monday's post.

158. SAMUEL PEPYS TO JAMES HOUBLON

St Helen's

16 August 1683

SIR

I write this with an expectation that it will be my last from this or any other port of our own coast: the weather, after a season of very bad, being this morning become very fair and favourable, so as we hope to put to sea the next tide. I expect, therefore, that my next will salute you from a greater distance, in order to my sooner doing it at a nearer; which, nevertheless, by this loss of time, I cannot now think will be sooner than October or November, the time you so kindly wished for me, in regard of the Michaelmas flaws, which will then, I hope, be over.

I owned, by the last post, my receipt of yours of the 11th, but so imperfectly, for want of time, that to supply it I cannot but mention it again, as bringing such a cargo with it of kindnesses of all sorts, sizes, and prices, and this to a market so overstocked already with commodities of the very self-same kind and mark, that, I vow, I should think it would turn you most to account that I sent you them in specie back again, were it not that being of a quality never subject to perishing, I will adventure to keep them by me, in hopes that one day or other I may be able to find you some return for them that may at least make you a saver, for a profitable servant I despair of ever being to you.

Tell your little congregation in the Forest that I value their prayers more than I would those of a whole convocation of mercenary priests, or that wretched choir of repining nuns their mother and I visited at Gravelines. Therefore, pray encourage them to pray on, that from the effects of their good wishes for me they may know what rate to put upon them hereafter, when they shall come to the bestowing them on others whose names are yet unknown.

Let the gentlewoman of the house know that I would not for the world divert one thought of her from her painters and joiners, because I would not stand chargeable with the want of one nail's driving at my coming back. Only, if (while she's too busy to do 't for me) God Almighty shall give ear to my praying for her, she may depend upon all that the blessings a friendship so obliged as mine is can prompt me to ask for on her behalf, or her good-nature, if at leisure, would lead her to for me.

As for yourself, because I can say nothing that can in any degree answer either your own general goodness, and the infinite instances you have given of particular applications of it to me, or my just and inexpressible estimations of both, I must leave it to Him who is only privy to all, to show you, by the continued affluence of his blessings upon you and yours, that good deeds, how unable soever they were that had the benefit of them, never wanted retribution.

Should it be my good fortune (which nothing yet appears to promise me) to see Lisbon, I know not which will have the ascendant over me, – the present good favours of Mr Houblon, or the memory of my past interest in Tom Hill, or those good stars which I am indebted to for both. But this I am sure of, namely, that you have given me a recommendation to Mr Bulteel that will secure me in the credit and benefit of all three.

And now for my present business and the work I am going upon. Though I must not deny to you that, since my last, I am let into the knowledge of the service his Majesty is pleased to reserve for my execution, and shall, by the grace of God, give the same, and possibly more, obedience, both passive and active, to it, than I might have done had my mean advice been pre-consulted in it; yet do I remain under no more liberty than before of communicating it, and therefore rest confident of your excuse in my not opening it to you. This only I think myself obliged for your ease to repeat to you, that I neither know nor think anything designed in it that may give any disquiet to the Spaniards, or interrupt the peace and security of our merchants with them.

Which having said, I must leave you to time for the knowledge of more; and, with my most zealous prayers to Heaven that all the good ejaculations of you and yours towards me may, in their effects, concentre upon themselves and you, whatsoever my fate in this uncertain enterprise may be, I remain,

Dear Mr Houblon,
Your most obliged, affectionate and
faithful servant,
S. PEPYS

Before the fleet left Plymouth, and the correspondence with James Houblon and others continued, there was one more remarkable chapter in the saga of Pepys, the Popish Plot and Colonel Scott. A letter reached Pepys on 22 August 1683 from a contact called John Gelson in Skeen, Norway. Pepys copied the letter with its revelations, had it endorsed by witnesses and sent it ashore to be filed for future reference on his return. Although dated earlier than Pepys's letter to James Houblon (above), in view of the time it took to reach Pepys it has been placed here in the sequence.

159. JOHN GELSON TO SAMUEL PEPYS

Skeen
12 July 1683

SIR

I cannot think of the civilities I received from you at Newcastle without a great sense of my obligation, and am very glad of any occasion to express my gratitude as well as duty, and do therefore give you the trouble of an adventure I met with.

The other day at Christiania I saw the infamous Colonel Scott who I believe was not well pleased to see me, because that he might be conscious that I knew him to be otherwise than he had insinuated in these parts, an opinion among the most eminent, and falling upon him with a great deal of freedom about the villainous practices that has of late years been in our nation, he as freely acknowledge himself a tool much used, as well as a cabinet councillor about the business, and told me many things about the same.

The one that hope to be your successor in the Secretary's employment put him upon contriving your destruction, and that what he did was merely upon that account, and that they designed to take away your life, but that the said person found he was not like to succeed in case they had proceeded.

That their design was to destroy the government and make themselves kings, or rather tyrants, and for that end did all they could to bring an odium and hatred upon his Majesty and family, and by their fictions to delude a giddy and unthinking people.

That their party was of three sorts. Those that wanted offices and were disappointed, those that were enemies to the government of church and state, and tools that the other two brought over to be of their side.

He told me many particulars of their cabals and debates.

That Oates did acknowledge to him he swore that the King was to be killed merely to get a party of such that were dear lovers of the King, and to make the Papists more odious that they might the better serve their ends by them, and in a fit tine would have brought in his Majesty to have given Commissions for the destroying his Protestant subjects.

That they set up the Duke of Monmouth for no other end than the dividing his Majesty's friends.

That the Protestant cause was used only to make a party of the zealously blind.

That they struck the government through the side of the Romanists. That they had no other way to destroy or wound it.

That my Lord Shaftesbury promised great settlement to him to make parties in the West and elsewhere, and that he had spent much time, speeches etc. for that purpose.

That the said Ld S. did appoint him to order and manage the Irish witnesses etc.

That he particularly knows those that were the principal actors in the brave Protestant cause (as they called it), the authors and spreaders of the infamous treasonable libels, particularly the History of the Black Box, and many other discourses which possibly might be thought troublesome, which I the rather waive with other matters at this time, because I hope in September to wait upon you in London. In the meantime, if to make any particular enquiry of him be desired, upon the least notice I will endeavour my utmost to procure a satisfaction.

Mr Margerum, an Ipswich Master of a ship, hath engaged to give this into your own hand, and saith he is suddenly to return into these parts, and if he comes not into this place will carefully send anything to me, and by an express if desired. If you please to honour me with a line, please to direct for me at Mr Cornishe's in Skeen, being

Sir, Your most humble and faithful servant
JOHN GELSON

160. SAMUEL PEPYS TO JAMES HOUBLON

Tangier

14 October 1683[3]

DEAR SIR

I little thought to have spoken to you at this distance, but so it is, and must be submitted to, however unpleasant.

My last was of the 17th of September, from before this place. The same day we landed, though without a formal publication of our errand till yesterday; when, in a full assembly, my Lord Dartmouth first communicated the contents of his commission from the King, for withdrawing all his forces and subjects from this place, rendering it desolate. Which proving, (as it hath long been apprehended,) the real purpose of all this secret, and fleet, you will not wonder that, even by the King, it was made a secret to me, when he required my service in accompanying Lord Dartmouth; for nobody can imagine I should at this time of day knowingly re-embark in an affair so public, of so hazardous success, so remote from all the little, to a knowledge of which I dare pretend, and so subject to common censure as this will necessarily be. Not but that, as far as I may say it, without taking on me the advocateship of a matter I was not called upon for adviser, much less in a business resolved on by my Prince, I shall take upon me to say that the reasons my Lord Dartmouth hath offered as the grounds of these his Majesty's resolutions, are such, as make it much less easy to justify those councils that led the King to the first acceptance of, and subsequent expenses on this place, than those by which he is now determined to put an end to them.

The particulars I shall take another time to open, and some considerations of my own, (in addition to all my Lord hath used,) which are much fitter for discourse than paper. This only I shall at present add, (for I yet take no pleasure in this subject,) that greater prudence, justice, and diligence I never yet observed in any management, than is daily shown by my Lord Dartmouth on this occasion; nor greater danger at the same time run, of being misunderstood by the multitude, than he is subjected to therein. The difficulties he hath to contend with, from the vigilance of a Moorish army at our gates, straitness of provisions, and other wants within, sufficient to disorder any man of less presence of mind. But, as I hope he will surmount them, so I foresee I shall be able to give you in a few days (by an express we shall be sending for England) a tolerable view of my expectations of the event of this service, and the time wherein it will show itself. In the mean while, I have the present satisfaction of being able to tell you that the part which (besides the general service which by the King's command my Lord of Dartmouth do sometimes call for from me in my advice) is particularly reserved for me herein, in conjunction with a worthy sober gentleman, Dr Trumbull, is the inquiring into, and stating the business of the several proprieties of the inhabitants of this place in the lands and houses here; for which his majesty proposes, most graciously, just reparation. In which commission though I am, at this time, and poor Mr Hewer in another, relating to the accounts between the military men and citizens, under a pressure of business equal, at least, to all that ever you knew us in at Derby House; yet, it is to me, a satisfaction, that it is an office

---

[3] The date is uncertain. In the Tangier Diary, P wrote to Houblon on 5 October, but says here that the last letter to Houblon was dated 17 September. In the next letter of 19 October he says his last was dated 14 October. Either P is wrong, or the confusion arose from the difference between the Julian and Gregorian calendars.

wherein I have it, equally in hand, to serve the King against impostures from them whose demands are so apt to fly too high, as the poor proprietors against others, whose want of tenderness might betray them to making offers of satisfaction too low. Both my duty and charity meet with a good degree of content.

It will look, I know, a little gravely, that I did not mix something of ordinary occurrences in this paper, nor, less necessary, sprinklings of questions and answers, foreign and domestic. But, to tell you the truth, I am at this very moment upon winding up a great many poor people's pretences, who have very little time to turn themselves in. Therefore, in general, only be pleased to know that (God be praised !) I am in most perfect health; full of just remembrances of all my friends and their friendships in England, and yours in the front of all; greedy to make an end here, in hopes of making a step over to Spain, while our sulphurmongers are preparing a Doomsday for this unfortunate place. Particularly sensible of the kindness of Mr Gough, which pray own to him, and to the rest of your friends at Cadiz, in their most ample instances of readiness to assist me, if I can get to them; and no less troubled for my mishap in not being in condition (by the task I have thus upon my hands here) to show the civility I ought to have done at Mr Gough's accidentally coming to Tangier upon our first entrance here, and his sudden departure.

And, now, I end with prayers for you and your dear tribe, to every of whom ten thousand blessings. And so God send us a good meeting! Adieu

Your most affectionate,

and ever most faithful humble servant,

S. PEPYS

161. SAMUEL PEPYS TO JAMES HOUBLON

Tangier

19 October 1683

SIR

My last was of the 14th, to Cadiz, under Mr Gough's cover. I am almost impatient to hear of your and your family's health, without which I have not above half the pleasure of my own. But our work advances so fast, that now I doubt a little of having anything from England before our coming away, being in full hopes of finishing all in a month, if the Moors in the fields just without our gates, and, by the help of their hills, in full view of all we are doing, will give us leave; which we do not expect, nor are in much pain about it, our military men thinking themselves secured, with the help of our fleet, against all the force of Barbary. What they do, it is supposed, they will reserve to the moment of retreat out of the town, when, on springing our mines, and thereby overthrowing our walls, it will be flung open. The inhabitants are daily shipping themselves off; many families already on board, and one ship gone with the sick and cripples.

Today embark the Portugueses, having full satisfaction in ready money, for all their proprieties. In eight days we pretend to have removed the whole of the townspeople. Then begins the destruction of the town; that is to say, the diswalling [of] houses, whose materials (the wooden part at least) will be applied to the mines. The number is great, and the work heavy, especially that of Mr Sheeres on the Mole, proving, by the difficulty to destroy it, such a piece of masonry as, our engineers say, was never yet put together in the world. I have been myself an eyewitness with how much less trouble they cut through the pieces of rock than the plaster with which he hath bound them together.

Mr Hewer (who gives you and your lady, as Mr Sheeres also does, his most humble services) is at this time paying the garrison. My own part (as, I think, I have already told you) is, adjudging the civil proprieties between the King and the burghers. In that, I trust in God, I shall leave as little dissatisfaction on the proprietors' part (governing myself by doing as I would be done by) as it is expected I should prevent any impostures on his Majesty.

For the main of the errand on which I accompany Lord Dartmouth, I first say to you, that I am not at all solicitous concerning the thanks I am likely to meet with from the world, the King my master's command being all the warrant and payment I look after. It being a service I neither chose, nor was privy in the least degree to the King's purposes in, at the time of my leaving England, I shall leave it (as I ought) to be answered for by those who advised it. But so much I shall never disown of my opinion at this day concerning it, namely, that at no time there needed any more than the walking once round it by daylight to convince any man (no better-sighted than I) of the impossibility of our ever making it, under our circumstances of government, either tenable by, or useful to, the crown of England. Therefore it seems to me a matter much more unaccountable how the King was led to the reception, and, afterwards, to so long and chargeable a maintaining, than, at this day, to the deserting and extinguishing it. Towards your fuller satisfaction in which, I here send you the substance of my Lord Dartmouth's discourse to this city at the opening of his commission. You will find not a few (yet far from all, or the most weighty) of the arguments in justification of his Majesty's procedure herein to be given, when you and I meet. In the meantime, (unless you find these otherwise published, as possibly you may, by order of the court,) pray let them not go abroad, but keep them till my coming, I having no other copy.

I thank God I am well, and would be at any cost to be sure that you and all my little friends are so. I have sent them my service by a line to their mother, and beg you will let the young gentlemen have the like from me by word.

I would not wish my sweet W. or little Jemmy here; for, with sorrow and indignation I speak, it is a place of the world I would last send a young man to, but to hell. Therefore, on God's account as well as the King's, I think it high time it were dissolved. But if I get time to visit Spain, it would compensate all the fatigue of my journey thus far, to have either or both of them with me. So God keep us all, and send us a contentful meeting.

Yours most affectionately
S. PEPYS

A few days later Pepys collected letters from home, brought across to Tangier from Cadiz. He compiled a second Diary during the trip, which includes this comment. 'Blessed be God! All friends well, and writing mighty kindly, moved me with joy, yet trouble; to be so far and long from them' (24 October 1683). He disliked Tangier, disapproved of the governor Colonel Percy Kirke whom he regarded as a vulgar and drunken oaf, and the way in which the whole place was given over to corruption and decadence. Pepys spent some of his time sorting out the finances of the colony, assessing what money was owed to whom and what was public or private expenditure. Meanwhile, on 1 December 1683 Pepys sailed to Cadiz aboard the *Montague*. One of the reasons was the possibility of a Moorish attack on Tangier, but Pepys was also anxious to take the opportunity to travel a little more widely. The weather soon deteriorated with high winds, heavy rains and then floods which put paid to some of Pepys's plans to explore the region. Pepys found himself temporarily stuck in Spain, which he found extremely frustrating.

162. SAMUEL PEPYS TO LORD DARTMOUTH

St Lucar
5/15 January 1684

MY LORD

Your lordship hath had, I am sure, too many other instances of the ill condition of the weather since my leaving you, to be surprised that I should be offering excuses for my being no further from you than this place, the season having been such, notwithstanding the hopes I had, in former letters, expressed to your lordship, of the contrary, as not in all this time to have given me two dry days together to look out of doors in, till Monday last, when I did immediately set out for Porto Santa Maria, and thence hither. From whence I am going, though the weather is becoming wet again, towards Seville, where I will endeavour, with all despatch, to run through, as I have done here, what that place will afford me of entertainment, and return to your lordship.

This unfortunateness of the season, and the loss of time occasioned by it, renders my journey of much less satisfaction to me than you were pleased to design it should; though this consideration of the weather do at the same time mind me of the little service my attendance would have been of to your lordship at Tangier, had I been still there.

Extremely afflicted I am for the miscarriage of the victuallers; though, I trust in God! you will find a sufficiency remaining to answer all your occasions, if the weather would but favour us. God send to your lordship a happy issue thereto!

My Lord,
Your lordship's most obedient and faithful servant,

S. PEPYS

Mr Hewer gives your lordship his most humble duty.

163. LORD DARTMOUTH TO SAMUEL PEPYS

Tangier
11 January 1684

DEAR SIR

You will easily imagine the condition we have been in here, by the ill weather you have been witness of where you have been; but yet God be thanked I we have struggled in it so far, that the Mole is totally destroyed; nay, much more than you will imagine, till you see it, which, I hope, will be as soon as conveniently you can; for, when the Alcade and I come to treat of slaves, I shall want both your advice and assistance (for which I must ever acknowledge myself already sufficiently indebted,) and Mr Hewer for paying and accounting the money. Pray, make no scruple of taking any man-of-war (that is, of his Majesty's fleet) to bring you hither when you think fit to command her; and I send you enclosed an order, that you may please to put in the commander's name when you can come to me; for nothing they can pretend (if the ship be in condition,) can be of more service to his Majesty than bringing you hither, whose judgment and kindness I have an entire confidence in, being from my heart,

Your most obliged and faithful friend,
and humble servant
DARTMOUTH

As Atkins has drawn the order, no Commander's name need now be added, so that you may apply it to whom and when you please. But remember Harry Williams is my old friend, and, since he is in hopes of making his fortune, I would not injure him.

164. SAMUEL PEPYS TO LORD DARTMOUTH

Seville
3/13 February 1684

MY LORD
I beg your lordship to believe me in saying, that I never suffered, through my whole life, so great a disappointment in any undertaking wherein I had proposed to myself particular satisfaction, as I have and do in this my journey to Spain; not so much from what I am prevented in by the weather, of the content I hoped it might have been of to me here, as from my being so much longer detained from the service of the King and your lordship at Tangier. Not that I have the vanity of thinking all I can do so considerable in any degree to either, as your lordship, in your excess of kindness, are pleased to write concerning it; but that, if less or more, I would have nothing to blame myself for, of neglect in that in which I desire to acquit myself with so entire a duty towards his Majesty, and personal regard and affection to your lordship,

But here the weather hath been such, that after having finished, in six days, all my curiosity aimed at, and could perform in this place, I have been, by the height of the floods, kept out of any capacity of quitting it. The ways, by land, have become wholly unpassable; and the river so overflowed, that notwithstanding all endeavours used for preventing it, by locking its gates, and damming up all other inlets, above one-third of the place within the walls hath been drowned, so as many persons are said to have been famished for want of access for provisions; nor is there believed to be ten dates more left within it for the whole town.

Nor was it before this morning that your letters of 11th of January could reach me, the weather, notwithstanding many public processions for its amendment, continuing still what it hath been ever since my arrival, it being now above eighteen days that I have had a boat waiting for a servant to carry me down to St Lucar. Nor shall a moment be lost than can be saved: on this I beg your lordship to depend; and that, consonant to the order with which, for my convenience, you are pleased to furnish me, I will immediately embark for Tangier from Cadiz, observing your direction in favour of Captain Williams.

Mr Hewer, who is under the same affliction with me, presents your lordship his most humble duty; and also by this post, according to your commands, sends letters to Mr Gardener about the cables, powder, and pitch, that no time be lost in their despatch, if the goods be to be found.

To my former uneasinesses, I have not wanted the consideration of the several difficulties and distresses to which your lordship, from the same cause, may have been exposed. But a great deal thereof is, I thank God! removed by the notice your letters give me of the great advancement in the work of the Mole, and coming in of the greatest part of your ships: nor will I despair but a little time will finish all there, and bring thither for your further commands,

My Lord,

Your lordship's most obedient and faithful humble servant,

S. PEPYS

Pepys eventually managed to arrange passage to return home at the beginning of March 1684 and reached Portsmouth a month later on 3 April. Despite his years in the Navy Office, the experience had told him far more about the Navy and its workings. This emerges in his Second Diary, which includes descriptions of how Navy ships were being used to carry money and goods for profit. Pepys commented that 'on the whole, it is plain this business of money, which runs through and debauches the whole service of the Navy, is now come to the highest degree of infamy, and nobody considers it'.[4] It was a problem he had been aware of since the beginning of his career, but became particularly conscious of it in the 1670s. The carriage of bullion for merchants in Royal Navy ships for protection had led to the transportation of other goods for merchants in return for payment. Of course the Navy's captains were thus less disinclined to risk their profitable cargoes by becoming embroiled in any military action. In 1674 Pepys had had a Captain Haddock prosecuted for carrying a cargo 'on terms of freight for his own benefit'.[5]

Now, nearly ten years later, things had apparently scarcely improved, despite Pepys's endeavours. In his notes on his experiences in Tangier he considered the prospects bleak in a depressingly timeless observation, noting that 'in this age and all past, both in the Navy and other offices, the effects of ignorance and corruption run in a circle, and return at their proper periods to the same pass again and again. Corruption spoiling, or negligence rendering good institutions in office useless ...'[6]

Partly as a result of Pepys's report, the Commission for the Admiralty was wound up. Samuel Pepys was made Secretary for the Affairs of the Admiralty of England in May 1684. It was the highest official position he was ever to reach. Six months later, at the end of November 1684 he was made President of the Royal Society. Despite the allegations made against him in the past his personal prestige, in every sense, was at its climax and led ultimately to the achievements of the Special Commission of April 1686 to October 1688, which Pepys presided over. It would repair, refit and reform the Navy and serve as his final great contribution.

This uncharacteristically long-winded letter contains interesting information about the problems faced by the commander of a ship, including dealing with 'cripples' onboard and a drunken lieutenant. The main subject though is finding a position for Pepys's nephew Samuel Jackson. Only a short excerpt of this letter has ever been published before. News of young Samuel's progress can be found in Letter no. 189.

165. SAMUEL PEPYS TO CAPTAIN JOHN TYRRELL

1 November 1684

SIR

This will I hope find you arrived with your ship at Portsmouth, and that at your arrival you found her in all things ready to executing commands you have received from his Majesty and that I shall hear from you on Monday next of what (if anything) you want towards it; there being nothing that I remember wanting from

---

[4] 16 February 1684
[5] Quoted by Bryant ii, 125.
[6] 7 March 1684, printed by Chappell 1935, 222.

hence of anything you have mentioned to me, unless it be the order you have desired for the easing of some of your unnecessary volunteers(?) and your cripples in which I have not indeed had opportunity of receiving his Majesty's pleasure, nor I hope will that be made any obstruction to your departure in case all things else be ready. Nevertheless I will endeavour to obtain the King's directions and orders in it against(?) Thursday's post, and venture the sending it to you, that it should come too late.

I remember you did also instance to me something touching the idle and drunken behaviour of Lieutenant Davey but have given me nothing in writing about it, so as I have not ground enough to make the complaint which I otherwise should in duty do concerning him to the King, who I'm sure will encourage no such libertines in his service, and least of all be at the charge of bearing such a man extra that has not virtue enough to entitle him to be borne in his ordinary service. Nor does it stand with your duty to pass by with silence, his Majesty being so injured, especially where at the beginning of the voyage you have reason to foresee that you shall not be able to give him that certificate of his good behaviour which you know he must come to you for, at the end of it. Wherefore if you find him like to continue what you in your discourse describe him to me to be, you'll do well to let me know it that I may disabuse his Majesty and desire his directions concerning him. For as long as I have the honour of serving the King, I'll never (by the grace of God) hear of any debauchery stirring in the Navy (let who will be guilty of it) without doing my part towards its correction. No more than I will ever be guilty of suffering virtue and diligence to pass unrewarded as far as any interest of mine can prevent.

What I have to add, is the telling you that it is not 24 hours since it came into my thoughts to give you a little trouble in a matter relating to myself, and extremely sorry I am that it did not occur to me sooner, so as to have given me opportunity of propounding to you while in town. But as late as it is, I will propose it to you now, but yet so, that if you don't approve of it I will be presently satisfied in your telling me so. The business is this. I have a nephew, my own sister's son, a boy of between 15 and 16 years old, who I have for some time bred in town to writing and arithmetic in order to the making him a seaman, it being my purpose to bind him apprentice to some Turkey or East India merchant. For though he is the nearest of kin to me of any relation I have next his mother, yet I'll make a seaman of him, so as that if he be capable, he shall be able to earn his living that way as much as if he had not a farthing to trust to either of his own or from me. For which reason I don't intend to enter him into the King's service, but breed him as I think I have heard you say you yourself were, to know all the work and trade of a seaman, first in the merchant's. The truth is, he is in his nature very good and well inclined, but heavy and backward in his learning. For which reason I did intend to have had him passed six or twelve months long at school before I sent him aboard. But having such an opportunity as this of having him go with a friend, under whom he will be kept to good discipline and work, I have determined with myself to have him go this voyage with you. The voyage itself encouraging me also in it, together with the hopes I have that the variety of it may lend to the enlivening him more than letting him stay longer on shore, since I do intend to make the sea his trade. Nor do I think it will be any hindrance to his learning, forasmuch as he may return to the perfecting of that with a master when he comes back.

Now I would not have you mistake me by thinking that I intend to give you any occasion of care or trouble for him, for I know you have enough of that kind already, it being my full intent not to have him looked upon as a volunteer, so as that you think I should expect to have him sit at your table, or treated with any kind of ceremony, but that he should be received or looked upon with really as your servant, nor if he comes shall he understand that I send him upon any other terms. And between you and I, were you here when it might be done, I could be willing that he might pass the formality of his being actually bound to you by indenture at the Tr[inity] H[ouse] as your servant. Not that I would fasten him upon you, so as to be a standing trouble to you, but take him from you at the end of the voyage. But that he might thereby be the further led to the looking upon himself as under the obligation of a servant to you, the better to imprint upon him the necessity of his duty, obedience and application to everything that may make him a seaman from the lowest office that he can begin with. Besides too that by this means of his coming as you servant there will be no ground for any of the volunteers saying, that while they were discharged a new one of my own was entertained.

This is what I propose to you, and shall adventure so far to go on with it, as that he shall be ready to go away from here by Thursday's coach next. So that if either you are gone before or that by Wednesday's post you shall think fit to advise me to forbear it, there shall be no harm done, for I'll stop his coming upon Thursday, it not being my mind that you should stay one hour from sailing in expectation of him, or that you should make any difficulty of advising me to let this alone in case upon any considerations you shall think that better. For upon my word I should much rather be guided upon it by you than by myself. But if neither of those things happen then I shall hold my mind of sending him down with the coach on Thursday so furnished with everything necessary for one in the condition I thus design him to be in, that he shall have nothing to stay for at Portsmouth but to come onboard you with my letter(?) to(?) your purser for the giving him his help in all common supplies that shall happen in the voyage so as he may be no occasion of charge, or care to yourself. And indeed of all the gentlemen that now serve the King I will now own it to you, there is not one with whom I would either be so free in reference to them or contented with as well to myself, as to offer this to them but you. With which and with wishes of all good fortune to you I remain

Your truly affectionate and humble servant
S. PEPYS

The youth is healthy, strong and I hope after a little use will prove apt for his trade and the labour of it though (as I have said) not so forward and pregnant at his books as I could wish.

Apart from copies of letters preserved by Pepys and now at Magdalene, there are few letters available from 1684 and on into 1685 in the Pepys-Cockerell or Rawlinson papers. However, the 1889 Davey Catalogue (see Introduction) included a number of letters from this period, mostly from John Evelyn, making it likely that other letters from around this time have been dispersed and probably lost The Evelyn letters are fully published in *Particular Friends*. They include a remarkable sequence from July and August 1685 when Evelyn sought Pepys's help in identifying and punishing anyone from the Royal Naval Dockyard who had helped the unnamed nephew of Sir John Tippetts elope with his daughter Elizabeth.[7] Pepys's replies have not survived, but it came to nothing anyway as Elizabeth soon caught smallpox and died. Private affairs aside, public events were equally dramatic

---

[7] The full texts are published at PF C21–3.

and with implications for Pepys. In early 1685 Charles II died. The Duke of York succeeded to the throne as James II but his Catholicism meant that opposition to his rule was already established. Before long Pepys was referring to 'evil days' and knew that his loyalty to James would exact a heavy price. Pepys had entered the last days of his public career.

Pepys was not unusual amongst his peers in being impressed by talented youngsters. Edward Southwell, whose adult career was as successful as his precocious childhood promised, was a source of particular admiration. His father was Sir Robert Southwell, the diplomatist and later President of the Royal Society. In the letter Pepys asks about a 'Mr Wentworth', related to Thomas Wentworth, first Earl of Strafford and Lord-Deputy of Ireland in 1641. There may be some connection with the rebellion led by the Duke of Monmouth in the summer. After capture Monmouth was executed on 15 July 1685 but before the axe fell, one of the crimes he was urged to admit to was committing adultery with one Lady Harriet Wentworth. A Sir Peter Wentworth (1592–1675) was MP for Tamworth in the Parliament of 1641, and this may be the man to whom Pepys refers. The musical entertainment Pepys mentions at the end of the letter is now unknown but is believed to have been by John Dryden who had composed something similar in 1682 when the Duke and Duchess of York returned from Scotland.

166. SAMUEL PEPYS TO SIR ROBERT SOUTHWELL

10 October 1685

SIR

I can't but thank you for the acquaintance you have recommended me to; and yet I am ready to wish sometimes you had let it alone. For I can't put a book or paper into his hand, out of a desire to entertain him, but he makes me sweat with one confounding question or other, before I can get it from him again; even to the putting me sometimes to more torture to find the gentleman a safe answer, then ever Sacheverell or Lee did. Only to day (I thank him) he has used me very gently, upon occasion of two papers I got him to read to me, the one an account I have lately received from Algiers of the whole proceeding (by way of journal) of the French fleets there; the other, the statutes designed by Sir William Boreman for the government of his new Mathematical School at Greenwich, in imitation of that of the King's at Christ-Hospital. Wherein asking our young man his advice, as Sir W. Boreman does mine, he has given it me with great satisfaction, without putting me to any pain about it; only I have promised to carry him down with me next week, when I shall be desired to meet the founder upon the place. And indeed it is a deed of the old man's very praiseworthy. And for the young one, you may be sure I'll keep him my friend (as you counsel me) for fear of his tales. For o' my conscience the knave has discovered more of my nakedness, then ever you did, or my Lord Shaftsbury either. In a word, I do most heartily joy you in him, and (as evil as our days are) should not be sorry, you could joy me in such another.   And so, God bless your whole fireside, and send you (for their sakes and the King's) a good occasion of removing your three parts a little nearer us. I do most respectfully kiss your hands and am

Your most faithful, and most humble servant

S. PEPYS

If you have had any occasion of knowing either here or in Ireland one Mr Wentworth, a branch of the great Lord Deputy's, who has (or is said so) an estate of about eight or nine hundred pounds per annum in the latter, and was a fellow-member of ours towards the latter end (as I take it) of the long Parliament, (a good sober gentleman in appearance, but at that time a great Ante-Courtier) pray give me a little light concerning him both as to the character of the man and his estate, there being an overture depending between him and a relation of a friend of yours and mine, wherein it imports as much to know the truth of both.

Tonight we have had a mighty music-entertainment at court for the welcoming home the King and Queen. Wherein the frequent returns of the Words, *Arms, Beauty, Triumph, Love, Progeny, Peace, Dominion, Glory* &c. had apparently cost our Poet-Prophet more pain to find rhymes than reasons.

In late 1685 Pepys's principal concern was the state of the fleet. On 26 November the Navy Board produced an estimate of £132,000 to repair rotten planking. Pepys charged himself with the task of producing proposals to solve the desperate state of the fleet. In the middle of this he received a letter from John Evelyn's wife Mary to propose a new housekeeper for him, in an effort to repay Pepys for his support during their daughter's elopement the previous summer.

167. MRS MARY EVELYN TO SAMUEL PEPYS

Sayes Court
29 November 1685

SIR

Mr Evelyn will have me trouble you this way with my thoughts concerning a person I believe very well qualified to perform that care in your family you were pleased to mention some time since to him; I have considered as well as I am capable what kind of person you ought to have, and if I were so happy to have pitched some one (such as I am sure so good as master deserves) I should be infinitely glad. It is one I have known in several conditions; she is not in so prosperous a way as formerly, yet in no want; has no charge of children, one only daughter and that provided for, and from her; she has a husband, but he is absent by consent for many years; so that she is almost a free woman; ever very neat, an excellent housewife, not ungentile, sightly, and well behaved, yet of years to allow the necessary experience and prudence to direct in a family, and preserve respect. I will not enlarge too much; but if you are not provided and dare hazard the little skill I have upon this account, I would recommend her to your favour, and hope to have credit by her. I am sensible of many obligations, and your kind concern in our great afflictions was so obliging, I must ever own it as becomes

Your most humble servant
MARY EVELYN

The woman concerned was probably Mrs Fane, hired in January 1686. She was sacked for her sharp tongue in 1687 but rehired at Mary Skinner's behest.[8] Pepys was now reminded of another favour to the Skinners (see Letter no. 155). Thanks to his intervention Peter Skinner was by this time being trained properly in seamanship, rather than the treatment of a 'common seaman'. He was onboard the *Happy Return* commanded by Thomas Fowler.

---

[8] Pepys adored her but found her 'bitterness and noise of tongue ... insupportable'. See his letter to Houblon of 10 July 1689, printed by Howarth pp. 202–3 (nos. 195–6).

168. PETER SKINNER TO SAMUEL PEPYS

To the Honourable Samuel Pepys Esquire Secretary of the Admiralty
At the Admiralty Office in York-Buildings London humbly present these

Plymouth Sound
29 November 1686

HONOURABLE SIR

I hear make bold to give my humble service to your honour (being this day arrived in Plymouth Sound) and my acknowledgements of the great favours, I have received from you, and by your honour's means; more especially by seeing a part of the world, and the small improvement I have made in the art of navigation, to the which I will endeavour shall be to your honour and service.

And further I desire your honour's excuse for the weakness of so green a youth, that being not capable of expressing my sense of gratitude as I ought to your honour, but hope time and your honour's patronage [and] encouragement will spring forth a more fragrant fruit in him, who is

Your honour's most obliged and most obedient servant to utmost breath

PETER SKINNER

Start (Point)   30 November 1686

HONOURABLE SIR

When I wrote this letter to your honour we did expect to set into Plymouth Sound but the wind coming up the NNW and NW b N° blowing fresh we could not fetch in, so were forced to come to an anchor under the Start[9] from whence I suppose the Captain will send a man and a horse up to Plymouth to see if there be any orders for him if not he designs to set sail for the Downs, so hoping your honour will pardon the mistake I subscribe myself   Honourable Sir

Your honour's most obedient servant

PETER SKINNER

Pepys's health had always been a matter of serious and academic interest to him. On 7 November 1677 he had composed a detailed account of his precise state of health that day. By 1686 Pepys was once again worried about it. On 22 June 1672 he had written to his brother-in-law to warn him against being too dependent on what Pepys could offer him because of what might happen (Letter no. 81). Now the time had come once more to reiterate that advice. At this time he was serving on the Special Commission, which Pepys had established to reform and refit the Navy, a capacity in which Balthazar performed as well as Pepys could hope.

169. SAMUEL PEPYS TO BALTHAZAR ST MICHEL

11 December 1686

BROTHER ST MICHEL

I cannot but thank you (though in few words) for your kind enquiry after my health by yours of the 7th instant. It was not without very much ground, that in one of my

---

[9] Start Point, a few miles along the coast from Plymouth. Even today it is difficult to enter Plymouth Sound with a +20 knots wind from the wrong direction as here. 'NNW and NW b N°' is an abbreviation for a wind blowing from the north-north-west alternating with one blowing from the north-west by north where 'b' means 'by' and '°' means direction (pers. comm. T. Johnstone-Burt OBE, RN, then commanding HMS *Ocean*).

late letters of general advice to you, I cautioned you against depending upon any support much longer from me, I then feeling what I now cannot hide, I mean, that pain which I at this day labour under (night and day) from a new stone lodged in my kidneys, and an ulcer attending it, with a general decay of my stomach and strength, that cannot be played with long, nor am I solicitous that it should.

This satisfaction I have as to your own particular, that I have discharged my part of friendship and care towards you and your family, as far as I have been, or could ever hope to be able, were I to live twenty years longer in the Navy; and to such a degree, as will with good conduct enable you both to provide well for your family, and at the same time do your King and country good service. Wherein I pray God to bless you so, as that you may neither by any neglect or miscarriage, fail in the latter, nor by any improvidence (which I must declare to you I am most doubtful of and in pain for) live to lament your neglect of my repeated admonitions to you touching the latter. This I say to you, as if I were never to trouble either you or myself about it more; and pray think of it as such, from

Your truly affectionate brother and servant,

S. PEPYS

The question of Captain Thomas Fowler's various troubles first arose in 1683. John Evelyn wrote to Pepys on 10 August that year, just as Pepys was about to set off for Tangier about these problems but considered Fowler to be of good character.[10] In 1686 Fowler, then commanding the *Happy Return,* had taken Peter Skinner to sea on Pepys's behalf, along with another young man called Robert Holmes. Holmes was a debauched individual and Pepys feared his influence on the young Skinner. He wrote to Fowler to express his concerns and then again shortly afterwards when he was told that Fowler had forgotten his rank when addressing Lady Trumbull, wife to Sir William Trumbull then ambassador in Constantinople, whom he was bringing home.[11] Fowler replied with incredulity.

170. SAMUEL PEPYS TO CAPTAIN THOMAS FOWLER

Captain Fowler
Happy Return, *Downs*

22 December 1686

SIR

I have your letter of the 19th, together with the account which you give me therein at full length of the occasions that have happened of those misunderstandings which have been between my Lady Soames and yourself which how far it may be of satisfaction to me upon your reading, or to any other that is qualified for making a true and impartial judgment of it, it is of no use for me I hereto declare, but rather I hope to leave the doing of you right in it, to my having a proper opportunity given me of doing it to the King himself, who as he ought principally to have his satisfaction in it first provided for, so is he the best able to discern between who has been in the most right or wrong in the matter. But this mishap you will not be able to

---

[10] PF C17.

[11] P's letter of concern about Holmes's effect on Skinner is quoted from by Bryant (iii, 166) who gives an incorrect date, confusing it with P's subsequent letter about Lady Trumbull given in full here. For Holmes's pedigree see Letter no. 181, and p. 261, below.

avoid no more than anybody else that has a quarrel with a fair lady, that her report will prevail among the ladies, whatever it does elsewhere. As an instance of which you must know that my Lady Trumbull has had such impressions made upon her concerning you from the account she has met with of your goodness knows what usage to my Lady Soames, that you may as well expect to persuade a child to meet a bulbeggar in the dark as my Lady Trumbull to venture herself in a ship with Captain Fowler. So that the King has been prevailed withal to appoint another ship for that voyage and (as far as I can judge) I don't think you have any reason to be sorry for it, nor consequently (seeing that it is over) to give yourself any more care about the differences between my Lady Soames and you, the King not having been pleased upon all this noise to express any change of his opinion touching your capacity of serving him as a seaman, and for a courtier I don't think he ever took you for any or thought the worse of you for being none. With which I remain

Your servant
S. P.

171. Captain Thomas Fowler to Samuel Pepys

To the Honourable Samuel Pepys Esquire
Secretary of the Admiralty
present these By M. Skinner

Downs
24 December 1686

HONOURABLE SIR

This comes to accompany Mr Skinner whom I have sent up with Captain Sanderson, and must give the following character of him, that I never found any ill inclinations in him but always good natured, and very obedient to all commands and directions which have been given him, I hope this voyage has done him much good and that he will in some good measure answer your expectations. I never showed him any ill example, neither did I suffer any others to do it, therefore hope he will be careful to keep in your favour, and have respect to his future well-being.

I received your letter last night for which I humbly thank you. I must confess I am a little troubled to be represented for such a monster as my good Lady Soames has made me, I wish Sir William Trumbull and his Lady all happiness and a safe passage to Constantinople and hope his Majesty after two voyages I have made (almost to my ruin) will be pleased to look upon me, with a favourable aspect and consider my condition, which is but very ill at present, and likewise that you will be pleased to continue your favours to

Honourable Sir
Your most faithful humble servant
THOMAS FOWLER

I earnestly beg (if you think it convenient) that I may have leave to come up although for a few days.

From 1664 to 1668 Pepys had taken advantage of the opportunities offered by Mrs Bagwell to enjoy her sexual favours. In return he was prepared to write letters of introduction for her husband, William Bagwell, to advance his career as a ship's carpenter.[12] At the time Mrs Bagwell was probably in her early twenties. Two decades later, she was still trying to solicit Pepys's attentions. Pepys was no longer interested and pointed out to Bagwell, who clearly felt he had been passed over for two recent positions, that his wife's constant visits to Pepys's office on her husband's behalf were wasted and involved unnecessary expense.

172. SAMUEL PEPYS TO WILLIAM BAGWELL

7 January 1687
MR BAGWELL
I am your friend and always have and will be so, your service to the King well deserving it. But I cannot pretend to be able to do everything that is desired of me, even by those that do deserve it well, there being a much greater number desiring and waiting for employment than the Navy can find opportunity of satisfying. And when opportunities do fall, I would not have it thought that the dispersal of them lies in mine or any other's hand but the King's, upon my showing him the several testimonies which each man brings of his abilities and their qualifications.

And hence it is, that I advised Mrs Bagwell, as I do everybody else, not to lose their time in attending, at least upon me, because that occasions them but an increase of expense in staying in town, and does them no advantage after once they have informed me in their case and request. Which is the reason that the greater part of his Majesty's favours of this kind are done to persons that know nothing of it till word is sent them of its being done. This I thought fit (out of my old friendship to you which I have no reason to alter) to say to you for removing the apprehension you seem to be under of my backwardness to do you kindness on occasion of the late vacancies of a Master Shipwright's and Assistant's place which you shall have no cause ever to doubt, it being as much my pleasure as duty to do good (as far as I am able) to any good man, and such have long and still know you to be, remaining

Your truly affectionate friend to serve you
S. P.

From this point on William Bagwell and his wife disappear from history. Britain's commercial future depended on armies of merchants and civil servants tolerating the privations of remote colonial postings. Pepys's friend Sir John Wyborne had been sent out with a small force to India to deal with piracy on behalf of the East India Company, and to collect the King's half share of seized ships and goods. Wyborne, and his wife, were dismayed by the place. This miserable letter arrived to describe Bombay to Pepys, following a similarly miserable one from Lady Wyborne.[13]

---

[12] See pp. 61–2, and Letter no. 54. P had written a letter of recommendation to Brouncker for Bagwell on 17 December 1681 (MS Rawl A194.261; quoted by Bryant ii, 372).
[13] Printed by Smith 1841, ii, 58–9, doubtless inaccurately.

73. SIR JOHN WYBORNE TO SAMUEL PEPYS

Bombay
14 January 1687

EVER HONOURED SIR

This comes by Captain Tyrrell, of his Majesty's ship *Phoenix*. (I) hope it will arrive safe, and find you and all good friends in better health than it leave me and my wife, neither of us being well. My wife's indisposition is occasioned mostly by melancholy; we not finding matters here according to expectation, but much the contrary. Captain Tyrrell will inform you, if God sends him safe home, how he has been treated, and how I am like to fare.

The people of this place pretend abundance of loyalty, but that is all. The greatest part hate anything or any man that belongs to the King; no man being valued here, but those that come out as factors or writers, at five pounds a year salary. You know did not come out of England on those terms.

The commission his Majesty was pleased to grant, and you to send me, into the Downs, empowering me to collect his moiety of all ships seized, and condemned as prizes, with all goods under the same circumstances, I think will turn to a very small account. Since my arrival, several ships and their goods have been seized and condemned as prizes. I have demanded an account of their produce from Dr St John, Judge of our Admiralty Court, who has been at Surat and Swally ever since I came into this country, and condemned the prizes there. My commission runs, to collect the moiety of such ships or goods as shall be condemned on this island. So they condemn all that is taken at other places.

Sir, I humbly beg you to send me his Majesty's commission, to collect all his said moiety, that are seized on and condemned within the North of India, from Cape Comorin to the Gulf of Persia. My commission from the Company runs so as Vice Admiral of those seas.

Please to let me have authority to call for an account of all forfeitures disposed of at Surat or Swally [Suvali] since the date of my new commission from his Majesty, which may turn to a good account; and I shall not be more hated for bearing this commission than I now am, though getting nothing by it. However, nothing shall trouble me as long as I hear our good Sovereign Lord and Master is in health, and I have so good a friend at Court as you.

This I must say, were I in England again, and knew this place as well as I now do, I would rather plough and thresh for bread, than come Deputy Governor to India The place of itself is well enough; but the people, most of them came out of England broken merchants, or very needy, and generally very proud. The usage Captain Tyrrell had, would have broken many a man's heart. I am sure I am the worse for seeing it, and could in no way relieve him, but sat down and condoled with him.

This island produces nothing but coconuts, rice, and salt, which is no rarity, but brings to the Company a good revenue. Our Captain-General adheres to all stories carried to him, and abundance of ill-men tell him abundance of lies, which cause a misunderstanding between us; but I hope when he comes hither, he will be better satisfied with me than now, and will find out the roguery of some about him and me. I have not a man on the island to whom I can communicate any secret, but all the country knows it; but with your kind assistance at home, I don't question but all will end well Sir Josiah Child is very much mistaken in several men here, in whom he puts great confidence.

I pray God Almighty to preserve you in life and good health. With mine and my
wife's most humble service to your good self and all friends with you, I am,
                              Dear Sir,
                    Your honour's most obedient
                    and ever obliged humble servant,
                        JOHN WYBORNE

I am well assured the King has but a few loyal subjects in these parts.

Another letter accompanied this one, sending Pepys a present from Bombay and a further
one a week later describing the inhabitants.[14] John Matthews was clerk to Captain Thomas
Fowler onboard the *Happy Return*, in fact a ship formerly commanded by Wyborne. The
context is unclear but seems to be a reply to one implying dissatisfaction by Pepys at the
standard of training afforded Peter Skinner.

174. JOHN MATTHEWS TO SAMUEL PEPYS

To the honourable Samuel Pepys Esq Secretary of the Admiralty.
At theAdmiralty Office in York Buildings London.
These humbly present   From onboard his Majesty's Ship
                                               Happy Return in the Downs
                                               21 January 1687

I stand engaged to your so many favours, so that I hold it a breach of thankfulness
this long to omit any duty, which may approve me not ungrateful. And though I am
unworthy, I am proud of your Honour's favour, which you were pleased to confer
upon me. In the admitting me to be an instructor of the worthy young gentleman Mr
Skinner, which I performed with all opportunities, and shall hereafter be ready to let
him be a partaker, in any part of what I profess. Let but your Honour, or him name
the thing, in [which] I can be any further serviceable: I now shall be more readier
then (with faithfulness) myself.
    My want of power to satisfy so great a debt, makes me accuse my fortune. But if
out of your Honour's bountiful and generous mind, you think a free surrender of
myself, a full payment, I'll gladly tender it, with my soul full of thanks; and shall
always be
                        Most honourable sir
                        Your most humble and highly obliged servant
                            JOHN MATTHEWS

In late 1686 another row blew up between Pepys and his emotionally reckless brother-in-
law. Balthazar had finally come from Tangier, that 'hellish torrid-zone' as he called it in a
letter of 27 June 1683. By 1686 he was Commissioner at Deptford and Woolwich but it
seems he had had a row with a 'nasty woman' (presumably Pepys's housekeeper Mrs Fane.

---

[14] Printed by Smith, ii, 63–4. Wyborne's eventual fate has not been traced.

ᵣr possibly Mary Skinner) over his debts. Pepys suspected he was being lied to, and warned ᵢim, but his tone was conciliatory.[15]

75. SAMUEL PEPYS TO BALTHAZAR ST MICHEL

27 January 1687

ƷROTHER

 have received your letter of the 24ᵗʰ, and have said my say. Upon your own head be ₜ, if in deceiving me, you at length find the effect of it to the ruin of your family. I ᵢm sure I have nothing to lead me to these jealousies concerning your conduct, by ᵢny fears on their and your behalfs, and desires of your good. Nor have I my ᵢnformation but from them that bear you goodwill; besides that your running on the ᵢcore for this saddle seems very little to consist with the good husbandry you would ᵢe thought to walk by. But I have done; and shall be glad to see you and without ᵢnger as you call it, though it deserves another name; it being too painful thing to me ᵢo write at all, and much more upon a subject so unpleasant to me as this is, would ᵢny care for you have suffered me to be silent. But you have said and undertaken for ᵢo much in this your last letter, that it ought to put me at full ease concerning you, ᵢnd therefore trusting God and you for the event, and your family to the ᵢonsequences of it, you may rest secure against my ever giving either you or myself ᵢny more trouble of this kind either by pen or word, so that you may freely visit me, ᵥhen ever your business will permit it, and be welcome.

Your truly affectionate brother and servant

S. PEPYS

ₜ was just as well that Pepys had found a way to close the matter. A few days later Ʒalthazar's pregnant wife Esther died after a miscarriage caused by an accident. The news ᵢame first from Balthazar's clerk, Abraham Tilghman. For once Balthazar's emotional state ᵢeems appropriate.

₁76. ABRAHAM TILGHMAN TO SAMUEL PEPYS

Deptford
9 February 1687

ₕONOURABLE SIR

Ꮃhilst Commissioner St Michel is drowned in tears, and his spirit sinking under the ᵢense of so heavy a loss, I am by him commanded to acquaint your honour that this ᵢfternoon about one, his lady fell in travel, was about two delivered of a son; but the ᵦirth of the child became the death of the mother, for within a quarter of an hour after, her soul expired; and hath left a husband and numerous family bleeding under (I think) the saddest accents of sorrow I ever saw.

I most humbly beg leave to subscribe honourable Sir

Your honour's most obedient and most humble servant

ABRAHAM TILGHMAN

---

[15] The letters of 27 June 1683 and 24 January 1687 are in Heath, nos. 163 and 165.

177. BALTHAZAR ST MICHEL TO SAMUEL PEPYS

Deptford
14 February 1687

HONOURED SIR

After my having paid the last devoirs to my dearest wife, and as soon as so great grief for so great a loss could permit, I have thought it my duty in the very next place to return you my most humble thanks, for your so generous and kind letter o the 9th instant which I'll assure you (most dear and ever honoured sir) was (in the depth of my bleeding heart's sorrow) the greatest comfort and cordial, that could ever be given me, which being the effects of your always usual goodness and favours, I shall to my life's end, with the uttermost of power ever study to obey your commands and follow every [one] of your counsels, not letting the least hint of your wise advices slip my most exact observation; I am, sir, stopped with a torrent o sorrowful lamentation, for oh God I have lost, oh I have lost such a loss, that no man is or can be sensible but myself: I have lost my wife, Sir, I have lost my wife; and such a wife, as your Honour knows has (may be) not left her fellow, I cannot say any more at present being overwhelmed, wherefore I most humbly beg your pardon and excuse for these ill, and nonsensical lines, as well as for the giving you trouble therewith: and concluding with my continual prayers to the Heavenly God for your dear health, prosperity, and welfare; beseeching the continuance of your favours remain

Your most dutiful and obedient servant

B. ST MICHEL

Pepys's former tutor at Magdalene, Samuel Morland, had been royal Master of Mechanic since 1660. Now he came to Pepys for help. Deep in debt, he had been conned into marrying a woman of modest means, believing she was wealthy. To add insult to this self-inflicted injury, she presented him with an illegitimate child she had had not long before the marriage.

178. SIR SAMUEL MORLAND TO SAMUEL PEPYS

19 February 1687

SIR

I went about three or four days since to see what the Commissioners of the Navy had done upon the order you sent them, relating to the new gun carriages etc but met with none but Sir John Narbrough who told me your order expressed a trial o shooting to be made like that at Portsmouth, which was impracticable at Deptford because shooting with powder only was no trial, and shooting with bullets too dangerous, and therefore his opinion (which he did believe would be the opinion o the whole Board) was that to each new carriage should be the addition of a windlass and also the false truck at the end of the carriage, and that all the other things a eyebolts, tackles etc should be left as they are in the old carriages, till such time as a full trial be made of the new way both at sea, and in a fight, and then what shall prove to be useless in the old way may be wholly left off, and laid aside.

I would have waited on you with this account myself, but I presume you have 'ere this time heard what an unfortunate and fatal accident has lately befallen me o which I shall give you an abbreviat.

About three weeks or a month since being in very great perplexities and almost
distracted for want of monies, my private creditors tormenting me from morning to
night and some of them threatening me with a prison, and having no positive answer
from His Majesty about the £1300, which the late Lord Treasurer cut off from my
pension, so severely, which left a debt upon me which I was utterly unable to pay,
here came a certain person to me whom I had relieved in a starving condition and
for whom I had done a thousand kindnesses, who pretended in gratitude, to help me
to a wife, who was a very virtuous pious and sweet dispositioned Lady, and an
heiress who had £500 per annum in land of inheritance, and £4000 in ready money
with the interest since nine years, besides a mortgage upon £300 per annum more,
with plate, jewels, etc. The devil himself could not contrive more probable
circumstances then were laid before me. And when I had often a mind to enquire
into the truth, I had no power, believing for certain reasons that there were some
charms or witchcraft used upon me. And withal believing it utterly impossible that a
person so obliged should ever be guilty of so black a deed as to betray me in so
barbarous a manner, besides that, I really believed it a blessing from Heaven for my
charity to that person, [I] was about a fortnight since, led as a fool to the stocks, and
married a coachman's daughter, not worth a shilling, and one who about nine
months since was brought to bed of a bastard. And thus I am become both absolutely
ruined in my fortune and reputation, and must become a derision to all the world.

My case is, at present, in the spiritual court, and I presume that one word from
His Majesty to his proctor, and advocate and judge would procure me speedy
justice, if either our old acquaintance or your Christian pity move you I beg you to
put in a kind word for me and to deliver the enclosed into the King's own hands,
with all convenient speed, for a criminal bound and going to execution is not in
greater agonies then has been my poor active soul since this befell me, and I
earnestly beg you to leave in three lines for me with your own porter what answer
the King gives you, and my man shall call for it. A flood of tears blind my eyes, and
can write no more but that I am

Your most humble but poor distressed servant

S. MORLAND

The saga continued into the following year (Letters nos. 186 and 188). In 1687 Sir John
Tippetts served on the Special Commission for the Navy (1686–8) in between two bouts of
service as Surveyor of the Navy. Pepys thought highly of him, a relationship potentially
compromised when Tippetts's nephew (perhaps John or Robert Tippetts, who were clerks in
the Navy Office) eloped with John Evelyn's daughter Elizabeth in July1685 (see PF C20–
22). This letter to the Navy Board is about the claim made by the mother of a seaman killed
on active service at Tangier.

179. SAMUEL PEPYS TO SIR JOHN TIPPETTS ETC

25 February 1687

GENTLEMEN
At the desire of Mr Penn, this serves to accompany the bearer, mother (as she
alleges) to a shipwright slain in the year 1680 by a great shot from the Moors at
Tangier, who lays claim to the provision made in the Navy for the mother of persons
slain therein, grounded upon that Establishment by which the relations of seamen of
the King's ships slain in the land service of that place are to be provided for in the

same manner as if they had been killed aboard. But the execution hereof, and the judging of the reasonableness of the claim being left to your Board, I have only out of respect to our old friend Mr Penn wrote this to conduct the woman to you, whose case you will have all fitting regard to, remaining Gentlemen,

Yours &c.

S. P.

In the spring of 1687 the celebrated eunuch singer Giovanni Francesco Grossi, known as 'Cifacca', was in London. Mary, Lady Tuke, wrote to tell Pepys that Cifacca would perform at his house, as indeed he did. It was an enormous privilege, and a mark of Pepys's reputation as a music lover.

180. MARY, LADY TUKE TO SAMUEL PEPYS

2 March 1687

SIR

I showed your answer to Mr Dies, who is so well satisfied with your excuse, that he hopes Signor Cifacca will find it as reasonable as he does; and be willing another day the next week to give you an hour or two to hear him sing, he also designs to bring Baptiste with him to play upon the harpsicall, I having told him you have the best in England and are a great lover of music. He told me he should think himself happy if he could by any of his endeavours contribute to your satisfaction, it not being in his power to acknowledge the great favour you have done him as he ought tomorrow morning he will send for your letter to the captain, and is extremely pleased you will be so kind to recommend the young gentleman by word of mouth if your business will give you leave in the beginning of the next week to hear Signor Cifacca, pray give me notice, that he may be prepared for it, but do not fancy (as some do) that he expects a present, for I would never propose so mercenary a thing did I believe he had such a thought, you may have the pleasure to hear him sing without putting yourself to charge, in other places, and I should be ashamed to put an obligation upon him at your cost. I only designed it as a diversion for yourself and your friends, of which number I hope to make up one, for I must ever own myself

Your most obliged humble servant

M. TUKE

Pepys wrote to Evelyn a few weeks later to invite him to Cifacca's performance on 19 April 1687.[16] Evelyn was most impressed by the music but thought Cifacca 'a mere, wanton effeminate child; very coy and proudly conceited'. Lady Tuke, unfortunately, was unable to attend since her father had just died.

Problems caused by Thomas Fowler continued to be an issue. The writer here is identified in the letter's endorsement as 'Lady Holmes to Mr Pepys about her son's pay'. This woman is Margaret, née Lowther, the widow of the deceased naval commander Sir John Holmes younger brother of the more famous naval commander Sir Robert Holmes who never married. The young (and disreputable) Robert Holmes had been sent to sea with Fowler along with Peter Skinner at Pepys's request, but now it seems that Fowler had failed to pay

---

[16] PF C37.

the lad's wages causing his mother palpable irritation. 'Mr Stone of Deal' has not been identified, but was presumably a naval official dealing with seamen's pay-tickets.

181. MARGARET, LADY HOLMES TO SAMUEL PEPYS

For Mr Secretary Pepys at his house
in York Buildings

31 March 1687

SIR

I give you this trouble not to beg your favour but justice in ordering Captain Fowler to deliver my son's ticket to Mr Stone of Deal. I have often sent to the Captain by letter for it, and so has my son. I presume he does nothing contrary to your pleasure therefore [he] begs you will command him to deliver Robert Holmes' ticket to Mr Stone and you will oblige

Sir
Your humble servant
M. HOLMES

By late summer in 1687 Captain Thomas Fowler had died, leaving his wife in dire straits as she confronted his impatient creditors. At this point Mary Evelyn, John Evelyn's wife, intervened and wrote to Pepys on Mrs Fowler's behalf.

182. MRS MARY EVELYN TO SAMUEL PEPYS

For Mr Secretary Pepys at the
Admiralty in York Buildings

Sayes Court
7 September 1687

SIR

It will not misbecome me to condole with you the loss of one for whose good I have so often importuned you in his lifetime. I will not altogether justify his proceedings (all men have their infirmities) but he was unfortunate in a great many of his endeavours, and especially in those which should have redeemed him from clamour and domestic troubles, which now more and more appear, by daily pretenders to considerable sums. These add affliction to the real sorrow of his widow, who laments (as she ought) the loss of her husband, and her want of power to be just to all. Though in order to it (as far as the arrear to due to the Captain, and her household goods will extend) she freely resigns to her creditors. More is not in her power, and the little provision remaining for her and her child, obliges me (and I am sure I shall have Mr Evelyn's leave) to give you her trouble, to consider her present case with the same favour and kindness, you have hitherto showed, in assisting with your advice, what may be reasonably offered in her behalf, to move his Majesty to pity her condition by some small pension towards her subsistence. I dare not name the sum; but any competency would be a welcome charity and could not be bestowed on a person more prudent and deserving, and who has none of those too-general failings of our sex to answer for, either pride, or vanity. A better wife no man ever had; she has suffered enough with great patience and discretion to his natural reservedness. The chagrin which proceeds from a necessitous condition, seldom makes a man easy at home; and that temper which seemed morose, might (possibly) be put on as a sense to the knowledge of those concerns, which might afflict a wife whom he had reason to love and cherish. But be it what it could, there never was prosperity enough in nine years time, to make him happy. I add no more, but that he spent his life and health in his Majesty's service, nor should I say so much, or press your good, and generous nature as I do; but that I am assured (by many instances) how just, and obliging you are to your friends, and most particularly to her who is

Sir, your most obliged, and most humble servant

MARY EVELYN

Pepys obliged (see Letter no. 184 below). Amongst Pepys's interests was collecting of engravings and historical medals. In this he was undoubtedly encouraged by John Evelyn who, like many of the two men's educated contemporaries, regarded such a collection as a reflection of, and tribute to, the men they admired. Evelyn later produced a book, *Numismata* (1697) on the subject. In 1687 Henry Slingsby, former Master of the Mint and who had a variety of money troubles, offered Pepys his collection. A list of the twenty-five available medals was attached,[17] coming to a total of £43. Slingsby's estimate of the medals' investment potential was close. The Breda medal of 1667 he priced at £1 9s (£1.45), guessing it would make £6 9s to £11 9s after Roettier's death, the equivalent today of at least £420 to £745. This medal presently sells for around £400–600.

183. HENRY SLINGSBY TO SAMUEL PEPYS

11 October 1687

SIR

You being my ancient friend and good acquaintance, I cannot do less than offer to put into your hands a general collection of all the medals made by Roettiers, of which I had an opportunity to choose the best struck off; and I am sure so full a collection no man in England has besides myself, which you shall have at the same rate I paid for. When Roettier happens to die, they may be worth five or ten pounds more, and yet are not to be had, many of the stamps being broke and spoiled. I have sent you the list to peruse, which if you approve of, I shall much rejoice at. If not, pray return the list again, for I have several friends will be glad to have them of

Sir, your very affectionate friend and humble servant

H. SLINGSBY

If you desire any of the King's and Queen's coronation medals, I have six of them that I can spare at 6s each.

In the spring of 1688 the unhappy affair of Captain Thomas Fowler's widow had a happy resolution. Pepys (and perhaps others) had interceded on Anne Fowler's behalf. The letter is endorsed, 'Mrs Fowler, widow of Captain Fowler, her letter of thanks to Mr Pepys for one hundred pounds obtained by him for her of the King as his charity to her and her children'. The money was equivalent to around at least £7000–10,000 today.

---

[17] Not shown here, but the list of medals is published in the Braybrooke text of the Diary and Correspondence (various editions).

184. MRS ANNE FOWLER TO SAMUEL PEPYS

Greenwich
14 April 1688

HONOURED SIR

The King's most gracious bounty and charity I have received and because I am very sensible I have found the effort of his Majesty's favour by no other means but through your mediation I presume to render you my most humble thanks praying for his Majesty's health and happiness and for continual prosperity to your worthy self. I remain

Your most obedient and humble servant
ANNE FOWLER

On 11 December 1682, Dr Nathaniel Vincent of Clare Hall, Cambridge, wrote to Pepys about his secret cipher, which he called *Cryptocoiranicon*. It involved an invisible ink that allowed the text to be read briefly before disappearing. A secret process allowed it to be read once more. This was supposed to make it secure from interception, being read by the courier and so on. He was anxious to profit from the invention. Pepys had written back on 23 December 1682 to say that he thought kings and the like were far too dependent on their secretaries to deal with anything written, and that the secretaries had their own established methods.[18] He could also see no point in a 'secret method' that had to be made available to everyone who needed to read a message. He also doubted a method that meant only short passages could be read before disappearing again. Nonetheless Pepys was open to being convinced that the method had such overwhelming virtues that it was worth considering investing in. Pepys was prepared to advance some cash for its development.

185. DR NATHANIEL VINCENT TO SAMUEL PEPYS

Clare Hall
12 May 1688

HONOURED SIR

The best returns being in some cases the slowest, I do but now, in acknowledgment of your noble present of five and twenty pieces for enriching my little study, humbly acquaint you that I have determined the first part of my thanks shall be a second part of the earliest payment of my respects to you, and an enlargement of my *Conjectura Nautica*. I have not yet finished it, but shall dispatch it as soon as you can expect it, and before you can have leisure to peruse it. In the meantime I reckon myself obliged to tell you; that you may command not only my magnetical experiments, or either of the inventions whereof I showed you a specimen; but likewise, either for your worthy self, or if you need it not, for any other secretary of state, my discovery of a cipher as easy, as it is useful and secure. It requires no more trouble to write and read it than one's own hand. It may be fully acquired by once reading over a direction of less than twenty lines, and is undecipherable by any rules in that art yet extant; and by the addition of one of my experiments, which will scarce double the labour of writing it. I do believe no mortal pains or skill can detect it. I remain Sir

Your most entirely devoted humble servant

NATHANIEL VINCENT

---

[18] Both letters are printed by Howarth, nos. 131 and 132.

It was early 1687 when Samuel Morland first wrote to Pepys about how his desperate financial situation had led to him being been tricked into marrying a woman of no means and with debts of her own, and an illegitimate child (Letter no. 178). Getting rid of his now-unwanted wife had proved a problem, but fortunately he had been informed that she had been committing adultery with Sir Gilbert Gerard. This is probably the second baronet who succeeded his father in 1687.

186. SIR SAMUEL MORLAND TO SAMUEL PEPYS

For the Honourable Mr Secretary Pepys
at the Admiralty Office in York Buildings

17 May 1688

SIR

Being of late unable to go abroad by reason of my lame hip, which gives me great pain, besides that It would not be safe for me at present, because of that strumpet's debts, I take the boldness to entreat you, that according to your wonted favours of the same kind, you will be pleased, at the next opportunity, to give the King this following account.

A little before Christmas last, being informed that she was willing, for a sum of money, to confess in open court, a pre–contract with Mr Cheek, and being at the same time assured both by her, and my own lawyers, that such a confession would be sufficient for a sentence of nullity, I did deposit the money, and accordingly a day of trial was appointed. But after the cause had been pleaded, I was privately assured that the judge was not at all satisfied with such a confession of hers, as to be a sufficient ground for him to null the marriage, and so that design came to nothing.

Then I was advised to treat with her, and give her a present sum, and a future maintenance, she giving me sufficient security never to trouble me more. But her demands were so high, I could not consent to them.

After this, she having sent me a very submissive letter by her own advocate, I was advised both by several private friends, and some eminent divines, to take her home, and a day of treaty was appointed for an accommodation.

In the interim, a certain gentleman came on purpose to my house to assure me that I was taking a snake into my bosom, forasmuch as she had for six months last past, to his certain knowledge been kept by, and cohabited with Sir Gilbert Gerrard as his wife and besides had the pox etc. Upon which making further enquiry, that gentleman furnishing me with some witnesses, and I having found out others, I am this term endeavouring to prove adultery against her, and so to obtain a divorce, which is the present condition of

Your most humble and faithful servant,

S. MORLAND

The next episode in the saga is below (Letter no. 188). Pepys was an inveterate book buyer. Unlike modern collectors, he preferred to replace first editions with later, revised, versions. Robert Scott, the bookseller of Little Britain near St Paul's, here writes to Pepys with news of books he has obtained for his client. The books referred to are: Edmund Campion, Meredith Hanmer and Edmund Spenser, *View of the State of Ireland* (Dublin 1633), and Alexander Barclay, *Ship of Fools* (1508) – a translation of *Narrenschiff* by Sebastian Brandt. 'Old Harding's Chronicle' is a reference to John Hardyng, author of *The Chronicle*

... from the Firste Begynnyng of Englande, unto the Reigne of Kyng Edward the Fourth.
John Evelyn had a copy, printed in 1548, which Pepys had probably examined.

187. ROBERT SCOTT TO SAMUEL PEPYS

30 June 1688

SIR

Having at length procured Campion, Hanmer, and Spencer's *History of Ireland*, folio, (which I think you formerly desired) I here send it you with two very scarce books besides viz. *Pricœei defensio Hist. Britt.* quarto, and old Harding's *Chronicle*, as also the old *Ship of Fools* in old verse by Alex Berkley priest, which last, though not scarce, yet so very fair and perfect, that seldom comes such another, the prices you will find dear, yet I never sold it under 10s, and at this time you can have it of a person of quality, butt without flattery I love to find a rare book for you, and hope shortly to procure for [you] a perfect Hall's *Chronicle*.

I am Sir, Your servant to command
ROBERT SCOTT

Campion, Hanmer and Spencer, fol.	0 : 12 : 0
Hardings chronicle 4°	0 : 6 : 0
Pricœei defens. Hist. Britt. .	0 : 8 : 0
Ship of Fools fol.	0 : 8 : 0
	1 14 : 0

Pepys's library has of course been preserved intact at Magdalene College, Cambridge, transferred there on the death of his nephew John Jackson according to Pepys's instructions in 1723. Meanwhile Samuel Morland finally achieved his divorce in July 1688.

188. SIR SAMUEL MORLAND TO SAMUEL PEPYS

For the Honourable Mr Secretary Pepys
at the Admiralty Office in York Buildings

19 July 1688

SIR

I once more beg you to give yourself the trouble of acquainting his Majesty that upon Monday last, after many hot disputes between the doctors of the civil law, the sentence of divorce was solemnly pronounced in open court against that strumpet for living in adultery with Sir Gilbert Gerard for six months last past, so that now, unless she appeal (for which the law allows her fifteen days), I am freed from her for life, and all I have to do, for the future, will be to get clear of her debts which she has contracted from the day of marriage to the time of sentence, which is like to give me no small trouble (besides the charge) for several months, in the Chancery, and till I get cleared of these debts, I shall be little better then a prisoner in my own house. Sir, believing it my duty to give his Majesty this account of myself and of my proceedings, and having no other friend to do it for me, I hope you will forgive the trouble thus given you by

Your most humble and faithful servant
S. MORLAND

Samuel Morland survived until 1695, but went blind in 1692. We can only assume that he spent his latter years with some peace of mind.

Samuel Jackson was Pepys's elder nephew. He and his brother John were intended to be the principal beneficiaries of Pepys's estate. However, Pepys wanted Samuel to be prepared for adulthood 'as if he had not a farthing to trust to' as he explained on 1 November1684 when writing to a Captain Tyrrell, then commanding the frigate *Phoenix*, requesting that the lad be trained as a cabin boy. Pepys was already concerned that he was 'heavy and backward in his learning' (see his Letter no. 165). This letter is the next we hear of him.

189. SAMUEL JACKSON TO SAMUEL PEPYS

This to the Honorable Samuel Pepys Esquire
At the Admiralty Office in the Strand London present.

From onboard the *Foresight*
20 July 1688

HONOURED SIR

This day we arrived at the Downs from the wreck though with the loss of our commander, Sir John Narbrough, who died upon the 26th of May last: and as though fate had decreed him to lie there after he had settled all his matters with the masters of vessels who were permitted to work on the wreck upon certain conditions we had orders to sail upon the 25th of the same May and as we were weighing our anchor the small bower cable broke and all the arguments Captain Stanley, Lieutenant Hubbard and the rest of the officers could use proved altogether ineffectual for Sir John was resolved not to leave the anchor behind him: though unfortunately left him, whereupon we plied to windward all day and at evening came to an anchor as near the buoy as conveniently we could and got it aboard. But at 3 of the clock next morning death put a period to his life and in the evening we celebrated his obsequies in a manner as suitable to the occasion as the place and company would admit.

Honoured Sir, I hope I have made such a progress in the art of navigation by the assistance of one Matthew Jane, the yeoman of the powder room, to who I am very much engaged for his voluntary pains and trouble in instructing of me that I do not doubt but to give your honor ample satisfaction therein. May it please your honour the present gunner Christopher Mercer, who was appointed by Sir John to act in that station, is a person to whom I am extremely obliged for his kindness and civility during the time of this voyage. He was seven years gunner's mate aboard the *James* galley under the command of Captain Shovell and hath a very large certificate: whom if your honour is pleased to vouchsafe your favour I do not doubt but he will give you sufficient satisfaction concerning his sobriety, loyalty and abilities for that employ as may render him capable thereof, and which I humbly request. Sir, I should not have dared to have given you this trouble had not your honour's transcending goodness and to avoid the sin of ingratitude been the chief motives that encouraged me thereto humbly craving your pardon. For this bold presumption and hoping that your honour will put a favorable construction upon these lines and fearing least by too much prolixity I should become troublesome I subscribe myself

SAMUEL JACKSON

Samuel Jackson went on to take care of Pepys's Brampton property. In 1701 he was made one of his principal heirs. However, he married against his uncle's will shortly afterwards. For this misdemeanour Pepys deprived him of any legacy apart from a £40 annuity.

The year 1688 was of course one of the most decisive in English history. Pepys was at the heart of crucial events. In June Pepys was a witness at the trial of the Seven Bishops, who refused to read out the King's Declaration of Indulgence. Expressed as a declaration of universal religious tolerance it was interpreted as another step on turning England into a Catholic country once again. The tide changed forever when James II's wife, Mary of Modena, gave birth to James Stuart on 10 June. Until then the succession would have passed to his Protestant daughter Mary, married to her cousin Prince William of Orange. The birth of a boy took precedence and presented England with the prospect of a dynasty of Catholic monarchs. Within a month political opponents of the crown had offered the throne to William of Orange. It was essential that the Navy was prepared to face an invasion.

190. SAMUEL PEPYS TO CAPTAIN CLOWDISLEY SHOVELL

To Captain Shovell
Dover, *in the Downs*   Admiralty
                                                      17 August 1688

In answer to yours of the 16th I am to let you know that his Majesty has very lately altered the measures he had before taken about the fleet's going to the westward service now requiring their being kept together (for some time at least) where they now are. So that I don't see how it can consist with his service at this time any of his officers should be absent from their duty; nor do I think his Majesty would receive any motion for such leave very kindly at this conjuncture. And therefore in hopes that your private affairs may without great injury to you dispense with your not being here for some time, I shall yet forbear to move his Majesty till I know from you whether, notwithstanding what I have here said, you shall continue to desire it. And if you do, I will not fail to do my part whatever the success thereof be, though for the sake of the King's service I could wish your occasions would not put you at present upon desiring. Which is all at present from

Yours &c.
S. P.

191. SAMUEL PEPYS TO CAPTAIN ANDREW COTTON

To Captain Cotton, Navy Yacht
                                                      Windsor
                                                      21 August 1688

CAPTAIN COTTON
If this finds you in the River of Thames as probably it may (my Lord Dartmouth having just now acquainted the King with his having seen you there or at London on Saturday last), this comes by his Majesty's special command lo let you know that (all other occasions being set apart) it is his pleasure that you do immediately apply yourself to take the first advantage of wind and weather after receipt hereof for your proceeding with his vessel under your command to the coast of Holland as far as Goeree, there, and from thence this way to visit that coast in order to the making of the Dutch fleet or what ships of war of those Provinces you can discover to be come out and now lying or moving anywhere along the coast; using your utmost care and diligence in making the best observations you can concerning them either to number, force or ought else fit for his Majesty's notice and which you can come near enough to descry without coming so near as to be commanded by them. And

this having done you are with the like diligence to repair back into the River of Thames there to give me an account of these his Majesty's commands in order to my informing the King thereof. To whom your speedy and effectual execution of the same is at this time of the utmost importance.

I am etc.

S. P.

On 30 September 1688 William of Orange accepted the invitation to take the throne of England, but news had already reached James II a week before that the Dutch were preparing to invade. William made overtures to the Royal Navy, stating that those who supported him would be favoured. James II appointed Dartmouth to command the fleet at sea since he was both loyal and a Protestant, in the hope that this would wrong-foot William's plans to win the Navy over. James also tried to reverse some of the pro-Catholic measures and examples of arbitrary government he had introduced. For example, Catholic magistrates were replaced with Protestants and a proclamation was issued that restored corporations to their ancient rights. It was too late.

William's fleet set sail on 19 October but was driven back by a storm. He left again on 1 November and reached Torbay on the 5th. William was unopposed partly because unfavourable winds had prevented Dartmouth from engaging him, but it was also true that William was largely regarded as a liberator rather than an enemy. A Dutch packet-boat carrying information about the Dutch fleet was captured and the papers sent to Pepys in London. At this point in time there seemed to be some grounds for optimism though Dartmouth's reply makes it clear the initiative had already been lost – the Dutch force had landed unopposed, Dartmouth had no idea what his orders were, and several ships had already defected to William.

192. SAMUEL PEPYS TO LORD DARTMOUTH

Admiralty
Saturday midnight, 10 November 1688

MY LORD

Mine of last night, (enclosing one from his Majesty,) acknowledged the receipt of your lordship's of the 8th current, brought me by Mr Hodder, with a bag of letters taken in a Dutch packet-boat.

This comes express, by the same hand, to let your lordship know, that partly from an apprehension that the said papers, and more especially the list of their fleet, which, with the plan of their camp, you sent me under your own cover, were not long enough in your hand to make any leisurely reflection thereon; and partly, that neither his Majesty nor you might want the benefit of what, by any observations, I could collect from the same.

I have been endeavouring to make the most exact comparison I can of his Majesty's force now at sea under your lordship, with that of the Prince under Admiral Herbert. The result, as containing somewhat no less welcome than surprising, I thought it my duty to represent to his Majesty (as I did this evening at the Cabinet,) showing that, contrary to the impressions universally received touching the inequality of the two fleets, greatly to the advantage of the Dutch, as superior both in number and force to yours, the odds in number is very inconsiderable, and in quality (as much as there is any) appears to incline to his Majesty's side. For the credit of the list on which this comparison is founded, his Majesty and my lords do not find any reason for questioning it, as observing the same, together with the plan of the army, to have been sent under cover of the letter, which came together with them from your lordship to me, designed for the use of the Elector of Brandenburg. Which being so, his Majesty hath, with the advice of my lords, commanded me to give your lordship by express (as I now do by the hand of Mr Hodder) the same I have now mentioned, they deeming it of very great importance to his Majesty that your lordship should, without delay, have it before you, in order, first, to your satisfying yourself in the validity and justness of my calculation; and then, that your lordship, on considering all circumstances, may, according to the fullness of the power lodged in you from his Majesty on that behalf, proceed to make such use thereof as you shall conceive most conducing to his honour and service.

What I have to add, my Lord, is, with relation to the vessel wherein these papers were found, and the fly-boat taken with the soldiers. Touching which, and what other like vessels may happen to be brought in, you desire to be directed as to their disposal. Wherein I am to let your lordship know that you may very soon expect his Majesty's resolution more amply under his own hand, he having been pleased at present to command my signifying to your lordship in the meantime, that he would not in anywise have anything done on his part upon so small an occasion as that of making prize of a poor merchant vessel or two, taken up by pressing or hire, as transports only, and which, in their true value, can be to him hardly worth their keeping, but may, untimely, give countenance to acts of violence on their side, of much greater prejudice to the trade of his Majesty's subjects, and his own revenue depending thereon, and draw on other consequences which his Majesty seems most desirous of avoiding. I am,

My Lord, Your lordship's most faithful and obedient
servant,
S. PEPYS

Postcript.—Near one in the morning

MY LORD
I am just now come from his Majesty, who, after perusing and approving what I have here wrote, was pleased to bid me add for your information, in case you should think of anything that way, that he hath not heard anything of the Dutch fleet's being removed from Torbay, where they were at their army's descent: more than that, some of their vessels with stores and guns which were at Exmouth are gone to Topsham.

You will find enclosed the Dutch list of their fleet, with a translation in English of the letter accompanying it, and the land camp, and my comparison of the two fleets.

193. LORD DARTMOUTH TO SAMUEL PEPYS

The Downs
11 November 1688

I am extremely sensible of your care and kindness to me, in yours of the 8th instant under your own hand, and this day I received the effect of yours by a letter from his Majesty which hath extremely eased my very sorrowful heart, you know I have long been hardened to ill usage, and though my Lord Sandwich is often in my thoughts, yet I can scarcely forbear thinking of pushing more then my own reason would otherwise prompt me, for I have good reason to believe the list of their ships before you, was made before the storm which drove them first back and that their flags changed into bigger or that they had their last supply of ships, yet I call God to witness no concerns of myself makes me so uneasy as the thoughts of the unnatural usage his Majesty meets with, and all his affaires are anxiously before me, pray endeavour to let mine this night to the King be answered effectually as soon as possible, for this step I am going to make is of the greatest consequence, Sir Jo. Berry and Davies seem mighty averse to it, and what is become of the ships from the river I can not imagine, I thought to have bettered myself by coming hither, but to my great disappointment I find my loss in the *Montague*, *Centurion*, and *Assurance*, greater then any recruit I am likely to have, so that nine and twenty men–of–war is all I am likely to depend on and several of them in no very good condition, I have great confidence that George Aylmer and Gifford will make good haste to me pray, encourage them and whatever ships are fitting to make the best dispatch they can, you know how far I am victualled and that must be thought on timely, cables, anchors, sails, and longboats must be sent for this time of the year we shall always be upon the losing hand, and the weather is one of my greatest and constantest enemies I am to expect. I have no answer to mine yet from you of the 8th; and I would be glad to know what I am to do with any vessels fall into my hands and how to proceed with all Dutch ships, for as yet you know I am in the dark my instructions being only if I had met them upon their invading. Sir, I can never enough acknowledge your share in my sufferings even from Tangier to the Long Sands Head etc but I am heartily

Your most obliged humble servant,

DARTMOUTH

Events were moving fast and James knew his hours left as King were numbered. Pepys managed to combine loyalty with self-interest on 17 November when he went with the King to Windsor and reminded him of the £28,007 2s 1¼d owing to him from the crown since 1679.[19] It was a reminder of Pepys's self-serving side, and his eye for detail, that he was so pedantically precise about the sum. James II wrote to the Lords Commissioners of the Treasury to advise they paid it. The money never was, and it remained specified as a debt in Pepys's will. James's support was trickling away by the moment. On 22 November John Churchill, the Duke of Grafton, and more troops abandoned James at Salisbury and defected to William. On 26 November James returned to London to find his daughter Anne had left the night before. John Churchill's loyalty was also in question.

194. LORD DARTMOUTH TO SAMUEL PEPYS

Resolution, Spithead
28 November 1688

SIR

The intelligence and order accompanying yours of the 26th, received by express at ten, Tuesday night, being such as require privacy and my very particular regret, is the reason I give you this answer apart from my general letter concerning the fleet.

I am much surprised at the Princess of Denmark's withdrawing herself, with the manner of it, and the malicious insinuations, you inform me, of ill-disposed people,

[19] Tanner 1925, 246, n. 3. The sum was enormous, equal to at least £2 million today.

as if she had been forced away by papists, all which, I fear, are heavy burdens, and great occasions of trouble and disquiet to our master, whom God preserve and direct to such counsels and resolutions as may remove, or at least alleviate these dismal and most dreadful anguishes of spirit, which I know he must labour under in the present unfortunate conjuncture of his affairs, to which I pray God grant so happy an issue as may put his Majesty in safety, his great mind at ease, and the whole nation and people out of that ferment and crisis of dissatisfaction to his government, which, from the too many nobles and great men ungratefully deserting him, appears to be so universal.

I have deliberated, very thoughtfully, on his Majesty's order for seizing and securing Captain Churchill at Plymouth; sending a frigate on that errand being to run the danger of her being intercepted by the Dutch fleet, who, by the last information, were cruising off the Start. If he be fallen into their company, it is impossible to retrieve him; and, if revolted, it may be reasonably concluded he has prepared his ship's company to make a desperate and resolute resistance; so that it will be a hard task for a single frigate to master him when, probably, now, some of the men may not be so well-disposed to it as I could wish. I have therefore resolved to send only the *Quaker* ketch, with orders to Captain Churchill to use his utmost diligence to join me. If he be found at Plymouth out of command, and be honest, (which is to be doubted), he will, on receipt of this order, take the first opportunity of coming; but if he be under command, the commander of the said ketch shall carry my request to my Lord Bath, with a copy of his Majesty's order for seizing him, and sending away the ship, if he apprehend she may be trusted with the company and the officers she has; if not, to continue there till further measures and resolutions shall be taken about her.

In the meantime, it may not be amiss if his Majesty think fit, and it be safe to venture it by hand, that my Lord Bath have the same directions sent him that way.

I shall order such vessel as I send, if he meet the Dutch fleet, and cannot avoid their examination, to make away with his dispatches, (unless he can secure them), and proceed to Plymouth, giving my Lord Bath a verbal account of the errand he comes to him on, and return with what dispatch he can, that I may be thoroughly informed in this matter; a good success and issue whereto, and all other his Majesty's affairs, are and shall be not the only prayers, but the most earnest desires of, Sir,

Your most humble servant,

DARTMOUTH

In fact Churchill had gone over to the Prince of Orange on 24 November, though he had sworn loyalty to James only a few days before. Despite voting publicly for a regency, he also persuaded Anne, Princess of Denmark, that William should rule England for life. James was now forced to treat with William but he took steps to clear the way for his family's escape. Pepys wrote down James II's cryptic orders to a Captain William Sanderson on 4 December 1688. The Count de Lauzun's 'company' was the Queen and Prince James.

195. JAMES II (via SAMUEL PEPYS) TO CAPTAIN WILLIAM SANDERSON

For Captain William Sanderson Commander
of our yacht the Isabella

4 December 1688

JAMES REX

Our will and pleasure is, that, upon sight hereof, you receive on board our yacht the *Isabella*, whereof you are commander, the Count de Lauzun, with his company, baggage and servants, and him and them having so taken on board you, you are to transport them, with the first opportunity of wind and weather, to such port of Flanders or France as he shall desire. Where having landed them, you are to return with all expedition to Margate, there to attend our further order. Given at our court of Whitehall this fourth day of December 1688.

By his Majesty's Command
S. PEPYS

The Queen and her baby son left England on 10 December. On the 11th James tried to follow them but was caught en route at Sheerness and held at Faversham. He was released on William's orders. By 18 December William had reached London. He granted permission for other members of the royal family to leave. Pepys was obliged to administer these facilities. The Countess of Sussex was Charlotte Fitzroy, one of Charles II's illegitimate children.

196. LADY SUSSEX TO SAMUEL PEPYS

Tuesday (four o'clock)
18 December 1688

SIR

My brother Grafton has spoken to the Prince of Orange for the *Mary* yacht, to carry me to Calais, and my goods and servants to Dieppe, and to set out tomorrow.

Wherefore, I only beg the favour of your dispatch, and you will oblige your humble servant.

FITZROY SUSSEX

In the middle of the upheaval, Will Hewer wrote to assure Pepys of his loyalty. In an ever-changing world, his relationship with Pepys was one of the most resilient.

197. WILL HEWER TO SAMUEL PEPYS

Wednesday night
19 December 1688

HONOURED SIR

I humbly thank you for yours of this afternoon, which gives me great satisfaction, and hope this afternoon or evenings audience will prove to your satisfaction, which I do heartily wish and pray for, if not, I know you will cheerfully acquiesce in what ever circumstance God Almighty shall think most proper for you, which I hope may prove more to your satisfaction then you can imagine. You may rest assured that I am wholly yours, and that you shall never want the utmost of my constant, faithful, and personal service, the utmost I can do being inconsiderable to what your kindness and favour to me, has and does oblige me to; And therefore as all I have proceeded from you so all I have and am, is and shall be, at your service.

I have no reason to complain as yet of any hardship, but tomorrow I shall know the utmost and then I shall wait on you remaining, in the meantime

Your ever faithful and obedient servant,

W. HEWER

James II was allowed to escape on 22 December and made his way to France. Pepys of course knew that he was professionally doomed, though he remained in post, now carrying out William's orders. Nevertheless, for the moment uncertainty pervaded everything, particularly in Dartmouth's cabin. Pepys, aware he had only a little time left in office, abandoned even thinking about what might happen. He took offence at the way Dartmouth had sent his private secretary, Phineas Bowles (who would succeed Pepys), directly to the Prince of Orange to find out the state of the fleet rather than going via Pepys.

198. LORD DARTMOUTH TO SAMUEL PEPYS

To Samuel Pepys Esq, Secretary of the Admiralty
at the Admiralty Office in York Buildings

Spithead
28 December 1688

SIR

I received yours, and have answered them as fully as I could at present; but I beg leave to write you this with my own hand, to assure you the only reason I sent up Mr Bowles, proceeded wholly from not hearing from you, and no disrespect or any design of mine; for I should be very ungrateful if I were capable of making any unkind return to you.

I doubt not but utility will help us both, though in this miserable distraction, and the grief I am in for my master, with being at such distance from affairs, and kept so much in the dark by my friends. They all write that they think I have better accounts from other hands, and in the meantime I am the most in the dark of anybody.

Pray deny me not your private and friendly advice, by which I shall be glad to govern myself; and I hope we may be yet helpful to one another. I am sure all things shall be done on my part as becomes

Your obliged and affectionate friend
and humble servant
DARTMOUTH

199. SAMUEL PEPYS TO LORD DARTMOUTH

2 January 1689

SIR

I thank you with all my heart for your last of 28th December, under your own hand; for, I must own, I thought your usage of me, in the particular you mention, somewhat unnatural, especially at a juncture so little needing it from one's friends. But, my Lord, you have done yourself and me right in the trouble given yourself for my satisfaction. I assure you, nothing on't shall longer stick with me; but, on the contrary, a desire of rendering your lordship all the faithful services that, during the little remainder of my abode here, I shall be able to pay you. I send you herewith the Prince's pleasure in supply of what I wrote you last night, both to Plymouth and the

Downs. In the latter, I presume, this will find you, and that, in a few days more, I shall kiss your hands here.

It will be matter of great content to me, if I may be able by any means to be of use to your lordship, though I have given over even thinking on't for myself.

I am, my Lord,

Your lordship's most affectionate and humble servant

S. PEPYS

Dartmouth remained true to James II, and unlike some of his contemporaries never pursued self-interest by finding some accommodation with William. He was accused of conspiring against the new regime and was sent to the Tower where he died in 1691. Under the circumstances, it was not surprising that Pepys lost his Harwich seat in the election of January 1689. News arrived from a Minister of Harwich and a member of Pepys's campaign team to tell him what had happened, and urging Pepys to look to the next election.

200. HIPPOLITUS DE LUZANCY TO SAMUEL PEPYS

For the Honourable Samuel Pepys Esq at the Admiralty London

Harwich

18 January 1689

SIR

I have been desired by your friends to send you the enclosed paper; by which you may easily be made sensible, how we are overrun with pride, heat, and faction; and unjust to our selves to that prodigious degree, as to deprive ourselves of the greatest honor and advantage which we could ever attain to, in the choice of so great and so good a man as you are. Had reason had the least place amongst us, or any love for ourselves, we had certainly carried it for you. Yet if we are not by this late defection altogether become unworthy of you, I dare almost be confident, that an earlier application of the appearing of yourself or Sir Anthony Deane will put the thing out of doubt against the next Parliament. A conventicle set up here since this unhappy liberty of conscience has been the cause of all this. In the meantime my poor endeavours shall not be wanting, and though my steadfastness to your interests these ten years has almost ruined me, yet I shall continue as long as I live

Your most humble and most obedient servant,

DE LUZANCY

An Account of the Election at Harwich January 16, 1688–9

The candidates, Sir Thomas Middleton, a very worthy gentleman, agreed upon by all parties, and one Mr John Eldred; the Town Clerk declaring that Samuel Pepys, Esq., should not be entered, except some appeared personally for him, which being done immediately, he was at last set down.

The Common Council were so hot for the other, that, without hearing any reasons, nothing would serve but a present election. But, before they voted, the Mayor and several of the Aldermen arguing strongly that many of them could not be electors; some not being qualified according to law, others being open dissenters from the church, amongst whom a kind of Quaker, four lately taken in the room of four who were absent, and turned out without any warrant; it was learnedly answered that, by the King's late proclamation, they were put *in statu quo* in 1679; to which reply being made, that the King's proclamation did really restore them who were then electors, but did not give them any power to choose any new members, especially their charter not being restored, which was their warrant to act by, they not knowing so much as where the said Charter is, all was overruled by noise and tumult. They took the paper where they were, to write down their votes, and carried it out of the Court; upon which the Mayor presently adjourning, two of the Aldermen went out, which made the others return into Court, and there give their votes: presently after, the following protestation was put into Mr Major's hands—

Mr Mayor—'We humbly conceive that the present choice of Mr Eldred to serve in the Convention is illegal, as to that part of it wherein the new electors are concerned; it being visible, that so long as we have no charter to chose them by, they are unwarrantably chosen. For, though his Majesty's proclamation restores us again to the same state we were in, in 79, and does qualify them who were then actually chosen, it does not appear to us, how, without the Charter being *actually* restored to us, which it is not at this present, the then electors can chose any new ones; so that their very choice is deficient in itself; and according, we humbly desire Samuel Pepys, Esq., to be returned with Sir Thomas Middleton, Knight; protesting against the choice of the said Mr Eldred, and desiring withal that this our said protestation may be entered and returned to the Convention, to be there examined with our further allegations against the said election.'

Mr Smith, the Town Clerk, took the said paper angrily; threatened a schoolmaster, whom he thought had copied it out, to imprison him; said it was a libel, flung it out of the Court, and proclaimed the said Mr Eldred duly chosen. As they carried him up and down in the streets, one Mr John Wertbrown cried out, 'No Tower men, no men out of the Tower!' which was echoed by nobody; most of the freemen, and particularly the seamen, being wholly against such a choice, and declaring that had they bin concerned in it, they would have chosen Mr Pepys.

This account is exactly true.

Pepys's career in Parliament was over, and he never contested a seat again. A few days later a remarkable letter was delivered to Pepys from The Hague. Nothing about the writer of the following letter is known, yet it seems that Deborah Egmont had once been in Pepys's service. Arthur Bryant speculated, but thought it improbable, that she might have been the Deborah Willet of the Diary years, the young woman hired as a companion for Elizabeth Pepys in 1667. The arrangement ended in catastrophe when Elizabeth caught her husband in a compromising position with Deborah on 25 October 1668.

It is hard to see who else this woman could be, or why she should have contacted Pepys unless she felt she had some other call on his goodwill. The original letter is written in a loose, open hand and apparently in some haste but the letters are well formed and the spelling a good deal less haphazard than that of many of the writer's contemporaries. The only significant exception is Will Hewer's name, given in the original as 'Yūres'. The surname Egmont/Egmond is Dutch, so perhaps this Deborah had married a Dutchman and lived in The Hague until plans were made to come back to England during the Revolution. However, there is another possibility given the discovery that the Skinner family originated in Egmond in Shropshire. She may somehow have been linked to the Skinners and through that route had come into Pepys's service and benefited from his patronage.[20] Unfortunately this woman is otherwise untraceable and we are unlikely ever to know who she was for certain. The name 'Mr Dispontain' is also otherwise unknown but is probably a corrupt form of the French name 'Spontain', perhaps 'de Spontain' and possibly a French contact Pepys had come to know while amassing evidence to clear his name in 1679. But this is mere speculation.

[20] See p. 114.

201. MRS DEBORAH EGMONT TO SAMUEL PEPYS

Squire Pepys York Buildings

The Hague
30 January 1689

HONOURED SIR

Having had formerly the honour to serve you, [I] hope you will be pleased to be kind to the bearer hereof, which is my husband, in all you can. I am to come to England as soon as possible I can. Meantime I do beseech you to advise and assist my dear husband in what you in your prudence and wisdom and goodness thinks best, having heard his request. My service to yourself and Mr Hewer and his mother and aunt and the whole family. Please to pardon my boldness assuring you that whatever you do for my husband shall be thankfully taken from your humble servant

DEBORAH EGMONT

Mr Dispontain hath his love to you.

Nothing in Pepys's surviving papers exists to confirm who Deborah Egmont was, and what – if anything – Pepys did in response to her request for help. Perhaps the most telling fact is that Pepys preserved the letter.

On 13 February 1689 William III and Mary II were declared joint monarchs of England, with the succession passing to Mary's sister Anne. In the Rawlinson manuscripts is a series of documents prefixed with a title page stating that they are copies of 'entries of all the Acts of his Highness the Prince of Orange prepared by Mr Pepys, relating to the Admiralty and Navy, from the time of his Coming to Whitehall and Entrance upon the Government, to that of Mr Pepys's Voluntary ceasing to act further therein'.[21]

On 20 February 1689 Pepys resigned his position as Secretary of the Admiralty and a few weeks later on 11 April William III and Mary II were crowned the new monarchs of England. By May Pepys was back in prison, but now at William and Mary's pleasure, under suspicion as a supporter of James II.

[21] MS Rawl A186.

6 Between Business and the Grave: 1689–1703

THE GLORIOUS REVOLUTION was the making of many men. Those who had opposed James II usually found that the new regime presented them with opportunities. Some men with a flexible sense of loyalty, like Sidney Godolphin, breezed through the transition with ease and continued their careers. But those who had been loyal to James and remained so, inevitably found that their time was up. Pepys had continued in his post into early 1689 but agreed to resign. Men Pepys trusted and counted as his friends, like Will Hewer and Anthony Deane, also left office. This meant that while one door was firmly closed on the past, another was thrown open to the future. Pepys was frustrated and angry about being forced out, but his vast reserves of self-belief, which had stood him in such good stead before the Brooke House Committee in 1669 and during the Popish Plot in 1679, were still thoroughly intact.

Pepys therefore embraced the prospect of an active retirement in close company with his intellectual friends. He also continued with the research on his *Navalia*, a project on which he had been working for years and for which John Evelyn (and others) had been bombarding him with material for longer than he probably cared to remember. In fact the book never appeared, though many of the papers he had accumulated survive in his library. There was something more pressing. Pepys recognized that he was now totally exposed to his old enemies. He focused his efforts on just a small part of the *Navalia*, which he called *Memoires Relating to the State of the Royal Navy of England, For Ten Years, Determin'd December 1688*. It was the only book he ever produced and served as a defence of his second Secretaryship, the achievements of the Special Commission of 1686–8, and also Anthony Deane and Will Hewer. Devised as a pre-emptive strike against 'a strong combination' that planned to attack him and 'discrediting the same', it appeared in June 1690. The text starts by pointing out the parlous state of the Navy by May 1684 when only 24 ships were actually at sea, and none of them more than a fourth-rate (50–60 guns) vessel. The rest of the Navy was 'so far out of repair' that costs to remedy the situation were estimated at £120,000 when available stores amounted to just £5,000. As far as Pepys was concerned the culprits were the Commissioners of the Navy between 1679–84. The book closes by tabulating the dramatic improvement four years later, listing ships now repaired, under repair or at sea. Fifteen third-rates were now at sea and all the second- and first-rates were repaired or being repaired. Although the improvements are largely beyond doubt, today it is recognized that the 1679–84 Commissioners were compromised by a chronic shortage of funds, Restoration politics and Charles II's haphazard government.

Meanwhile, Pepys was imprisoned with Hewer and Deane between May and June in 1689 on a warrant issued by the Earl of Shrewsbury. He was imprisoned again briefly in July 1690. Thereafter he was more or less left alone and apart from a half-hearted effort to seek another seat in Parliament in February 1690 he made no further effort to take part in public life.

While Pepys was in prison a family row exploded. Balthazar wrote to Pepys in a letter that even by his standards was inexcusably abusive though he interspersed his rage with the usual vows of loyalty and respect. Balthazar, recently remarried, clearly thought little of one of Pepys's household. Heath believed this was Mary Skinner, but it is far more likely to be the 'insupportable' housekeeper Mrs Fane.[1] She presumably made her feelings clear to Balthazar while Pepys was in prison, occasioning this remarkable letter.[2] To be fair to Balthazar, his loyalty to Pepys as a member of the Commission of 1686–8 meant that he had lost his position too.

202. BALTHAZAR ST MICHEL TO SAMUEL PEPYS

For the Honourable Samuel Pepys Esquire
At his house in Buckingham Street York Buildings

28 May 1689
HONOURED SIR
After my late having groaned under some troubles (on my private account) which at this unfortunate juncture of time have proved extreme heavy and grievous to me; I understand that by the malicious inventive ill offices of a female beast, which you keep, I am like also to lie under your anger and disgrace (to me more insupportable than the former) but I hope, and humbly pray, (though she told me impudently, and arrogantly, you scorned to see me) that with your generous usual goodness, wisdom, manhood, and former kindness you will not damn him unheard who should joy to hazard (as in duty bound) his dearest blood for your service. The meanwhile, returning your honour my most humble and hearty thanks for the petition you sent me, and for all the other your many favours I remain
Your ever dutiful and most faithful humble servant
B. ST MICHEL

No reply from Pepys is known, or indeed any other letters to Balthazar though the latter continued to write to Pepys. In 1683 Mary Skinner's mother Frances had written to Pepys about her son Peter's inadequate naval training. Pepys interceded on the family's behalf (Letters nos. 155 and 168). Unfortunately, by 1689 young Skinner appears to have decided that he could get through life without Pepys's patronage. Frances Skinner wrote again.

203. MRS FRANCES SKINNER TO SAMUEL PEPYS

10 June 1689
MOST HONOURED SIR
I am in the heaviest affliction that ever I was since I was born about this graceless son of mine that he should abuse and sleight so good a master as you have been to him. I did look upon him to be the greatest staff and comfort of my old age being brought up under so worthy, wise and good a man as you are and have been to him but let me earnestly beg and entreat of you with bitter weeping tears for his father's sake that is dead and gone that had the greatest desire in the world of his last that he should be brought up with you. Dear Sir, do not turn him going if he be not gone and if he be gone upon his humble submission take him under your protection again. Oh

---

[1] Heath 1955, 223, n. 2, but see p. 179, and P to Houblon in Howarth, no. 195.
[2] Probably not for the first time. See Letter no. 175.

would to God that you had caned him that you had broken all his bones limb from limb. I humbly thank you for what you have done for him already and pray for you.

Your very humble servant
FRANCES SKINNER

Sir, I beseech you for Christ his sake do not let him be ruined for if he goeth away from you he will be ruined body and soul.

A letter (no. 206) from Peter Skinner pleading contrition followed that autumn. Meanwhile Pepys, Deane, and Hewer were released from the Tower on bail.

204. JAMES VERNON TO SAMUEL PEPYS

Whitehall
15 June 1689

SIR

My Lord Shrewsbury commands me to acquaint you that he can now discharge you from confinement if you think fit to give bail for your appearance the first day of the next term; and if the notice be any way grateful to you, I am glad I have the signifying of it, who am, Sir,

Your faithful, humble servant,

JAMES VERNON

Sir Anthony Deane and Mr Hewer may have the same benefit; I hope I may trouble you to let them know so much. The bail that has been given by Colonel Graham, Mr Harpe, and some others, has been £1000, the principal, and £1000 for one or more sureties.

Once out of prison Pepys seems to have decided to send money to Balthazar. The usual grovelling letter from Balthazar followed.

205. BALTHAZAR ST MICHEL TO SAMUEL PEPYS

For Mr Samuel Pepys Esquire
At his house in Buckingham Stree York Buildings
Per penny post paid

6 August 1689

HONOURED SIR

Whatsoever your pleasure, or displeasure is towards me; I shall never fail of my duty to you-wards while I live, being (besides my natural inclination) thereto obliged, by all the deeds of gratitude I can ever be capable of, which I will show to the hazard of my life, whensoever your service, or commands may call for the same; the meanwhile I having just now received the enclosed, which (after above four months absence, and silence) being very infinitely welcome to me, and believing your ever generous goodness to be still such, that it is no less also to you have therefore, thinking it my duly, made bold to give you the trouble of its perusal; and remain

Your honour's most dutiful faithful and humble servant
B. ST MICHEL

The disgraced Peter Skinner wrote to Pepys in September.[3] Pepys's reply expresses his disappointment about what he regarded as an abuse of the help that had been offered, and worse that he is no longer in any position to offer further help.

206. PETER SKINNER TO SAMUEL PEPYS

Portsmouth
27 September 1689

MAY IT PLEASE YOUR HONOUR

If tears and sighs and the unfeigned sorrows of a perplexed and uneasy mind can make any impression upon your honour's good nature to pardon my offending you; If the low submission and prostration of a slave cast at your feet can move any pity in your tender breast, look upon me with eyes of compassion and suffer a compassionate relenting to possess your mind; let the former kindness you was pleased to express towards me plead on my behalf, that you would restore me from banishment, that you would once more admit me to your presence that there I may obtain the favour of excusing, or at least of confessing and begging pardon for the crime of which I stand charged before you and as an expiation thereof undergo any punishment you shall doom me to, except that of being forbidden to approach the darling of my repose, the centre of all my happiness and all my earthly felicity. And so in hope you will look kindly upon this my low submission, I remain

May it please your honour, your honour's most penitent and
afflicted servant

P. SKINNER

207. SAMUEL PEPYS TO PETER SKINNER

These for Mr Skinner at Portsmouth 17 October 1689

YOUNG MAN

Mr Harman coming to me this day to take his leave of me, I gave him this in answer to that which he brought me from you of the 27th of the last and serves only to tell you that if good words would have controlled[?] me you would never have had occasion to have write to me as you therein do. Therefore don't think that that will now do anything with me. For your sister's sake and in hopes of your being of the same righteous disposure of mind with her, you know I entertained, cherished and encouraged you and was at no contemptible charge in doing it. And this out of a pure desire of doing you some good and enabling you to do some more. This I did while you were at the same time using all the way[?] you could to frustrate both mine and your poor sister's hopes [and] cares concerning you. What the event of it to you will be I shall not now add anything to what I have heretofore said to you by way of prophecy about it. This only I shall tell you that you are not to flatter yourself with any further expectation from me, the condition I am now in not furnishing me with opportunity of being anyway further useful to you, did you deserve it. And as to the seeing me till I have more assurance and from yourself that you behave yourself worthy of it by a steady sobriety and industry of life and the effect of it in your being able to return the past kindnesses of your friends to you by yours to those of your relations who may want it rather than by the misspending of what you have levied up from their former favours to you be drawn (without success) to come to

---

[3] For Skinner's career see also nos. 155, 168, 203, 206 and 207, and Smith ii, 239–40.

them for more. This I say to you as one that still for your own sake wish you well though at the same time I but own to you that till your actions convince me of the contrary I shall despair of my wish

Your very loving friend

S. P.

With the benefit of maturity and experience, Peter Skinner was later able to look back on his behaviour around this time. In December 1702 he wrote to Pepys reflecting on his former actions (see Letter no. 257).

Meanwhile, since the summer of 1680 when Pepys, Deane and Hewer had been released, the three men had had to confront the time that lay ahead. A letter from Deane set the tone for many of the years to come.

208. SIR ANTHONY DEANE TO SAMUEL PEPYS

Worcestershire

29 October 1689

SIR

These are only to let you know I am alive, I have nothing to do but read, walk and prepare for all chances attending this obliging world, I have the old soldier's request, a little space between business and the grave, which is very pleasant on(?) many considerations, as most men towards their later ends grow serious, so I in assuring you that am Sir   Your very humble servant

A. D.

209. SAMUEL PEPYS TO SIR ANTHONY DEANE

23 November 1689

SIR

I am alive too (I thank God) and as serious (I fancy) as you can be and not less alone; and yet (I thank God too) I have not one of those melancholy misgivings within me that you seem haunted with; for the worse the world uses me the better I think I am bound to use myself; nor shall any solicitousness after the felicities of the next world (which yet I bless God I am not without care for) ever stifle the satisfactions arising from a just confidence of receiving (some time or other even here) the reparations due to such unaccountable usage as I have sustained in this. Be therefore of my mind (if you can) and be cheerful; if not enjoy yourself your own way and in your devotions think of your friend whom you have so outstripped from their not being able so easily to fall out with themselves as you have done. I kiss Mrs Hunt's hands with a thousand respects and am her and

Your faithful humble servant

S. PEPYS

Pepys's release from his second imprisonment was partly occasioned by his health. The order for his liberation, dated 14 July 1690, stated that thanks to an 'ulcer in his kidneys ... unless he be speedily enlarged from his present confinement he is in danger of death'. By June that year his one and only book, *Memoires Relating to the State of the Royal Navy*, had been published. He sent John Jackson with a presentation copy for John Mountagu, son of his long-deceased patron, the Earl of Sandwich. Surviving examples of the presentation copies show that Pepys had gone through each one and corrected any remaining typographical errors in his own hand.

210. DR JOHN MOUNTAGU TO SAMUEL PEPYS

Trinity Hall, Cambridge
9 December 1690

SIR

I humbly thank you for the present you was pleased to send me by your nephew. It is a subject I shall very much delight to peruse by reason of the near alliance I once had to it by my father, and particularly for the sake of its author, to whose friendship I am so much indebted and for whose knowledge and experience in our naval affairs it may justly be said that the whole nation is your debtor too. I am very sorry that a person so greatly experienced in all those affairs should not be continued in the service of the public, but, Sir, since it is, I cannot call it your but our misfortune not to enjoy the advantages of so eminent a service. All the world in the meantime must own the generosity of your temper, that whilst you are retired, you still are desirous to promote the public welfare of the kingdom.

Sir, Your very affectionate, obliged, humble servant,

JOHN MOUNTAGU

211. SAMUEL PEPYS TO DR JOHN MOUNTAGU

20 December 1690

SIR

You have said much too much in favour both of my present and me; but if it were fit for me to admit there were anything either in the one or the other worthy the good word you bestow on them, you know and I most gratefully acknowledge whose memory alone it is that I owe it to, I mean my noble Lord your father's, and in deference to which I believed myself bound to make you in particular privy to what I have been doing relating to the Navy since (I thank God) I have had no more to do in it.

I am, Honoured Sir, Your ever most obedient servant,

[S. P.]

One consequence of leaving office was obviously a loss of salary. Although Pepys was not as honest as he liked to think himself, there is no doubt that unlike many of his contemporaries he had never seriously profited from his position, though he had maintained a close interest in his financial affairs from the beginning of his career. He now found it necessary to call in debts. This was a balance of a loan of £400 to the dramatist Sir Robert Howard, of which 200 guineas had already been paid. In practice a guinea's value was prone to extreme fluctuation at the time, since gold was circulating at a premium. The 200 guineas were therefore potentially equal to as much as £300. It is not known if Pepys recovered the outstanding amount.

212. SAMUEL PEPYS TO SIR ROBERT HOWARD

York Buildings
1 July 1691

SIR

My late freedom from public has given me opportunity of looking a little into my private affairs. And therein it has been my hap to meet with a paper I have long been at a loss for. I mean, the note you were pleased to give me for the £400 which at your desire I accommodated you with in the year 1676, upon an occasion of your going to Newmarket, and of which you soon after repaid me by the hand of Mr Hewer 200 guineas, as appears by his entry thereof upon the said note.

I have chosen to make use of the same hand to attend you herewith; assuring you that having now nothing coming-in of what I then had, your present ordering me the remainder will be a great pleasure to,

Your old humble and most faithful servant
S. PEPYS

Another crucial change in Pepys's life was that he was no longer an automatic source of patronage. For a man accustomed to the status and respect his influence over who filled positions earned him, the effect of his new impotence was both humiliating and even insulting. Some of those to whom he had shown favours in the past now repaid him by spurning him. Amongst these was James Southerne, once a clerk in Pepys's office, then Clerk of the Acts himself and now Secretary of the Admiralty.

213. HENRY COMPTON, BISHOP OF LONDON TO SAMUEL PEPYS

15 December 1691

SIR

When I tell you I write in behalf of an eminently honest man, I hope you will pardon more easily my importunity. The bearer, Mr Nutt, though I have very little or no acquaintance with him, is one that I highly value for two actions of his life very unusual in this age. When upon the credit he had given the King, Charles II, he found himself sinking from an estate of ten or twelve thousand pounds to nothing, he returned back to the value of £3000 of money just then put into his hands, telling his creditors that he was no longer responsible. His other action was more generous than this. For being called to witness the title of a gentleman who has not wherewithal to reward him, and being himself not worth a groat, he refused to keep back his evidence, though he was offered a very considerable reward by the other party which would have supported him all his life. Upon these merits it is that I would beg of you to use your interest with Mr Southerne to bestow some clerk's or other place under the Admiralty upon him, to get him bread. If it were for my brother I could not with more concern entreat you in this particular to oblige, Sir,

Your most obedient humble servant,
H. LONDON

214. SAMUEL PEPYS TO HENRY COMPTON, BISHOP OF LONDON

York Buildings
18 December 1691

MY LORD

I have received your Lordship's commands with the deference due thereto, and shall gladly endeavour to execute them with efficacy to the benefit of the honest gentleman (my old kind acquaintance) whom your Lordship is on so honourable inducements pleased to favour, in case you shall continue to require it of me after I have, in duty to yourself as well as faithfulness to him, observed to your Lordship: That however unnatural it may seem to your Lordship, as it does to all who know it, I have been so far from meeting with any marks of Mr Southerne's remembering himself to have been my servant, and by me (and me alone) raised to the condition of a Master in the Navy that, on the contrary, if there be one man in it that has under this Revolution shown me not only most neglect but most despite on all occasions wherein my name has been made use of, it is he. So that I cannot think it anything less than a betraying of this good man's suite for me to pretend to any capacity of furthering it with Mr Southerne.

If nevertheless from any special inducement (not appearing to me) Mr Nutt shall think my mediation may be of any moment to him in this case, I both will and ought to make it my business to render it so. And this not only for the sake of your Lordship's commands (though they were alone sufficient) but from arguments also within my own cognizance as an Officer of the Navy, privy more than most to what this honest gentleman and his family might challenge of favour from the Crown for the credit he has heretofore given it as a merchant, when the Navy most needed and could least find it from other hands.

This (my Lord) I beg your receiving as the only honest return I (to my great trouble) find myself in present condition of giving in this case till I shall be further directed concerning it by your Lordship; being with all possible sincerity of respect,

My Lord,
Your Lordship's most dutiful and most obedient servant,
S. PEPYS

Perhaps even Balthazar St Michel came to realize that what Pepys had himself predicted long before – his inability to offer his brother-in-law significant assistance – had now come about. The last known letter from Balthazar records his receipt of some sort of allowance through an intermediary, a device resorted to by Pepys after his brother-in-law's abusive letter of 28 May 1689 (no. 202). The letter is the usual rambling profession of loyalty and gratitude combined with a self-pitying account of his ailments. It ends with a postscript requesting some secondhand clothes.

215. BALTHAZAR ST MICHEL TO SAMUEL PEPYS

For Mr Samuel Pepys at his house in Buckingham Street
In York Buildings near the Strand, these London

20 March 1692

MOST EVER HONOURED SIR

Ever since the knowledge of your generous goodness, favour, kindness, and charity, signified to me by Mr Boudler, it hath pleased God so to have afflicted me with such sickness, and tormenting pains all over my body, with the addition of the yellow jaundice, and other distempers (which the wants, and hardships, my late misfortune hath occasioned my groaning under,) as but two days ago, it was thought, I should never more have seen light in this world: but this being the first day (since my foresaid terrible illness) that I have been able to hold up my head, and pen, I could, nor would not let slip the opportunity which (by this little respite I have) God hath been pleased to afford me that so I might with true gratitude, give your honour my most dutiful and humble thanks for the same, which I do from the very bottom of my heart and soul, and assuring your honour that though (to my last breath) I will ever own to have had the best part of my life, support, and bread, by your only favour and goodness; yet this late generous act of yours hath (to me-wards) out done all the former, for that at this pinch, in this my latter age, and groaning under such circumstances of afflictions, and miseries of body and mind, which none but the Great Divinity, and myself knows, and indeed such, as I am sure hath no parallel; you ware pleased to relieve me. For which as I again, return your honour my everlasting dutiful thanks; so shall also my daily prayers, be ever to the Heavenly God, not only to repay you 1000-fold, but also that his divine Majesty would ever keep your dear body and soul to Everlasting life and Glory. I am

Your honour's poor afflicted
but most faithful humble
and dutiful servant

B. St Michel

If you have an old spare cast-off morning gown, peruiques, and some like cast-off large cloak-coat, which things you could spare without the least inconveniency to you, if you would spare them to your afflicted servant they would be very welcome and with millions of thanks, and to have a bundle made up, and by a porter to have it privately left for me, at Trinity House, Water Lane, at Mr Hunter's.

Pepys spent the summer of 1692 withdrawn from his friends, claiming to have gone to the country. In fact he had stayed working on his papers, so assiduously that he had ended up with a swollen leg. He wrote to Thomas Gale apologizing, recalling that he abandoned his friends on the Tangier expedition, called here the 'excursion to Spain'. He also alludes to depression, a theme he returned to later (Letter no. 234). Pepys's friend Mrs Steward is mentioned several times. Her identity is discussed in the introduction to Pepys's letter of 20 September 1695 (no. 230).

216. Samuel Pepys to Dr Thomas Gale

15 September 1692

Dear Sir

I have paid otherwise so dear for it that I will trust my friends as to any further chastisement for a fault that I was never guilty of but once before, and that was when I with as little manners left them for six months upon an excursion to Spain as now I have done (they know as little whither) for near three, without either asking or taking leave. But there are some things that won't bear ceremony, and must be done as that and this was or not at all; namely, where the extravagance of the doing is obvious to everybody but the expediency to none but oneself. This led me about that time ago to dive all at once under water, no body knew whither (but into the country), without ever appearing above it, till now that I would be glad to do it and cannot. The secret is this. I have (as you know) been every year for now three or four, subject to such a sort of surprises and disquietings from powers above me, without any prospect of ever being less so, that, upon the last trial I had of them, I resolved (when ever that was over) to put myself into a condition of meeting them with less uneasiness by ridding myself quite through of all that might on like occasions give me any anxieties, and above all in relation to my papers that I have so many years been tumultuously gathering and laying by, without a vacancy of hand or head ever to garble, sort, or putt into order for use either to myself or any that come after me; though I have several times since my recess from business attempted it, but with a plain conviction that nothing but a direct sequestering myself from all the world for a while would do it. And this I resolved to delay no longer, but at the charge of £30 for the colour only of a country-house, have shut myself up entirely here at home (even to the surmounting all considerations of good nature or good manners towards either friends or myself) to this day, that I have gained so much of my satisfaction aimed at as to have no more left to do than what by the grace of God I can now hope to compass with some regard to both; I mean, first to my friends, and at the head of them to yourself, whose kind enquiries after me and endeavours of visits as well as my best Mrs Steward's do with a great deal of reason bestow my first reflections upon and pay my earliest thanks for; which I beg you to accept by this, and to do me the good office also of communicating them to her, that you may together sit upon me and the extravagancy of this proceeding of mine before I am exposed to either of your reproachings singly; for I must own I have used you (as she calls it) very indiscreetly, i.e. so as I ought and do take shame to myself for.

And now as to this self of mine, I have indeed been soundly punished for it; my constant poring, and sitting so long still in one posture, without any divertings or exercise, having for about a month past brought a humour down into one of my legs, not only to the swelling it to almost the size of both, but with the giving me mighty pains, and disabling me to this day to putt on a shoe on that foot. Not but that since I allowed myself freedom to take some physic (which I have done twice this week) the pain is in a great part gone and the swelling abated, but not so as to have yet suffered me to step a step from the beginning of it but from my chamber to my study upon the same floor; Nor doubt it will before Saturday next, when I will (if God please) endeavour to meet you in my little parlour at a dish of tripes, if my ill usage of you will permit it on your side. Against which time I have (from a letter of his, which I have not answered neither) some hopes Mr Evelyn, who knows not yet where I am but gives you his wonted kind remembrances, may be in the way of waiting on you too.

Having thus shown myself impudently to you, one would think I might not need any mediator to any body else. But indeed Mrs Steward is so bitter a gentlewoman and bowelless, that I know the first word she saith will be the wishing my right leg as bad as my left for using her as I have done, and I know not how to blame her. Therefore pray assail her first on my behalf, and stroke her violence (if you can) till you have got her to name a time when you will together come and eat a dish of atonement with me. For I am now in a state of longing again, and the first fit of it is to see her, and to see her with you, that I may do it safely.

After this, give me leave to enquire after your health and your whole family's, and to continue to profess myself,

Your most humble and most faithful
affectionate servant

S. PEPYS

I am the more in want of an advocate with Mrs Steward for your countrywoman Mrs Lee's being gone into the north.

Edward Southwell was the son of Sir Robert Southwell (1635–1702), the diplomatist and by 1690 principal secretary of state for Ireland and President of the Royal Society 1690–5. He had just been appointed clerk to the Privy Council at the age of 22 and was likely to follow a career like those of William Cecil (1520–98), Elizabeth I's chief minister, and his son Robert Cecil (1563–1612), hence the suggestion that Pepys was accustomed to referring to him as the 'young Cecil'. Pepys clearly delighted in his relationship with the young man, regarding him with enthralled respect and as a kind of protégé. The work by Hooke referred to is possibly Hooke's analysis of hydrography, presented to Pepys on 24 March 1686 during his term as President of the Royal Society.

217. EDWARD SOUTHWELL TO SAMUEL PEPYS

16 May 1693

SIR

I am afraid your young Cecil may disappoint you, as many other of your old friends have done, unless you help to build him up by some of those excellent materials which you have in plenty and at your command.

My father bid me tell you that Dr Hooke's scheme about naval matters was presented you towards the end of your being President. And it was writt with some emulation to Sir William Petty's discourse called a *Treatise of Naval Philosophy in 3 Parts*[4]. And you will see in the Transaction now sent you a small sketch of what Sir William did, and at my Father's persuasion, in 1685.[5] And they are such heads as seem well worthy to be enlarged upon by the sons of that science. For as we are grown into a greater rate of building, ii were but suitable that men grew also taller in their skill. But for Dr Hooke's paper, if the hints aforesaid cannot discover it, you shall be assisted with farther information from him who takes it for great honour to be esteemed, Sir,

Your most humble servant

EDWARD SOUTHWELL

Part of Pepys's correspondence with Edward Southwell has only recently come to light. This letter survives as a loose secretarial copy, now in private hands. It is endorsed 'Mr Pepys to Mr Southwell, newly a clerk of the Council; part compliment, part business'. The contents include a mention of a letter from William Cecil, apparently in Pepys's possession. Pepys had a large number of sixteenth-century letters and manuscripts, passed to him by John Evelyn in order to assist the great naval history Pepys always planned to write but never did. These papers are now at Magdalene College, Cambridge. Evelyn had inherited them from his father-in-law, Sir Richard Browne, sometime clerk to the Privy Council (as

---

[4] Published 1691.
[5] *What a complete Treatise of Navigation should contain* (compiled 1685, published 1693).

Edward Southwell now was himself). The letter in question cannot be identified for certain but was possibly that of 28 May 1564 from George Nedham to William Cecil concerning the navigation potential at Emden in Holland.[6]

218. SAMUEL PEPYS TO EDWARD SOUTHWELL

York Buildings
5 July 1693

SIR

I follow you as soon as I can with my *Peccari* for yesterday's faults; not doubting my living long enough to give your greatness opportunities enough of revenge, by turning me off as slightly. But remember you would have it so.

With this, I send you two papers; one by commission from Mr Evelyn to be delivered to the old gentleman, whom I would have you strip, even while alive, of every state-virtue he has; it being but equal, that while he presses you thus into business, he grudge you none of his furniture for it. Not that I think you want an ample stock of your own. But time has some lessons which it keeps for its own teaching only, unless you can and will borrow them of a friend that has paid for them. I say Will [Hewer]. For 'twas not Solomon's faults, that I learnt too late, nor shall be mine if you do so too. To shun being too righteous, as much as being too wise. There's one of them.

The other paper is to yourself, and brings a piece of work with it. It is an extract of a letter of a predecessor of yours one William Cecil, that contains a naval note I would be glad to improve; by knowing what (if anything) is to be found in the Council books of that time relative to the matter therein mentioned, and which bespeaks its being soon followed by something from the Council Board.

Whether these books be within your reach, or to be come at at all; I know not But if they be, pray grant me this as the first cast of your office; wherein I do with all my heart pray God to bless you, and rest

Your most affectionate and hereditary humble servant
S. PEPYS

In 1693 Pepys received a disturbing letter from Isaac Newton. It was one of several sent by Newton, then aged 51, to friends in which he cut ties and made various allegations. In a letter to John Locke, Newton said that he had believed Locke was attempting to 'embroil' him 'with women'. This is now recognized as evidence for Newton suffering a bout of psychosis which lasted eighteen months and which was characterized by paranoid delusions. It has never been possible to identify the cause.

219. ISAAC NEWTON TO SAMUEL PEPYS

13 September 1693

SIR

Some time after Mr Millington had delivered your message, he pressed me to see you the next time I went to London. I was averse; but upon his pressing consented, before I considered what I did, for I am extremely troubled at the embroilment I am in, and have neither ate nor slept well this twelve month, nor have my former

[6] HMC pp. 22–24.

consistency of mind. I never designed to get anything by your interest, nor by King James's favour, but am now sensible that I must withdraw from your acquaintance, and see neither you nor the rest of my friends any more, if I may but leave them quietlv. I beg your pardon for saying I would see you again, and rest your most humble and most obedient servant,

IS. NEWTON

Happily, Newton soon recovered. On 15 October he wrote to John Locke to say that 'The last winter by sleeping too often by my fire I got an ill habit of sleeping and a distemper which this summer has been epidemical put me further out of order, so that when I wrote to you I had not slept an hour a night for a fortnight together and for five nights together not a wink.' Newton and Pepys were exchanging amicable letters on the complicated issue of mathematical probability (see no. 222).

Meanwhile, on 29 September 1693 Pepys was robbed by highwaymen. The incident is unmentioned in the extant correspondence, and is only known from Old Bailey session papers. It is an insight into what Pepys carried about his person.

220. SAMUEL PEPYS AND JOHN JACKSON ROBBED 29 SEPTEMBER 1693

Old Bailey Session Papers 2–9 December 1693

Thomas Hoyle and Samuel Gibbons, gentlemen, were both tried upon two indictments for a Robbery on the Highway, committed on Michaelmas Day last; first upon Samuel Pepys Esq, secondly upon John Jackson Esq. Mr Pepys gave evidence, That as he was riding to Chelsea in his coach, accompanied with Mr Jackson and his lady, and some other ladies, on the 29th of September last, in the dusk of the evening three persons (having their faces covered with vizored masks) met his coach, (being all on horseback) and holding a pistol to the coachman's breast and holding a pistol to the coachman's breast, and another against Mr Pepys, commanded the coach to stand, demanded what they had, which Mr Pepys readily gave them; which was a silver ruler, value 30s, a gold pencil value £8, five mathematical instruments, value £3, a magnifying glass, value 20s, a gold and silver purse, value 10s, two guineas and 20s in money, these were Mr Pepys' goods and money. The things they took from Mr Jackson were, a silver hilted sword, value 50s, a hatband, value 2s etc. Mr Pepys and Mr Jackson could not swear the prisoners were the men that robbed them, because they were masked; Mr Pepys conjured them to be civil to the ladies, and not to affright them, which they were; and by their demeanour of themselves, my Lady Pepys saved a bag of money that she had about her; Mr Pepys desired them to give him a particular instrument that was of great use to him; and one of them told him, 'Sir, you are a gentleman and so are we; if you will send to the Rummer Tavern at Charing Cross tomorrow, you shall have it there'. Mr Pepys did send, but there was nothing left. Another witness for the King swore, that the prisoners were two of the three that committed the robbery, for that Mr Hoyle had oftentimes solicited him to go abroad with him to take a purse; at last he told them he would; and at the same time, viz. on the 29th of September last, they went upon this design; but this witness shifted the matter, under some pretence of an accidental business, and so they went away by themselves; but however he immediately followed them, with a purpose to see what they did: and he saw them stop the coach, and commit the robbery; and they pulled off their masks after they had done the feat, and he saw their faces plainly. The man that let them the horses swore, that they had three horses of him about the same time, about Michaelmas Day, and that Mr Hoyle hired them, and that they returned back about six o'clock in the evening. They were taken at Westminster in a short time after, and Mr Hoyle had a pencil about him, which was Mr Pepys his pencil; they were taken at the Rummer Tavern in Charing Cross.

The Prisoners called some witnesses, who said, that they were elsewhere when the robbery was done; and Mr Hoyle urged that he was sworn against out of revenge, and a malice that was ingrafted in the bosom of one of the witnesses, upon account of a former quarrel that happened betwixt them about beating a boy. Other evidence on his part, declared that he was sick, and had taken physic, he further said that he was an officer in the army, and never wronged any person, neither man woman, nor child. Mr Gibbons said, that he mounted the Guard at the same time which he called a corporal to declare; but it was presumed he might do so, and yet be in the robbery too. He being asked how he came by the pistols? He said he bought them to go to Flanders. The evidence was very particular for the king against them: So the jury having considered the matter very distinctly, they brought in a verdict, that they were both guilty of felony and robbery. [Note. Received sentence of death.]

Oddly, this unpleasant experience went unmentioned in a letter Pepys wrote to Arthur Charlett the next day. One of his abiding interests was collecting engraved portraits, an enthusiasm he shared with John Evelyn.[7] Evelyn may have encouraged Pepys but he was already looking out for prints as a young man.[8] Accumulating portraits of the great, famous or merely curious, was almost a *de rigueur* activity for someone like Pepys wished to express his recognition and appreciation of their world by collecting their likenesses. Unlike Evelyn, Pepys did not actively encourage artists and seems to have had little exper knowledge in the field.

221. SAMUEL PEPYS TO DR ARTHUR CHARLETT

York Buildings
30 September 1693

SIR

I own with all the thankfulness I am able your favours shown me when here, and those you pursue them with from Oxford. Nor had I taken all this time for doing so had I been earlier instructed how to direct myself to you in it; your being come to Oxford remaining uncertain to me, till you were pleased to tell it me in yours of the 28th.

Your heads, even to Mother George's, are a very welcome addition to my collection, and accordingly it must acknowledge you its benefactor; but 'tis confident enough at the same time to call you its debtor too, for Dr Hammond's Dundee's, Dr Fell, Allestree and Dolben's, and I think for Mr Woods, and D Pococke's. Forgive the clamminess of my memory on this occasion; for I can't help laying up every word that sounds that way, and much less can I forget names like

---

[7] See for example his letter to Evelyn of 25 September 1690, PF D7, and Der Waals, 1984. Evelyn published a book on the subject: *Sculptura* (1661).
[8] Diary 1 January 1662.

these, the want of which (if to be had) were alone enough to blast all I pretend to in it. I cannot therefore be ashamed to pray your aid in reference to them, if within your power; or direction, whither else I may apply myself for them, if they are not: For in all my searches after this commodity I do not remember that any one of them ever occurred to me in this whole town; nor of your own, neither, which I would less be without then my own, if your good will to mankind has at any time been strong enough to obtain of you a graving of it.

I have a particular set of thanks to pay you for your university prints, I mean, those of Loggan's work, not to be found in the ordinary volume of them; whereinto I have therefore caused them to be inserted, and thereby through your kindness rendered it much more valuable to me.

Your late public exercises are what I have last to give you my acknowledgements for, and that you think so much more gently of my gusto towards them, then of that of our excellent Captain Hatton's. In which nevertheless I shall adventure upon disappointing you so far, as to respite the giving you any aim at my thoughts of them, till I can at the same time entertain you with his too.

The account you give me of Mr Wood's No-Mortification, and the further kicks he means to expose his teeth to from the Heels of Truth, makes me yet more covetous of his picture, if it be to be had. For he is in more senses then one an original, but such a one, as I can much better bear the being without, then the copy.

I would to God your next would tell me of something this town could enable me to furnish you with, in exchange for all or any part of this; and beshrew your good nature if you know what, and do not. For you will force me else to what of most earthly things I would least willingly do, I mean, unbespeak the continuance of a kindness I cannot repay. I am

Honoured Sir

Your most faithful and obedient servant

S. PEPYS

I have recovered my mistake, since I made it, in applying Loggan's name to the works of Burgher; for which I pray your pardon.

In late 1693 Pepys exchanged letters with Isaac Newton on probability. Apparently Thomas Neale had monopolized educated conversation in London on the subject. Pepys's letter was carried by a Mr Smith, writing master at Christ's Hospital in which Pepys took a great interest. In 1673 he had helped set up the Royal Mathematical School, and became a governor in 1675. Newton's reply is one of the best-known letters in the Pepys correspondence. In view of his recent breakdown, he seems to have been delighted by the chance to renew his friendship with Pepys.

222. SAMUEL PEPYS TO ISAAC NEWTON

22 November 1693

SIR

However this comes accompanied with a little trouble to you, yet I cannot but say that the occasion is welcome to me, in that it gives me an opportunity of telling you that I continue most sensible of my obligations to you, most desirous of rendering you service in whatever you shall think me able, and no less afflicted when I hear of your being in town without knowing how to wait on you till it be too late for me to do it.

This said, and with great truth and respect, I go on to tell you that the bearer, Mr Smith, is one I bear great goodwill to, no less for what I personally know of his general ingenuity, industry, and virtue, than for the general reputation he has, in this town (inferior to none, but superior to most) for his mastery in the two points of his profession, namely, *Fair-Writing* and *Arithmetic,* so far (principally) as is subservient to accountantship. Now so it is, that the late project (of which you cannot but have heard) of Mr Neale, the groom-porter his lottery, has almost extinguished for some time at all places of public conversation in this town, especially among men of numbers, every other talk but what relates to the doctrine of determining between the true proportions of the hazards incident to this or that given chance or lot.

On this occasion it has fallen-out that this gentleman is become concerned (more than in jest) to compass a solution that may be relied on beyond what his modesty will suffer him to think his own alone, or any less than Mr Newton's to be, to a question which he takes a journey on purpose to attend you with, and prayed my giving him this introduction to you to that purpose, which, not in common friendship only but as due to his so earnest an application after truth, though in a matter of speculation alone, I cannot deny him, and therefore trust you will forgive me in it, and the trouble I desire you to bear at my instance, of giving him your decision upon it, and the process of your coming at it. Wherein I shall esteem myself on his behalf greatly owing to you, and remain,

Honoured Sir, Your most humble and
most affectionate and faithful servant,
S. P.

THE QUESTION

A—has 6 dice in a box, with which he is to fling a 6.
B—has in another box 12 dice, with which he is to fling 2 sixes.
C—has in another box 18 dice, with which he is to fling 3 sixes.
Q—Whether B and C have not as easy a task as A at even luck?

223. ISAAC NEWTON TO SAMUEL PEPYS

Cambridge
26 November 1693

SIR

I was very glad to hear of your good health by Mr Smith, and to have any opportunity given me of showing how ready I should be to serve you or your friends upon any occasion, and wish that something of greater moment would give me a new opportunity of doing it so as to become more useful to you than in solving only a mathematical question. In reading the question it seemed to me at first to be ill stated, and in examining Mr Smith about the meaning of some phrases in it he put the case of the question the same as if A plaid with six dyes till he threw a six and then B threw as often with 12 and C with 18 — the one for twice as many, the other for thrice as many sixes. To examine who had the advantage, I took the case of A throwing with one dye and B with two, the former till he threw a six, the latter as often for two sixes, and found that A had the advantage. But whether A will have the advantage when he throws with 6 and B with 12 dyes I cannot tell, for the number of dyes may alter the proportion of the chances considerably, and I did not compute it in this case, the problem being a very hard one. And indeed, upon reading the question anew, I found that these cases do not come within the question. For here an advantage is given to A by his throwing first till he throws a six; whereas the question requires that they throw upon equal luck, and by consequence that no advantage be given to any one by throwing first. The question is this:

A has 6 dyes in a box, with which he is to fling a six.
B has in another box 12 dyes, with which he is to fling two sixes.
C has in another box 18 dyes, with which he is to fling three sixes.
Q. Whether B and C have not as easy a task as A at even luck ?

If this question must be understood according to the plainest sense of the words, I think that sense must be this:

1. Because A, B, and C are to throw upon equal luck, there must be no advantage of luck given to any of them by throwing first or last, or by making anything depend upon the throw of any one which does not equally depend on the throws of the other two. And therefore to bar all inequality of luck on these accounts, I would understand the question as if A, B, and C were to throw all at the same time.
2. I take the most proper and obvious meaning of the words of the question to be that when A flings more sixes than one he flings a six as well as when he flings but a single six and so gains his expectation, and so when B flings more sixes than two and C more than three they gain their expectations. But if B throw under two sixes and C under three, they miss their expectations, because in the question 'tis expressed that B is to throw 2 and C three sixes.
3. Because each man has his dyes in a box ready to throw, and the question is put upon the chances of that throw without naming any more throws than that, I take the question to be the same as if it had been put thus upon single throws.

What is the expectation or hope of A to throw every time one six at least with six dyes?

What is the expectation or hope of B to throw every time two sixes at least with 12 dyes?

What is the expectation or hope of C to throw every time three sixes or more than three with 18 dyes?

And whether has not B and C as great an expectation or hope to hit every time what they throw for as A hath to hit his what he throws for?

If the question be thus stated, it appears by an easy computation that the expectation of A is greater than that of B or C; that is, the task of A is the easiest. And the reason is because A has all the chances of sixes on his dyes for his expectation, but B and C have not all the chances on theirs. For when B throws a single six or C but one or two sixes, they miss of their expectations. This Mr Smith understands, and therefore allows that if the question be understood as I have stated it, then B and C have not so easy a task as A; but he seems of opinion that the question should be so stated that B and C as well as A may have all the chances of sixes on their dyes within their expectations. I do not see that the words of the question as 'tis set down in your letter will admit it, but this being no mathematical question, but a question what is the true mathematical question, it belongs not to me to determine it. I have contented myself therefore to set down how in my opinion the question according to the most obvious and proper meaning of the words is to be understood, and that if this be the true state of the question, then B and C have not so easy a task as A. But whether I have hit the true meaning of the question I must submit to the better judgments of yourself and others. If you desire the computation, I will send it you.

I am, Sir,

Your most humble and most obedient servant

ISAAC NEWTON

Further, lengthy, letters followed on the subject.[9] Isaac Newton sent the computation he offered, on 16 December, and the correspondence carried on into 1694.

In 1695 James Houblon set out on a journey to the Continent. Since 1694 he had been a director of the newly founded Bank of England. Pepys wrote with what little news he had, including a reference to the bullion crisis that was leaving the country seriously short of silver and gold coinage.

224. SAMUEL PEPYS TO SIR JAMES HOUBLON

9 July 1695

DEAR SIR

Length is no commendation to a letter from him that has nothing to do to you that have a great deal. Therefore in brief, I received great pleasure from the safeness of your passage and arrival at Antwerp; owning no less thanks to you for my share in the knowledge you gave your friends of it. We are all well here, as we pray you may ever be. The town yields no news; the season emptying it of men as the Bank (we thank you) does of money, some gold only excepted, and that very dear bought. You won't think it news (I know) that Mr Willmer sings at this day upon the hustings to my Lord Mayor, the Aldermen, and Sheriffs, the very same song (the burthen you may perhaps remember, Liberty, Privilege, and Property) that themselves joined-in with him to Sir John Moore but few years since. But I have something just come to my hand that I can't but take for news. I am sure 'tis so to me, notwithstanding all I pretend to of knowledge in the history of the Navy of England, and this I enclose you, with a hearty commitment of you to God's protection, and rest,

Your most faithful and obedient servant

S. PEPYS

More news would shortly arrive from Houblon giving an eyewitness account of the Siege at Namur (Letter no. 229). Meanwhile another side to Pepys's interest in mathematics and improving the standards of seamen threw up problems. In the 1670s Pepys had been a prime mover in establishing the Royal Mathematical School at Christ's Hospital. He was made a governor on 1 February 1676. The idea was that public funds should be invested in training

---

[9] Printed by Tanner 1926, i, nos. 55–61.

up navigators who could serve in the Royal Navy or in the Merchant Service. The school's fortunes fluctuated, depending on the quality of the teacher.

Despite Pepys's efforts he found that all too often teachers were appointed who had no interest in actually educating the boys of Christ's Hospital, preferring research instead. The problems did not abate, and continued well into Pepys's old age. He was frustrated by John Reeves, an administrator at the Hospital, who seems to have been incompetent and unhelpful. This was followed by a complaint from a new and competent teacher about having incompletely-trained boys being pulled out of the school to work prematurely. These letters were preserved amongst the archives of Christ's Hospital but have now passed to the British Library.

225. SAMUEL PEPYS TO JOHN REEVES

Mr Reeves of Christ's Hospital

5 August 1695

MR REEVES

I have long expected (you know) the particulars you promised me, making out the state of the House as you laid it before the Court in the General Account of its debts and income in February last. I do not doubt of you having it ready by you, and therefore shall desire either my seeing you with it, or you sending it me, tomorrow morning about 9 a clock.

And pray let me at the same time have the names of any of the children of our Foundation, whom you understand to have been advanced to the charge of Commander, Lieutenant, or Master in any of the King's ships, since the account you have me thereof in March was twelvemonth; and the like as to the advancement of any of them in the Merchant Service. For I would unwittingly want the knowledge of anything that may do the Foundation honour; while I meet with so many that tend (I greatly fear) to the prejudice of it. I am

Your assured friend
S. PEPYS

226. JOHN REEVES TO SAMUEL PEPYS

6 August 1695

HONOURED SIR

I confess myself in arrear to what you directed and promised. I have searched but can scarcely find the exact particulars of the general accompt of debts and yearly income presented in February last, and have reason to believe some of our Committee did take the same away with them, but in some further time shall most readily tender the same in the best manner I can tell you.

As to the advance of the Mathematical Scholars in his Majesty's service or otherwise, until some of them come home, it seems to be difficult to give a just accompt thereof, but as soon as maybe, you may expect the same from

Your Honour's most humble servant
JOHN REEVES

This was hardly the reply the frustrated Pepys wanted and wrote in a subsequent letter on 7 August to another Christ's Hospital official that it was a letter 'I know not of myself how to interpret'. A few days later an unexpected new problem arose. Isaac Newton had recommended Samuel Newton (no relation) as a suitable new mathematics master for the school. A conscientious man, Samuel Newton was annoyed to find himself being forced to allow boys to be taken from the school before they were ready for the sea. He wrote to Pepys to complain about 'this injurious cancer' in a frank letter that challenged the social protocols of the day.

227. SAMUEL NEWTON TO SAMUEL PEPYS

To the Honourable Samuel Pepys Esq
York Buildings London

Christ's Hospital
8 August 1695

HONOURED SIR

The letter which Pemberton brought me from your Honour arrived about two in the afternoon yesterday and about four (or two hours after) comes Sir Matthew for a boy, to be put out the next week. I told him, I have none ready, so he expressed if there were none ready he must have one unready, because he has promised one to a Sea Captain and that he would answer (I think he said excuse) the boy's unpreparedness to the Trinity House.

It grieves me to the very soul when I reflect upon such inconsiderate actions; and that the most famous Mathematical School (dedicated to charity) should be thus torn in pieces by one man, who were he sensible of the injury he does, would blush to think of such doings. These proceedings will bring down the honour and reputation of this famous nursery, to the level of an Abcdarian and every common tarpaulin who never knew either the usefulness or sweetness of Mathematical learning will run down our poor children brought up in a royal foundation; and in this the school which was erected on purpose to improve our English seamen in arts and sciences (particularly navigation) will fall under the lowest degree of contempt.

Let Heaven direct your Honour to find out some proper expedient to stop this injurious cancer; that the children in after times may have a thankful remembrance of your goodness to them in opposing such practices as will lead to the ruin of their education.

Your Honour's
Most humble servant
S. NEWTON

I hope to have my answer to your Honour's excellent letter ready to kiss your hands sometime the next week.

Pepys had little choice but to chide Samuel Newton for being so forthright. He suggested that there was little more the young man could do other than accept the situation and do his best by the boys, certifying the skills they had reached in the time available.

228. SAMUEL PEPYS TO SAMUEL NEWTON

8 August 1695

MR NEWTON

I have your letter of this morning and am satisfied of there being but one way of setting matters right in the business of the foundation you are so concerned for; and that is by showing the House at once, that the whole of it (from end to end) is at this day wrong; and it is to no purpose to think of rectifying it by retail, where the whole in every part is equally faulty. And this, as the best service I can ever hope to do it, I am preparing myself for, and not far (I hope) from accomplishing it.

All then which I think to be now needful to return to you upon your present complaint, is, the giving you my opinion, what may be fit in your place to do upon it, with respect to Sir Matthew Andrews; who not only is your superior, and so not decently to be contended with by you, but the person whom you find in a special manner depended upon by the House in the business of disposing of the children, and moreover has the honour of being Master at this time of the Trinity House, where the King by his Letters Patents has placed the last judgment of the children's proficiencies and fitness to be sent abroad; and so there seems no room left in either respect for you doubting their being informed in the design or moment of the foundation. Besides, as it now happens, the Treasurer your immediate superior, is out of the way, nor any court or committee within your reach to appeal to, in case you found yourself so to do.

As to what therefore you are in this case to [do] towards Sir Matthew Andrews, in case he shall think fit to press in his purpose of disposing presently some of your boys to sea, notwithstanding your having acquainted him with his unreadiness yet for it, according to the rules prescribed you. My opinion is, that you are in the first place to apply yourself with all the diligence you can to improving the child in all the principal points as far as ever the little time allowed you for it will enable you; and that being done, to give Sir Matthew a certificate under your hand, in the decentest terms you are able, of the several heads of science wherein you can safely assent the child's being instructed, not sparing to do the child full right in the same, submitting it to Sir Matthew Andrews and the Gentlemen of the Trinity House, to make such use thereof on his behalf as they shall see fit. This much, he demanding it, I think you in duty bound to do. And more than that, after the profession you tell me you have made to him, I will presume he will not ask nor expect from you.

I am your very humble servant
S. PEPYS

I thank you for what you promised me next week.

James Houblon was present when William III's army recaptured Namur on 1 September. He was a member of a party of Bank of England officials en route to Antwerp to establish a branch. As the gateway into Holland, recovering Namur was a major strike in the war against France. Houblon wrote to Pepys to describe the scene, though that letter is lost. Pepys was clearly fascinated by Houblon's account, having spent much of the summer locked away on his papers (which included the Christ's Hospital correspondence above). There had been a tragedy. 'Mr Godfrey' is Michael Godfrey, first deputy-governor of the Bank of England who was killed observing the siege from the trenches when the party passed through Namur.

229. SAMUEL PEPYS TO SIR JAMES HOUBLON

6 September 1695

DEAR SIR

If I have been longer than in good manners I should have been in my return to your late cheerful account of our martial improvements; pray answer for it yourself, in putting me in expectation of the minute you there seemed so determined in relating to Namur. Not but that 'tis come; but if this be all you mean by our overtaking the French in their way of reckoning by minutes, God help us; since what you call minutes, would any where else pass for months; at least not for French minutes months. Monsieur Bouflers indeed was taken to a minute; but I don't think you any more thought then of his capture, than I, or your poor colleague Mr Godfrey (whose fate I truly pity) when he surveyed the siege. God be thanked you were not all alike curious nor yourself in particular; whom I pray God always protect.

Where this is to meet with you I know not, as having made another dive for some time, that is, shut myself up among my papers (for there's no work to be done without it sometimes) so as to be become a stranger to everything out of my own house; my first sally being this moment towards yours, with this, and to inform myself of the best part of my concerning, namely, your health and family's. Which I trust I shall meet with a good account of, and (as the welcomest circumstance of it) that you are 'ere this looking homeward.

Other matters can't but go well (you will conclude) when I tell you, that I have for sometime had nothing in my ears but ringing of bells, huzzas, and crackling of bonfires, Which some time or other must terminate in a peace, and I hope 'tis not far off. In the meantime God keep you in his protection, and send us a happy meeting. I am ever dear Sir,

Your most faithful and most
humble and affectionate servant
S. PEPYS

The next letter, a retained copy, to Pepys's friend Mrs Steward contains several contemporary references. The main subject under discussion was legacies to children at Christ's Hospital. The reference to 'our losses at sea' means the loss of more than a hundred English merchant ships to French privateers during the current war with France. This explains the shortage of muslin mentioned. The lack of a 'good' shilling refers to how by 1695 circulating coinage was largely made up of clipped and worn medieval hammered coins. The new milled coinage produced since early 1663 had been mostly hoarded or melted down causing an ongoing crisis in cash, restricting everyday commerce. The great recoinage did not start until 1696.

Mrs Steward herself is unknown apart from Pepys's references and a mention in Evelyn's diary. Although Pepys refers here to Mrs Steward's frequent correspondence with him, unfortunately no letter from her has survived that might have clarified her first name. Although the original manuscript was examined for this book, no further information could be found.

She is usually described as the sister of Elizabeth, Lady Mordaunt, and was presumably the woman called Lady Mordaunt's 'sister Johnson' in the Diary (9 March 1669). Lady Mordaunt was the daughter of Nicholas Johnson and his wife Elizabeth (née Turner) and was christened at St Gregory-by-St Paul in June 1645. Her mother Elizabeth Turner was the sister of John Turner (1613–88 or 89) of Kirkleatham, Yorks, who married Pepys's cousin Jane (1623–86) in 1648. Her 'sister Johnson' may be the Jane Johnson who was christened at St Gregory-by-St Paul on 23 April 1652, the daughter of Nicholas Johnson and, this time, a woman named Katherine.

Although the death of Mrs Elizabeth Johnson has not been traced, or a second marriage for Nicholas Johnson, or the marriage of a Jane Johnson to anyone called Steward/Stewart/Stuart, it does seem possible that 'Mrs Steward' was in fact Elizabeth Mordaunt's half-sister, unless her mother 'Katherine' is an error. Not only is her name Jane the same as that of Pepys's cousin, her aunt (or step-aunt), but Mrs Steward and Pepys became godparents to John Evelyn's granddaughter, also Jane, on 12 January 1692. This circumstantial association suggests that Jane Johnson was probably Mrs Steward.

However, since Mrs Steward's husband is never mentioned or even alluded to, it must be assumed that he died very young and she never remarried. Since she was not included amongst the mourners at Pepys's funeral, she probably died between 1695 and May 1703.

230. SAMUEL PEPYS TO MRS STEWARD

20 September 1695

MADAM

You are very good, and pray continue so by as many kind messages as you can and notices of your health; such as the bearer brings you back my thanks for, and a thousand services.

Here's a sad town, and God knows when it will be better, our losses at sea making a very melancholy exchange at both ends on't; the gentlewomen of this (to say nothing of the other) sitting with their arms across, without a yard of muslin in their shops to sell, while the ladies (they tell me) walk pensively by, without a shilling (I mean, a good one) in their pockets to buy.

One thing there is indeed that comes in my way as a Governor to hear of which carries a little mirth with it, and indeed is very odd. Two wealthy citizens are lately dead, and left their estates, one to a Bluecoat boy and the other to a Bluecoat girl in Christ's Hospital. The extraordinariness of which has led some of the Magistrates to carry it on to a match, which is ended in a public wedding, he in his habit of blew-satin, led by two of the girls, and she in blue, with an apron green and petticoat yellow, all of sarsenet, led by two of the boys of the House, through Cheapside to Guildhall chapel, where they were married by the Dean of St Paul's, and she given by my Lord Mayor. The wedding-dinner it seems was kept in the Hospital hall. But the great day will be tomorrow, St Matthew's; when (so much I am sure of) my Lord Mayor will be there, and myself also have had a ticket of invitation thither, and if I can will be there too. But for the other particulars must refer you to my next; and so,

Dear Madam, Adieu.

Bow-Bells are just now ringing Ding-Dong; but whether for this I cannot presently tell; but 'tis likely enough. For I have known them ring upon much foolisher occasions, and lately too.

Late in 1695 Colonel John Scott, the charlatan, rogue, master of disguise, and key player in the case against Pepys during the Popish Plot returned to England. The identity of Pepys's correspondent, Edward Wright, is unknown.

231. EDWARD WRIGHT TO SAMUEL PEPYS

10 November 1696

HONOURED SIR

Colonel Scott (your prosecutor) is again come for England. When he arrived first he was in the habit of a Dutch skipper, which disguised him very much. But now he has got good clothes and a periwig. He was at a friend's house of mine some few days past, and pretended he had got his pardon for killing the coachman, but he tells me he does not believe it. This I thought good to acquaint you of because, Sir, I am,

Your most humble servant,
EDWARD WRIGHT

232. SAMUEL PEPYS TO EDWARD WRIGHT

[10/11 November 1696]

MR WRIGHT

I give you thanks for your information this morning, which I should be glad you could enlighten yourself further in, and particularly as to the pardon, and that you would do me the favour to communicate the same to me; who am,

Your very affectionate friend to serve you,
S. PEPYS

233. EDWARD WRIGHT TO SAMUEL PEPYS

12 November 1696

HONOURED SIR

I have done to learn as much as I can since the other day. Colonel Scott about nine weeks ago came to England in seamens' habit; he was not seen by anybody I know till about sixteen days ago, and then he appeared in pretty good habit and a bob wig on, and pulled out a parchment with a broad seal to it and said it was his pardon, and desired that man to get him a silver box made to put it in. But he never since see him. I called this morning at his house; he tells me that the Colonel was there yesterday but he was not at home. Whether it was a pardon or no he cannot tell; Kings does not use to grant pardons before convictions unless it be to noble men, – to the Duke of Buckingham for killing my Lord Shrewsbury, or the like this present King did to Colonel Beverage for killing Mr Danby, and to some other outlaws that he brought along with him. But the Colonel has always been obnoxious to him; when he was in Holland he ran away with his regiment's money and hanged in effigy. Besides I have employed a particular friend of mine to search the Hamper Office and the Petty Bag Office, where all patents of that nature passes, and for sixteen terms past there has been no such patent past. I am informed that he lodges in Gray's Inn by two people that he has told so to. If I can anyways further serve your Honour, no person shall more faithfully do it than, Sir,

Your most humble servant,
EDWARD WRIGHT

I had like to [have] omitted this one thing: When he returned out of Holland again he told my friend he had a bill from the Bank of Amsterdam of £100 upon the Bank here and could not get his money. He is not a bit altered, not as to his person and carriage.

Julia Shelcross (or Shallcross), née Boteler, was related to Mary Skinner through her father's marriage. Her stepmother was Mary's aunt. This draft letter, transcribed in full here for the first time, is the only surviving part of Pepys's correspondence with her. It emerged in a 1937 sales catalogue, having been previously unknown, though it is plain from the original manuscript that it was probably once amongst the Pepys-Cockerell papers. Endorsed 'a letter of respect only' it includes an explicit reference to Pepys's self-imposed isolation. Significantly, Pepys also refers to the *Anatomy of Melancholy* (1621) by Robert Burton (1577–1640), now considered to be a pioneering work in the analysis of human cognition, and in particular, clinical depression. It may well be that at this time, his career over and after a bout of illness in the summer and autumn of 1697, Pepys did experience what we would now recognize as depression. However, although he possessed a copy of Burton's work, the 'quotation' does not appear to be from it and could not be traced.[10]

This draft originally bore the address 'York Buildings' but Pepys struck this out, either because he sent the letter from somewhere else, probably Clapham, or because he never sent it at all. The letter has a number of crossings-out, alterations and insertions and the exact intended word order in one or two places is consequently uncertain.

234. SAMUEL PEPYS TO MRS JULIA SHELCROSS/SHALLCROSS

18 November 1697

MADAM,

Mrs Skinner has shown me how indelible the impressions are of your generous friendship, not towards her only, but to myself too, notwithstanding all the unreasonable courses of silence and neglect that I have taken to render myself unworthy of them. Not that I would lead your ladyship from my own calling it so, to think it really neglect, there being no lady upon Earth towards whom I either would or ought more to shun that guilt than yourself. But indeed Madam the world and I have been strangers a great while, even to the working myself as much out of the memory of that, as I have reason (if I could) to get that out of mine.

But since it is my better fortune, notwithstanding this, not to be forgot by your ladyship, pray be so good, as with your remembrance[11] to think me worthy of your commands, if anything can be at this day though left, wherein my poor services may be worth your calling for.

It would have been too much for me to have troubled your ladyship with this, had I not had some pretence to it, from a command of Mrs Skinner's, to give you her most humble services, she having been for these two days, as she is at this hour, in great disorder and pain. But I hope it is the effect of the sudden severity of the season only, and that she will soon be in a condition herself of acknowledging to you the favour of your last, and possibly of taking the benefit of it, by a visit, in the approaching Holy Time, if her health will bear it.

As to other matters, Madam, let me state them to you in one stanza of Mr Burton's (I think it is)

---

[10] Pers. comm. Dr R. Luckett. The text of Letter no. 216 also seems to allude to depression.

[11] 'with your remembrance' is an abbreviated insertion, and its intended place is not certain.

> When I see a discontent
> Sick of the faults of government
> Whose very rest and peace disease him
> 'Cause given by those that do not please him
> Methinks that Bedlam has no folly
> Like to the politic melancholy.

My mention of Mrs Skinner's visit to your ladyship gives me occasion of adding, that I hope it will not be long unfollowed by another to some friends of yours and ours a great way further off, and myself possibly her guide. If that should fall out, I should not then despair, but you might think of some commands that I might be fit for.

Dear Madam, Adieu

Thomas Gale was distantly related to Pepys by marriage. Gale's wife Barbara, whom he married in 1674, was the granddaughter of Talbot Pepys of Impington, himself son of John Pepys (d. 1589) by his second marriage. Samuel Pepys was John Pepys's great-grandson by the latter's first marriage. Gale had been Professor of Greek at Cambridge from 1666–72, when he became high master of St Paul's School, a post he held until 1697, and a member of the Royal Society from 1677. The two men became close friends and remained so even when in 1697 he was elevated to the position of Dean of York, by which time his wife had been dead for nine years.

235. SAMUEL PEPYS TO DR THOMAS GALE, DEAN OF YORK

York Buildings
9 March 1699

SIR

Having made my way to you by Colson your York-Carrier now near fourteen days since, who has (I hope) delivered you Dr Bentley's reply to Mr [Charles] Boyle (then fresh from the press) with expectation of a great deal ready to follow it from several quarters; allow me to assure you (not in excuse for, but to prevent your thinking my silence singular towards you) that I am now writing the first letter that has gone from me, but into France, since I had last the pleasure of waiting on you here. So much am I fallen, farther than ever I was, from the gusto of any satisfaction to be fetched from without doors, since by the separation or other avocations of the few friends I had remaining of them whose conversations were my just delight, I have so little left me of it within; and what with your Iamblichus, Stobaeus, Eugubinus, and two or three more domestics of your recommending, I can make shift to entertain myself better by myself, than at this time of day to be looking out for new acquaintance. Besides that (to tell you the truth) a friend of this sort at York is little other than a Death's Head to me here; the distance of the one filling me with contemplations as ghastly as the presence of the other. Especially when I think of the new set of thoughts, which with this change of life, business, conversation and abode must 'ere this have got possession of you. But I won't despair, but there may be something yet behind, that may bring you southward again, and set me once more at your feet, where I have so long delighted to be.

Mr Evelyn's visits are still very kind and ever valuable. But what with the common effects of age, with the addition of some late domestic cares, and one of them now depending in Parliament upon an unhappy misunderstanding between the two brothers, are becoming less frequent and less lively too, than you and I have known them.

Dr Bentley's *Phalaris* has taken him up wholly for many a day, as I think I had not seen him above three or four times in eight or ten months, till since his being delivered thereof, which set him at liberty to see me last Tripe Day; but with his head still embroiled, and for ought I hear, likely to continue so. Nor indeed (whatever the reputation of his learning may be advantaged by it) has he governed himself, either in the matter or in the style of his new work, as if he had a mind ever to have it otherwise. No advantage of cause (if he has that) seeming able to justify his forgetting at once the difference of quality, age, character, and interest (as he has done) between his adversary's and his own. But it has not arose from the want of my being his early remembrancer in them all; as one whose learning I cannot but have a partiality for, though it be very coarsely managed by him, which soon or late he'll be glad to mend.

Mrs Skinner is greatly your servant and so is my nephew with the greatest respect; who have made a tour of three months to Paris and its environs, and thence through Flanders to Antwerp, and so home, with great pleasure, and I hope to my nephew's solid benefit.

I have myself had an uneasy winter, so as to have been kept on this side my threshold for three months past, but the spring is upon its entry, and will (I hope) in a little time set me at liberty.

As late as it is, pray take my most thankful acknowledging for yours of August, and as soon as you can afford it me, let me know how you and all my cousins do; how this retirement of yours (for so I must call it, though few else will) agrees with you; and when (if ever) I may hope for your drawing this way again, your six months' residence being long out, and another far advanced. I am with great truth Dear Sir

Your most humble faithful and affectionate servant
S. PEPYS

Mr Hewer has for some time been very ill, and not much otherwise yet, saving that he's got (we hope) beyond danger

John Dryden was a friend of Pepys, but unlike him Dryden became a Catholic under James II, which John Evelyn called 'no great loss to the [Protestant] Church'.[12] In 1698 Pepys had dined with Dryden and encouraged him to produce his own edition of some of Chaucer's works. This appeared in 1700 called *Fables Ancient and Modern; Translated into Verse from Homer, Ovid, Boccace, and Chaucer.* Here Dryden writes to Pepys to thank him for the suggestion.

---

[12] Diary 19 January 1686.

236. JOHN DRYDEN TO SAMUEL PEPYS

For Samuel Pepys, Esq.
At his house in York Street   14 July 1699

PADRON MIO

I remember, last year, when I had the honour of dining with you, you were pleased to recommend to me the Character of Chaucer's Good Parson. Any desire of yours is a command to me; and accordingly I have put it into my English, with such additions and alterations as I thought fit. Having translated as many fables from Ovid, and as many novels from Boccacio and Tales from Chaucer, as will make an indifferent large volume in folio, I intend them for the press in Michaelmas Term next. In the meantime my parson desires the favour of being known to you, and promises, if you find any fault in his Character, he will reform it. Whenever you please, he shall wait on you, and for the safer conveyance, I will carry him in my pocket who am

My padron's most obedient servant,
JOHN DRYDEN

237. SAMUEL PEPYS TO JOHN DRYDEN

14 July 1699
SIR

You truly have obliged me; and possibly in saying so, I am more in earnest then you can readily think; as verily hoping from this your copy of one Good Parson, to fancy some amends made me for the hourly offence I bear with, from the sight of so many lewd originals.

I shall with great pleasure attend you on this occasion, when ere you'll permit it; unless you would have the kindness to double it to me, by suffering my coach to wait on you (and who you can gain me the same favour from) hither, to a cold chicken and a salad, any noon after Sunday, as being just stepping into the air for two days.

I am most respectfully
Your honoured and obedient Servant,
S. P.

News of Dryden's death in 1700 was sent by Pepys to his nephew John Jackson (Letter no. 242), who had left for his Grand Tour in October 1699. This letter was written while Jackson was still in England, waiting for a favourable wind at Shoreham-on-Sea in Sussex to sail to the continent. It is an affectionate letter that reminds Jackson of the need to make courteous references to Pepys's circle. The eclipse mentioned had occurred on 13 September and was a substantial partial eclipse of the sun. It was scarcely visible across much of England thanks to dense cloud. Pepys received this information in a letter from Dr John Wallis, Professor of Geometry at Oxford, and it is this that Pepys had enclosed a copy of with the letter to John Jackson. The rest of the letter discusses material sent from Amsterdam to Pepys by his cousin Roger Gale. These include an unidentified book by Christian Kortholt, the *De Formulis* by the seventh-century monk Marculfus, of great interest to Pepys as the book had a collection of templates for official documents.

238. SAMUEL PEPYS TO JOHN JACKSON

These for Mr John Jackson,
at Mr Luck's house at Shoreham in Sussex   London
                                                                         17 October 1699

NEPHEW

I write as one that would be sorry it should find you in England to read. But the wind must be obeyed. I thank you for my knowing that you are so far well, and nothing but that to hinder your going further. Your friends are all well, and take kindly your remembrance of them, particularly Mrs Skinner and Mr Hewer, Sir James Houblon's family, etc. And because I shall have frequent occasion of saying this or something like it, let it for my ease be all and always understood so by you under these two words, – Your friends, etc., – unless I say the contrary, as on all just occasions I will. But you must not be so laconic, it being a necessary respect to be heeded on your side that your friends may find their names mentioned by you, when in proof of it I shall sometimes see it needful to show it. I mind your observations touching the little delight you are like on any score to take in your staying where you are; but 'tis better at the worst to wait there for a good wind than be beating it to no purpose at sea with a contrary one.

I send you for your present diversion what I have lately received from Dr Wallis about the eclipse, and 'twill serve as something on that topic when you are elsewhere.

The manner of my sending you abroad does throughout show you my reliance upon your conduct, and therefore you shall owe it to yourself if ever I appear doubting it.

Yesterday I received from our cousin Gale, Marculfus (so that that old hole is stopped), and with it a supply of seven score title-pages, none contemptible but many very good, sequel to any I have but the French, and not one (upon my first view) that I had before; and the charge of them and book and all (a thick quarto) but 24s 8d. With which I am now brim-full as to that work, unless you shall find Dr Shadwell has already picked up anything, or shall, that is very curious, soon enough to be forwarded hither with Mrs Skinner's goods. But pray fail not to give him my services and thanks for what was brought me two days since by Mr Prior's clerk, viz., Alais's copy-book, a thing I mightily wanted and wished for. If Marculfus and Kortholtus were in his commission, pray advise him of my being now supplied therewith.

I shall be in daily pain for your loss of time till I hear you are gone, which God make happy to you.

                                   Your ever affectionate Uncle,
                                              S. PEPYS

One of the more curious subjects to turn up in Pepys's later correspondence is the subject of 'second sight' and the world of fairies in late-seventeenth-century Scotland. This had become a topic of major interest amongst English intellectuals and scientists who came to regard Scotland as a conveniently accessible repository of reported paranormal happenings.[13] Robert Boyle was one of the leading figures in the pursuit to collect and record as much data as possible about the phenomena in Scotland. The Scottish cleric Robert Kirk compiled his own account of them in his *Secret Commonwealth*, composed in

---

[13] See Hunter 2001.

1691 but which remained unpublished until 1815. Pepys joined in the debate and solicited information for himself. Some of what he received borders on the incomprehensible, partly thanks to his prolix correspondent's reliance on a barely-literate servant.

239. GEORGE, LORD REAY TO SAMUEL PEPYS

Durness
24 October 1699

HONOURED SIR

Conform to my promise in my last, I send you all the information I could make in those things you recommended to me. I have just now received my Lord Tarbat's answer, and shall copy what is to the purpose.

'I remember that several years ago, in answer to a letter of Mr Boyle's, I did write to him as to the second sight, a copy whereof receive herein [en]closed. If you please, return it after using it.

Since that time I was not much in the north, nor did I make any enquiry on purpose, and what I had occasion to hear thereof differed not considerably from what I heard formerly.

One of them was of a footman of your great grandfather's, who was mightily concerned upon seeing a dagger in the Lord Reay's breast. He informed his master of the sight, who laughed at it. Some months thereafter, he gave the doublet which he did wear when the seer did see the dagger in his breast to his servant, who did wear or keep it two years, and then did give it to this footman who was the seer, and who was stabbed by another in the breast when that doublet was on him. My Lord, you may enquire further in the truth of this. Some things (though nothing demonstrative) persuade me still to suspect that the qualities of the eyes and air in these places may contribute much to this sight, for as to the emission of species, especially from moving bodies, beings, are little to be doubted, but that the species should flow from things before they exist, whilst they are only potential as to the circumstance wherein they are seen, requires a new system of philosophy for explicating it.

My Lord, as to the salt beef, I have eat salt beef in the castle of Borthwick (which is within eight miles of Edinburgh, and I presume that it is the reladeall(?) that you have heard of) which both the house keeper and others told me to be above 200 year old and still keeped in that place, and I doubt not there is of it as yet there. All the gentlemen about that place concur in the testimony, for those living have heard it related by their grandfathers as never to be doubted of its being of so old a date. It would not appear to the eye to be other than a soft wood, but when boiled it is evidently discerned to be flesh. And there is testimonial proof sufficient to extend it beyond Harry the Eight; that is, I have heard old men of good and untainted veracity assert that their grandfathers did affirm it to be esteemed wonderful old.

I wish for a particular accompt of the sea fowl which builds in earth holes like rabbits. I apprehend it to be the same which is called lyres in Orkney; you have them in Ileand Henda.'

Sir, this is the answer I had from my Lord Tarbat, and receive here enclosed a copy of the letter he sent to Mr Boyle.

I informed myself of the truth of the story about my grandfather's footman, and find it literally true; as also of another much of the same nature, which I shall give you an accompt of because that I had it from a sure author, being a friend of my own of unquestionable honesty, to whose father the thing happened, and who was witness to it all himself.

John Macky of Dilril having put on a new sheet [suit] of clothes, was told by a seer that he did see the gallows on his coat; which he never noticed, but some time thereafter gave the coat to his servant, William Forbes, to whose honesty there could be nothing said at that time, but was shortly thereafter hanged for theft with the same coat about him; my informer being eye witness to the execution, and heard what the seer said before.

I have heard several other stories, but shall trouble you with no more than what has happened since I cam to this country.

There was a servant woman in Murdo Mckye's house, in Langduale on Strathnewer in the shire of Sutherland told her mistress she saw the gallows about her brother's neck (who hade then the repute of an honest man), at which her mistress being offended, put her out of her house. Her brother, having stolen some goods, was sentenced to be hanged the 22 August 1698; yet by the intercession of several gentlemen, who became bail for his future behaviour, was set free (though not customary by our law), which made one of the gentlemen, called Lieutenant Alexander Mackay, tell the woman servant that she was once deceived, the man being at liberty. She replied, 'he is not dead as yet, but shall certainly be hanged'. Accordingly he began to steal of new, and being catched was hanged the 14th of February 1699.

I was this year at hunting in my forest, having several Highlanders with me, and speaking of the second sight, one told me there was a boy in company that saw it, and had told many things which fell out to be true; and having called him, he confessed it. I asked him what he saw last. He told [me] he had seen the night before such a man by name, who lived thirty miles from that place, breaking my forester servant's head. The servant overhearing, laughed at him, saying that that could not be, they being very good friends. I did not believe it then, but it has certainly happened since.

These stories with what is contained in my Lord Tarbat's letters, are the most sufficient to prove the second sight of any ever I heard. And the people are so much persuaded of the truth of it in the Highlands and Isles, that one would be more laughed at for not believing it there than affirming it elsewhere. For my own part I do not question it; though but a small ground to persuade others to the belief of it. But I dare affirm, hade you the same reasons I have, you would be of my opinion. I mean, had you heard all the stories I have, attested by men of honour not to be doubted, and been eye witness to some of them yourself, as the breaking of the man's head, foretelling of an other's death, and another story which the same boy told me long ere they happened.

There was a blind woman in this country in my time who see them perfectly well, and foretold several things that happened; which hundreds of honest men can attest. She was not born blind, but became so by accident, to that degree that she did not see as much as a glimmering, yet saw the second sight as perfectly as before.

I have got a manuscript since I came to Scotland, called *An Essay of the Nature and Actions of the Subterraneans and (for the most part) Invisible People*, heretofore going under the names of elves, fauns, and fairies, or the like, among the low-country Scots, and termed [... *lusbartan*....][14] amongst the Tramontans or Scottish Irish, as they are now described by those that have the second sight, and now, to occasion further enquiry, collected and compared by Mr Robert Kirk The author of this treatise was a parson. I received a letter this day from a friend I employed, promising me his acquaintance, which I'm very covetous of, being persuaded it will give me much insight in this matter. And yet after giving a very full accompt of this second sight, [he] defends that there is no sin in it, upon several reasons too tedious to relate; but when ever I have occasion I shall send you a copy of the book. He is not of my Lord Tarbat's opinion as to the quality of air and eyes.

There is a people in these countries surnamed Mansone who see this sight naturally, both men and woman, though they commonly deny it, but affirmed by all their neighbours. A seer with whom I was reasoning on this subject, finding me very incredulous of the truth of what he asserted, offered to let me see them as well as himself. I asked if he could free me from seeing them thereafter, and he saying he could not put a stop to my curiosity. The manner of showing them to another is, the seer puts both his hands and his feet above yours, and mutters some words to himself, which done, both sees them alike.

This is, Sir, all the information I can send you on this head 'till I have occasion to send you the formentioned treatise.

I could never hear anything of the salt beef save what my Lord Tarbat tells of the beef of Borthwick, which several other [illegible]. You never heard of these fowls called lyres mentioned in my Lord Tarbat his letter. It's a gray fowl, short-winged, of the size of a teal, with a bill like a maverale.[15] They build in holes of the earth like rabbits, but not above three foot in. The young ones are commonly catched by a hook tied to the end of a stick, which by turning the stick about entangles in the nest and so pulls it and the young out. It's almost all fat, and so luscious that they are seldom eaten till they be salted. I have them in Island Henda, but never see one of them. There are several other fowls on this coast and many things in the country that deserve a particular description, but I had never time, though my inclinations were never so good.

There is a loch called Duntelchaig, on McKintosh his land two miles above Loch Ness, on a height, which was never known to freeze before Candlemas (save once, nineteen years ago), but freezes very hard then with the least frost.

Loch Ness minds me of a man I see at Inverness selling peats for fire. He is 125 year old, yet comes six miles back and fore in one day twice a week to sell those peats. The oldest man in that country told me that he was a very old man when he was a child.

There is a kyle in the Harris a mile long which runs the winter half of the year (that is to say, from September to March) northerly, and from thence to September again southerly; I have forgot the name of the kyle.

The bones said to be found in the court of the Earl of Argyll's house at Inverary of a monstrous bigness was but a romance.

I cannot possibly tell you whether the clay goose be suppositious or not, though all this countrymen affirm it for a truth. I have seen myself an old mast of a ship come in on the shore full of large holes, as if made by worms, whereinto there sticks a shell within which there is a small thing which resembles a fowl in every thing; in

---

[14] Mostly illegible text giving various Celtic terms including *lusbartan*, 'elf'.
[15] Mallard?

a warm day the shell opens and the fowl would seem to thresh their wings. But many of undoubted honesty assure me they have seen a fowl with wings, feathers, feet, and tail, sticking to a tree by the bill, but wanted life. The shell falls away when they come to perfection, as an egg breaks, and they stick by the bill till they get life. Those that were seen sticking to the tree was as long as a small chicken. They engender only in fir trees. I have seen several after they came to perfection, but not sticking to the tree. There will be hundreds of them sticking to one old mast or plank of a ship.

I spared no pains (when my troublesome affairs gave me leisure) to satisfy your curiosity, and am sorry that I can't do it as much as I would, Dear Sir, though I used my endeavour, but be sure if I can get any information in this or anything else that is curious, that I won't fail to acquaint you of it. I would be content to know the reason why the lake never freezes till a certain time, and freezes with the least frost then. I can easily conceive why it should not freeze at all, as many in this country never doe. And what can occasion the running of the forementioned kyle the one half of the year southerly and contrary the other half, seeing the ocean at both ends of it (being only a mile long) flows and ebbs as other seas. And if a fowl can reasonably engender out of a fir tree by lying in the sea. you'll say not, but if real, as I'm almost persuaded, what can be [the] occasion of it ?

I expect you'll acquaint me how soon you receive this. And be persuaded that I am, Honoured Sir,   Your most humble servant,

REAY

I made use of a servant to write this, because my own hand is not very legible, which occasions it's being so very uncorrect, and that I have not time scarcely to look over it.

240. SAMUEL PEPYS TO GEORGE, LORD REAY

To be left with Robert Menies at the Bill-Chamber in Edinburgh

York Buildings
21 November 1699

MY LORD

I can never enough acknowledge either the honour or favour of your Lordship's letters of the 10th and 24th of the last.[16] Could I have foreseen the least part of the fatigue my enquiries have cost your Lordship in the answering, I should have proceeded with more tenderness in the burthening you with them. But since your Lordship has had the goodness to undergo it, I cannot repent me of being the occasion of your giving the world so early a proof of what may further be expected from a genius so curious, so painful, so discerning, and every way so truly philosophical as your Lordship has herein shown yours to be. In the exercise whereof I cannot (as an old man) but wish you a long life and a happy, to the honour of your noble family, your country, the whole commonwealth of learning, and more particularly that part of it (the Royal Society of England, dedicated to the advancement of natural knowledge) whereto your Lordship is already become a peculiar ornament.

---

[16] Reay's letter of 10 October is printed by Tanner 1926, i, no. 114.

And now, my Lord, for the matter of your letters. They carry too much of observation and weight in them to be too easily spoken to; and therefore shall pray your Lordship's bearing with me if I ask a little time for it.

This only I shall not now spare to say; that as to the business of the second sight, I little expected to have been ever brought so near to a conviction of the reality of it as by your Lordship's and the Lord Tarbat's authorities I must already own myself to be. Not that I yet know how to subscribe to my Lord Tarbat's charging it upon some singularity of quality in the air or eye of the persons affected therewith. Forasmuch as I have never heard of other consequences of any indisposure in the medium or organs of sight than what related to the miscolouring, misfiguring, diminishing, or undue magnifying of an object truly existing and exposed thereto. Whereas in this case we are entertained with daggers, shrouds, arrows, gibbets, and God knows what, that indeed are not; and consequently must be the creatures of the mind only (however directed to them) and not of the eye.

Nor yet, as to the reality of this effect, would I be thought, my Lord, to derive this propension of mine to the belief of it, to the credit only which I find it to have obtained among your neighbours the Highlanders; for that it has been my particular fortune to have outlived the belief of another point of faith relating to the eyes, no less extraordinary nor of less universal reception elsewhere, than this can be in Scotland. I mean, the *mal de ojo* in Spain; with a third touching the sanative and prophetic faculty of the *Saludadores* there. As having heretofore pursued my enquiries thereinto so far upon the place, as to have fully convinced myself of the vanity thereof, especially of the latter, from the very confessions of its professors.

But, my Lord, where (as in the matter before us) the power pretended to is so far from being of any advantage to the possessors as on the contrary to be attended with constant uneasiness to them, as well as for the most part of evil and grievous import (and irresistibly so) to the persons it is applied to, in consequence whereof (as your Lordship well notes) your seers are both desirous to be themselves rid of it and ready to communicate it to any other that will adventure on't; I say, these considerations, joined to that of its being so abundantly attested by eye-witnesses of unquestionable faith, authority, and capacity to judge, will not permit me to distrust the truth of it, at least till something [more] shall arise from my further deliberations upon your Lordship's papers leading me thereto than I must acknowledge there yet does. In which case I shall give myself the liberty of resorting again to your Lordship, praying in the meantime to know how far I have your leave to make some of my learned friends partakers with me in the pleasure of them, and of what your Lordship has been pleased with so much generosity to promise me of further light upon this subject from the manuscript lately come to your Lordship's hand; a copy of which will be a most welcome and lasting obligation upon me from your Lordship.

I should now go to the rest of your excellent remarks upon the beef, the geese, the loch, the peat-man, and the kyle; nor shall an iota of them drop. But they have all of 'em their peculiar weight; and I would not so soon requite your Lordship's late fatigue in writing with a greater from myself in reading; and therefore (for your Lordship's sake only) choose rather to respite it to the next; remaining,

With most profound respect,

Your Lordship's most obedient servant,

S. PEPYS

Pepys soon found himself suffering more physical pain. The wound caused by the surgery to remove his bladder stone in March 1658 had suddenly and unexpectedly reopened, occasioning the need for an emergency operation. It had delayed his ability to reply to Jackson's various letters.

241. SAMUEL PEPYS TO JOHN JACKSON

York Buildings
8 April 1700

NEPHEW

Believing that after so long silence as this since my last to you of the 11th of March last, it would be of no less satisfaction to you than I bless God it is to me to be able to give you under my own hand the occasion of that silence, and this welcome account of its removal; I have chosen (as the most, I think, I yet think it convenient to put myself to the trouble on this occasion of doing) to make use of Mr Lorrain's for what follows. Which is to acquaint you that it has been my calamity for much the greatest part of this time to have been kept bed-rid under an evil so rarely known as to have had it made a matter of universal surprise, and with little less general opinion of its dangerousness: namely, that the cicatrice of a wound occasioned upon my cutting for the stone, without hearing anything of it in all this time, should after more than forty-year-perfect cure, all on a sudden, without any known occasion given for it, break-out again, so as to make another issue for my urine to sally at, besides that of its natural channel. A thing (as I have said before) never till now heard-of, and calling for an operation for its cure every whit as extraordinary, by requiring the wound that has been so long asleep to be a-new laid open again and re-healed, which it has been, and after that a second time; but both unsuccessfully.

But I have great hopes given me that what has been since done upon the third breach will prove thoroughly effectual; I being (I thank God) once more upon my legs, and though my long lying in bed will cost me possibly some time for the removal of my weakness, yet I am in no doubt of recovering my first state very soon, and in particular, as to yourself, of writing to you more at large by the very next post, by my answering your several of the 3rd, 9th and 20th of March (the two former from Naples, the last from Rome),[17] for all which I shall now only thank you, and tell you in general that I am thoroughly satisfied with every step of your proceedings mentioned therein; it being my purpose to dispatch this by this night's to meet you at Venice, with a copy thereof forwarded at the same time to Leghorn, directed to your several correspondents there; not doubting but that to Leghorn will come seasonably to you, in case that to Venice should fail, which I am not without some apprehension of, our friends here having not thought fit to communicate to me these your letters or any other papers during my late illness, but the rather respiting the same till this very day that they conceive they might with least trouble to me do it. With which, recommending you as before to the next post, and my constant good wishes for the happy progress of your journey, I rest,

Your most affectionate Uncle,
S. PEPYS

---

[17] Dates given by P are the continental ones. The letters are dated Feb 21/3 March, Feb 27/March 9, and 9/20 March, printed by Tanner 1926, i, nos. 184, 188, and 193.

Though the pain and trouble occasioned me by this evil about the parts immediately concerned therein have been very great, yet my chirurgeon (Mr Charles Bernard, a man of fame in his profession) never expressing the least doubt of my cure, and not having in the whole time suffered one quarter of an hour's sickness of stomach or elsewhere, I have not thought it of any use to interrupt you and the business you are upon with any imperfect tidings thereof till now that I can report it as a thing past.

Soon afterwards Pepys moved out to Clapham to recuperate. He was pleased to hear that Jackson had had an audience with the Pope, 'The Old Father', but sorry to hear that Jackson had not had time to copy any of Henry VIII's letters held in the Vatican Library.

242. SAMUEL PEPYS TO JOHN JACKSON

Clapham
9 May 1700

NEPHEW

I have been here four days, and by Mr Hewer's kindness am, with Mrs Skinner and a good part of my family, likely to have the benefit of its whole summer's airing, and with great encouragement already given me to expect very good effects from it. This whole family also is full of their respectful mentions and kind wishes towards you.

You are by your last of the 24th April (for which I thank you) from Rome, which I observe plainly to have been opened and resealed by the way, at this time at Venice, as being the evening, both here and there, of the Ascension; where I wish you all the satisfaction you expect. But not knowing what your stay is likely to be there, am in doubt how otherwise to write to you but (as I said in my last of the 29th of April) to Leghorn, as having already wrote three to you to Venice, which I trust will all meet you there.

I am mightily pleased with your having seen the Old Father, and been partaker of an Audience from him before your coming away; and shall now with pleasure hear of your motions homeward, and your seeing with the same satisfaction what remains for your visiting, by land and sea, in your way thither.

Your disappointment about Henry VIIIth's letters I am sorry for, but hope your memory will suffice to clear the few doubts we have upon the copy we are already masters of. My next shall bring you all I am likely to have of advice to you towards your proceeding homeward from Leghorn, as not knowing where to meet you after your going thence, but as you shall from time to time give me aim; therefore pray be earlily and constantly foresighted therein.

I am in hourly hopes, however, of one more of yours from Rome at your quitting it, with some notices of the view you then had of your next motion.

I am, I thank God, greatly recovered, and in a fair road towards being perfectly so; as your friends all about me are, and inquisitive after your being the like.

Our Great Seale is put *pro interim* into the hands of the two Chief Justices and Chief Baron, till the King has further deliberated touching the disposal thereof; wherein he seems to precede at this time very thoughtfully. For other matters, I must pray you to content yourself with the public prints.

And so, with my own best wishes, and the respects of all your friends, I bid you Adieu, and rest,

Your affectionate uncle,
S. PEPYS

Sir Peter Daniel in this neighbourhood is newly dead; and so (I am just now told) is Mr Dryden, who will be buried in Chaucer's grave, and have his monument erected by the Lord Dorset and Mr [Charles] Mountagu.

Sir Godfrey Kneller had come to England in 1675 and first painted Charles II in 1678. In 1684 he painted Samuel Pepys, a portrait which was just one of many that he produced of men in Pepys's circle. This letter from Arthur Charlett discusses ongoing and prospective commissions, including those of the family of the great mathematician John Wallis.

243. DR ARTHUR CHARLETT TO SAMUEL PEPYS

University College
6 October 1700

HONOURED SIR

I received your most obliging letter at Soundess, a great manor of John Wallis, Esq.,in the woods next Nettlebed, and communicating the contents to him, he said that for the further encouragement of Sir Godfrey Kneller, he would be willing to be at the charges of having his father's, his own, his son, and two daughters, viz., five heads in one piece, as the Dean of Christ Church should direct.

I am just now informed that Sir Godfrey Kneller has drawn our Chancellor the Duke of Ormonde at full length, which the Duke has some thoughts of bringing down himself, and 'tis very probable Sir Godfrey may come with his Grace, he having done so only for his pleasure twice or thrice within these three years. I must also add that Dr Wallis was a little out of order last night (though I fear we shall have much a do to hinder him this morning from Church, the Earl of Rochester being also to be there), to whom I then read your most obliging inclinations. He seemed (to say the truth) very fond and pleased with the thoughts of having his picture presented to the University by your hands, Mr Pepys and the late Lord Chancellor Somers being the two persons most in his honour and estimation.

I will not be positive, but am apt to believe that Sir Godfrey Kneller may have more business if he pleases, and the last time he was with me he seemed desirous to have some of his art visible in the gallery. He is Doctor of Law with us; 'tis possible a decent application to Dr Radcliffe might persuade him to give the picture of King Alfred, the founder of his old College, Dr Aldrich having long since designed a head for him. I am very much in arrears to you for a thousand civilities which I have time only now to acknowledge to be due from.

Sir, Your obedient servant,

ARTHUR CHARLETT

A book of verses is ordered for you.
My very humble service to Mr Hewer.

Pepys grew excited at the prospect of his nephew's homecoming as the autumn of 1700 began to merge into winter. He brought John Jackson up to date with news of his circle. John Evelyn and his extended family had recently been to visit. Evelyn's entire expectations had dramatically altered in 1699 with the death of, first, his only surviving son, John Evelyn junior, and then his elder brother George. This meant that Evelyn inherited the family estate at Wotton, near Dorking in Surrey, and focused all his attention on making sure that his grandson, also John Evelyn, survived to inherit in due course. It seems that James Houblon had been ill but the news was now better. Unfortunately, the news would not stay good.

244. SAMUEL PEPYS TO JOHN JACKSON

To Mr John Jackson,
at Sir William Hodges and Company, in Cadiz

Clapham
8 October 1700

NEPHEW

My last was of the 16th of September to Cadiz (for I have no whither else to follow you to) owning my receipt of yours of the 31st of August and 5th and 9th of ditto September, to all of which I then gave you answer, together with a copy of my then last, of the 28th of August; as I now do of that of the abovesaid 16th of September, being rather willing to pay for a double one than have you bear the want of any single letter at this distance.

Since then, I have had two from you of the 15th and 24th of September from Marseilles,[18] importing your return thither, and the ill effects of your improvident excess upon fruit, which alone was the occasion of all that has befallen the Earl of Exeter's family, in the death not only of himself and of one or two more of his train, but the endangering all the rest, by a bloody flux; from which my Lady herself and her son Mr Cecil have but hardly escaped. And what the like misgovernment might have ended in to you, has not given me small care 'till, after one and twenty days silence, I was eased in it by yours of the 1st of October,[19] which came most welcomely to my hand last night, giving me the very glad tidings of your being so far recovered as to be then embarking for Barcelona, upon a ship and with a commander to your liking, and under an assured expectation of a satisfactory voyage. In all of which both myself and your other friends here take very great content, hoping that this will find it to have succeeded accordingly, and you before the arrival of it well arrived at Cadiz, and that you have there found my worthy friends Sir William Hodges with my Lady and family in like good health. Whose furtherance and direction you are (I trust) by this time possessed, if not actually entered upon the execution of, in your journey towards the Court of Spain, which (by what we newly hear) you are likely to find in great *discompuesto* upon the death of the King, and will give you a very different scene, and perhaps never a whit the less entertaining one, from what you would have found there; and probably, too, shorten your visit to a place that at the best you will hardly think deserving a long one. On which last consideration I shall very soon think of writing to you to Lisbon, as the only next place I have in my eye to meet you at.

Your friends (and particularly myself) are, I bless God, in perfect health here, excepting only my excellent friend Sir James Houblon (who yet is at this time better) and Mr Hatton, from whom I am specially to note to you the content he owns his having had in his perusal of your collections for me; adding (to give it you in his own words) that had he known so much of your virtuoso-ship as he says he now does, he should have minded you of one thing which he is sorry to find unmentioned by you, viz., the *lapis fungifer* or stone that produces mushrooms, which is to be had at Naples, and no where else that he knows of; wishing that you would yet send to your correspondent there (for he depends upon your having provided yourself of

---

[18] P gives the continental dates on Jackson's letters. See Tanner 1926, ii, nos. 288, 294, 300, 303, and 308. P's letter of 28 August is not extant, but that of 26 August is (ibid., no. 296).
[19] Ibid., no. 315.

one) for some of them, as what would be a welcome rarity to yourself and friends here. Besides which, he observing your having taken care for some Lazarolls for me, wishes that you would this winter-season procure to be sent hither by shipping from Naples some young trees of the several kinds there, where, he says, they are almost as common as haw-trees here, producing a pleasant fruit, and such as would thrive very well at Clapham. This I tell you from him, and leave you to take what notice you see fit of, as being myself wholly a stranger to the matter, what ever you may now be after having been upon the place.

The 20 *louis* you have taken up more at Marseilles shall be duly answered.

I hear nothing yet of the *Benjamine*.

I can hardly forbear, any more than I know you can do, to wish your having been at Rome at the death of the Pope; but who can help it, or could then have reasonably bid fairer for it than you did?

If this reaches you before or during your being at Lisbon, I must give it you in charge to find out and wait upon my Lady Tuke, one of the Ladies attending my once Royal Mistress our Queen Dowager there; a lady for whom I bear great honour, and of whose health and satisfactory present state I should most gladly hear. Nor (if she should offer you the honour of kissing the Queen's hand) would I have you to omit (if my Lady Tuke thinks it proper) the presenting her Majesty in most humble manner with my profoundest duty, as becomes a most faithful subject, and one who continues daily to pray for her Majesty's prosperity, health, and long life.

Let my Lady also know that her and my old good friends Mr Evelyn and his Lady did me within these ten days the honour of coming over to me hither from Wotton, with their whole family of children, children-in-law, and grandchildren, and dined with me; where her Ladyship's health was duly remembered, and from whom I understood the fair lady Mrs Tuke's being lately well returned to England; though by their yet being under their summer's recess in the country, they have not yet had the satisfaction of seeing her. But that will be now soon over with us all, when I also shall hope for the honour of kissing her hand.

And with this I commit you to God's protection, and rest,

Your most loving Uncle,

S. PEPYS

Dr David Gregory had, by the age of thirty, been appointed Savilian professor of astronomy at Oxford in 1691, having been professor of mathematics at Edinburgh since 1683. Arthur Charlett here seems to be forwarding a summary or outline of a prospective book of Gregory's for Pepys to comment on. This can only be Gregory's *Astronomiae Physicae et Geometricae Elementa* ('Elements of Astronomy, Physics and Geometry'), which was published in 1702.

245. DR ARTHUR CHARLETT TO SAMUEL PEPYS

University College
15 October 1700

HONOURED SIR

I send you here enclosed a scheme of Dr Gregory's, not yet in any other hand, with a desire that you would, with the freedom of a man of honour and a scholar, peruse, examine, correct, alter, and improve it, as may make the design most beneficial to youth (especially of the nobility and gentry) and redound most to the honor of the University and our professors and the promotion of learning.

Dr Wallis having been for several days confined within his house, I know he must be very busy with his pen, and is I think writing somewhat by way of letter recommending the teaching and study of Mathematics within the two Universities (with preference I guess to other places) in which I hope he will insert this proposal of Dr Gregory's, and print it afterwards in the Transactions. Your remarks and observations will be very welcome to,

Sir, Your most obedient servant,

AR. CHARLETT

I hope you have taken notice in our Book of Verses of the compliment to Signor Verrio and Sir Godfrey Kneller in the same page.

246. SAMUEL PEPYS TO DR ARTHUR CHARLETT

These for the Reverend Dr Charlett at University College Oxford

Clapham

29 October 1700

REVEREND SIR

As impatient as I am to be among my old friends again (as you know who called them) my books; my friends on this side the water are obstinately bent to prevent it, as long as there is one mouthful of serene air to be hoped for this season; and therefore to render my stay in it the less burthensome to me, have put me upon several little excursions of late into the neighbourhood, that must excuse my no sooner acknowledging (as I now most thankfully do) and answering, your too kind letter of the 6th instant, and a later of the 5th.

Be assured, that I won't be three days in town (and that at farthest can't now be ten days off) before I fall to work with Sir Godfrey Kneller, with the materials you have given me, to procure his compliance with what we have to ask of him; the state of my own present health making me as solicitous to secure to myself the honour of doing it, as that of my reverend and learned friend the doctor's makes it unfit, with respect to his satisfaction (since he is pleased to take it so) to yours, and to the university's, that any time should be lost in the having it done. And a most welcome pleasure it would be to me, to think, that what I do herein could pass for the least instance of that veneration, which I should be glad to have opportunities of showing greater marks of, towards him. Nor should this (as you know) have been to do now, had not the hopes you and I had entertained of tempting him some time or other down by water to York Stairs, kept me under an expectation (by your favour) of getting it done here.

Nor would I despair of what you have in wish, and perhaps in view, about King Alfred's head from Dr Ratcliffe; but I have a word to say to you first upon it, if you would employ me to him in it.

I have not yet seen your book of verses, and so can make you no present return upon your compliment therein to our two painters.

I know not which of your misreckonings to find fault with most; that of our learned doctor's, in placing me on so near a level in any respect with our late great Chancellor the Lord Somers (the first Maecenas of the age), or yours, in thinking me a fit man to be asked questions upon anything that has passed the thought of the most learned professor and my most honoured friend Dr Gregory. Nevertheless, leaving the former's to be answered-for among the venerable frailties of his age and goodness of nature, I cannot be so squeamish or remiss in the labour, as not to take another post (having a little foreign work extraordinary for this) to see whither it be possible, for any one useful thought to occur to me, that could escape Dr Gregory, upon a subject so noble, and of which he is so absolute a master.

I am ever Dear Sir

Your obliged and obedient Servant

S. PEPYS

Pepys had occasion to write twice to Arthur Charlett on 5 November 1700. While writing a much longer epistle concerned with music, the sad news of the death of Sir James Houblon arrived.

247. SAMUEL PEPYS TO DR ARTHUR CHARLETT

Clapham

5 November 1700

DEAR SIR

I was gone through half the enclosed when I was seized with the tidings of the death of one of the oldest and most approved friends I had in the world, Sir James Houblon, a worthy merchant, Alderman and one of the Burgesses for this City; by which I have been kept under a full stop to the finishing it, till now that having with great affliction seen him laid where within these ten months he had much more reason to have expected his first leaving me, I have made shift to go thorough it, and as it is must pray your pardon for it, remaining, Reverend Sir,

Your most obedient servant

S. P.

You not requiring it, I upon second thoughts keep your learned paper with me; but so as to be at your ready call if you want it.

In 1701 Dr Hans Sloane was secretary to the Royal Society. Pepys wrote to him about a Monsignor Bellisono of Rome who wanted to start correspondence with the Royal Society. John Jackson had written to Pepys on 6 April 1700 about Bellisono who was 'universally read, very communicative, free in his sentiments of the government both of the Church and State here, and wonderfully fond of all strangers, but more particularly the English'.[20] Nothing else is known about him. This is one of several letters between Sloane and Pepys that survives amongst Sloane's papers in the British Library.

248. SAMUEL PEPYS TO DR HANS SLOANE

York Buildings

8 January 1701

SIR

I am led by some conversation I have just now had with our learned friend the bearer Mr Monro, to repeat what I have heretofore said to you, in relation to the most learned and celebrated Monsignor Bellisono at Rome. His character is so universally

---

[20] Tanner 1926, i, 315.

known and honoured, that I will not so much as suppose you a stranger to it; only I think it becoming me, to give you so much of it as comes to me from a gentleman, a member of our own society, to whom he has expressed his most regardful esteem of the same, and desire of the honour of his admission thereinto, in order to a correspondence, that that gentleman Mr Jackson tells me he believes may be truly useful to the Society; adding, that besides his known urbanity and respectfulness as well as communicativeness to all strangers, he is observed to express himself to none more so then to the English. On all which scores, I make it my motion and request to the Society by your hand (because, as you well know, utterly unable at this time to do it personally, as I otherwise ought and should have done) that the said Signor Bellisono may be thought worthy, and have the honour he desires, of being admitted into the number of the Fellows of the Royal Society.

With which, and the telling you, that I shall not fail in my duty of attending the service thereof, as soon as ever my health shall enable me to do it, I rest

Sir Your most humble servant

S. PEPYS

John Jackson sent his uncle a great many letters from his Grand Tour, most of which consist of bland descriptive accounts of the sights he had seen. This particular example is more dramatic and includes his eyewitness account of Philip (Felipe) V of Spain's entry into Madrid, which involved a disaster. Philip, grandson of Louis XIV of France, had been declared King of Spain on 24 November 1700 following the death of his uncle, Charles II of Spain. At the time, Jackson had no idea he was witnessing a crucial moment in history Under the Partition Treaty of 1698 the Spanish crown was supposed to pass to the Archduke Charles of Austria. The prospect of a powerful Spanish-French combination meant that Britain now formed an alliance with Austria, the Netherlands, Portugal and Denmark, and the War of the Spanish Succession broke out. It would not end until the Treaties of Utrecht in 1713 and Rastatt in 1714. In view of the epic consequences, an equally memorable and ironic part of the letter is Jackson's description of the king's 'filthy old coach'.

249. JOHN JACKSON TO SAMUEL PEPYS

Madrid

13/24 February 1701

HONOURED SIR

Long looked for is come at last. On Friday the 18th, about 4 in the afternoon, Felipe V made his entry here; not with much pomp, but a most surprising concourse of coaches and people. For several miles, I might say leagues, out of town the road was so thronged that his Majesty was scarce able to make his way through; having according to the Spanish manner, no guards before his coach, but only the Magistrates with their white wands. He designed to have mounted on horseback at some distance from the town, as was generally expected, but seeing the dust and crowd he had to encounter with, very prudently waved it, though to the disappointment of abundance that perhaps would otherwise have staid at home, and particularly the ladies, who were very numerous and the richest in clothes and jewels I ever saw. As a sad proof of the multitudes I speak of, no less than forty men, women, and children were trod under foot and killed out-right in their return through the gate; and above 100 are said to be now languishing under their bruises and dying daily. Diverse of the dead I saw myself lying, heads and tails, in a little neighbouring chapel, where they were putt till known and carried away; among the rest were a friar and a priest. I believe the like accident has not been heard of, nor would it cost so many lives to take the very town of Madrid. The occasion is somewhat differently told, but the most received account is this: that the officers of the customs, suspecting the people to take the advantage of this confusion for running of goods, so soon as the King was entered shut the gates upon them; and afterwards opening them again on a sudden, the foremost fell, and upon them the next, and so on, to the number I have mentioned at least, and were immediately smothered without redress. Certain it is that the mob had this notion of it, for the same evening they came and plundered the Guardas' lodge, burnt all their registers before their door, and set fire to the house itself; but it went no further than the smoking the walls a little and damaging a window. The next morning also they assembled again, and we were apprehensive of the consequences, but by noon they drew quietly off without doing more; and for their satisfaction I am told the Guardas have been put in prison, and the King has granted pensions to those poor families who suffered by this disaster.

His Majesty went directly to the Atocha to sing *Te Deum*, and thence to his Palace of the Retiro; where in the evening he was entertained with fireworks prepared in the outermost court for this occasion, and performed at least as well as ours upon the Peace [of Ryswyck, 1697], though not thought to be extraordinary for Spain, where they are very expert in this art. The rockets and other smaller fires were in abundance; and the principal part which concluded the whole was an engagement between a castle and four men-of-war, which were contrived to move, and though [they] plaid their parts very well, were at last overcome. At the same time there were also illuminations quite through the town, and these continued three nights together. Whoever had seen the Spaniards this day only, would have concluded them a very drunken people, having taken their cups very freely, and laid aside all gravity. They were generally pleased with the person of the King at first sight; but by putting-on the *golilla* with his whole court on Sunday last he has entirely won their hearts. He hunts and shoots every day, and by this means, and a free admission to his court, is already become very well known to his people.

What is to be excepted against in his entry is, the coming in no parade or order; his Majesty in a filthy old coach of the late King's; without Guards; his better sort of attendance, some on horseback, and some in coaches at ½ an hour's distance from one another; and divers of the inferior sort attending the baggage in so very ragged clothes as exposed them extremely to the scorn of the Spaniards. But this indeed was not the entry we have all along talked-of. That will not be till after Lent, and some say till May; for which triumphal arches are preparing and bulls in feeding, with other things which our friends would make us believe to be worth the staying for, but I cannot, at least, if you should think them so, might return from Lisbon time enough to see them. For which purpose only I troubled you with a small letter yesterday by the Groyne, in order to have the favour of your answer in due time at Lisbon. I had been gone 'ere this from hence, had my companion used the same diligence as myself; but having not, I fear It will be Sunday before we set out for Seville.

The change of ministers here I shall not trouble you with, you not being acquainted with the names of either side. The Cardinal is the do-all. The Spaniards expect war, and wait only for some notice of the countenance of our new parliament before they speak more plainly.

Permit me to trouble you with my humble service to Mrs Skinner, Mr Hewer and family, Captain Hatton, Mr Houblon's, etc., and remain,

Honoured Sir, Your most dutiful and obedient nephew,

J. JACKSON

Despite the pleasure Jackson's news brought him, Pepys was frequently in no condition to enjoy it. In the early summer of 1701 Pepys was ill again, though he soon recovered. Friends wrote to express their relief.

250. CAPTAIN CHRISTOPHER HATTON TO SAMUEL PEPYS

11 July 1701

SIR

Excess of joy is, Sir, equally difficult to be expressed as that of grief, and therefore I am no more capable to declare how much I rejoice to hear of your recovery than I was to express how sensibly I was afflicted at the news of your late sickness. But be assured, Sir, none of your most faithful servants and sincerely affectionate friends do more cordially congratulate your recovery than I do who, having so often experienced your readiness to oblige, was encouraged thereby to take the liberty to send so small a present as a few cakes of chocolate. But be[ing] convinced that there cannot be better made, I hoped it might not be unacceptable to you. I am, Sir,

Your most faithful and humblest servant,

C. HATTON

Give me leave to take the liberty herein to present my very humble service to Mrs Skinner, to whom I am infinitely obliged for informing me of the state of your health. And I can never fail to pay all due respect to good Mr Hewer and worthy Mr Jackson, of whose safe arrival I impatiently long to hear.

Pepys continued to commission portraits of his friends, to be painted by Sir Godfrey Kneller. The mathematician, John Wallis, now in his 85th year, wrote to thank Pepys.

251. DR JOHN WALLIS TO SAMUEL PEPYS

Oxford

24 September 1701

SIR

You have been pleased to put an honour upon me which I could not deserve nor did expect; to send so worthy an artist as Sir Godfrey Kneller from London to Oxford to hike my picture at length, and put the charge of it to your own account. I wish it may be to your content. It had been more agreeable to my circumstances if you had commanded my attendance to wait on you at London, which I should have readily obeyed, if my age would permit it. Till I was past fourscore years of age, I could pretty well bear up under the weight of these years. But, since that time, it hath been too late to dissemble my being an old man. My sight, my hearing, my strength, are not as they were wont to be. Though I have no cause to complain of God's Providence, through whose goodness I do yet enjoy as much of ease and health as I can reasonably expect at these years. And though you and some other friends are pleased to think me not quite unserviceable; yet I must not so far flatter myself as not to think but that it doth better become me to conceal the infirmities of age than to expose them.

I have endeavour[ed] to express to Sir Godfrey the sense I have of your undeserved favour by treating him with the respect due to a person of his quality. And if I have been therein defective, I desire it may be imputed to the absence of my daughter, who is my housekeeper, but chanced to be now out of town; whereby I was obliged to depend on servants. I know not what to return for your great kindness but the humble thanks of, Sir,

Your obliged and very humble servant,

JOHN WALLIS

In this, his last known letter to John Evelyn, Pepys is concerned with encouraging Evelyn to allow his grandson to travel abroad as an essential part of his education. In 1699 Evelyn's only surviving son, John Evelyn junior, had died. Later the same year Evelyn's elder brother George died too. Since George had no surviving sons, the family estate at Wotton therefore passed to John Evelyn, now eighty years old. Evelyn was concerned that his grandson (also called John Evelyn) took no risks, as the sole surviving male heir. In November 1700 the youth had caught smallpox but to his grandfather's incalculable relief he had recovered.

252. SAMUEL PEPYS TO JOHN EVELYN

Clapham
24 December 1701

DEAREST SIR

Dover Street at the top and J EVELYN at the bottom had alone been a sight equal in the pleasure of it to all I have had before me in my two or three months by work of sorting and binding together my nephew's Roman marketings: and yet I dare predict that even you won't think two hours thrown away in overlooking them, whenever a kindelier season shall justify my inviting you to't.

What then should I have to say to the whole of that glorious matter that was enclosed in your last? Why truly, neither more nor less than that it looks to me like a seraphic *How d'you* from one already entered into the regions you talk of in it, and who has sent me this for a *viaticum* towards my speeding thither after him. Which, as the world now is and you have so justly described: and being bereft (as I now am) of the very uppermost of my wonted felicities here, in your conversation and that of a very few virtuous friends more, I should be in very good faith much rather choose to obey you in by leading, than staying to follow you.

I am, for public good's sake, as truly sorry as you for your friend's withdrawing; wishing only that I could as easily satisfy myself how he ever came-in as why he now goes-out.[21]

I fully agree with Mr Evelyn (your excellent Grandson) in his thinking it no longer worth his while to stay where he is; and do the like with you too in your next thoughts concerning him; if (which I could not easily wonder at, he being indeed a jewel) your and my lady his grandmother's tendernesses have determined against venturing him further from home. But since you ask it, I cannot but in faithfulness

---

[21] Sidney, Lord Godolphin. He had just resigned the post of Lord Justice, to which he had been recently appointed.

tell you that were he mine, and (if it were possible) ten times more valuable than he is, I should not, even for his and my family's sake, think the hazard of sending him abroad (tomorrow before next day, with a pass) for four or five months, through Holland and Flanders to Paris and so home (a tour that by the aid of your instructions I myself, when time was, and with a wife with me, dispatched in bare two; and to a degree of satisfaction and solid usefulness that has stuck by me through the whole course of my life and business since). I say, I should not think it a hazard fit to be named with that of his being, when your and my lady's heads shall be laid, and himself possibly engaged in conjugal and domestic encumbrances tempted to do, what the deference which he cannot but by this time see paid to your selves from all the politer world on the account of the distinguishing perfections eminently raised in you from your foreign education, in addition to your native must naturally, and therefore unavoidably, prompt him to; I mean, of looking abroad, when (I say) his home concernments may possibly much worse bear it.

Nor have either of you (I trust) any ground to doubt a much longer continuance through God's favour, among your friends here than is necessary for your seeing this over, and him well returned (before midsummer next) to prosecute (and all in very good time) the course you are now designing him at the common law. Thereby, with the furniture you have already given him, to qualify himself for making another-gate's figures, upon the bench, in parliament, in the ministry, and every other the most sublime conversation, than any one among all that I have ever had the fortune to meet with, of those we call *Country-Gentlemen* purely English; and this, as little as you are willing to see it in yourselves, I am sure you know to be so.

Nor do I overlook what you note to me of Mr Finch's thoughts herein in the case of his son, whom for my lady his mother's sake, as well as his illustrious father's, I cannot but be a most affectionate well-wisher to: but should rather join with him in them when I reflect upon my friend his father-in-law Sir John Bankes's unfortunate conduct upon the like occasion;[22] were it not for my having been but too privy to the Occasions of it, and my being well assured of their being all abundantly provided against, in both your cases.

In a word, though it may look like a little overweening in me, yet I know not how to mistrust the validity of a doctrine that I have lived under more than thirty years continued proof of the truth and usefulness of; and that raised, not from borrowed but my own immediate notices of the different grace as well as reality of performances in persons of the highest forms, no less then greatest eminence, in every of the stations above-mentioned; between those (I say) whose knowledge has been widened and refined by travel and others whose observations have been stinted to the narrow practice of their own country. Nor am I without the satisfaction of being so far at least confirmed herein from the little experiment I am just come from making upon your dutiful servant my nephew Jackson: that though he be hardly yet at home after a near two years' tour, through Flanders, France, Italy, Spain, and Portugal, and through the Mediterranean by sea back, I shall struggle hard to give him two months' leisure within the next summer to finish his travels with Holland, for the sake of the many eminent particularities to be met with at this juncture: that were never to be seen together there in any Age past, nor possible may ever again be in any to come: a sight, in one word, that, as late as it is, I should hardly think too

---

[22] The meaning here is uncertain, but may refer to when Bankes's son had travelled to France (Evelyn, Diary 25 August 1676).

ate even for myself to covet, had I you to wait on thither, for I am (in spite of this instance) with inseparable respect, My ever honoured Mr Evelyn,

Your most affectionately faithful
and obedient servant,
S. P.

Mrs Skinner prays to be thought no less so to my Lady; nor either myself or nephew servants to the young gentlemen I have been here shooting my bolt about; nor Mr Jewer to you all; with wishes of a happy Christmas.

In fact Evelyn never took Pepys's advice and his grandson was prevented from travelling. Evelyn finally secured a marriage for him in September 1705, more than two years after Pepys's death.

On 8 March 1702 William III died after falling from his horse. Almost exactly six months earlier, his father-in-law, the deposed James II had died in France. William was succeeded by his sister-in-law Anne, who ruled as the last Stuart monarch. Pepys was more immediately concerned with Kneller's portrait of John Wallis. This was something he had commissioned, but it seems it had been completed as a full-length figure (rather than a portrait) at Arthur Charlett's behest without Pepys being told. Pepys had expressed what seemed like annoyance to Godfrey Kneller, though Pepys was appalled at the thought he had done any such thing. A rapid exchange of letters followed to clear the matter up, with Pepys explaining how his poor health had kept him virtually confined indoors for two years.

53. Sir Godfrey Kneller to Samuel Pepys

24 March 1702

SIR

I sent a letter writ by Dr Wallis when I came from Oxford, in which I suppose he acknowledged your favour for him. And I did acquaint you then of what I had done, of which you approved in your letter to me, and were very much pleased and delighted with what I had done by order from you of Dr Charlett's message. Which letter of yours made me proceed and finish that picture, and I will send a copy of the letter to show at any time if required, and hope I have done my part, believing Dr Charlett as a divine, and knowing you an entire gentleman of a noble, generous mind, or else I should hardly [have] left my home and business for Oxford's conversation sake, and wish you had given me any one hint in your letter of disliking what I had then done, and I would have kept the face (as I only then had done) for myself without putting any figure, as I have done all myself to it, or had any more west of time. Which I perceive in your present letter you wonder at, and shall leave it to what you think fit, of which no body can be a judge like yourself. And I can show I never did a better picture nor so good a one in my life, which is the opinion of all as has seen it, and which I have done merely for the respect I have for your person, fame, and reputation, and for the love of so great a man as Dr Wallis, as you know, and besides being recommended by a message from you of Dr Charlett, a head in Oxford; which if all be rightly considered, I hope to have no blame on ether account, but to be thanked, and allowed to own myself,

Your obedient and faithful real humble servant,
G. KNELLER

254. SAMUEL PEPYS TO SIR GODFREY KNELLER

Clapha■
24 March 170:

SIR

For God's sake (my old friend) look once more over my letter of yesterday, and te■ me what one word there is in it that should occasion any one syllable of what m■ man brings me from you this morning in answer to't.

I said indeed (but without the least shadow of dissatisfaction, much less relatin■ to you) that I was surprised at the manner of our learned friend's proceeding with m■ upon this picture. And I dare take upon me the prophesying that so will you to■ when you come to know why; which I told you yesterday you should soon do; an■ had now done, had you been pleased but by two words to satisfy me in what yo■ telling me of the picture's being very much expected at Oxford led me to ask of yo■ As I therefore hereby again do; remaining, with the same thankfulness I fir■ expressed to you upon Dr Wallis's notice of your respect shown me on th■ occasion, Sir,

Your truly obliged and most humble servant,
S. PEPYS

255. SIR GODFREY KNELLER TO SAMUEL PEPYS

25 March 170:

SIR

I ask your pardon for misapprehending; and as to the picture being desired, I mea■ no more but that several from Oxford have only wished to see such a picture in the■ Gallery, where Dr Aldrich intends to get more he hopes, and to make it fine as yo■ may imagine with great and learned men their pictures in full length; which is all ■ might have mentioned, for none of them are so ill-bred for to pres such a prese■ from you, but expect your leisure, and so will I. For I know no one living kno■ better nor can judge truer of manners and what is truly civil than yourself on a■ occasion, and I hope you do believe none shall observe your command nor be mo■ sincere and real than I am, and ever must be,

Sir, Your obedient and most obliged humble servant,
G. KNELLER

256. SAMUEL PEPYS TO SIR GODFREY KNELLER

Clapha■
26 March 170:

SIR

I know not how better to become even with you for the kind satisfaction you hav■ been at the trouble of giving me, than by trying to give you the like in reference ■ my late sending you the same question twice, that could not but look impertine■ enough on my part to have asked you once; and pray take it as follows.

I have long (with great pleasure) determined, and no less frequently declared it ■ my friend Dr Charlett, upon providing as far as I could by your hand toward■ immortalizing the memory of the person (for his name can never die) of that gre■ man and my most honoured friend, Dr Wallis, to be lodged as an humble present c■ mine (though a Cambridge-man) to my dear aunt the University of Oxford.

Towards this I have been long consulting with Dr Charlett, and not without hopes of getting this reverend gentleman once more up to town; and since (through his age) those hopes have sunk, I have flattered myself with others, namely, of being able some time or other, in a vacation, to prevail with my friend Sir Godfrey Kneller to make a little country-excursion for me and do it upon the place; with a design indeed of waiting on you myself thither.

But so it has fallen-out that by an unexpected return of an old evil, the stone, I have been ever since under a continued incapacity, for these two years and more, of stirring-out of doors, and at length was forced for life (as Dr Charlett knows) to be brought hither, where I still am and am likely to be; but with some hopes given me by Mr Hewer and some other of our friends the last year of seeing you here. And so this matter has stood, till Dr Wallis (by your own hand) gave me from Oxford the very first word of my having (as he words it) sent you down thither, and of the work's being done.

Now as much satisfied as I must again and again own I am with the extraordinary instance of respect I have received from you in it, I submit it to you to judge of the reasonableness or unreasonableness of my surprise at the manner of my friend's proceeding with me therein, when I have told you that Dr Charlett did me the favour of a double visit here, about the month of August last, with promise of a third, and bringing Dr Aldrich with him before his return to Oxford; which I greatly expected, in order to the considering of some way (under my present distance from town) how to supply it to you in reference to this matter. Instead of which I have not only never heard one word of or from him to this day, but without the least mention, either of your name or anything at all of the picture at either of his forementioned visits. You have been pleased to tell me, to my no small confusion (for I swear it still looks like a dream to me) of his message from me to you and what you have been doing upon it. But pray take it along with you that I say it is no unpleasing dream to me, but what I shall venture very hard (as soon as the weather shall favour it) to come by chair and pay you my real thanks for; remaining,

Your ever most affectionate and most humble Servant,
S. PEPYS

The naval career of Peter Skinner, Mary's brother, had been an issue for Pepys since 1683 at least, and a source of great offence.[23] By 1702 Mary and Peter's mother was dead. Peter chose to write to Pepys to ask for his help in managing the money he had inherited and to ruminate on his former behaviour and ingratitude. The letter is not dated to an exact day.

257. PETER SKINNER TO SAMUEL PEPYS

December 1702

HONOURABLE SIR

The time is now drawing near which makes me consider how frequently your Honour has cast an eye of your extraordinary goodness and bounty upon me, many years past, upon a New Year's Day; and what gives me a great occasion to thank Heaven for such an exceeding blessing of your Honour's happy life to this time. Beseeching heaven not to cut it shorter, by how much the more we adore it; but that your Honour may commence and finish this ensuing year, and many a one, with all the health and felicity my tongue and pen can set forth, and to continue the same so

[23] Letters nos. 155, 168, and 206–7.

long as you shall desire; for your kindnesses to me have been so far above my merits that they are even above my gratitude, if that were to be judged by words, being not capable to express it.

When I reflect upon the deportments of my youth, I find that I have behaved myself so ill, according to what I understand, that I am unworthy to approach your Honour for any favour. But I shall study a nobler way of acting than what I have hitherto done, and produce a repentance of all my folly by abandoning, diverting, and turning my thoughts from the consideration of anything in itself but what shall tend to the serious exhortation of your Honour when I received the glory of being admitted into your presence at Foxhall, continuing in the same mind, solemnly declaring to perform those commands your Honour conjured me to.

Lastly, as your Honour has been the only pillar whereon the kingdom of my happiness was erected, and by whom upheld, so let me implore so much compassion from your Honour (this last time) as to take under your care the hundred-pounds which I have entreated my honoured sister Mary (chief executrix of my mother's will) to pay into your hands when she receives the same, and that your Honour will be so charitable as to manage it for me, towards my future and only dependance; and, as in duty bound, shall ever pray as becomes,

Honourable Sir,
Your most obedient and most humble devoted servant,
PETER SKINNER

Whether Pepys obliged or not, we do not know. In April 1703 Pepys made his last gesture of familial loyalty to Balthazar St Michel in one of the last letters he ever composed. He wrote to Sir George Rooke, then commanding the fleet, and gave it to Balthazar to deliver it himself. It is a simple plea that in return for his loyalty and unpaid service, Balthazar be afforded some 'protection'. By now Pepys was seriously and terminally ill. John Jackson copied the letter into Pepys's archives for him though Pepys was well enough to look it through and make some amendments. The letter is not dated to an exact day.

258. SAMUEL PEPYS TO SIR GEORGE ROOKE

April 1703

SIR

I have too long outlived my relation to the Navy to pretend to any remains of interest in, or even being remembered by many who have now (with yourself) the honour of being at the head of it, I retain nevertheless (as I always shall) the same degree of concernment for its prosperity, and respectful regard to the persons of its present directors; and therein particularly of yourself, with whom I have had the honour of the longest acquaintance, as well as the strongest obligations of ancient friendship with your honoured father and family.

The remembrance of which encourages me to putt into your hand the first and only request relating to the Navy that I have ever appeared in since my retirement from it. Nor should I have now done it in this, upon any less moving occasion than that of the unhappy bearer, Mr St Michel, heretofore one of its commissioners, who is now addressing himself to the Queen for the relief in all time past and at this day universally enjoyed by persons under his circumstances of age and length of service. Which, what they more particularly are in his case, I refer you for information to the enclosed copy of his petition to her Majesty; with this only addition thereto from myself, that as I am an immediate witness of the truth of every line of it relating to his services and employments mentioned therein, and of his ever laudable and approved acquittal of himself in them, so have I most convincing inducements for pitying him under the hardship of being so unaccountably and for so many years together wholly overlooked in the Navy, and with his numerous family exposed to and continued in a known state of want, notwithstanding the constant proofs he has (inferior to no man) given of his steadiness in the established religion, his obedience to the present Government, and industry in that useful piece of public trust for the seamen of England which he has been all this while continued in (without penny-salary) as an Elder Brother of the Trinity House.

I therefore take leave, as in a case truly worthy of you, to recommend this unhappy gentleman and his cause to your kindness and protection, as the same shall be brought within your notice, either before the Queen, his Royal Highness the Lord Admiral, or the gentlemen of your honourable Board: assuring you that I am most sensibly afflicted for the severities of it, and shall ever most thankfully own whatever you shall at this my instance be pleased to do in favour of it; remaining, with the utmost respect,

Honoured Sir

Your most faithful and most humble servant

S. P.

On 19 April Pepys was informed by doctors of the seriousness of his condition. On 26 May, he died in Will Hewer's house in Clapham. John Jackson sent an account of his passing to John Evelyn. A few days later Jackson forwarded the mourning rings intended for Evelyn and his grandson, because neither had been able to attend the funeral at St Olave's.

259. JOHN JACKSON TO JOHN EVELYN

Clapham

Friday night, 28 May 1703

HONOURED SIR

'Tis no small addition to my grief, to be obliged to interrupt the quiet of your happy recess with the afflicting tidings of my uncle Pepys's death; knowing how sensibly you will partake with me herein; but I should not be faithful to his desires if I did not beg your doing the honour to his memory of accepting mourning from him, as a small Instance of his most affectionate respect and honour for you. I have thought myself extremely unfortunate to be out of the way at that only time when you were pleased lately to touch here, and express so great a desire of taking leave of my uncle, which could not but have been admitted by him as a most welcome exception to his general orders against being interrupted: And I could most heartily wish that the circumstances of your health and distance did not forbid me to ask the favour of your assisting in the holding-up of the pawl at his internment, which is intended to be on Thursday next; for if the *Manes* are affected with what passes below, I'm sure this would have been very grateful to his.

I must not omit acquainting you, Sir, that upon opening his body (which the uncommonness of his case required of us, for our own satisfaction as well as public good) there was found in his left kidney a nest of no less than seven stones, of the most irregular figures your imagination can frame, and weighing together 4½ ounces. But all fast linked together and adhering to his back, whereby they solve his having felt no greater pains upon motion, nor other of the ordinary symptoms of the stone. The rest of that kidney was nothing but a bag full of ulcerous matter; which, irritating his bowels, caused an irresistible flux, and that his destruction. Some other lesser defects there also were in his body, proceeding from the same cause. But his stamina in general were marvellously strong, and not only supported him under the most exquisite pains, weeks beyond all expectations, but, in the conclusion, contended for near forty hours (unassisted by any nourishment) with the very agonies of death, some few minutes excepted before his expiring, which were very calm.

There remains only for me, under this affliction, to beg the consolation and honour of succeeding to your patronage, for my uncle's sake, and leave to number myself with the same sincerity he ever did, among your greatest honourers, which I shall esteem as one of the most valuable parts of my Inheritances from him; being also with the faithfullest wishes of health and a happy long life to you,

Honoured Sir,
Your most obedient and most humble servant,
JACKSON

Mr Hewer, as my uncle's executor, and equally your faithful servant, joins with me in every part hereof. The time of my good uncle's departure was about ¾ past 3 on Wednesday morning last.

260. JOHN JACKSON TO JOHN EVELYN

Clapham
5 June 1703

HONOURED SIR

To what I troubled you with by Thursday's post, I have, by this messenger, only to add the repetition of my humblest thanks for the honours you have been pleased to do me; and to beg your own and young Mr Evelyn's acceptance of the enclosed memorials of my good Uncle Pepys; whose body was last night interred in the parish church of St Olave's Hart Street by the Navy-Office,

I am, with profoundest respect, honoured Sir,
Your most faithful humble servant,
JACKSON

Samuel Pepys remains buried in St Olave's, alongside the body of his wife Elizabeth, who had been laid there more than thirty-three years earlier. John Jackson fulfilled the terms of his uncle's will. Jackson also inherited much of Mary Skinner's estate when she died in 1715, which was also the year in which Will Hewer died. The fate of Balthazar St Michel, perhaps the most durable individual in the correspondence, is unknown. He died some time after 1710. On Jackson's death in 1724 the library, as Pepys had intended, was transferred to Magdalene College along with many of his papers, letterbooks, and of course the Diary. Here they have remained a source of curiosity ever since, doubtless as Samuel Pepys intended, and prove the absolute truth of his motto.

Mens cuiusque is est quisque
'The mind of each man is the man himself'
Cicero. *De Republica* vi.26

Personalities mentioned in the letters

This alphabetical lists most of the individuals (but not monarchs) mentioned in the letters, whether correspondents of Pepys or cited in the texts. The sources used to compile the biographical details include information in the letters themselves, the diaries of Pepys and Evelyn, and the editorial notes prepared by their respective editors.[1] Not all dates are known for all individuals. Other sources include the Dictionary of National Biography, and Burke's Peerage and Baronetage, and online genealogical resources.

ALBEMARLE, Duke of. See MONCK, George

ALCOCK, Mark. P's cousin. His mother Elizabeth (née Pepys) was P's great-aunt.

ALLESTREE, Dr Richard (1619–81). Fought for the Royalists in the Civil War. Canon of Christ Church, Oxford 1660, chaplain to the King in 1663, regius professor of divinity 1663–79 and from 1665 provost of Eton College.

ANDREWS, John. Probably a servant in the John Crew (q.v.) household.

ANDREWS, Sir Matthew. Master of Trinity House 1695–6.

APSLEY, Sir Alan/Allen (1616–83). Friend of the Duke of York, and treasurer of his household 1662–83.

ATKINS, Samuel. P's clerk in 1679. Accused of being implicated in the murder of St Edmund Berry Godfrey (q.v.).

BAGWELL, William. Possibly the William Backewell christened at St Botolph's, Bishopsgate, 14 November 1630, son of William and Margaret. A ship's carpenter at Deptford and then Harwich, with whose wife P maintained sexual relations in return for her husband's promotion. Mrs Bagwell, hitherto unidentified, may be possibly Judith Campion, who married a William Bagwell at the same St Botolph's on 26 September 1658.

BANKS, Sir John (1627–99). Merchant and friend who P first met in 1664 but became close to later. Banks supported P in 1674.

BARNWELL, Robert. Edward Mountagu's steward at Hinchingbrooke.

BARTON, Mr ___. Probably Thomas Barton. Barton lived in Brampton and sold his house to Robert Pepys, Samuel's uncle.

BATES, Dr ___. A doctor who treated Jemimah Sandwich in January 1660.

BATH, Lord. See GRENVILLE, John

BATTEN, Sir William (1601–67). Surveyor of the Navy 1660–7 and one of the principal figures in the Diary and correspondence during the Second Dutch War. He and P were rivals. P considered Batten corrupt and incompetent.

BEARD, Thomas(?). Identified by Latham and Matthews as the 'Huntingdon carrier' perhaps better 'courier'. Diary 14 March 1660: 'old Beard'.

BENNET, Henry, Earl of Arlington (1618–85). Secretary of state 1662–74.

BENTLEY, Dr Richard (1662–1742). Scholar, chaplain to the bishop of Worcester 1690, prebendary of Worcester 1692, keeper of royal libraries 1694. In 1697 he proved the Greek *Letters of Phalaris* (the part-mythical ruler of Agrigentum) to

---

[1] Latham and Matthews have in rare instances (e.g. the birth date of John Creed q.v. see vol. X, 79) made errors. These have been corrected here.

be forgeries, which humiliated the editor of a 1695 edition, Charles Boyle (q.v.). This occasioned a bitter 'scholarly' dispute characterized by the trading of insults and watched by the educated public including P with fascination.

BERKELEY, George, Lord (1628–98). Ninth Baron Berkeley and (1679) first Earl. Pepys knew him slightly in the Diary period, probably through the Royal Society. On 14 October 1668 Pepys saw his cart experiment. Councillor for Foreign Plantations and on the Committee of the East India Company.

BERNARD, [Elizabeth], Lady. Probably the wife of Sir John Bernard (1630–79), an adviser and friend of P's.

BERRY, Major-General James (*fl.* 1655). Parliamentary soldier on Council of state.

BERRY, Sir John (1635–90). Naval commander who led a squadron against the French and Dutch 1667. Knighted for his performance at Sole Bay 1672. Commanded the *Gloucester* in 1682 when it was wrecked with great loss of life, nearly killing the Duke of York. Vice-Admiral of squadron sent to Tangier 1683.

BLAKE, Robert (1599–1657). Parliamentary admiral from 1649 who pursued Rupert's (q.v. 'The Prince') fleet to the Mediterranean. Defeated, and then was defeated by, the Dutch in 1652. In 1655 defeated a Turkish pirate fleet. In 1657 beat a Spanish fleet at Santa Cruz but died on the way home.

BOREMAN, Sir William (1612–86). Clerk to the Board of Green Cloth, members of which oversaw the management of the royal household.

BOTELER, Sir Francis. See SHELCROSS, Julia

BOUFLERS, Monsieur, *recte* Louis François, Duc de Bouflers, Marshal of France (1644–1711). The event concerning him at the Siege of Namur referred to in Letter no. 229 from P to Sir James Houblon is otherwise unknown.

BOWLES, Phineas (d. 1714). Dartmouth's private secretary in 1688. Succeeded P as Secretary of the Admiralty in 1689.

BOYLE, Charles (1676–1731), later fourth Earl of Orrery and grandnephew of Robert Boyle (q.v.). His undergraduate edition of *The Letters of Phalaris* contained a pointed criticism of Richard Bentley (q.v.) and occasioned an exchange of bitter mutual insults called by Swift 'The Battle of the Books' watched with fascination by men such as Pepys.

BOYLE, The Honourable Robert (1627–91). Chemist, natural philosopher and theologian. Pioneer of the experimental method. Member of the Royal Society.

BRANDRITH, Henry. Served on Committee for Safety under the Commonwealth.

BRISBANE, John (d. 1684). Deputy Treasurer of the Fleet 1665, Judge Advocate-General 1672–80 and then Secretary to the Admiralty 1680–4 during P's interregnum. In 1679 secretary to the embassy in Paris, where he helped P secure evidence to rubbish Col. John Scott's (q.v.) claims.

BROOKE, Sir Robert (1637–69). MP for Aldeburgh. His accidental death in the Rhône occasioned P's unsuccessful attempts to be made candidate for the seat.

BROUNCKER, William, second Viscount (1620–84). First president of the Royal Society 1662–77. Interested in mathematics and shipbuilding. Commissioner of the Navy 1664–79, and Admiralty Commissioner 1681–4.

BROWNE, John. Storekeeper at Harwich.

BUNN, Captain Thomas. Naval commander serving under the Commonwealth, and 1660–1. Commander of the *Essex* in 1660.

BURROUGHES, William. William Penn's clerk.

BUTLER, James, first Duke of Ormonde (1610–88). Lord Lieutenant of Ireland under Charles I and Charles II.

BUTLER, James, second Duke of Ormonde (1665–1745). Chancellor of Oxford University 1688. Fought extensively for William III and Anne.

CARTERET, Sir George (1610–80). Vice-Chamberlain to the Household 1660–70, Treasurer of the Navy 1660–7, Master of Trinity House 1664–5, and member of the Tangier and Fishery Committees. His son Philip married Jemima Mountagu, daughter of Edward Mountagu, first Earl of Sandwich (q.v.).

CHARLETT, Dr Arthur (1655–1722). One of P's closest friends. Master of University College, Oxford, from 1692.

CHILD, Sir Josiah (1630–99). A former naval storekeeper at Portsmouth who became chairman of the East India Company. His brother, Sir John Child (d. 1690), went out to India in the EIC's service and was governor of Bombay 1685.

CHURCHILL, John, first Duke of Marlborough (1650–1722). Soldier. Served at Tangier, as envoy to the Prince of Orange in 1678. Travelled with Duke of York to Holland 1679, and to Scotland 1679–82 and was wrecked with him in the *Gloucester*, acting as go-between with York and the King. Defeated the Monmouth Rebellion 1685, and went over to the Prince of Orange 1688. Served under William III and Anne, climaxing in the victory at Blenheim 1704.

CIFACCA, see GROSSI

CLARKE/CLERKE, Capt. Robert (d. by 1688). Commander of the *Speaker* and other vessels. He gained his experience under the Commonwealth and in the 1660s was considered a very competent commander, but earned criticism in 1667 for letting the Dutch steal the *Monmouth* from the Medway.

CLAY, Capt. Robert. Officer commanding *Sapphire* in 1660. He is unmentioned in the Diary yet was clearly known personally to P.

CLAYPOOLE, Elizabeth, Lady (1624–58). Cromwell's daughter and wife of John Claypoole, Master of the Horse, then Lord of the Bedchamber under Cromwell.

CLERKE, Capt. Robin. Commander of the *Speaker*.

CLERKE, Mr ____. Injured on the *Mountague*, probably in the Battle of Sole Bay 28 May 1672. P describes him as a friend. He was possibly husband of Mrs Clerke, P's Greenwich landlady from October 1665–January 1666.

COCKE, Captain George (1617–79). Merchant and Navy contractor. He and P dealt over the prize-goods in 1665. P did not trust him.

COLE, Mr ____. Timber merchant

COLEMAN, Capt. William (d. 1681). Commander of *James*, Collector at Plymouth.

COMPTON, Henry, Bishop of London (1632–1713). Opposed James II and supported the Prince of Orange. Bishop of London.

COOPER, Sir Anthony Ashley, first Baron Ashley and first Earl of Shaftesbury (1621–83). Fought for the king until transferring to Parliament in 1644. Served as a councillor of state but opposed Cromwell's government. In December 1659 he negotiated for the Restoration. Major player in the opposition under Charles II, using fears of Catholicism to stoke the Popish Plot and oppose P.

COTTON, Captain Andrew. Officer commanding the Navy yacht in 1688.

COVENTRY, Sir William (1627–86). Secretary to Lord High Admiral 1660–7, Commissioner of the Navy 1662–7. MP for Great Yarmouth 1661–79. A close colleague of P's, and supported P's reforms. Instrumental in the fall of Edward Hyde in 1667. Lost office when Clarendon's enemies turned on him.

CREED, John (c. 1635–1701). Deputy-treasurer of the fleet 1660–3, secretary to the Commissioners for Tangier 1662. P's rival for Mountagu's favour.

CREW, Mrs Anne. See WRIGHT, Anne, Lady

CREW, Edward (1630–57). John and Jemimah Crew's eldest son.

CREW, John (1598–1679), Mountagu's father-in-law. Sat in Parliament in 1654 until excluded until February 1660. Created Baron Crew of Stene in 1661. Married Jemimah Waldegrave on 24 February 1622 at Stene.[2]

CROOKE, Sir Henry. Clerk of the Pipe in the 1650s.

DANIEL, Sir Peter. Sometime Sheriff of London, and MP for Southwark

DE BADES, Marquis ____. The Marquis de Bades was a boy captured off Cadiz when Blake (q.v.) seized Spanish treasure ships in 1656. His father, the Viceroy of Peru, his mother and sister, were all killed. The plan had been to ransom the boy off, but meanwhile Mountagu handed him over to the Pickerings (q.v.).

DEANE, Captain Anthony (1638–1721). Master-shipwright at Harwich from 1664, and at Portsmouth 1668. A close friend of P's and as a member of the Navy Board 1675–80 helped with P's programme of shipbuilding. In 1679 imprisoned with P, jointly accused of selling naval secrets to France as part of the hysteria surrounding the Popish Plot. A pall-bearer at P's funeral.

DELAVALL, Sir Ralph (d. 1707). His seat, referred to in the letter of 28 May 1682, was at Seaton Delaval.

DESBOROUGH, Major-General John (1608–80). Parliamentary soldier.

D'ESTRÉE, Comte Jean (b. 1624). Admiral and Marshal. Blamed for inaction in the Battles of Sole Bay 28 May 1672, and Texel 11 August 1673.

DOLBEN, Dr John (1625–86). Canon of Christ Church, Oxford, from 1660. Dean of Westminster 1662–83, Bishop of Rochester 1666, Archbishop of York 1683–6.

DOLING, Thomas. In 1660 a messenger to the Council of State, and a friend of P's.

DORSET, Lord. See SACKVILLE, Charles

DOWNING, George. George Downing (1623–84), formerly scout-master-general of Cromwell's army in Scotland and MP for Edinburgh in 1654. By 1656 a Teller of the Receipt of the Exchequer where P was on his staff 1656–60.

D'OYLY, Edmund. Possibly a son or relative of Edward Doyley (1617–75)

DOYLY, Sir William (1614–77). Commissioner for Sick and Wounded Seamen.

DRYDEN, John (1631–1700). Poet and scholar. P encouraged him to produce his own version of some of Chaucer's works, published in 1700.

DUTTON, Sir Richard. Friend of P's and listed amongst his mourners in 1703.

'EDWARD, Mr'. See Montagu, Edward, second Earl of Sandwich.

EGMONT, Deborah. Nothing about this woman is known unless she was, as Bryant suggested, possibly the former Deb Willets of the Diary years. Elizabeth Pepys caught P with her, and the drama was graphically described by P in the Diary.

EVELYN, John (1620–1706). Savant best known then for books on trees and gardening, and also numismatics, architecture and naval history. Commissioner for Sick and Wounded Seamen and Prisoners of War during the Second and Third Dutch Wars. One of P's oldest friends and most prolific correspondent.

EVELYN, John (1655–99). Son of the diarist. Gifted linguist. Commissioner of the Revenue in Ireland 1692. Father of Evelyn's grandson of the same name.

EVELYN, Sir John (1682–1763). Grandson of the diarist and friend of P's.

EVELYN, Mrs Mary (c. 1635–1709). Wife of John Evelyn (q.v.), the diarist.

---

[2] Latham and Matthews (vol X, 80–1) place the marriage in 1648 despite this postdating the birth of their daughter Jemimah, later Countess of Sandwich, by 26 years, and may in fact be referring to the marriage of their son John Crew the younger (1622–71).

FAGG, Colonel Sir John (d. 1701). Commissioner for Charles I's trial. Arrested for helping Haselrig and Morley 1659. MP for Sussex under the Commonwealth, and Steyning, Sussex 1661–1701.

FAIRBORNE, Sir Palmes (1644–80). Governor of Tangier 1676–8, and builder of the mole. Killed in a battle with the Moors.

FANE, Mrs. P's housekeeper. Hired c. January 1686. Considered loyal and reliable but to have a vicious tongue. Probably fell out with B. St Michel (Letters nos. 167, 175, 202). Sacked 1687 until Mary Skinner insisted on her re-engagement.

FEAKE, Christopher (*fl.* 1645–60), a Fifth Monarchist and opponent of Quakers. Criticized Cromwell in 1653 and imprisoned.

FELL, Dr John (1625–86). Dean of Christ Church, Oxford 1660, Bishop of Oxford 1675. Encouraged Oxford students to oppose the Monmouth Rebellion of 1685.

FINCH, Heneage (1647–1719). Younger son of Sir Heneage Finch (1621–82), first Earl of Nottingham. Served as leading counsel for the Seven Bishops, 1686. MP for Oxford University. Privy councillor 1703, Earl of Aylesford 1714.

FISHER, Payne (1616–93), known as 'Pagan Fisher'. Poet who eulogized Cromwell, and later Louis XIV of France in a pangyric given to P. See Diary 14 July 1660.

FITZROY, Charlotte, Countess of Sussex (1664–1718). Daughter of Charles II and Barbara Villiers, Duchess of Cleveland. Later the Countess of Lichfield.

FITZROY, Henry, first Duke of Grafton (1663–90). Son of Charles II and Barbara Villiers. Fought at Sedgemoor 1685. Declared himself loyal to James II but went over to William III. Killed while fighting for him at Cork in 1690.

FLEETWOOD, George (*fl.* 1650). Regicide on Council of State. Escaped execution.

FULLER, Dr Thomas (1608–61). Author of the *History of the Holy War* (1643). Chaplain to Charles I, and travelled to The Hague in 1660 to greet Charles II.

GALE, Roger (1672–1744). Son of Thomas Gale (q.v.). Antiquary and later Commissioner of Excise 1715–35. First vice-president of Society of Antiquaries.

GALE, Dr Thomas (1635–1702). Master of St Paul's School, then Dean of York 1697–1702. P's close friend and cousin through marriage.

GARRAWAY, William (1617–1701). An enemy of P's who challenged his seat in Parliament 1674, his shipbuilding plans 1675 and 1677, and encouraged the campaign against P in 1679. Supported the Glorious Revolution.

GAUDEN, Sir Denis (1600–88). Navy Victualler 1660–77, Surveyor-General 1660, and Alderman 1667–76. Ruined by the failure of the government to pay him.

GELSON, John. An acquaintance of P's based in Norway in 1683 but formerly employed in the Earl of Arlington's office.

GEORGE, Mother. Alice George of Oxford, said to have been 141 when she died in 1691, two years before P acquired an engraving of her.

GERRARD, Sir Gilbert. Samuel Morland's disastrous marriage was to a woman who was also cohabiting with a Sir Gilbert Gerrard, probably not the one who died 1687 but perhaps his son, Sir Gilbert Cosin-Gerard (1662–1730). In 1686 Gerard senior had seen John Evelyn in an attempt to arrange his son's marriage with Evelyn's daughter Susanna (diary 1 March 1686).

GODFREY, Sir Edmund Berry (1621–78). JP for Westminster, found dead a month after Titus Oates (q.v.) made his claims before him about the Popish Plot. Various executions followed forced confessions

GODFREY, Michael (d. 1695). Nephew of Sir Edmund (q.v.). Financier and first deputy-governor of the Bank of England, killed at Namur en route to establish a branch at Antwerp.

GODOLPHIN, Sidney (1645–1712). Managed to serve under James II and William III. Baron Godolphin 1684, commissioner of the Treasury 1687, head of the Treasury 1690–6, Lord High Treasurer 1702–10.

GOFFE, Captain __ . Probably served in Mountagu's regiment.

GOUGH, Richard. Cadiz-based associate of Houblon's (Chappell 1935, 12, 18, 26).

GRAFTON, Duke of. See FITZROY, Henry

GRANTHAM, Sir Thomas (*fl.* 1684). Naval commander who brought ships from Virginia during the Third Dutch War. Later commanded the East India Company ship *Charles II* and served under William III and Anne.

GREGORY, Sir Edward. Clerk of the Cheque at Chatham 1665. Knighted 1689 and made Navy Commissioner at Chatham 1689–1703.

GREGORY, Dr David (1661–1708). Professor of mathematics at Edinburgh 1683–91, Savilian Professor of Astronomy at Oxford 1691, and author of *Astronomiae Physicae et Geometricae Elementa* (1702).

GRENVILLE, John, Earl of Bath (1628–1701). Fought for the Royalists in the Civil War. Governor of Plymouth 1661. Privy councillor in 1689.

GROSSI, Giovanni Francesco (1653–97). Known as 'Cifacca', a celebrated eunuch singer who performed at P's house in 1687.

GUY, Captain Thomas. Probably the soldier who was in the Dunkirk Garrison 1659–60, or alternatively the Captain Thomas Guy who commanded the *Assurance* in 1666 (see Diary 28 October 1666).

HADDOCK, Sir Richard (1629–1715). Fought in Second and Third Dutch Wars, Commander in the Nore 1682, Commissioner of Victualling 1683–90.

HAMMOND, Dr ____ . Probably John Hammond, archdeacon of Huntingdon.

HARBORD, William (1635–92). MP for Thetford and chairman of the Parliamentary committee that compiled the evidence against P and Deane in 1679. He later supported William of Orange and accompanied him to England in 1688. Also referred to in the original correspondence as HARBERT and HERBERT.

HART, Major Theo. Served in Mountagu's regiment 1657–60 and probably served as paymaster. He paid P money owing to him on 28 November 1660 (Diary).

HASELRIG, Sir Arthur (d. 1661). Parliament soldier, and councillor of state throughout the Commonwealth. Opposed Cromwell's rule, and Lambert. Arrested at the Restoration and died in the Tower.

HAYES, Sir James (d. 1693). Secretary to Prince Rupert. 1666–72, and Fellow of the Royal Society 1663–84.

HAYTER, Tom (d. 1689). Clerk in the Navy Office by 1660. Succeeded P as Clerk of the Acts in 1673, serving jointly with John Pepys until 1677. Secretary of the Admiralty 1679–80, Comptroller of the Navy 1680–3, assistant to the Comptroller 1682–6 and late 1688.

HEEMSKIRKE, Laurence van. A Dutch captain who claimed that he had a secret method to double a ship's speed. On 13 May 1668 it had been decided England would pay him £20,000 for this. Pepys thought this 'folly' since it would be impossible to keep the method a secret (Diary for that day).

HERBERT, Admiral Arthur (1647–1716). Served in Second and Third Dutch Wars, commanded fleet relieving Tangier 1680. Opposed repeal of Test Act in 1687. Commanded William's 1688 invasion fleet. Made Earl of Torrington 1689. Career ended in 1690 when he held back in an engagement with the French.

HERBERT, Philip, fifth earl of Pembroke (1619–68). President of council of state 1652, Councillor for Trade and Navigation 1660.

HERVEY, Sir Thomas (1625–94). Extra-Commissioner of the Navy 1665–8, and MP for Bury St Edmunds 1679–90.

HEWER, Will (1642–1715). Worked under P from early on, acting as P's clerk and manservant. By 1674 he was chief clerk, and Judge Advocate-General in 1677. His journey with Deane in 1675 played a major role in the accusations against P in 1679. Served on the Special Commission of 1686–8 and fell with P in 1689. Noticeable for having accumulated considerable wealth. Accusations of his corruption had been made against him, strenuously denied by P, but his affluence remains unexplained. P lived with him at his various houses in York Buildings and Clapham and died at the latter in 1703.

HEWSON, Colonel John (d. 1662). A regicide who escaped after the Restoration and died abroad. A former shoemaker, he was mocked in the run-up to the Restoration as a 'cobbler'.

HILL, Thomas (1630–75). Merchant, associate of the Houblons and friend of P's. Based in Lisbon. Introduced P to Cesare Morelli (q.v.).

HINCHINGBROOKE, Lord. See MOUNTAGU, Edward, second Earl of Sandwich.

HINGSTON, John (1612–83). Served as musician to Charles I and Charles II and in between as state organist for Cromwell. Evidently his skills overcame any concerns about where his loyalties lay.

HODDER, Mr ___. Presumably an official in the Navy Office in 1688, who carried letters between Lord Dartmouth and Pepys.

HOLLAND, Captain Philip. Although he fought in the First Dutch War, during the Second Dutch War he was to change sides and even took part in the Battle of the Medway in 1667. Later captured but agreed to serve as a spy.

HOLLIER, Dr Thomas. Surgeon at St Thomas's Hospital who operated on P's bladder stone on 26 March 1658.

HOLMES, Margaret, Lady. Known as 'Peg'. Wife and widow of Sir John Holmes (c. 1640–83), the naval commander. Petitioned P on her son's behalf who was at sea with Thomas Fowler. She was sister of Anthony Lowther, and not therefore to be confused with Anthony's wife Margaret (née Penn), also known as Peg.

HOMEWOOD, Edward. Privately employed clerk in the Navy Office in 1663. Probably the Mr Homeward who was Clerk of the Survey at Chatham in 1675.

HOTHAM, Sir John. Mentioned in Hewer's letter of 16 Novmber 1680 (no. 143) this must be Sir John Hotham (d. 1689), 2nd bt, and grandson of Sir John Hotham, executed 1645 by Parliament for negotiating with the Royalists.

HOUBLON, Sir James (1629–1700). One of P's closest friends, whom he came to know through his invaluable knowledge of trade and shipping. A wealthy man, he actively supported P financially and with amassing evidence for the defence in 1679 and 1690. P was also close friends with Houblon's family.

HOWARD, Henry (1628–84). Baron Howard of Castle Rising 1669, and sixth Duke of Norfolk 1677. Friend of John Evelyn's. His home, Arundel House, was used by the Royal Society as its meeting place.

HOWE, William. Formerly in the service of the Earl of Sandwich, he became Treasurer of the Fleet 1664–5. By 1666 he had gone into the legal profession and by 1680 was living in Barbados. His wife was P's god-daughter, who has until now remained unidentified but a Sarah Bartlet married a William Howe at St Katherine-by-the-Tower on 18 September 1670 and this is probably her.[3]

HYDE, Henry, first Earl of Clarendon (1609–74). Lord Chancellor 1658–67. His daughter's marriage to the Duke of York enhanced resentment for, and jealousy of, his position and he fell in 1667.

HYDE, Henry, second Earl of Clarendon (1638–1709). Lord Privy Seal 1685. Opposed William and Mary, and imprisoned 1691.

HYDE, Laurence, Earl of Rochester (1641–1711). Second son of Edward Hyde, first Earl of Clarendon. Commissioner of the Treasury 1679. Privy councillor and first lord of the Treasury 1679–85. Lord High Treasurer 1685, dismissed for anti-Catholicism 1687. Privy councillor 1692. Patron of John Dryden (q.v.).

INGOLDSBY, Colonel Sir Richard (d. 1685). One of the regicides, then MP for Buckinghamshire. Pardoned after the Restoration.

JACKSON, John senior (d. 1680). Husband of P's sister Paulina. A farmer from Ellington near Brampton. Poor management of his affairs meant Paulina and later P had to intervene. Even so, at his death in 1680 P was obliged to sort out an accumulation of debts.

JACKSON, John junior (1673–1723). P's favoured nephew and heir. After graduating from Magdalene in 1690 he worked for P as a secretary and clerk. From 1699–1701 he was dispatched on a Grand Tour for his education and to accumulate books for his uncle's library. After P's death he maintained and completed the library and arranged for its transfer to Magdalene on his death.

JACKSON, Paulina (1640–89). P's sister, and mother of his nephews Samuel and John junior (q.v.). She also took her father John in after 1667 when his wife died. Considered bad-tempered and charmless.

JACKSON, Samuel (1669–*post* 1714). P's eldest nephew. Sent to sea in 1684. By 1694 he was managing P's Brampton estates. In P's 1701 will he was left all the Huntingdonshire property. Shortly afterwards he made a marriage of which P disapproved and was cut out of the will apart from a £40 annuity. His wife had died before 1714 when he remarried. His date of death is unknown.

JOHNSTON, Sir Archibald, Lord Warriston (1610–63). Scottish statesman, supported Parliament. Member of Committee for Safety. Executed 1663.

JONES, Colonel John (d. 1660). A regicide and Cromwell's brother-in-law. Governor of Anglesey in 1657. Executed after the Restoration.

JONES, Sir William (1631–82). Lawyer, MP for Plymouth, and supporter of the Exclusion Bill. P heard about his death while in Scotland after the shipwreck of the *Gloucester* in 1682.

KEN, Dr Thomas (1637–1711). Dartmouth's chaplain on the Tangier trip of 1683–4 but later Bishop of Bath and Wells (1685–91).

KINGDOME/KINGDON, Captain Richard. Commissioner at the Prize Office 1656, 1665–7, Comptroller of Excise 1666. Noted for financial acumen.

KNELLER, Sir Godfrey (1646–1723). German-born artist who arrived in England 1675 and proceeded to become the principal portrait painter of his time,

---

[3] Latham and Matthews were unable to trace her (vol. X, 199). However, this Sarah's father was Robert Bartlet, perhaps a brother or cousin of the Nick Bartlet P describes as Sandwich's former servant at sea (Diary 31 January 1660), though this could not be confirmed. Nick Bartlet is probably the man christened at St Margaret's, Westminster on [...] July 1627, the same church in which Sandwich, and later P, were married. A Sandwich connection would explain P's being her godfather.

remaining as popular after 1689 as he had been before. P's commission of a portrait of John Wallis is a major theme of the late correspondence.

KORTHOLT, Christian (1633–94). Professor of theology at Rostock, and Kiel.

LAMBERT, Major-General John (1619–83). Lambert's influence swayed Cromwell from accepting the crown. Imprisoned and executed after the Restoration.

LAURENCE/LAWRENCE, Lord Henry (1600–64), Lord President of the Council of State 1654–9.

LAWRENCE, Dr ___. Dartmouth's physican on the journey to Tangier in 1683–4.

LAWSON, Admiral Sir John (d. 1665). Admiral in the Parliamentary fleet. Cooperated with Monck (q.v.) during the Restoration as Vice-Admiral of the fleet in 1660. Served as Vice-Admiral in the Second Dutch War.

LEGGE, George (1648–91), first Baron Dartmouth. Various appointments include Master of the Horse to the Duke of York 1673, Master-General of Ordnance 1682, and created Baron Dartmouth 1682. His actions at the wreck of the *Gloucester* in 1682 ensured the Duke of York's survival at the expense of others. Opposed William III and sent to the Tower in 1691 where he died.

LENTHALL, William (1591–1662). Speaker of the House of Commons 1640–7. He subsequently supported the Restoration.

LOGGAN, David (1635–1700). Artist and engraver, made engraver to Oxford University from 1669.

LORRAIN, Paul. Secretary on P's staff, responsible for (amongst other things) copying letters. He was working for P by 1680. In 1700 he was working at York Buildings and protesting to P that his conscientious efforts were not being appreciated (letter to P 12 October 1700, published by Tanner 1926, ii.329).

MACKENZIE, George, first Viscount Tarbat (1630–1714). A member of William III's government but actively interested in the phenomenon of 'second sight'.

MAIDSTONE, John. MP for Colchester.

MALLARD, Thomas. Viol player and composer who served Oliver Cromwell. Subsequently he joined Sandwich's staff and sailed to Portugal with him.

MARCULFUS (*fl.* 7th century AD). His *Formularies* were the most important collection of model forms of official documents (formularies) from the Frankish empire, compiled c. 650 and edited by French scholar Jérôme Bignon (1589–1656) for a 1613 edition.

MARYON, Joseph (d. 1710?). Fellow of Clare Hall, Cambridge. P calls him cousin, but how the two were related is unknown.

MATTHEWS, John (i). In 1687 clerk to Captain Thomas Fowler commanding the *Happy Return*. Possibly the same as the John Matthews who was Clerk to the Privy Seal Office in 1660.

MATTHEWS, John (ii). Huntingdon schoolmaster and remote cousin of P's who supervised the education of Samuel and John Jackson (q.v.).

MAY, Baptist (1628–97). York's servant, Keeper of the Privy Purse 1665–85.

MEADOWS, Mr ___. Probably Philip Meadows (1626–1718), knighted in 1658. Ambassador in Portugal in 1656, Sweden in 1658. Later served on royal commissions, and wrote about naval supremacy and the Swedish–Danish war.

MEDOWES (*recte* MEADOWS?), Mr ___. Unknown. Presumably a kersey supplier?

MENNES, Sir John (1599–1671). Royalist soldier, and later naval commander under Rupert. Comptroller of the Navy 1660–71 and a major figure in P's Diary. A weak administrator, his position was compromised by the extraordinary financial problems the Navy faced in the Second Dutch War. In 1667 he was obliged to delegate his work to Brouncker and Penn, but was kept in post to save face.

MERES, Sir Thomas (1635–1715). MP for Lincoln 1659–1700. Commissioner of the Admiralty 1679–84. In 1685 he attempted to pass a bill that would have compelled foreigners to accept the English liturgy.

MIDDLETON, Colonel Thomas (d. 1672). Commissioner of the Navy at Portsmouth 1664–7, Surveyor of the Navy 1667–72. P recorded his 'bad keeping of the Surveyor's books and papers' (NWB, pp. 157–8, and 165).

MILDMAY, Sir Henry (d. 1664). Formerly Master of the Jewel House under Charles I but joined Parliament in 1641, subsequently serving on a number of state councils. Sentenced to life imprisonment in 1660.

MONCK, George, first Duke of Albemarle (1608–1670). Fought for the Royalists but in 1647 went over to Parliament, fighting in Scotland and then as admiral in the First Dutch War. Despite being trusted by Cromwell he accepted Royalist overtures in 1659 and opposed the army's expulsion of Parliament. Negotiated with Charles II and oversaw the Restoration. Effectively commander-in-chief during the Second Dutch War. First Lord of the Treasury 1667.

MONRO, Mr. A friend of John Jackson junior's who passed on a letter from Monsignor Bellisono to the Royal Society.

MOORE, Sir John. London merchant, and Lord Mayor 1681.

MOOTHAM, Capt. ___ . Commander of the *Foresight* in 1660.

MORDAUNT, Elizabeth, Lady (1645–87). Widow of Sir Charles Mordaunt, (d. 1665 – Latham & Matthews give George in error) (1) and then (2) Francis Godolphin (1629–72) of Coulston. After the latter's death she reverted to the title of her higher-ranked first husband. Her second husband was distantly related by marriage to Margaret Godolphin, subject of an obsessive friendship with John Evelyn. Lady Mordaunt was sister of Mrs Steward/Stewart (q.v.) and daughter of Nicholas (b. c. 1615) and Elizabeth (née Turner) Johnson. Christened 10 June 1645 at St Gregory-by-St Paul, eight days after the death of a sister of the same name at the age of one year. The pair were close friends of P's, and related to him by marriage through his cousin Jane (1623–86) whose husband was John Turner (1613–89) of Kirkleatham, Yorks (and not his brother Sir William Turner as stated in error by Latham and Matthews, X, 249), the brother of Elizabeth Turner. In 1682 she had suffered an acute 'fit of the stone' (Hewer to P, 25 May 1682; Smith i, 298). Evelyn's letter to P (see PF C39) discusses the news of her death in October 1687. William Glanville, Evelyn's brother-in-law, said she had been called 'the best-humoured woman in the world' (letter to Lady Mordaunt, 25 August 1673, printed by Smith 1841, ii, 144–5).

MORELLI, Cesare. Musician and singer in P's household, born in Flanders but educated in Rome. Recommended to P by Thomas Hill (q.v.) in 1673. His Catholicism was a useful stick for P's opponents to beat him with in 1679.

MORICE, Sir William (1602–76). Secretary of state 1660–8, privy councillor 1660.

MORLAND, Sir Samuel (1625–95). Diplomat and mathematician, and inventor of arithmetical machines and a hydraulic pump.

MORLEY, Colonel Herbert (1616–67). Although a soldier for Parliament in the Civil War he refused to help try the king, and was opposed to Cromwell. A councillor of state in 1659, he restored Parliament in December. Refused to take part in negotiations for the Restoration but purchased a pardon.

MOUNTAGU, Catherine (b. 1661). Youngest daughter and child of Edward and Jemimah, Earl and Countess of Sandwich. Married Nicholas Bacon of Suffolk.

MOUNTAGU, Mr Charles (1661–1715), created Earl of Halifax 1715. Author of a parody of Dryden's *The Hind and the Panther*, called *The Town and the Country Mouse* (1687). In 1692 as a lord of the Treasury he established the process of national debt, in 1694 he oversaw the creation of the Bank of England and became Chancellor of the Exchequer. In 1695–6 he administered the Great Recoinage.

MOUNTAGU, Edward (1625–72), first Earl of Sandwich. His mother Paulina was the daughter of P's great-grandfather John by his second marriage. Fought for Parliament, but joined Monck (q.v.) for the Restoration for which he was created Viscount Hinchingbrooke and Earl of Sandwich. Negotiated the marriage treaty with Portugal for Catherine of Braganza. His triumph at the Battle of Lowestoft (1665) was soured by the management of prize goods and he was made ambassador to Spain. He was killed in the Third Dutch War when his ship, *Royal James*, was set on fire at Sole Bay by the Dutch in 1672, though another version has him being drowned while carrying his flag to another ship.

MOUNTAGU, Edward, second Earl of Sandwich (1647–88), Lord Hinchingbrooke from 1660. Eldest son of Edward Mountagu, first Earl of Sandwich (q.v.). Married Anne Boyle, fourth daughter of Richard Boyle, Earl of Cork, and niece of the scientist Robert Boyle (q.v.). In childhood known as 'Mr Edward' by P.

MOUNTAGU, Mr Edward (1635–65). Son of the second Baron Mountagu of Boughton, and cousin to Edward Mountagu, Earl of Sandwich.

MOUNTAGU, Jemimah, countess of Sandwich (1622–). Daughter of John and Jemimah Crew. Married Edward Mountagu 7 November 1642 at Westminster.

MOUNTAGU Mistress Jemimah (b. c. 1645). The eldest daughter of Edward and Jemimah Mountagu, and not to be confused with her mother. Married Philip Carteret, son of Sir George Carteret, in 1665.

MOUNTAGU, Dr John (1655–1728). Son of Edward Mountagu, first Earl of Sandwich. Master Trinity College, Cambridge 1683, vice-chancellor 1687.

MOUNTAGU, Sidney (1655–1727). Second son of Edward Mountagu, first Earl of Sandwich. Married Anne Wortley of York. His daughter-in-law was the celebrated Lady Mary Wortley Montagu (1689–1762).

MUSGRAVE, Sir Christopher (1632–1704). Lieutenant-General of the ordnance 1681–7, MP for Carlisle 1661–90, and later Westmorland and Appleby.

NARBROUGH, Sir John (1640–88). Naval commander in the Second and Third Dutch Wars. Commissioner of the Navy 1680–7.

NEALE, Thomas (d. 1699). Master and worker of the Royal Mint 1678–99.

NEWTON, Isaac (1642–1727). Scientist, mathematician, designer of telescopes. In 1693 suffered a psychotic breakdown. Warden of the Mint 1695, Master of the Mint 1699. President of the Royal Society 1703. Knighted 1705.

NEWTON, Samuel. Mathematics master at Christ's Hospital in 1695. No relation to Isaac Newton (apparently), but was recommended by him.

NORTH, Sir Francis (1637–85). Lawyer, made Solicitor-General and knighted 1671. MP for King's Lynn and Attorney-General 1673. Chief Justice of Common Pleas 1675–82. Lord Chancellor 1682. Created first Baron Guilford 1683.

NORWOOD, Colonel Henry (1614–89). A Royalist who helped negotiate the Restoration. Deputy governor of Dunkirk in 1662, and Tangier 1665–9, and Tangier Commissioner 1673–80. P rented a house at Parson's Green from him.

OATES, Titus (1649–1705). Converted to Catholicism 1677 to amass 'evidence' against Catholics. In 1678 claimed to have uncovered the 'Popish Plot' in which Charles II was to be murdered and England ruled by Jesuits. Believed by a credulous public and administration, reinforced by the murder of Sir Edmund Berry Godfrey (q.v.), resulting in around 35 executions. Subsequently fell from favour, tried for perjury 1685, imprisoned for life but released 1689.

ORMONDE, Duke of. See BUTLER, James

OSBORNE, Sir Thomas (1631–1712). Treasurer of the Navy 1671–3. Created Earl of Danby 1674. His later involvement in secret negotiations for the Treaty of Dover with Louis XIV meant he fell under suspicion during the Popish Plot. Imprisoned until 1684. Supported the accession of William and Mary. Created Marquis of Carmarthen 1689, and Duke of Leeds 1694.

PASTON, Sir Robert (1631–83). MP for Castle Rising 1661–73. Created Viscount Yarmouth 1673, Earl of Yarmouth 1679.

PEMBROKE, Lord. See HERBERT, Philip

PENN, Sir William (1621–70). Commissioner of the Navy 1660–9. P resented his extensive experience at sea and disliked him. He worked hard during the Second Dutch War and served at the Battle of Lowestoft. Implicated in the prize goods scandal. An attempt to impeach him was abandoned.

PEPYS, Elizabeth (née St Michel) (1640–69). P's volatile wife born 23 October 1640 at Bideford, whom he married when she was fifteen. Her father Alexander St Michel was a Huguenot. Their relationship was punctuated by disagreements of various sorts, and affected by her health. P was frustrated by this, and her indulgences, though he clearly loved her. This failed to prevent his relentless sexual relationships with other women, amongst whom Mrs Bagwell and his wife's servant Deb Willets were the most significant. In 1669 P took Elizabeth and her brother to France and the Low Countries. Soon after returning in late October, she died from a fever and was buried in St Olave's, Hart Street. P was buried beside her in 1703.

PEPYS, John senior (1601–80). P's father. Worked as a tailor in London 1615–61, moving to Brampton when he inherited property from his brother Robert (q.v.). After his wife died in 1667 he moved in with his daughter, Paulina Jackson (q.v.), and depended on her and P to administer his affairs.

PEPYS, John junior (1641–77). P's younger brother. After taking a degree at Cambridge he was made Clerk of Trinity House in 1670 with P's influence. In 1673 he became joint Clerk of the Acts with Tom Hayter. On his death P had to settle £300–worth of debts John had incurred with Trinity House.

PEPYS, Paulina. See JACKSON, Paulina.

PEPYS, Robert (d. 1661). P's uncle. He probably worked for the Mountagues at Hinchingbrooke. Former militia service led to him being known as 'the Captain'. Childless, he left his Brampton property to P's father John, but his stepsons exploited complications in the will to secure a share for themselves. Other complications over land tenure resulted in legal issues that dragged on for years.

PEPYS, Roger (1617–88), P's cousin, a lawyer and trustee of Sandwich's will.

PEPYS, Thomas (dates unknown), P's cousin. He was a turner, and had a shop in St Paul's churchyard. The Thomas Pepys described as 'cousin Pepys' in the letter of 11 December 1675 (no. 106) to Robert Buller is a different individual and his relationship to Pepys remains unknown.

PETERBOROUGH, Penelope Mordaunt, Countess of. Wife of Henry Mordaunt, second Earl of Peterborough (1624–97).

PETT, Peter (1610–72). Navy Commissioner at Chatham 1648–60, and 1660–7. Master shipwright at Chatham 1664–7. Pett belonged to a family that had held many posts in naval yards on the Thames from the 1650s and used their positions to build private fortunes. P believed Pett to be a poor manager.

PETT, Phineas (1628–78). Master-shipwright at Woolwich 1675.

PETT, Captain Phineas (1635–94). Master-shipwright at Chatham 1660–80. Comptroller Store Accounts 1680–6. Navy Commissioner Chatham 1686–8.

PETTY, Sir William (1623–87). A man with an extraordinary range of skills that included innovative ship design, mathematics, and a term as physician-general to Cromwell's army. A founding member of the Royal Society. Pepys admired him enormously.

PICKERING, Elizabeth, Lady (c. 1620–79). Wife of Sir Gilbert Pickering (q.v.) since 1640, and sister of Edward Mountagu, first Earl of Sandwich (q.v.).

PICKERING, Sir Gilbert (1613–68), MP for Northamptonshire.

POCOCKE, Edward (1604–91). Oriental scholar. Arabic professor at Oxford 1636, Hebrew professor 1648.

POVEY, Thomas (1615–1702). From 1660 Treasurer of the Duke of York's Household, and from 1661 Secretary and Receiver-General of the Committee for Foreign Plantations. Treasurer of Tangier 1663, but from 1665 Pepys took over the work and they shared the profit. In 1674 Povey's belief that P had pocketed the profits himself provoked an exchange of letters (see no. 97).

'PRINCE, THE'. Prince Rupert of the Rhine (1619–82). Third son of Elizabeth of Bohemia, eldest daughter of James I, and her husband Frederick V, Elector Palatine, and thereby first cousin to Charles II. One of the principal Royalist commanders of the Civil War. During the Second Dutch War he shared naval command with the Duke of Albemarle, and was vice-admiral in the Third Dutch War. First Lord of the Admiralty 1673–9.

'QUEEN DOWAGER'. Catherine of Braganza (1638–1705), Charles II's queen. She left England in 1692 and returned home to Portugal in 1693 eventually acting as regent for her brother Pedro 1704–5.

REEVES, John. A clerk at Christ's Hospital, whose failure in 1695 to produce accounts for P's perusal caused him some disquiet.

ROCHESTER, Earl of. See HYDE, Laurence

ROETTIER, John (1631–1703). Born in Antwerp, appointed chief engraver at the Royal Mint in 1661 and produced the new milled coinage of Charles II, James II and William and Mary, as well as a series of historical medals. A hand condition caused him to delegate most die engraving after 1689 to his sons. Sacked in 1697 after thefts of coin dies by his workers.

SACHEVERELL, William (1638–91). Anti-Catholic politician under James II.

SACKVILLE, Charles, sixth Earl of Dorset (1638–1706). Took part in Second Dutch War. Opposed James II and withdrew, returning in 1689 as Chamberlain of the Household 1689–97. Served as regent three times during William III's absences.

ST MICHEL, Balthazar (c. 1642–d. *post* 1710). Brother of Mrs Elizabeth Pepys (q.v.) and the beneficiary of P's familial loyalty. Muster-master on the *Henry* 1666, Muster-master at Deal 1670. In 1679 he went to Paris to obtain evidence against Pepys's accusers. Muster-master and Surveyor of the Victualling at Tangier

1680–2. Commissioner at Deptford and Woolwich 1686–8 and fell with Pepys in the Glorious Revolution. He continued to call on P for support.

SALMON, Mr. Correctly Solomon Soulemont, clerk to Sir George Carteret (q.v.).

SALWEY, Richard (1615–85). Parliamentarian, member of Committee of Safety and Council of State 1659. Commissioner of Navy 1659. Imprisoned 1663–4.

SANDWICH, Earl of. See MOUNTAGU, Edward

SAVILE, Henry (1642–87). Diplomatist and wit. Groom of the Bedchamber to the Duke of York 1665–72. In 1679 he helped P amass evidence against Colonel Scott. Commissioner of the Admiralty 1682–4, in the commission which caused P so much frustration. Nephew of Sir William Coventry (q.v.).

SCOTT, Dr ____. A doctor who treated Jemimah Mountagu, Edward and Jemimah Mountagu's daughter, for a neck deformity. See the Diary 23 January and 1 February 1660, and 16 July 1665.

SCOTT, Caroline, Lady. Daughter of Lady Carteret and wife of Sir Thomas Scott.

SCOTT, Colonel John (*fl.* 1654–96). Blackguard, opportunist and adventurer. In 1679 he provided 'evidence' of P's Catholicism and treachery to support the claims by Oates in the Popish Plot. In 1683 Scott turned up in Norway. He was next heard of again back in England in 1695.

SCOTT, Robert. Bookseller of Little Britain, St Paul's, London. See also PF C7, p. 115, n. 4, where Evelyn comments on one of P's shopping forays to Scott's.

SEIGNELAY, Marquis de. Secretary to the French Admiralty. In 1679 P and Anthony Deane were charged with having given Seignelay secrets about the state of the Royal Navy when Deane visited France (see Letter no. 102). Getting Seignelay to deny this was crucial to P's case.

SHADWELL, Dr John (1671–1747). In 1699 physician to the English ambassador at Paris. In 1709 he became physician extraordinary to Queen Anne and remained in post into George III's reign. Knighted 1715.

SHALLCROSS, see SHELCROSS

SHEERES, Henry (d. 1710). An expert in ordnance, he supervised the destruction of the Tangier mole in 1683–4. Knighted 1685 and made Master of the Ordnance.

SHELCROSS/SHALLCROSS, Mrs Julia (c. 1635–1725). Julia Shelcross, née Boteler, was the daughter of Sir Francis Boteler and his first wife Anne Cokaine. Mary Skinner, P's housekeeper, was brought up in the Boteler household, since Sir Francis's second wife Elizabeth was her aunt. Julia married Francis Shelcross (b. 1630) on 10 April 1656 at Tewin, Hertford. He died on 26 February 1681. She remained close to Mary Skinner and travelled to France with her, and Pepys's nephew John Jackson in 1698. She was named in Mary Skinner's will of 1715, and died herself on 13 March 1725 at Tewin aged around ninety.

SHEPLEY, William. A steward of the Mountagues at Hinchingbrooke.

SHOVELL, Sir Clowdisley (1650–1707). Naval commander, who saw action at Sole Bay (1672), Tripoli (1676), in the campaign against Barbary pirates (1677–86), Barfleur (1692) and commanded the Channel fleet on and off between 1696 and 1703. Comptroller of victualling 1699–1704. His arrogant rejection of a seaman's advice that his fleet was in the wrong position led to the wreck of the *Association* and other vessels in 1707 off the Scilly Isles with total loss of life.

SHREWSBURY, Earl of. See TALBOT, Charles

SKINNER, Daniel senior (b. c. 1619). It has been said he came from Essex. However, he seems to have been born in Edgmond, Shropshire, as was his wife

Frances (née Corbet) whom he married in 1644. He was a member of the St Olave's congregation, and father of Mary Skinner (q.v.), P's housekeeper, and her brothers Daniel and Peter (q.v.). He and his wife seem to have greatly disapproved of their daughter's relationship with P in its early days.

SKINNER, Daniel junior. Son of Daniel and Frances Skinner, and brother of Mary (q.v.). He took his degree at Trinity College, Cambridge, in 1673. He worked for Milton and in 1676 asked P to recommend him for a diplomatic post in Holland. P was displeased to discover the Milton connection, since Milton's radical republicanism had made him an unpopular figure after 1660. His efforts to publish Milton's papers earned him Joseph Williamson's (q.v.) ire.

SKINNER, Mrs Frances (née Corbet) (1623–1702). Daughter of Robert Corbet and Frances Spencer. Wife of Daniel Skinner senior, born Edgmond, Shropshire.

SKINNER, Mrs Mary (1650–1715). Daughter of Daniel and Frances Skinner. Born in Dover, and christened at the French Church there as 'Marie Skinner'. Apparently P's common-law wife (called 'Lady Pepys' in Letter no. 220). Their relationship is implicit and never specified. However, Evelyn's letter to P of 6 July 1693 (PF D18) contains material that Tanner (1926, i, 68, n. 1) interpreted as possible evidence that P was seeking a suitable husband for her.

SKINNER, Peter (b. 1668). Brother of Mary Skinner (q.v.). Sent to sea in 1683 for naval training with P's help (Letter no. 155). In 1689 he decided to dispense with P's patronage (Letter no. 203), causing great offence. In 1702 he wrote to P ruminating on his foolishness (Letter no. 257).

SLANNING, Anne, Lady. Daughter of George Carteret and widow of Sir Nicholas Slanning (1606–43).

SLINGSBY, Henry (1621–90). Master of the Mint 1662–85, but suspended in 1680 for failing to keep his account up to date. Made to leave the Royal Society for letting his dues fall into arrears. Offered to sell P medals (Letter no. 183).

SOMERS, John, Baron Somers (1651–1716). Counsel for the Seven Bishops in 1688. Drafted the Declaration of Rights and became Solicitor-General. Helped plan the Great Recoinage of 1696 with Newton and others. Created Lord High Chancellor of England in 1697 but his close association with William III meant he suffered unpopularity amongst those who opposed the maintenance of a costly standing army. Forced to resign in 1700 but was acquitted after an attempt to impeach him. Later helped draft the Act of Union with Scotland in 1707.

SOUTHERNE, James. Began his career as a clerk under Pepys, rising to clerk in the Admiralty in the 1670s, Clerk of the Acts 1677–86 and then Secretary of the Admiralty 1690–4. He did not acknowledge P's help (Letter no. 214).

SOUTHWELL, Edward (1671–1730). Son of Sir Robert Southwell (q.v.). Clerk to the council 1699, followed his father in becoming secretary of state for Ireland 1702 and the served in a variety of posts under Anne and George I. MP for Rye 1707–11 and then MP for various other seats including Kinsale. P admired him.

SOUTHWELL, Sir Robert (1635–1702). Diplomatist. Ambassador to Cornwall 1665–8, secretary of state for Ireland 1690 and President of the Royal Society 1690–5. Father of Edward Southwell (q.v.).

STEWARD/STEWART, Mrs (Jane?). Sister of Elizabeth, Lady Mordaunt (1645–87), and daughter of Nicholas Johnson/Johnston (b. c. 1615). The pair were close friends of P's, and related to him by marriage through John Turner (1613–89) who was married to P's cousin Jane (1623–86). They lived together in Portugal Row on the south side of Lincoln's Inn Fields and dined regularly with Pepys.

Mrs Steward may have been Nicholas Johnson's daughter by a second marriage (a Jane Johnson, born 1652; see the discussion on. p. 226). Not to be confused with Frances Stuart, Duchess of Richmond, called 'Mrs Steward' in the Diary.

STRICKLAND, Frances, Lady, wife of Sir William Strickland, MP for Yorkshire.

SUSSEX, Countess of. See FITZROY, Charlotte.

TALBOT, Charles (1660–1718), twelfth Earl and only Duke of Shrewsbury. Assisted William III in 1688 invasion and made secretary of state in 1689, but maintained communications with James II. Issued the 1689 warrant for P's arrest.

TANNER, Thomas (1674–1735). Fellow of All Souls, Oxford 1696 and rose to become Bishop of St Asaph 1732–5. Author of *Notitia Monastica* (1695), about which he corresponded with P. His papers at the Bodleian appear to include other correspondence of P's.

TARBAT, Lord. See MACKENZIE, George

TAYLOR, Captain John (d. 1670). Master-shipwright at Chatham under the Commonwealth. Appointed Commissioner of the Navy at Harwich 1665–8.

TILGHMAN, Abraham (1651–1729). Balthazar St Michel's clerk at Deptford.

TIPPETTS, Sir John (*fl.* 1660–85). Master-shipwright at Portsmouth 1660–8, Commissioner of the Navy 1668–72, Surveyor of the Navy 1672–86, and 1688–92, Special Commissioner 1686–8. P thought highly of him, which became awkward in 1685 when Evelyn's daughter Elizabeth eloped with one of his nephews at the Deptford dockyard (see PF C21–23).

TONGE, Dr Israel (1621–80). Co-accuser with Titus Oates (q.v.) whom he met in 1676. Created the narrative construct of the 'Popish Plot' out of Oates's claims.

TRAFFORD, Mr ___. Mentioned in Letter no. 4. Otherwise unknown.

TREVOR(S), Sir John (1637–1717). Lawyer. MP for Castle Rising 1673 and thus P's colleague once P was elected, later MP for various other seats. Speaker of the House of Commons 1685, and 1690–5 when dismissed for taking bribes.

TREVORS, Mr ___. A naval official who in 1678 attempted to buy P's favour.

TRUMBULL, (Dr) Sir William (1639–1716). Clerk to the Signet 1683–1716. Travelled to Tangier with Pepys as Judge-Advocate, envoy to France 1685 and Turkey 1696–91, Lord of the Treasury 1694, Secretary of state 1695–7.

TUKE, Mary, Lady (d. 1705). Second wife of Sir Samuel Tuke (q.v.) and sister of Ralph Sheldon. A good friend of P's.

TUKE, Sir Samuel (d. 1674). Husband of Mary, Lady Tuke, and possibly a distant relative of John Evelyn's.

TURNER, Dr John. Rector of Eynesbury, Cambridgeshire, near Brampton on the other side of St Neots, and formerly chaplain to the Earl of Sandwich.

TYRRELL, Captain John. Officer commanding the *Phoenix* in 1684 when P asked for his nephew Samuel Jackson to be taken on board for his education.

VANE, Sir Henry (1613–62). An opponent of Cromwell, he had been imprisoned in 1656 for publishing a pamphlet against Cromwell's arbitrary government.

VERNON, James (1646–1727). Secretary to Anthony Ashley Cooper, Earl of Shrewsbury (q.v.) and later principal secretary of state 1698–1702 under William III. Previously he had been secretary to the Duke of Monmouth.

VERRIO, Antonio (1639–1707). French painter who decorated Windsor Castle for Charles II and James II, Hampton Court for William III and Anne, and various other stately homes of English noblemen. P appeared in his painting of Christ's Hospital 1685 (PC Sale Lot 10, illustrated in the sale catalogue).

WALLIS, Dr John (1616–1703). Friend of P's. Mathematician and professor of geometry at Oxford 1649–1703. Invented the symbol ∞ for infinity.

WALLOP, Robert (1601–67). Regicide, and councillor of state throughout the Interregnum until the Restoration. Imprisoned 1660–7.

WALTON, Colonel Valentine (d. 1661). Cromwell's brother-in-law, regicide, and commissioner for the government of the Army.

WARREN, Sir William (1624 – *post* 1689). Timber merchant, Master of the Drapers' Company 1668–9. In 1664 P effectively awarded Warren a monopoly of supplying timber to the Navy, arguing this was the best deal. However, Warren evaded freight charges resulting in a £44,000 debt to the government. Paid it off in 1679 and continued in business for at least another ten years.

WARRISTON, Lord. *See* JOHNSTON, Sir Archibald

WATERHOUSE, Nathaniel. Joint steward of the Household 1654–7, then Master of the Board of Green Cloth 1657–9

WERDEN/WORDEN, Sir John (1640–1716). Secretary to the Duke of York, and later Commissioner of Customs 1685–97 and 1702–14. Helped P's defence in 1679.

WHEELER, Mr ___. Unknown but probably employed in the stores with John Browne (q.v.). See Letter no. 45.

WHEELER, Sir William (1601–66). Mountagu's financial adviser. Knighted by Cromwell in 1657. A taxation expert, and elected to Parliament in 1640 and 1660.

WHITELOCKE, Bulstrode (1605–75), a long-serving parliamentarian and sometime commissioner of the great seal. Served on a number of commissions and committees, and was one of those who urged Cromwell to accept the crown. He had been governor of Henley for Parliament in 1644.

WILDE, John (1590–1669), 'the Recorder'. Lawyer, Recorder of Worcester 1646, Judge of Assize in various counties, Chief Baron Exchequer 1646–53, and 1660.

WILSON, Thomas (d. 1676). Clerk of the Cheque, Chatham 1661. Surveyor of the Victualling at London, 1665–7 and then Storekeeper until his death.

WOOD/WOODS, Anthony à (1632–95). Antiquary and historian, his best-known work being *History and Antiquities of Oxford University* (1674). He also wrote several other papers published posthumously.

WREN, Matthew (1629–72). Secretary to the Duke of York 1667–72.

WRIGHT, Anne, Lady (b. c. 1640–1708), née Crew. Daughter of John and Jemimah Crew, and sister of Jemimah, Countess of Sandwich. Referred to by P as 'Mrs Anne Crew' in letters of 1657. Married Sir Henry Wright on 23 March 1658 and P refers to her in Letter no. 9 as 'Lady Wright'. He called her 'a witty, but very conceited woman and proud' (Diary 20 November 1661).

WRIGHT, Edward. An acquaintance of P's who in 1696 provided intelligence about John Scott's having come into England again.

WRIGHT, Sir Henry (1637–64) of Dagenhams, Essex. A commissioner of Trade 1656–7 and MP for Harwich, he married Anne Crew on 23 March 1658.

WRIOTHESLEY, Thomas, fourth Earl of Southampton (1606–67). Lord Treasurer 1660–67.

WYBORNE, Captain Sir John. Officer commanding the *Happy Return* in 1682 during the calamitous wrecking of the *Gloucester*. Sent with a small force to Bombay in 1687 to suppress piracy and recover the royal share of prize goods, from where he sent P disconsolate letters (see no. 173).

Ships mentioned in the letters

The principal source is Colledge (1987).

Assurance. 42 guns. Built Deptford 1646. Sold 1698.

Centurion. 34 guns. Built 1650. Wrecked 25 Dec 1689 off Plymouth.

Dragon. 38 guns. Built Chatham 1647. Rebuilt 1690. Wrecked 1711.

Emsworth. 4-gun ketch. Built Emsworth 1665. Sold 1683.

Essex. 60 guns. Built Deptford 1653. Captured by the French in June 1666.

Falcon. 4th-rate, 42 guns. Built Woolwich as a 5th-rate and upgraded 1668. Captured by the French in 1694.

Flying Greyhound. 24-guns. Captured 1665. Sold 1667.

Foresight. 50 guns. Built Deptford 1650. Wrecked 4 July 1698.

Gloucester. 54 guns. Built Limehouse 1654. Wrecked 6 May 1682 off the Humber Estuary.

Golden Hind. Unlikely to be the privateer of 1577 and renamed 1578, though she was apparently extant in 1662. No other candidate.

Grafton. 3rd-rate, 70 guns. Built Woolwich 1679. Captured by the French 1 May 1707.

Greenwich. 4th-rate, 54 guns. Built Woolwich 1666. Rebuilt 1699 and 1730. Wrecked 1744 in Jamaica.

Guernsey. 22-guns. Built Walderswick as the *Basing* 1654. Renamed 1660. Broken up 1693.

Happy Return. 50 guns. Built 1654 as *Winsby*. Renamed 1660. Captured by French 1691.

Henry. 3rd-rate, 64 guns. Built as the *Dunbar* at Deptford 1656. Renamed 1660. Destroyed in an accidental fire 1682.

Hunter. Possibly the 3rd-rate 50-gun ship captured from the Dutch in 1672.

Isabella. 8-gun yacht. Built Greenwich 1683. Rebuilt 1703. Sold 1716.

James. Probably the 4th-rate 30-gun *James* galley. Built Blackwall 1676. Wrecked 25 Nov 1694

Katherine. 8-gun yacht. Built Chatham 1674. Rebuilt 1720. Sold 1801.

Mountague. Built Portsmouth 1654 as the *Lyme*. Renamed 1660. Rebuilt 1675, 1698 and 1716. Broken up 1749.

Naseby. See *Royal Charles*.

Nonsuch. 4th-rate, 48 guns. Built Portsmouth 1648. Captured by the French in 1695.

Phoenix. 5th-rate. Built Portsmouth 1671. Burned 1692 to prevent capture by the French.

Prince. 1st-rate, 100 guns. Built Chatham 1670. Rebuilt 1692 as *Royal William*.

Quaker. 10-gun ketch. Bought 1671. Sold 1698.

Resolution. 3rd-rate, 70 guns. Built by Anthony Deane at Harwich 1667. Rebuilt 1698. Wrecked 27 Nov 1703 off Sussex.

Royal Charles. 80 guns. Built 1656 as the *Naseby*. Renamed 1660. Captured 12 June 1667 at Chatham by the Dutch.

Royal James. 1st-rate, 100-guns. Built Portsmouth 1671. Blown up at the Battle of Sole Bay 28 May 1672, killing the Earl of Sandwich.

Royal Katherine. 2nd-rate, 82 guns. Built Woolwich 1664, rebuilt 1702. Wrecked 1760. Colledge (p. 188) states the ship was called *Katherine* only until 1696. However, it is plain from the letter of 17 Feb 1666 that she was already known as *Royal Katherine*.

Rupert. 3rd-rate, 66 guns. Built 1666 by Deane at Harwich. Rebuilt 170. Broken up 1769.

St Patrick. 4th-rate, 48 guns. Built Bristol May 1666. Captured 5 Feb 1667 by the Dutch.

Sapphire. 36-guns. Built 1651. Run ashore 1671 to avoid capture by the French.

Sovereign. 100 guns. Built Woolwich 1637. Rebuilt 1660 as *Royal Sovereign*. Rebuilt 1685. Destroyed by accidental fire 1696.

Speedwell. 20 guns. Built as the *Cheriton* 1656. Renamed 1660. Wrecked 1676.

Stavereene. Correctly *Stavoreen*. 4th-rate, 48 guns. Captured 1672. Sold 1682.

Principal dates

1633	23 Feb	Born at Salisbury Court near St Bride's, London
1644		Starts at Huntingdon Grammar School
1650	Jun	At Trinity College, Cambridge
	Oct	Transfers to Magdalene College, Cambridge
1654	Mar	Takes his degree
1655	1 Dec	Marries Elizabeth St Michel
1656	11 Mar	Extant correspondence begins
1658	26 Mar	Operated on for a bladder stone, celebrated annually thereafter
	3 Sep	Death of Cromwell
1660	1 Jan	Diary begins
	23 Mar	Sails with Mountagu to collect Charles II
	29 Jun	Appointed Clerk of the Acts
1665	15 Feb	Elected Fellow of the Royal Society
	22 Feb	Second Dutch War begins
	20 May	Appointed Treasurer for Tangier
	5 Jul	Moves household to Greenwich to escape the Plague
	27 Oct	Made Surveyor-General of the Victualling
1666	2 Sep	Great Fire of London begins
1667	31 Jul	End of the Second Dutch War
	22 Oct	Defends Navy Office before the Commons
1668	5 Mar	Defends Navy Office before the Commons
1669	31 May	Ends Diary
	Jun–Oct	Travels in northern France and the Low Countries
	10 Nov	Death of Elizabeth Pepys
1670	Jan-Feb	Brooke House Committee
	30 Mar	John Pepys made Clerk of Trinity House
1672	24 Jan	Made Elder Brother of Trinity House
	Mar	Third Dutch War begins
	7 Jun	Sandwich killed at Battle of Solebay
1673	29 Jan	Navy Office destroyed by fire. Moves to Winchester Street
	Jun	Appointed Secretary of the Admiralty
	4 Nov	Elected MP for Castle Rising (colleague: Sir John Trevor)
1674	Feb	End of Third Dutch War
		Moves to Admiralty Office at Derby House
1676	1 Feb	Made Governor of Christ's Hospital
	22 May	Master of Trinity House
1679	Feb	Samuel Atkins, P's clerk, accused of being an accessory in the murder of Sir Edmund Berry Godfrey

	Mar	Elected MP for Harwich
	May	Forced to resign Secretaryship. Imprisoned in the Tower
	Jul	Released on bail

1680	Feb	Released from bail
	Jun	Case against P dropped
	Oct	Death of John Pepys senior
1682	May	Accompanies Duke of York north and witnesses shipwreck
1683	30 Jul	Sets out for Tangier. Second Diary begins
	1 Dec	Second Diary ends
	Dec	Visits Spain
1684	Mar	Arrives home
		Re-appointed Secretary of the Admiralty
	30 Nov	Elected President of the Royal Society
1685	6 Feb	Charles II dies. Accession of James II
	Mar	Elected MP for Harwich
	Jul	Master of Trinity House again
1686	Mar	Special Commission for Navy begins
1687	Apr	Cifacca sings for P
1688	Sep	Prince of Orange prepares invasion
	Oct	Special Commission ends
	1 Nov	William of Orange lands at Torbay
	23 Dec	James II leaves for France
1689	Jan	Loses seat at Harwich
	20 Feb	Resigns Secretaryship
	May	Imprisoned at the Tower
	Jul	Released
	Aug	Resigns from Trinity House

1690	Jun	Reimprisoned in the Tower
	Dec	Publishes *Memoires*
1693	29 Sep	Robbed by highwaymen
1699	Oct	John Jackson's Grand Tour starts

1701	Jun	Moves permanently to Hewer's Clapham house
1702	Dec	Portrait of John Wallis presented to Oxford
1703	26 May	Death of Pepys
	4 Jun	Burial at St Olave's

1825		First edition of the Diary published by Braybrooke
1841		Smith's edition of letters and the Second Diary published
1926		Tanner publishes part of the Pepys-Cockerell correspondence
1929		Tanner publishes part of the correspondence 1662-79
1932		Howarth's edition of the correspondence and Second Diary
1933		Chappell's edition of some shorthand letters
1955		Heath's edition of the correspondence
1971ff		Latham and Matthews' definitive Diary edition begins
1997		P's correspondence with Evelyn published in full

Sources of the letters

For abbreviations, see p. 14. Each entry supplies the number of the letter in this edition, who from (or to), its date, the manuscript location (if known), and earliest previous publication apart from those indicated * for previously unpublished manuscripts. However, where the primary published source is an unreliable one (e.g. Braybrooke or Smith), this has been replaced by a later more reliable source wherever a later editor was able to publish a fresh transcription from the original manuscript.

Typically, outgoing letters *from* Pepys preserved in any Pepys archive (or strays like nos. 230 and 234), such as the Rawlinson manuscripts, are copies or drafts made by Pepys. Outgoing letters by Pepys preserved in other archives (such as no. 34) are usually the actual letters-sent. Incoming letters *to* Pepys are normally the original letter-sent where preserved in a Pepys archive, or in another that has been preserved (for example the Christ's Hospital letters now at the British Library). In some instances just a draft or copy made by Pepys's correspondent survives. However, this is usually only the case with John Evelyn and does not include any letters in this selection (see for example PF C41).

1 EARLY LIFE: 1633–60

1	Mountagu to P	11 Mar 1656	MS Carte 223	Howarth 1
2	P to Mountagu	27 Nov 1656	MS Carte 73	Howarth 2
3	P to Mountagu	11 Dec 1656	MS Carte 73	Howarth 5
4	P to Mountagu	8 Jan 1657	MS Carte 73	Howarth 6
5	P to Mountagu	5 Dec 1657	MS Carte 73	Howarth 7
6	P to Mountagu	8 Dec 1657	MS Carte 73	Howarth 8
7	P to Mountagu	22 Dec 1657	MS Carte 73	Howarth 10
8	P to Mountagu	26 Dec 1657	MS Carte 73	Howarth 11
9	P to Mountagu	20 Oct 1659	MS Carte 73	Howarth 12
10	P to Mountagu	22 Oct 1659	MS Carte 73	Howarth 13
11	P to Mountagu	3 Dec 1659	MS Carte 73	Howarth 14
12	P to Mountagu	6 Dec 1659	MS Carte 73	Howarth 15
13	P to Mountagu	8 Dec 1659i	MS Carte 73	Howarth 16
14	P to Mountagu	8 Dec 1659ii	MS Carte 73	Howarth 17
15	P to Mountagu	15 Dec 1659	MS Carte 73	Howarth 18
16	P to Mountagu	12 Jan 1660	MS Carte 73	Howarth 19
17	P to Mootham/Bun	27 Jun 1660	Unknown[1]	*

2 CLERK OF THE ACTS – THE DIARY YEARS: 1660–9

18	Clay to P	20 Aug 1660	SP 29/10.215	*
19	P to Mountagu	29 Aug 1661	MS Carte 73	Howarth 20
20	John Pepys Senior to P	10 July 1664	MS Rawl A182	Heath 7
21	Coventry to P	12 Oct 1664	MS Rawl A165	*

[1] Lot 493 Sotheby's 24 July 1995, and illustrated on p. 229 of the catalogue.

22	Pett to P	4 Apr 1665	NWB	Latham p. 115
23	P to Coventry	15 Apr 1665	PC MS p. 191	T1929.31
24	P to Coventry	20 May 1665	PC MS p. 214	T1929.36
25	P to Sandwich	27 May 1665	PC MS p. 218	T1929.38
26	Sandwich to P	29 May 1665	MS Rawl?	Braybrooke
27	P to Pett	16 June 1665	PC MS p. 223	Chappell xxvii
28	P to Sandwich	17 June 1665	PC MS p. 224	T1929.40
29	P to Coventry	1 July 1665	PC MS p. 227	T1929.41
30	P to Coventry	8 July 1665	PC MS p. 228	T1929.42
31	Middleton to P	25 July 1665	NWB	Latham p. 125
32	P to Coventry	5 August 1665	PC MS p. 233	T1929.43
33	P to Sandwich	7 August 1665	MS Carte 75	Howarth 21
34	P to Evelyn	9 August 1665	BL.1080	PF A3
35	P to Coventry	25 August 1665	PC MS p. 239	T1929.47
36	Sandwich to P	30 August 1665	MS Rawl A195	Howarth 23
37	P to Lady Carteret	4 Sep 1665	MS Rawl A195	Howarth 24
38	Evelyn to P	23 Sep1665	SP29/133.28	PF A4
39	Sandwich to P	1 Oct 1665	MS Rawl A174	*
40	Albemarle to P	11 Oct 1665	SP 29/134.115	*
41	P to Coventry	14 Oct 1665	PC MS p. 256	T1929.52
42	Sandwich to P	14 Oct 1665	MS Rawl A174	Braybrooke
43	P to Sandwich	25 Nov 1665	PC MS p. 308	Chappell xxxix
44	P to Coventry	17 Feb 1666	PC MS p. 370	T1929.93
45	P to Deane	8 Mar 1666	PC MS p. 373	T1929.95
46	P to Capt. Taylor	13 Mar 1666	PC MS p. 375	T1929.96
47	P to Deane	5 May 1666	PC MS p. 379	T1929.100
48	Navy Board to York	12 May 1666	PC MS p. 394	T1929.101
49	P to Hayes	7 July 1666	PC MS p. 390	T1929.103
50	P to York	25 July 1666	PC MS p. 400	T1929.105
51	P to Penn	19 Oct 1666	PC MS p. 408	T1929.107
52	P to Coventry	10 Jan 1667	PC MS p. 440	T1929.112
53	P to Chest Govs	2 Feb 1667	PC MS p. 454	T1929.114
54	P to Coventry	6 Feb1667	PC MS p. 454	T1929.115
55	P to Lady Sandwich	7 Feb 1667	MS Rawl A195	Howarth 27
56	Navy Board to York	31 Mar 1667	PC MS p. 471	T1929.118
57	Middleton to P	31 Mar 1667	PC MS p. 480	T 1929.119
58	Taylor to P	30 Mar 1667	PC MS p. 480	T 1929.119[2]
59	P to Coventry	11 June 1667	PC MS p. 491	T1929.124
60	P to Brouncker	1 July 1667	PC MS p. 493	T1929.125
61	P to Sandwich	7 Oct 1667	MS Rawl A195	Howarth 28
62	P to Deane	14 Dec 1667	PC MS p. 516	T1929.132
63	Brouncker & P to Chest	6 Feb 1668	PC MS p. 524	T1929.134
64	P to Sandwich	29 Sep 1668	MS Rawl A195	Howarth 29
65	P to Deane	24 Oct 1668	PC MS p. 545	T1929.142
66	P to Wilson	11 Dec 1668	PC MS p. 553	T1929.144
67	P to Deane	3 Feb1669	PC MS p. 569	T1929.150
68	P to Deane	4 Feb1669	PC MS p. 571	T1929.151
69	P to Deane	25 Feb1669	PC MS p. 574	T1929.153
70	P to Brouncker	11 Mar 1669	PC MS p. 581	T1929.154

[2] Nos. 57–8 are given here in the order the originals were read to the Duke of York and as published by Tanner.

3 CLERK OF THE ACTS – AFTER THE DIARY: 1669–73

71	P to Thomas Elliot	1 July 1669	PC MS p. 610	T1929.165
72	P to Evelyn	2 Nov 1669	BL Up Ant II	PF A29
73	P to BH Commrs	6 Jan 1670	BHP	NWB p. 325
74	P to Charles II	8 Jan 1670	BHP	NWB p. 330
75	P to Elliot	3 Mar 1670	PC MS?	Braybrooke
76	P to Richard Browne	26 Mar 1670	Upcott	Howarth 36
77	P to John Pepys Junior	26 Mar 1670	MS Rawl A182	Heath 10
78	P to Deane	2 May 1670	PC MS p. 643	T1929.183
79	B St Michel to P	11 June 1670	MS Rawl A195	Heath 11
80	Matthew Wren to P	9 Nov 1670	MS Rawl A174	Howarth 37
81	P to B St Michel	22 June 1672	PC MS p. 672	Heath 14
82	B St Michel to P	14 Aug 1672	MS Rawl A174	Heath 15
83	Henry Savile to P	14 Aug 1672	MS Rawl A174	Howarth 38
84	P to Howard	20 Aug 1672	PC MS p. 675	T1929.190 (encls)
85	Povey to P	31 Aug 1672	MS Rawl A172	Braybrooke
86	P to Savile	2 Sep 1672	PC MS p. 676–7	*
87	P to Savile	17 Sep 1672	PC MS p. 679	*
88	P to Middleton	17 Sep 1672	PC MS p. 680	*
89	P to Southerne	17 Sep 1672	PC MS p. 682	*
90	Hill to P	4/14 Apr 1673	MS Rawl A175	Howarth 40

4 SECRETARY OF THE ADMIRALTY: 1673–9

91	Coventry to P	25 Jun 1673	MS Rawl A191	Howarth 41
92	Howard to P	15 Aug 1673	MS Rawl A175	Smith i,140–2
93	P to Evelyn	23 Jan 1674	BL.1084	PF B10
94	B St Michel to P	8 Feb 1674	MS Rawl A185	Heath 21
95	Shaftesbury to Meres	10 Feb 1674	MS Rawl A172	*
96	P to Shaftesbury	15 Feb 1674	MS Rawl A172	Bryant ii, 113–14
97	Povey to P	3 Apr 1674	MS Rawl A172	*
98	Hill to P	27 Sep/7 Oct 1674	MS Rawl A175	Howarth 43
99	P to Hill	21 Nov 1674	MS Rawl A175	Howarth 44
100	Hill to P	21 Jun/1 Jul 1675	MS Rawl A175	Howarth 45
101	P to B St Michel	6 Jul 1675	PL AL iv.166	Heath 29
102	Hewer to P	12/22 Aug 1675	MS Rawl A175	Howarth 47
103	P to B St Michel	13 Aug 1675	PC MS p.713	Heath 30
104	Gibbon to P	27 Aug 1675	MS Rawl A185	Howarth 48
105	P to B St Michel	29 Aug 1675	PC MS p.716	Heath 31
106	P to Buller	11 Dec 1675	PC MS p. 723	T1929.205
107	P to Homewood	24 Dec 1675	PC MS p. 726	T1929.206
108	P to D Skinner	17 Nov 1676	PC MS p. 755	T1929.213
109	D Skinner to P	28 Jan 1677	MS Rawl A185	Howarth 54
110	Burton to P	9 Apr 1677	MS Rawl A185	Howarth 56
111	Houblon to P	3 May 1677	MS Rawl A185	Howarth 57
112	P to Ph Pett	22 Jun 1677	PC MS p. 768	T1929.215
113	P to Berkeley	22 Feb 1678	Unknown	Braybrooke
114	Berkeley to P	23 Feb 1678	MS Rawl A191	Howarth 59
115	P to Houblon	2 Nov 1678	PC MS p. 829	T1929.246
116	Houblon to P	3 Nov 1678	MS Rawl A175	Howarth 61
117	P to Houblon	4 Nov 1678	PC MS p. 830	T1929.247
118	Morelli to P	6 Nov 1678	MS Rawl A175	Howarth 63

119	P to Paulina Jackson	5 Dec 1678	PC MS p. 834	T1929.248
120	P to Trevors	18 Dec 1678	PC MS p. 836	T1929.249
121	P to Langley	6 Mar 1679	PC MS p. 878	T1929.272
122	P to D of York	6 May 1679	PC MS i.5	T1926.5
123	D of York to CII	12/22 May 1679	PC MS i.11	T1926.6
124	P to Norwood	30 May 1679	MS Rawl A194	*
125	Norwood to P	2 June 1679	MS Rawl A181	Howarth 72
126	P to Brisbane?	5/15 June 1679	MS Tanner 38.39	*
127	P to D of York	9 June 1679	PC MS i.12	T1926.8
128	D'Oyly to P	10 June 1679	MS Rawl A181	Howarth 74
129	P to D'Oyly	10 June 1679	MS Rawl A181	Howarth 75
130	P to B St Michel	28 July 1679	MS Rawl A194	Heath 75
131	P to Morelli	25 Sep 1679	MS Rawl A194	Howarth 76
132	P to Mrs F Skinner	24 Oct 1679	MS Rawl A194	Howarth 77
133	P to Povey	25 Feb 1680	MS Rawl A194	Howarth 80
134	P to B St Michel	8 Mar 1680	MS Rawl A194	Heath 116
135	P to Mrs Turner	24 Mar 1680	MS Rawl A190	*
136	P to J Pepys Sr	27 Mar 1680	MS Rawl A194	Howarth 83

5 RESTORED TO FAVOUR: 1680–9

137	P to Mrs F Skinner	1 July 1680	MS Rawl A194	Howarth 86
138	P to Howe	8 July 1680	MS Rawl A194	Howarth 87
139	P to Dr J Turner	3 Sep1680	MS Rawl A194	Howarth 92
140	Hewer to P	28 Oct 1680	MS Rawl A183	Howarth 95
141	P to Houblon	14 Nov 1680	MS Rawl A194	Howarth 98
142	Hewer to P	15 Nov 1680	MS Rawl A183	Howarth 99
143	Hewer to P	16 Nov 1680	MS Rawl A183	Howarth 100
144	B St Michel to P	21 Apr 1681	MS Rawl A183	Heath 138
145	Howe to P	15 June 1681	MS Rawl A183	Howarth 107
146	Maryon to P	8 Aug 1681	MS Rawl A194	Smith i. 265–6
147	P to Maryon	10 Aug 1681	MS Rawl A194	Howarth 109
148	Matthews to P	20 Oct 1681	MS Rawl A178	Heath 147
149	P to Matthews	12 Nov 1681	MS Rawl A194	Heath 149
150	P to Hewer	8 May 1682	MS Rawl A194	Howarth 123
151	Hewer to P	13 May 1682	MS Rawl A178	Howarth 124
152	Houblon to P	13 May 1682	MS Rawl A178	Howarth 125
153	P to Hewer	19 May 1682	MS Rawl A194	Howarth 126
154	P to Hewer	26 May 1682	MS Rawl A194	Howarth 128
155	Mrs F Skinner to P	25 Apr 1683`	MS Rawl A178	Howarth 133
156	P to Evelyn	7 Aug 1683	BL Up An II	PF C16
157	Houblon to P	11 Aug 1683	MS Rawl A190	Howarth 138
158	P to Houblon	16 Aug 1683	MS Rawl A190	Howarth 139
159	Gelson to P	12 Jul 1683	MS Rawl A190	Bryant ii, 399[3]
160	P to Houblon	14 Oct 1683	MS Rawl A190	Howarth 141
161	P to Houblon	19 Oct 1683	MS Rawl A190	Howarth 142
162	P to Dartmouth	5/15 Jan 1684	MS Rawl A190	Howarth 147
163	Dartmouth to P	11 Jan 1684	MS Rawl A190	Howarth 148
164	P to Dartmouth	3/13 Feb 1684	MS Rawl A190	Howarth 149

[3] This letter is deliberately placed later in the sequence since the date of its receipt by P (22 August) is more relevant than date of composition.

165	P to Tyrrell	1 Nov 1684	PL AL x.174	*
166	P to R Southwell	10 Oct 1685	Unknown	Howarth 154[4]
167	Mrs Evelyn to P	29 Nov 1685	HL Harvard	*
168	P Skinner to P	29/30 Nov 1686	MS Rawl A189	Howarth 155
169	P to B St Michel	11 Dec 1686	MS Rawl A189	Howarth 156
170	P to T Fowler	22 Dec 1686	PL AL xii.406–7	*
171	T Fowler to P	24 Dec 1686	MS Rawl A189	Howarth 158
172	P to Bagwell	7 Jan 1687	PL AL xi.531–2	Bryant iii, 166
173	Wyborne to P	14 Jan 1687	Unknown	Smith ii.60–2
174	J Matthews to P	21 Jan 1687	MS Rawl A189	*
175	P to B St Michel	27 Jan 1687	MS Rawl A189	Heath 166
176	Tilghman to P	9 Feb 1687	MS Rawl A189	Heath 167
177	B St Michel to P	14 Feb 1687	MS Rawl A189	Heath 169
178	S Morland to P	19 Feb 1687	MS Rawl A189	Howarth 161
179	P to Tippetts	25 Feb 1687	PL AL xiv.53	Bryant iii, App A
180	M Tuke to P	2 Mar 1687	MS Rawl A189	Howarth 163
181	M Holmes to P	31 Mar 1687	MS Rawl A.189	*
182	Mrs Evelyn to P	7 Sept 1687	MS Rawl A189	Howarth 170
183	H Slingsby to P	11 Oct 1687	MS Rawl A189?	Braybrooke
184	Mrs A Fowler to P	14 Apr 1688	MS Rawl A179	*
185	Vincent to P	12 May 1688	MS Rawl A179	Howarth 174
186	Morland to P	17 May 1688	MS Rawl A179	Howarth 175
187	R Scott to P	30 June 1688	MS Rawl A179	Howarth 177
188	Morland to P	19 July 1688	MS Rawl A179	Howarth 179
189	S Jackson to P	20 July 1688	MS Rawl A179	Howarth 180
190	P to Shovell	17 Aug 1688	PL AL xiv.349	Bryant iii, App B
191	P to Cotton	21 Aug 1688	PL AL xiv.366	Bryant iii, App C
192	P to Dartmouth	10 Nov 1688	MS Rawl A179	Howarth 185
193	Dartmouth to P	11 Nov 1688	MS Rawl A186	Howarth 186
194	Dartmouth to P	28 Nov 1688	Unknown	Smith ii.182–6
195	James II to Sanderson	4 Dec 1688	Maine HS	*
196	Lady Sussex to P	18 Dec 1688	Unknown	Smith ii.198–9
197	Hewer to P	19 Dec 1688	MS Rawl A179	Howarth 188
198	Dartmouth to P	28 Dec 1688	Unknown	Smith ii.200–1
199	P to Dartmouth	2 Jan 1689	Unknown	Smith ii.210–11
200	De Luzancy to P	18 Jan 1689	MS Rawl A179	Howarth191
201	Mrs D Egmont to P	30 Jan 1689	MS Rawl A179	Bryant iii, App E

6 BETWEEN BUSINESS AND THE GRAVE: 1689–1703

202	B St Michel to P	28 May 1689	MS Rawl A170	Heath 181
203	Mrs F Skinner to P	10 Jun 1689	MS Rawl A170	*
204	J Vernon to P	15 June 1689	PC MS i.34	T1926.17
205	B St Michel to P	6 Aug 1689	MS Rawl A170	Heath 187
206	P Skinner to P	27 Sep 1689	MS Rawl A170	Pepysiana 277
207	P to P Skinner	17 Oct 1689	MS Rawl A170	Pepysiana 278
208	Deane to P	29 Oct 1689	MS Rawl A170	Pepysiana 276
209	P to Deane	23 Nov 1689	MS Rawl A170	Pepysiana 276
210	J Mountagu to P	9 Dec 1690	PC MS i.42	T1926.25
211	P to J Mountagu	20 Dec 1690	PC MS i.44	T1926.27
212	P to R Howard	1 July 1691	PC MS i.52	T1926.34

[4] This letter is omitted from Howarth's list of sources, and it could not be located.

213	Compton to P	15 Dec 1691	PC MS i.54	T1926.36
214	P to Compton	18 Dec 1691	PC MS i.54	T1926.36
215	B St Michel to P	20 Mar 1692	PC MS i.60	Heath 188
216	P to Gale	15 Sep 1692	PC MS i.63	T1926.45
217	Southwell to P	16 May 1693	PC MS i.66	T1926.49
218	P to Southwell	5 July 1693	Private	*
219	Newton to P	13 Sep 1693	unknown	Turnbull iii
220	P robbed	29 Sep 1693	OBSessP	Pepysiana 46
221	P to Charlett	30 Sep 1693	Ballard I	Howarth 224
222	P to I Newton	22 Nov 1693	PC MS i.70	T1926.53
223	I Newton to P	26 Nov 1693	PC MS i.71	T1926.54
224	P to Houblon	9 July 1695	PC MS i.94	T1926.71
225	P to J Reeves	5 Aug 1695	BL AM 20732.152	*
226	J Reeves to P	6 Aug 1695	BL AM 20732.153	*
227	S Newton to P	8 Aug 1695	BL AM 20732.158	*
228	P to S Newton	8 Aug 1695	BL AM 20732.158	*
229	P to Houblon	6 Sep 1695	Pforz 105D	*
230	P to Mrs Steward	20 Sep 1695	PC MS i.96	T1926.72
231	Wright to P	10 Nov 1696	PC MS i.108	T1926.81
232	P to Wright	10/11 Nov 1696	PC MS i.108	T1926.81
233	Wright to P	12 Nov 1696	PC MS i.109	T1926.82
234	P to Mrs Shelcross	18 Nov 1697	PUL Bx 13 F Pepys	*[5]
235	P to Gale	9 Mar 1699	Pforz 105E	*
236	Dryden to P	14 July 1699	PL	Howarth 262
237	P to Dryden	14 July 1699	PL	Howarth 263
238	P to Jackson	17 Oct 1699	PC MS i.148	T1926.123
239	Reay to P	24 Oct 1699	PC MS ii.4	T1926.135
240	P to Reay	21 Nov 1699	PC MS ii.8	T1926.149
241	P to Jackson	8 Apr 1700	PC MS ii.98	T1926.205
242	P to Jackson	9 May 1700	PC MS ii.122	T1926.213
243	Charlett to P	6 Oct 1700	PC MS iii.76	T1926.323
244	P to Jackson	8 Oct 1700	PC MS iii.80	T1926.327
245	Charlett to P	15 Oct 1700	PC MS iii.84	T1926.331
246	P to Charlett	29 Oct 1700	Ballard I	Howarth 289
247	P to Charlett	5 Nov 1700	PC MS iii.105	T1926.350
248	P to Sloane	8 Jan 1701	BL Sloane 4038	Howarth 293
249	Jackson to P	13/24 Feb 1701	PC MS iv.41	T1926.419
250	Hatton to P	11 July 1701	PC MS iv.81	T1926.460
251	J Wallis to P	24 Sep 1701	PC MS iv.84	T1926.463
252	P to Evelyn	24 Dec 1701	BL Up An II	PF E14
253	Kneller to P	24 Mar 1702	PC MS iv.93	T1926.473
254	P to Kneller	24 Mar 1702	PC MS iv.93	T1926.474
255	Kneller to P	25 Mar 1702	PC MS iv.94	T1926.475
256	P to Kneller	26 Mar 1702	PC MS iv.94	T1926.476
257	P Skinner to P	Dec 1702	PC MS iv.119	T1926.499
258	P to Rooke	Apr 1703	PC MS iv.136	T1926.516
259	Jackson to Evelyn	28 May 1703	BL MS (Evelyn)	PF App 1.8
260	Jackson to Evelyn	5 Jun 1703	BL Deposit 9604	PF App 1.9

[5] A passage from this long-lost letter cited in a 1937 sale catalogue was included in PF, p. 235, n. 3, and copied from here by Tomalin, 454, n. 12. In 1997 its whereabouts could not be traced, and since it was not a priority the search was abandoned. Happily the facilities afforded by the Internet made it easily locatable at Princeton in 2005.

Glossary

This glossary covers only some of the terms and places mentioned in the letters. The extensive glossary appended to every volume of the Latham and Matthews' edition of the Diary is the definitive reference for the English used by Pepys.

ABCDARIAN	An ordinary school engaged in teaching only the very basics
ABROAD	outside, out of doors
ALCADE	Recte ALCALDE,a sheriff or justice
BALY	Correctly BAILIE, an archaic form of bailiff
BATTLEDOOR/ BATTLEDORE	Small racket used to hit shuttlecocks, though it can also mean a device used in washing linen.
BROOM	A type of shrub, usually used for fuel or tool handles
BUOY OF THE NORE	Mooring point in the Thames Estuary, north of Sheerness
CANDY MARSH	Perhaps Canvey Island, Essex
CHALOUPE	See Shallop
CHATHAM CHEST	A welfare fund for wounded and disabled seamen stored in a physical chest now preserved at the National Maritime Museum in Greenwich.
CHIRURGEON	Surgeon
COCKPIT	There were two Cockpits in Pepys's London: the theatre of this name in Drury Lane last recorded in use 1664; and the Cockpit in Whitehall Palace
COFFERER	Treasurer
COMBLE	Shower
DAGENHAMS	Also spelled DAGNAMS, the Essex country seat of Anne, Lady Wright, sister of Lady Sandwich
DEFALK	Reduce by deductions
DICHET	Probably ditches
DISCOMPUESTO	A state of discomposure
DOUBLOON	Spanish gold coin nominally equivalent to an English pound
FOXHALL	Now known as Vauxhall (south London) and formerly the site of a substantial pleasure garden
GENII	A reference to the generic Roman deity known as a 'Genius' (literally a spirit), usually applied to the god of a place, *Genius loci*, an object or an institution such as a military unit. Gibbon, P's correspondent, seems to regard the apparition as proof of the existence of ghosts.
GOLILLA	Spanish starched collar
GRACIOUS ST	Gracechurch Street, London
GRANADO/ GRENADO	Explosive shell
GROAT	Fourpence
GROYNE, THE	Corunna
HINCHINGBROOKE	Mountagu's seat
HOPE, THE	Probably part of Canvey Island, Essex
HUMOUR	The four fluids (humours) of the body: blood, phlegm, water and melancholy
KERSIES	*Recte* KERSEYS, trousers made from a kind of coarse woollen cloth called kersey, usually ribbed
LAZAROLLS	Medlar trees
LEAF OF ASARUM	Camphor-like substance obtained from the Asarabacca plant. Later used in snuff

LEET	Possibly a reference to the jurisdiction of a court leet, or in the case of the letter of 10 July 1664 probably a corrupt form of 'letter'
LIVORN(O)	Leghorn
LIVRE TOURNOIS	The 'Tournois' pound, a French unit of currency originally struck in Tours. By the 12th century its use was spreading across France and became the basic unit until the Revolution when it was abolished
LONG SANDS HEAD	Probably the sandbank of this name lying offshore between Harwich and Ramsgate
LUMBAR ST	Lombard St, London
MANES	Spirits of the departed
MASTER OF THE GREEN CLOTH	The Board of Green Cloth ran the Royal Household
MOIETY	A half share
MUSTER-MASTER	Naval official ensuring the actual crew of a ship corresponded with those on the muster list and who were being paid. Corrupt muster-masters maintained partly fictitious crew lists
NORE	The Buoy of the Nore, a mooring place off Sheerness
PATTEN	Undershoe made of wood to protect the wearer from mud
PECCANT	Faulty, incorrect, sinful
PECCARI	Sins
PERUIQUES	Periwig, a wig.
PIECE OF EIGHT	Spanish dollar, equal to 4 English shillings and sixpence
PISTOLE	Spanish gold coin equal to around 18 English shillings
PLAGUE-WATER	Cordial made of white wine and herbs, believed to have medicinal properties effective against the Plague. There were various recipes
PRICK	To set out music by notes ('pricks')
PRIVITY TO	Privy to, aware of.
RATTEENE	A thick woollen cloth
RENDERED	'Given way', as in Letter no. 60 regarding the chain at Chatham
RESENTMENT	A sense of appreciation or gratitude
ROCKER	Nursemaid or other person charged to rock a cradle
ROD	A unit of measure equal to 16½ feet (503 cm)
ROSIN	Variant spelling of RESIN
ST ELLEN'S ROAD	*Recte* St Helen's Road, a stretch of water off the Isle of Wight
SALUDADORES	Spanish charlatans of modest origins who claimed an ability to cure diseases through the properties of their saliva
SCOTTS HALL	Correctly SCOTT'S HALL, the home in Kent of Thomas Scott, husband of George Carteret's daughter Caroline
SENSIBLE	aware
SHALLOP	A sloop, a boat with one or two masts, sometimes equipped with guns
SO-ALL	Nevertheless
SOLE BAY	Southwold Bay
START POINT	Start Point, a few miles along the coast from Plymouth
TARPAULIN	Slang term for an ordinary seaman of the Royal Navy
THEORBA	Musical instrument: large lute with two necks and sets of tuning pegs
VIATICUM	Provision for a journey
WHITE YARN	Untarred yarn
YORK STAIRS	The watergate at the end of Buckingham Street where P lived at York Buildings. Both the gate and York Buildings still stand though the embankment of the Thames has left the gate high and dry in Victoria Embankment Gardens beside Charing Cross Station

Bibliography

DIARIES AND OTHER TEXTS

Braybrooke, R., Lord (ed.), 1825, *Memoirs of Samuel Pepys...and a selection of his private correspondence*, Colburn, London

Chappell, E., 1933, *The Shorthand Letters of Samuel Pepys*, Cambridge University Press

Chappell, E., 1935, *The Tangier Papers of Samuel Pepys*, Navy Records Society, Greenwich

Davey, S.J., 1889, *A Catalogue of Historical Documents and Autograph Letters including a large unpublished correspondence addressed to Samuel Pepys*, Catalogue no. 31, London

de la Bédoyère, G., 1997 (revised second edition 2005), *Particular Friends: The Correspondence of Samuel Pepys and John Evelyn*, Boydell, Woodbridge

de Beer, E. S., (ed.), 1955 *The Diary of John Evelyn*, Clarendon Press, Oxford

Heath, H. T., 1955, *The Letters of Samuel Pepys and his Family Circle*, Clarendon Press, Oxford

Howarth, R. G., 1932, *The Letters and Second Diary of Samuel Pepys*, Dent, London

Knighton, C. S., (ed), 2004, *Pepys's Later Diaries*, Sutton, Stroud

Latham, R., (ed.), 1995, *Samuel Pepys and the Second Dutch War: Pepys's Navy White Book and Brooke House Papers*, Navy Records Society, Scolar Press, Aldershot

Latham, R., and Matthews, W., 1971ff, *The Diary of Samuel Pepys* (11 vols), Bell, London

Robinson, H. W., and Adams, W., 1935, *The Diary of Robert Hooke 1672–80*, Taylor & Francis, London

Smith, Rev. J., 1841, *The Life, Journals, and Correspondence of Samuel Pepys Esq FRS* (2 vols), Bentley, London

Tanner, J. R., 1926, *Private Correspondence and Miscellaneous Papers of Samuel Pepys*, Bell, London (2 vols)

Tanner, J. R., 1929, *Further Correspondence of Samuel Pepys*, Bell, London

Turnbull, H. W., (ed.) 1961, *The Correspondence of Isaac Newton*, Vol. III Cambridge University Press

Wheatley, H. B., 1918, *The Diary of Samuel Pepys MA FRS. Supplementary Volume Pepysiana or Additional Notes on the Particulars of Pepys's Life and on Some Passages in the Diary*, Bell, London

BIOGRAPHIES

Bryant, A., 1933, *Samuel Pepys. The Man in the Making*, Collins, London

Bryant, A., 1935, *Samuel Pepys. The Years of Peril*, Collins, London

Bryant, A., 1938, *Samuel Pepys. The Saviour of the Navy*, Collins, London

Knighton, C. S., 2003, *Pepys and the Navy*, Sutton, Stroud

Ollard, R., 1974, *Pepys. A Biography*, Sinclair-Stevenson, London

Tanner, J. R., 1925, *Mr Pepys*, Bell, London

Tomalin, C., 2002, *Samuel Pepys. The Unequalled Self*, Viking, London

OTHER WORKS

Beal, P., 1987, *Index of English Literary Manuscripts*, Mansell, London

Colledge, J. J., 1987, *Ships of the Royal Navy*, Greenhill, London (and Naval Institute Press, Annapolis)

Der Waals, Jan van, 1984, 'The Print Collection of Samuel Pepys', *Print Quarterly* vol. I, no. 4, 236–57

Hunter, M., 1995, 'How to edit a Seventeenth-century Manuscript: Principles and Practice', *The Seventeenth Century*, vol. x, 277–310

Hunter, M., (ed.), 2001, *The Occult Laboratory: Magic, Science and Second Sight in Late 17th-Century Scotland. A New Edition of Robert Kirk's The Secret Commonwealth and Other Texts.* Boydell, Woodbridge

Pepys, S., 1690, *Memoires Relating to the State of the Royal Navy in England, for Ten Years, Determin'd December 1688*, Ben Griffin, London

Salmon, T., 1723, *The Chronological Historian*, Mears, London

Shelton, T., 1647, *Tachygraphy*, Cambridge (facsimile issued by the Augustan Reprint Society, William Andrews Clark Memorial Library, University of California, Los Angeles, 1970)

Index

This is a select index of correspondents and other persons mentioned in the letters. References are to the Letter number, NOT page number. Where the letter number is in **bold** this indicates that the person is the addressee or writer of the letter. Incidental individuals mentioned in passing are generally not indexed.